THE SCOTTISH MOUNTAINEERING CLUB JOURNAL 2018

A' Cioch. Photo: Grahame Nicoll.

THE SCOTTISH MOUNTAINEERING CLUB JOURNAL 2018

Edited by Peter Biggar

Volume 46
No. 209

THE SCOTTISH MOUNTAINEERING CLUB

THE SCOTTISH MOUNTAINEERING CLUB JOURNAL 2018
Volume 46 No 209

Published by the Scottish Mountaineering Club 2018
www.smc.org.uk/

© The Scottish Mountaineering Club 2018

ISSN 0080-813X
ISBN 978-1-907233-09-8

Typeset by Noel Williams

Printed and bound by Novoprint S.A., Barcelona, Spain.

Distributed by Cordee Ltd, 11 Jacknell Road, Hinckley, LE10 3BS.

CONTENTS

Suilven from Cul Mòr. Photo: Robert Durran.

ROOT OF ALL EVIL

By Murdoch Jamieson

A TRENCH FORMED AT the base of Far East Wall caused by my pacing back and forth unable to decide what to climb. John's jaw was on the ground. I had never seen Far East Wall in such fine mixed condition. John assured me he had done very little mixed climbing this season. He also reminded me, he hadn't climbed anything of this steep nature before. 'Oh right,' I said.

Beinn Eighe's Far East Wall. Photo: Murdoch Jamieson.

I had clocked *Root of all Evil* a few days previously when I was there with Iain Small climbing *Sundance*. But that was it, I never really thought much more. John and I had planned to climb *Rampart Wall* on Eastern Ramparts. We had planned a nice quick easy day and so that route fitted the bill. But, one thing I have learnt, when Far East Wall is 'in', you drop everything and get on it. As a modern mixed climber you need to be open to criticism about what you should and shouldn't climb. We all have our own ethics and I feel that a dirty, slow to dry and rarely climbed summer E2 is more acceptable that a 4 star, clean and regularly climbed E2 on that wall. Root of all Evil fitted the bill so off we went. Despite John voicing his concern he quickly said 'What the heck' in his Irish voice and agreed to get involved. John laid down the rules. He would do pitch one, I would

John Orr leading the first pitch of Root of All Evil, IX,8. Photo: Murdoch Jamieson.

John Orr following pitch two. Photo: Murdoch Jamieson

do pitches two and three and he would maybe consider pitch four. 'Fine' I said.

In its own right the entry pitch was a good solid VII,7. The first pitches of all the routes on the wall should not be underestimated and should come with a health warning. Fortunately I have escaped leading any of them. John was strapped in to a nice belay on a ledge, smug as what lay above looked rather athletic. Pitch two starts up a corner then moves right into the main corner system. The traverse left looked rather thin and exciting. I probed back and forth, unable to commit. Hmm. Eventually I committed to some thin but positive hooks and small edges for the feet. Some welcome deep pick slots were gained in the corner. But now the test on endurance began as the wall was beginning to show its true colours. Hell! Steep and strenuous with good slots for the tools but you are hanging on and blowing hard.

Arranging some solid gear, I began the exercise of executing some seriously strenuous moves up the corner. There certainly aren't any ledges to stand on, just little match sticks for the points of the crampons. The guide talks about belays three metres below the roof. I assumed there would have been a little ledge. Inching my way up, eyes peeled, this imaginary ledge never appeared. Maybe in summer there might be a nice hanging belay and one could smear one's feet on a little sort of ramp. Anyway, there was no ledge to chill out on, and creating a hanging belay

'Some wild moves left under the roof...' Jamieson on pitch three. Photo: John Orr.

one-handed with what was left of the rack whilst maintaining body tension to stay in the corner wasn't the easiest thing in the world. Eventually all was equalised and safe so I could sit back.

John began the process of following the pitch. He aired some doubts on his ability to follow, but his high standard of rock climbing fitness and technique shone through and he was cruising. With no real belay stance, it was easiest for John just to build something below me. I didn't envy his stance. I felt bad. At least I had a ramp to smear for my left foot, John had nothing. He just had to paste his feet on the walls.

Pitch three was a short 15m of summer 5c climbing. The guide talks about traversing the wall left below the roof then climbing up to gain its left side. For a winter ascent, the crack at the back of the roof seemed more appealing to under cling, or stein pull! Footholds again were scarce apart from a lone edge, the width of the side of a match box directly beneath the middle part of the roof. So up the corner I went, feet pasted on nothing. Again, the helpful nature of the quartzite allowed me to arrange good protection under the roof.

It was now a matter of leaving the sanctuary of the corner for some wild moves left under the roof, then surmounting its left side. It's all a bit of a blur, but it involved pulling hard with matching feet getting pumped. Somehow I found myself at the left side. I just had to pull round the roof and then traverse right across the wall above to gain the belay. As easy as it sounds, the positive nature of the cracks below vanished. I was left with just hooking blind edges, gear far below, it all felt a bit wild. A committing rock round an edge onto the belay felt like the living end, but at least a Rock-5 in a flared crack protected that. The belay ledge I was on was part of the existing route, *Hydroponicum*. I was hoping for a nice solid belay so I could just sit back and chill out. No, just a poor peg, poor wire, poor cam and another poor wire. It all equalised creating a less poor belay. Just as well there was a bit of rope drag and that John weighs less than me!

Of course it was getting dull now. I had been at the sharp end which meant we were moving at a snail's pace. John made the final rock-over onto my ledge with wide eyes. I looked at him, suggesting he had a look at the top pitch. He declined before I even finished. John voiced his concern and was adamant we should rapp down. The pitch above was still VIII in its own right. There was absolutely no way I was rapping down! I won't lie, I was a bit selfish. After those leads, I was not just going to bin the route. Having served my steep mixed climbing apprenticeship with Martin Moran, hard mixed climbing in the dark doesn't faze me too much.

Despite a cramping body, I re-racked, strapped the head torch on and quested off. In the fading light, I felt myself rush. The gear wasn't as obvious as below which slowed my pace. Down climbing, I had to take a moment. Nothing was said by either of us. At the time, I dare say John was hoping that I would have given up, but after so much investment, I couldn't. Off I went with an intense focus. This pitch was pretty rimed up and clearing took an age. Eventually as I gained height, the wall became friendlier and the angle began to ease.

I brought John up. Hats off to him as he was a frozen wreck. He had just endured three long belays, one of which was a full-on hanging belay with zero comfort. That in itself was probably harder than the climbing. It was 9 p.m. when we reached our bags at the summit cairn. John had work in Glencoe the following day while I had the painful joy of teaching kids 'V Knee, 1,2,3' at the climbing wall. I'm not sure who drew the short straw.

ON BEING SCARED

By Ian Crofton

We must travel in the direction of our fear.
John Berryman, 'A Point of Age'

WE'VE ALL BEEN frightened, or we'd all of us be dead. No one knows this better than the climber. A sudden fright prompts a quick instinctive reaction, the fight-or-flight response. The conscious mind is barely, if at all, involved. Evolution has determined that the interference of reason or will in the matter would only bring about catastrophe. So reason and will are bypassed. Instead, the sympathetic nervous system floods the body with hormones, readying it to deal with the perceived threat in an instant.

We will all have had an inkling of this when a foot unexpectedly slips off a hold. The sudden surge of adrenaline is experienced as a spurt in the stomach. It feels like panic. The adrenaline is preparing the body for immediate and energetic action. The heart and lungs quicken. Blood, fat and glycogen are harnessed for the almost exclusive use of the muscles. Fingers grip the handholds tighter. We are saved.

There are of course fears we experience as climbers that are conjured, not by instant chemical stimuli, but by reason and memory – even though such fears may grow beyond all rational bounds. Fear creeps up the spine when we feel we are not in control. When I'm roped up and leading and placing gear on good sound rock, my own will and conscious direction is in charge. But on some kinds of unstable terrain we feel at the mercy of chance, of the disorderliness and unpredictability of the territory. Reason and experience tell us to be afraid. If ever I have a climbing nightmare, it invariably involves either steep, slick grass, or horribly loose rock. Handholds crumble, feet skid, the insubstantial air below beckons, fingers try to grasp something, anything, and when that fails attempt to dig into the unsolid ground. Nothing can stop the fall but waking up.

Less rationally, many climbers will have suffered something close to vertigo on top of a high building, looking over the edge, however objectively safe they are. It is not just that one is neither roped nor belayed. It's the fact that one is not in command of one's own destiny. There are other kinds of terror to be found in the mountains, terrors that have nothing to do with the space beneath one's feet, terrors that were spawned in the bad dreams of childhood.

In late September 1975, when I was not yet 21, I found myself camped with a companion high on the southwestern side of Luinne Bheinn in the Rough Bounds of Knoydart. We were tired but content, having that day traversed Ladhar Bheinn. Our pitch was by a small burn, whose gentle trickles lulled us towards sleep – until we were alerted by other noises, close-by shufflings and snufflings. Something was brushing the outside of the tiny cotton tent. I held my breath. 'Must be a sheep,' I told myself, none-too-convinced. 'Or a deer.' Snuffle, snuffle. Sheep? Deer? Snuffle, snuffle. Witch, ghost, or man-eating monster? In the end, exhaustion overcame trepidation, and I drifted off to sleep. The next thing I knew our puny cotton tent was flapping and snapping fit to rip. Gusts of rain drilled on the fly sheet. Through the din I could pick up a steady background noise. It wasn't the rain, or the wind. The tiny burn beside which we'd camped was now roaring in full throat, rising ever closer to our pitch. We were faced into the teeth of an equinoctial gale. As the wind began to shred the tent, the rain found its way in. The creeping fear of the unknown that had beset me the previous evening was replaced by an adrenaline-fuelled rush to salvage the situation. In headtorch and underpants I ducked round the tent replanting pegs and tightening guys, before creeping back inside a thoroughly dampened sleeping bag.

The next morning the wind had diminished, and the rain at least partly abated. We pondered what to do. The sensible thing would be to head back to the car at the road-end at Kinloch Hourn the way we'd come, over the pass to Barrisdale and along the south shore of Loch Hourn. Our original plan had been to continue up Luinne Bheinn and over Meall Buidhe, then down to the head of Loch Nevis and back to Kinloch Hourn via the shores of Loch Quoich. We looked at the map. It seemed to us at the time (through some miscalculation I suppose) to be almost as far to go back as to go forward. So we decided to salvage what we could from the situation (including two new Munros) and press on. Further up the slopes of Luinne Bheinn we found an old boundary fence, and over this we draped our wet sleeping bags and the remains of the tent. Although the wind was fresh, it failed to achieve much in the way of drying, so we stuffed the soggy wreckage back into our sacs and continued. My diary notes that the day was 'windy, quite wet'.

Late that afternoon we descended to Carnoch[1], a remote and abandoned settlement on the boggy flats close to the head of Loch Nevis. The loch itself is a place as unsettling as its etymology is uncertain. Although 'Nevis' may be from Gaelic nèamh, 'heaven', it may also be nibheis, 'evil'. On that dark and gloomy evening it was the latter meaning that held sway. There was an indefinable air of dread at Carnoch, a sense of desolation that was enhanced by the two ruined crofters' cottages that stand there. Nothing was left apart from side walls and gable ends, a few roof beams and a sheet or two of corrugated iron. With the tent shredded, these ruins were the only shelter we were going to find for the night. If the bothy at Sourlies, less than a mile round the corner, was then habitable, we certainly weren't aware of its existence.[2] Having decided on one of

---

[1] This spelling is an anglicisation: the river which gives the valley its name is the Carnach as is recognised later in the article. (Hon. Ed.)

[2] The first edition of the MBA Handbook (1967) listed Sourlies but said that it offered *shelter only*. However, had the author but known, Sourlies was eventually renovated in the early '70s. There is a photo of it in *The Western Highlands*

the ruins at Carnoch as our home for the night, we set about rearranging the beams and sheets of metal to form some sort of roof over a corner facing away from the wind. The down in our sleeping bags was too dank to hold much warmth. So we spent an hour or so gathering heather and bracken from the slopes at the back of the flats. As twilight drew in around us, we piled up a nest in our sheltered corner under the makeshift roof, and burrowed ourselves in.

It is one thing to poo-poo the possibility of otherworldly malevolence at eleven o'clock in the morning. It is quite another thing to banish all thoughts of an ill-disposed spirit world in the deep dark of a windy September night, while bivouacked in a long-abandoned ruin near to the head of one of Scotland's perhaps more sinisterly named lochs. Who had lived at Carnoch? We did not know. Why had they left? We did not dare speculate. But through the ruined, empty doorway we could sense rather than see something stirring out there in the pitch-black night. I switched on my headtorch. Two eyes glinted back at me for a moment. And then they were gone.

The adrenaline released kept us from sleep. And then the wind got up again, and all thought of slumber was put to flight by the rattle and clang of corrugated iron overhead. My imagination envisaged a gust lifting a heavy metal sheet into the air, and then dropping it down like a guillotine onto our necks.

It was, in short, a bad night, draining much of the energy we would need the next day to walk the many miles back to Kinloch Hourn. There were then no paths, not even sheep paths, up the River Carnach, just the tracks of deer cutting intermittently through the tussocks. These were indeed the Rough Bounds. The glen at one point narrowed to a gorge, and we were forced to hop from boulder to boulder between the river and a rocky slope, sometimes swinging above the water clinging onto the thin branches of birch or rowan. Eventually we reached the dam at the southwest end of Loch Quoich. Our spirits lifted to find that from the dam there was a track heading the way we wanted to go. With a new lightness in our step we followed it, only to have our spirits dashed as the track suddenly made a right turn and dived down into the loch. The track must have predated the dam. The drowned village of Kinlochquoich lies beneath the dark waters: a drowned village, perhaps a drowned kirk, maybe even a drowned graveyard, a graveyard stuffed with the bodies of the affronted dead …

With the track no more than a memory, it was back into the Rough Bounds. By the time we reached the Abhainn Chòssaidh[3] it was beginning to get dark. There was no bridge over the wide river, not even boulders to jump across. We didn't bother to remove our boots, or our woollen

---

District Guide (1974) by Donald Bennet (illus. 39 between pp. 84–5). (Hon. Ed.)

[3] The author was lucky: this is a notorious river in wet weather. See e.g. p.170 of *The Corbetts*, Ed. Milne and Brown, (2017), where it is described as 'very dangerous'. (Hon. Ed.)

breeches, just plunged in and waded across, squelching the remaining miles to the road.

It was some kind of comfort to be back on tarmac, though our feet did not think so. Here and there in the darkness on the long walk down to Kinloch Hourn we sensed movements in the scatterings of trees on either side. We didn't dare to shine a torch, for fear of what we might see.

As we get older, we're not so easily spooked. The tapping on the dark windowpane turns out to be the twig of a shrub blown by the breeze; and in the loneliness of a winter's night no restless spirits roam – or if they do, we might welcome them as visitors from a past world to which we might ourselves soon return. Even by my later twenties I was disinclined to conjure up bogles and spectres from the dark. But, as it transpired, my sympathetic nervous system was still capable of overruling my rational will.

My second season in the Alps, in 1981, was on the southern, Italian side of the Bregaglia. Again it was September, and our valley base was a wild camp in the idyllic woods and meadows of the Val di Mello. Our first few routes were made from the Rifugio Gianetti, on the south side of Piz Badile. Then we planned to finish the trip at the south-eastern end of the range.

It's a long, beautiful walk up to the Rifugio Allievi. After several thousand feet of ascent we came level with the hut. As we approached, a man emerged from the interior and began to wave and shout from the terrace. It was the guardian. He said we must go back down, it was the start of winter, the hut was closed. We tried to plead our case. We were not Inglese, but Scozzese, we argued. This fact had been very much in our favour at the Gianetti Hut. Here it carried no weight.

A young woman cradling a baby appeared beside the guardian. She talked to him quietly. We could not hear, but it seemed she was putting our case. The guardian's posture relaxed then softened. He whispered, nodded, and in the end asked us in. Once he'd shown us where we should sleep, he invited us to eat with the family in their small kitchen. But, he said, he would be closing up in the morning and descending to the valley. We would have to sleep in the winter room after our climb.

Our objective was the Via Gervasutti, a magnificent TD up the south ridge of Punta Allievi. The guardian woke us early. As we pulled on jumper after jumper he thumped two large glasses of grappa down on the table where our otherwise modest breakfast was spread. 'You must drink,' he insisted. 'It will be cold today.' We did as we were told. The grappa was fiery. I winced, my throat shrank. But my stomach warmed with Dutch courage.

The Via Gervasutti was long – about twenty pitches up a soaring spire of a ridge. We were slow in those days on alpine rock, and as we climbed higher and higher the light began to go. A few flakes of snow fell, and by the time we reached the summit the moon was up. The first part of the descent was straightforward, but it was tricky negotiating the final steep scramble down a complex, verglassed ledge system towards the hut.

Ian Crofton on the crux of the Via Gervasutti (TD) on Punta Allievi.
Photo: Crofton Collection.

After sixteen hours on the mountain I was mightily relieved when the shape of the hut emerged in my torch beam. I breathed a sigh of relief. Exhausted, I stumbled up the side of the hut to the entrance of the winter room. I reached forward, turned the latch, began to open the door. I jumped back in horror. It was as if some unseen force had exploded in my face, throwing me back outside. Something – some monstrous shape – had moved in the darkness of the interior. My heart beat furiously, my breath came in spurts. I slammed the door shut. Shit, I thought. I was shaking, panting, my heart racing. Then I heard voices coming from the inside.

Sleepy voices. Sleepy voices speaking German. I paused, took stock of the situation, then cautiously opened the door again. Now there were lights.

'Good evening,' a voice said. 'I hope we did not frighten you?'

'Er, no, of course not,' I mumbled. 'It's just that it's been ... a very long day.'

'Good, good. Come in. There is plenty of room.' A bearded face approached me and offered me a mug. 'We have tea. Would you like some of this?' I suppose I gave a sheepish grin.

I've sometimes wondered why I reacted as I did when I opened the door. I hadn't been expecting anybody to be in occupation of the winter room. So my mind had envisaged an empty hut, and was shocked when a shadow moved. I acted before my reason could advise me that there were, after all, likely to be many other climbers out and about in the Alps that day, and that there was no reason at all why some of them should not be spending the night in the winter room of the Allievi Hut.

Instead of patiently attending to that slow process of reasoning, I had been manhandled by millions of years of evolution. These had short-circuited my deductive capacities and roared out 'Fight or flight!' I'd fled. Something unknown moving in the dark was most likely a predator – a lion, a cave bear, a sabre-toothed tiger. Or if not 'most likely' then 'quite possibly'. Best not to trouble the poor fool up there who thinks he's in charge, he'll just end up being eaten before he has worked out the odds, let alone had a chance to breed. Best just to fire off a burst of adrenaline and get him out of there. Pronto.

It had all happened in an instant. But it took me a long time to calm down. This, I understand, is the job of the parasympathetic nervous system – to restore the body to homeostasis, the state of metabolic equilibrium in which it can 'rest and digest'. The parasympathetic nervous system was meant to be flooding me with acetylcholine to calm me down and reset my controls. But, failing that, what I needed was not a cup of tea, however kindly offered. What I needed was a great big slug of single malt. Even a shot of gut-rot grappa would have done.

MOUNTAINS, BED BUGS AND FIRE LIZARDS:
a little walk through Corsica

By Helen Rennard

THE GR20 IS ONE of the world's most famous long distance trails, traversing diagonally through the island of Corsica from Calenzana in the north to Conca in the south for 180km. The trail is considered to be one of the most difficult of the GR (grand randonnée) routes, with much of it high up in the mountains on rocky terrain and with a total ascent of 13,000m over the 180km. Most of the first half, to Vizzavona, is spent up amongst granite spires. The southern half is easier and includes areas of forest, lakes and alpine pastures. Much of the northern section is at 1400m or higher. The highest point on the trail is 2607m, at Pointe des Éboulis. Along the way it is possible to ascend several of Corsica's highest mountains without too much of a detour, including Monte Cinto (2706m), the highest.

The simplicity of a walking holiday appeals to me; easy to organise (partly because no partner is needed) and I find that the walking itself can be meditative. The fact that the GR20 travels through Corsica also appeals to me. I like the idea of a journey with a different start and end point, as opposed to days out from the same base. For my GR20 trip I decided to go in the last two weeks of September 2017 when it would be cooler and quieter than the peak summer months but the refuges would still be open. I was content to approach it as a walking holiday rather than a mission so I planned to complete the sixteen stages in eleven days. The current record for running the GR20 is an amazing 31 hours 6 minutes, set on 4th June 2016 by François D'Haene of France. Interestingly for an ultrarunner, François is 6'4" (by comparison, Killian Jornet is 5'7"). Most of my planning was done using the 2016 Cicerone guide by Paddy Dillon with some additional information from websites and also Simon Love, who led a school trip there ten years ago.

My carefully planned walk, with nights booked at refuges, was based on the timings in the Paddy Dillon guide. So when I completed the first stage in half the guidebook time I realised that the timings were a bit off for me. My solution to this unexpected problem was not to alter my schedule but instead to sleep in late every morning, leave the refuge after everyone else was long gone and then set myself the challenge of overtaking as many people as possible over the course of the day. I enjoyed moving fast, half-running along with my backpack, I tend to be competitive when someone is ahead of me on a mountain, and I like sleeping, so this approach worked out well. It also gave me space to pack and get ready every day separate from the early morning rush. I completed most of the first half in one stage per day and linked stages for the second half.

Flying from the UK to Ajaccio, on the south west coast of Corsica, it

Rocky peaks and deep valleys: a typical view in the northern part of the GR20 looking south. Photo: Helen Rennard.

was easy to spot fellow GR20ers and later that day we were all rammed in together on the Trinicellu, the little train nicknamed 'the boneshaker' that rattles and clatters its way along a narrow gauge railway line from Ajaccio to Calvi in the north west and Bastia in the north east. This is regarded as one of the most scenic train routes in the world, travelling through the heart of Corsica's rugged interior. My view for the first half of the journey was of the back of other people's heads as more and more passengers crammed themselves in at each stop. Thankfully the crush subsided further north and I was able to get a seat and a view. After a number of wrong turns and dead ends getting out of Calenzana the following morning I eventually found the start of the GR20, with its distinctive red and white paint marks (these are at approximately 10 metre intervals, which is a lot of paint over 180km), and I was underway. Three and a half hours later I had arrived at my refuge for the night and was wondering what to do with myself for the rest of the day! Though when the morning's sunshine gave way to heavy rain which continued non-stop until the following dawn I was quite happy to have arrived at the refuge early. That was the only heavy rain of the whole trip.

On the first night a group of six young Latvians arrived at the hut as the evening meal was being served. They were in a bad way; soaked through, exhausted, mildly hypothermic and with enormous rucksacks containing two weeks' worth of food. One of their rucksacks weighed 30kg! I lent my sleeping bag to the girl shivering on the bunk next to me

The author on the summit of Monte Cinto 2706m Corsica's highest mountain.
Photo: Rennard collection.

as hers was completely saturated. I heard that the next day they had decided to turn back. Unfortunate for it to all have ended so early for them but I think a wise decision based on the state they were in after one stage. They reminded me of myself at that age, setting off into the hills with a ridiculously heavy rucksack.

The sun returned on the second morning and, apart from a few days of low cloud and drizzle, remained out for the rest of the trip. Most of the days were dry and sunny and it was warm enough to walk in t-shirt and shorts on all but the highest sections. The days in the northern half were the most satisfying, with stunning views of rocky peaks and spires and the Mediterranean in the distance and with an endless supply of granite slabs and boulders to bound across. From Vizzavona south the terrain became much easier but it was still interesting, with trails through forests of laricio and maritime pines, birch and beech, lush pastures with grazing cattle and wild ponies, and sparkling lakes. There was a beautiful scent in the forests which I think came from the maquis, a gorse-type tangle of vegetation for which Corsica is renowned. There was some unusual wildlife; walking through the forest to Bocca di Verdi I nearly trod on several Corsican fire salamanders (black with yellow blobs to warn off potential predators) which were sitting on the path.

Staying in the refuges was an interesting experience. They varied considerably in quality and hygiene levels, and also in the amount of personal space on bunks. Bed bugs were a problem in many of the refuges

The gentler side: evening outside the Refuge de Ciotulli du I Mori. Photo: Helen Rennard.

and this led to pandemonium at bedtime in the Refuge Manganu when someone shouted that they had seen one as everyone was settling down to sleep. In an earlier refuge the three Germans in my room insisted on sleeping with the light on, claiming that the bedbugs would only come out in the dark. This may have been true, but keeping the unshaded lightbulb on all night didn't lend itself to a good night's sleep. I slept outside that night. The best hut I stayed at was Refuge Tighiettu, on the southern side of Monte Cinto. This, a curious timber chalet construction supported partly on stilts, is situated on a rock spur with fantastic views down the valley, and had the most welcoming guardian and staff of all the refuges (some of the refuge guardians could be positively grumpy). Having made the (quickly regretted) decision not to take a tent with me I stuck it out with the refuges and was lucky enough to evade the bedbugs.

The food experiences were also interesting and vegetarians would struggle. An evening meal in a refuge was typically a plate of charcuterie and then a heavy stew or soup with black or brown lentils and great chunks of pork. Breakfast, evening meals and food for through the day (including cakes and biscuits made from Chestnut flour) could all be bought at refuges if you were prepared to spend money and take a gamble on what you would be eating. Some of the refuges have their provisions carried in by pony, which felt very rustic. The quality and also quantity of food did deteriorate in the refuges in the southern half of the walk and my waist belt was being tightened about as far as it would go by day eight or nine. The lowlight of the trip, from a food perspective, was in

'Fame for the salamander. It could so easily have ended very differently... as I very nearly trod on him.' Photo: Helen Rennard.

Vizzavona, when I had my first and last taste of Figaro (pig liver sausage). This was served in huge pieces hidden in a sludge of brown lentils. I was the only person staying in the gîte and the only person eating in the restaurant and was being regularly checked on by a very large and quietly intimidating proprietor during the meal. Too scared of him to dare leave the sausage, which is considered Corsica's speciality but was making me gag despite the amount of wine I'd drunk, I waited for him to leave the room and quickly smuggled it into a napkin to dispose of later. I was painfully conscious of the smell coming from my pocket as he waited for me to pay my bill.

Highlights of the GR20 for me included the views in the northern half; the feeling of freedom moving over seemingly unending expanses of dry grippy rock in the mountains; the peaks climbed off the main path – Monte Cinto, with blazing sunshine and sea views on the south side and fresh snow and streaks of ice on the north, Monte Ritondu (2622m) and Paglia Orba (2525m), the second and third highest mountains in Corsica respectively and a decent scramble to the summit on the latter; the wildlife and flora on the route; sitting out under the stars in the evenings; and arriving at Conca with aching legs but feeling fit, suntanned and happy to have completed the walk.

The other real highlight for me was the people I met and got to know along the way; there was a real sense of camaraderie along the route. All in all it was one of the best holidays I have ever had and I would highly recommend the GR20. I am looking forward to returning to Corsica in the future to explore other areas of the island.

EDINBURGH IN THE EARLY SIXTIES

By Robin Campbell

I WENT TO EDINBURGH from Perth in October 1960 and remained there until the summer of 1969. This put me in a good position to observe the very active climbing scene there, which kicked off with Marshall, Smith and their friends, moved on to the Squirrels Group and finished with the emergence of Dave Cuthbertson and Murray Hamilton. This is a personal account of my observation of the early years. Last year marked the 55th anniversary of Robin Smith's death, aged 23, on Mount Garmo in the Pamirs. Despite his short career Smith was Scotland's most potent and innovative climber since Raeburn, so he certainly deserves whatever can be added to his story by way of personal reminiscence – particularly since there are now so few climbers alive who knew him. His personal history is well described in Jimmy Cruickshank's biography, and others have written about his climbs in these pages and elsewhere. But Edinburgh climbing at the beginning of the Sixties was by no means just Smith.

What is perhaps missing from these various accounts of his life is a clear picture of the group of climbers of which Smith was one focus. The other focus was of course Jimmy Marshall. There were four other climbers who gave the group strength: these were the Currie trio of Dougal Haston, Jim 'Elly' Moriarty, and Jimmy Stenhouse – and Marshall's brother Ronnie. At the time of the group's domination of Scottish climbing, approximately 1958–62, all six were 'comfortable' at a similar high standard – around 5b in today's money, and although there were other Edinburgh climbers such as Graham Tiso and Andy Wightman, and the odd Glaswegian, who participated in the exploits of this Group of Six, their involvement was either very occasional or amounted to cup-bearing and rope-holding.

Smith, of course, climbed with an assortment of 'single use' partners from the University Mountaineering Club, men whom he cajoled into following him up routes that lay wildly beyond their experience and technique, giving them the best and worst days of their lives. It is a tribute to his personal charm that he remained on good terms with all of them, so far as I know. The 'odd Glaswegian' referred to above was of course usually John McLean, and had it not been for his close affiliation with and steadfast support for the Creagh Dhu Mountaineering Club, I'm sure that this strong and skilful climber would have participated much more fully with the Edinburgh group – and to their mutual advantage.

At any rate it was this Group of Six, together with McLean in Glasgow, who boot-strapped the general standard of rock-climbing here in the late 1950s and early 60s beyond the level achieved earlier by John Cunningham, Pat Walsh and their Creagh Dhu associates, and of course the Group – pulled along by Jimmy Marshall – also pushed winter-climbing standards up to and beyond the level achieved by Tom Patey and his Etchachan Club friends. Another potent factor in this boot-strapping was the Pierre Allain rock shoe, known as the 'P.A.' These were originally obtained beginning around 1957 – from Allain's shop in Rue St Sulpice, Paris, and orders placed in Edinburgh with climbers going to the Alps were filled on the return journey. From 1962 onwards, Graham Tiso's shop in Rodney Street supplied these as well as other vital products, such as 12-point Grivel crampons. Ronnie Marshall, a shipwright, had the necessary skills and workshop access to produce suitably shortened axes. Protection was primitive, a matter of slings over flakes or around jammed rocks, or fixed after a fashion with home-made nuts or knots in line. However, everyone – winter and summer – carried a hammer and a few pegs, to ensure a means of escape by abseil, and to provide the odd protection point.

I went to Edinburgh as an undergraduate in 1960. I already knew about these climbers, and had 'met' them once or twice in Glen Coe and at the CIC Hut. I put 'met' in quotes, because these were not the sort of people who strode up to you, shook your hand, and pronounced their names. They were more the sort of people who treated you as beneath notice, replied to your enquiries with silence or grunts, and stole your food and drink. Nevertheless, it was largely because of this powerful group that I went to Edinburgh University, with a view as much to improving my climbing as improving my knowledge. When I got there I soon fell in with Neil Macniven, a Fife climber whose standard was similar to mine, and who had gone to Edinburgh for the same misguided reasons. We were both studying Maths and Physics, and had rooms in Cowan House, the only men's student residence at the time, then situated in George Square. The present ugly University Library now stands there, fouling the space where Cowan House, and its neighbour Masson Hall (the only women's residence) once stood in Georgian splendour. Our teachers, A.C. Aitken, W.L. Edge, N.T. Feather, P.W. Higgs and R. Schlapp, other-wordly creatures of lofty eccentricity, served up incomprehensible pearls to uncomprehending swine. The universal teaching method in those departments was to turn your back on the swine, and scribble on the blackboard for 50 minutes. My first roped climb with Macniven may well have been McEwan's Hall, which we decorated with a rectorial banner. In the same campaign a Perth friend, whose secret I will keep, conquered the Old Quad dome by the ingenious method of wrapping a rope around it and twisting the ends so that it rode up the dome to the easy-angled upper slopes.

Macniven was slightly better than me (at Maths and Physics as well as climbing), and just as I had learned my trade – such as it was – on Craigie Barns, he had learned his on the Fife coastal crags and Dumbarton Rock while his parents moved between Kirkcaldy and Dumbarton. We were both well off the pace, however, and struggled to cope with VS leads, or anything north of Grade IV. We shared a second-hand motorbike, which died at Bridge of Orchy after an unsatisfactory variation to what is now

Neil Macniven on Salisbury Crags c. 1961. Photo: Robin Campbell.

Haar (Beinn an Dothaidh) in the winter of 1961. We visited Wales together
that Easter, and managed a few standard HVS routes, and then a couple
of new routes on Arran. The Arran routes are now despised and indeed
even deleted, but they got us noticed, and we were then allowed to sit at
the same table as Smith and whatever other Group of Six members or
hangers-on happened to be patronizing the facilities of the Old Quad
Common Room (now gone), Deacon Brodie's upstairs bar on the High
Street, or most commonly The Hall Bar on Bristo Street (demolished long
ago), and to speak when we were spoken to.

The Old Quad Common Room was a wonderfully large space at the back of the old University Courtyard, rather like a German Beer Hall without the beer, in which you could count on meeting any other idle undergraduate. You could spend a happy day there, drinking coffee, chewing the fat, and playing bridge, which substituted for the intellectual exercise we were supposed to be taking. It was in this Common Room that I listened to Smith and Haston hatching a plan to go winter-climbing in the Alps – executed, but a complete failure because of their inability to ski, and where I – showing unusual good sense – refused Smith's proposition to join him in an early-season First British ascent of The Eigerwand in June 1962. Deacon Brodie's was the trough used by the University Club, and the lunchtime meetings there were presided over by the amazing Tom Graham Brown, the 80-year-old hero of the Brenva Face. The Hall Bar, named for the McEwan Hall situated opposite, was a renowned primitive drinking den adjoining the University. 'Mine host' was a truculent and menacing individual named Willie, who kept a shillelagh below the bar for use on awkward customers. He served well-kept McEwan's Export from the wood at one and tenpence the pint – approximately 9p in today's debased coin, but offered no other comforts, and banned people routinely for excessive drunkenness or vomiting in the toilets. However, such minor offences merited only a week's exclusion. After achieving a sufficient degree of intoxication there, we would repair to the Barbecue on the south-east corner of Forrest Road for coffee and snacks (later turned into a bar named 'Doctors'), or to Willy's Restaurant in Forrest Road, which served Vienna Steak (i.e. a roll-less burger) peas and chips for two and thruppence (11p). Willy's was also the venue of choice for eating competitions in which contestants took turns to nominate the dish, the final bill being paid by the losers. I never took part, but once saw Brian 'Goofy' Wakefield defeat all-comers there.

Drinking in those days was regulated by rigid opening hours (11 a.m. to 2 p.m.; 5 p.m. to 10 p.m.) and in the duller regions of the year, the gap was sometimes bridged by a purchase from the off-licence and a few circuits of the town on the top deck of the Circle Bus. The Currie trio also favoured the Denmark Rooms (now a Japanese restaurant) opposite Wemyss Place on Queen Street, which served especially damaging strong lager at a reasonable price, but they were soon banned from these premises. The Sixties is often described as the decade where the British discovered sex, but in Edinburgh binge drinking seemed to loom somewhat larger.

The Group had no particular enthusiasm for training, but spent the odd evening at the Currie Railway Walls keeping arm and finger strength up to the mark. That classic Edinburgh training ground, the South or Little Quarry of Salisbury Crags, had largely been abandoned by them, since the difficulty level was considered inadequate, and it provided little in the way of strength training. Jimmy Marshall was, however, still a regular visitor to the Arthur's Seat crags on Sunday mornings. Macniven and I

Jimmy Marshall, Elly Moriarty and Jim Stenhouse exercising on the Currie Wa's c.1960.
Photo: Ronnie Marshall, SMC Image Archive.

became devotees of the Little Quarry, and had everything there licked by the end of the 1961 session. We got there by dint of some dangerous strength training with devices equipped with a stiff spring which you squeezed in each hand at lectures, or in the cinema, etc. until ligament damage threatened, or happened. I was particularly proud of my mastery of a variation of Athlete's Arête called 'Coupe Jacques' which was perhaps

5c, and I recall stunning Bugs McKeith some years later by smoothing up it in my Hush Puppies. Coupe Jacques was an unhealthy concoction served in the nearby Newington Café (still available) which climbers often visited after their morning workout. Climbing in the Queen's Park was forbidden for the stupid reason that it set a bad example to children (these were non-existent during school hours), and was made difficult by Her Majesty's Park Rangers, who threatened prosecution and attempted to take names and addresses. Their notebooks contained many entries for 'Bill Murray', 'Donald Bennet' and 'Hamish MacInnes'. Since these pests didn't begin their rounds until around 10 o'clock, most climbers visited the Quarry in the mornings.

Another important focus of activity, particularly in the dog days of spring and autumn, was the SMC Clubroom at 369 High Street. This was used responsibly for Lectures, Committee meetings and keeping up with events elsewhere via the Library, but also irresponsibly as occasional Hut accommodation when the last buses had gone, and for alfresco drinking parties organized by Smith, whom the Club had foolishly made Custodian. A keg of Export beer (88 pints) would be ordered from McEwan's, and carefully tended beforehand. I was an avid fan of so-called Modern Jazz, having listened throughout my teenage years to the Voice of America's Jazz Hour, presented every evening by Willis Conover on the massive valve radio in my bedroom. I was delighted to discover that Smith was also a fan, so these drinking parties swung along to the be-bop of the moment – Cannonball Adderley, Miles Davis, Thelonious Monk, Bobby Timmons, etc. The parties brought everyone together, and Creagh Dhu visitors frequently arrived from Glasgow and on one occasion Geoff Arkless and Geoff Oliver attended from Newcastle. Afterwards, we lay where we fell, wrapped in the Clubroom curtains. After one such debauch, Her Majesty visited St Giles' Cathedral opposite on the following morning. The police decided that several young gentlemen hanging out of the S.M.C. windows in their underwear while jazz blared behind them wouldn't quite do, and entered the premises to restore order. The Library was only opened by the Librarian, Robin Gall Inglis, at inconvenient set times. However, there was a simple traverse involving a downpipe, albeit across the abyss of Advocates Close, from kitchen window to the latchless Library window, so the more agile Clubroom visitors were able to make use of it at all times, and Robin Inglis endured a difficult few years. The Group's alpine exploits were also greatly assisted by Graham Brown, who gave Smith free access to his formidable Alpine library in his Manor Place flat, and provided suggestions for routes.

In the summer of 1962, Smith was killed on Mt. Garmo in the Pamirs, taking part in an ill-conceived British-Soviet expedition. This dire event knocked the stuffing out of all Edinburgh climbing, and the Group began to disintegrate shortly afterwards. But Macniven and I recovered well in 1963. In late winter we climbed Crow's Nest Crack on Buachaille in boots, stepping off névé at the bottom and onto it at the top. At Easter we toured the Lakes, shepherded initially by Geoff Arkless to Troutdale Pinnacle Superdirect, which we breezed up in boots, and then we managed North Crag Eliminate, Do Not, Kipling Groove, and several other noteworthy routes there. A visit to Ben Nevis yielded up Minus One Direct, Centurion and Sassenach. We went to the Alps with high hopes and foolish aspirations. When I arrived in Chamonix I was greeted by a grinning Haston, who had just come from the Eigerwand. After sorting out a tent in the Biolay campsite, we went on a giant bender in the Bar National to celebrate his success. The evening ended for me in the Chamonix Jail after throwing up in the public fountain. 'Robin à Boire' the constables called me. They fined me a paltry amount in the morning, and gave me breakfast – autres temps, autres moeurs. When Macniven turned up, we climbed a trivial ED on the Pte. Albert. Then he had the idea that we would repeat the Brown-Whillans route on the Blaitière. However, our knowledge of how to deal with flared holdless cracks was zero, and the Fissure Brown was completely beyond us. The outing should have ended there, but a French party appeared armed with huge wooden wedges with which the Fissure was soon disgracefully overcome. Compounding folly, we followed the French party, and after the Fissure Whillans, Macniven was struck on the head by their stonefall when we stopped to eat, and rendered comatose. There was a spectacular rescue that evening by Charles Bozon and René Novel of the ENSA to the accompaniment of a violent thunderstorm and blazing searchlights on the glacier. Neil died in the Argentière hospital a week after the accident, never recovering consciousness, and Bozon and Novel were killed in the Verte avalanche of 7 July 1964. This horrible catastrophe ended my interest in the Alps, and I didn't return there until 1975.

I hung on for a few days, encouraged by others to return quickly to the fray, but the weather had turned. Haston and Moriarty came back from a tour of the Dolomites, where they had been chauffeured by Norman Tennent. They had taken turns to cook: Norman had sourced fresh meat and vegetables from local markets, and prepared delicious meals; Dougal and Elly heated up tinned food stolen from supermarkets. Matters came to a head in the old chicken-shed at the Biolay where Norman was egged on to cook a giant mushroom omelette of 12 eggs in a collapsible frying pan, which duly collapsed at the vital moment of service, depositing the omelette amongst the ancient chicken faeces. As we hurriedly scraped with our spoons and plates, Norman fled into the night.

The 1963–4 session was a blank year for me, since I had to bear down a lot for the looming final exams. I moved into 20 Manor Place. Graham Brown had opened up the basement of his flat to members of the University Club, and I had one of the rooms. 'Goofy' Wakefield occupied a cupboard, which suited his spartan Yorkshire taste. This was a man who throughout 30-odd years of annual visits to Mont Blanc chose always to stay in the Chalet Austria – a derelict building on the Montenvers to Plan de l'Aiguille path – and to fetch his groceries by foot from Chamonix.

'Goofy': Brian Wakefield, An Teallach 1999. Photo: Robin Campbell.

Haston and Moriarty embarked on a doomed enterprise, a Climbing School venture based in Glencoe and fuelled by money supplied by Bev Clark. In the course of a year, three cars were written off by them, a Lotus Elan, a Ferrari and a Porsche, and early in 1965 Dougal mowed down three pedestrians in Glen Coe illegally driving the School van, and was sent to prison. Jimmy Stenhouse disappeared to England somewhere. The University Club moved its headquarters from Deacon Brodie's to Rutherford's Bar in Drummond Street. The Squirrels – a group of Edinburgh City natives – burst on the scene, emerging from the obscurity of the Hawcraig at Aberdour to make fine climbs in Glen Coe and Ben Nevis from their Hut at the Studdy. It was the end of an era of Edinburgh climbing, and the beginning of a new one.

STORM AND SUNLIGHT IN THE MOUNTAINS[1]

By Iain Smart

I FOUND MYSELF FOLLOWING the footpath that runs south through the wild country between Loch Torridon and Glen Carron. It was as fine a summer's day as you could wish for and I reached the summit of the pass in a mood to linger about just enjoying the colours of the landscape. This was a morning if ever there was one when God was in his heaven and all was right with the world. In Scotland, at least, this combination puts you on your guard. Nevertheless on this occasion I threw caution to the winds and spent a happy hour wandering about with an open mind. I found a niche by the side of a bright blue lochan where I must have dozed off.

When I awoke it was afternoon; the air had turned humid and towering cumulus clouds loured in the south-west. The vast landscape of colourful hills and distant horizons that had dominated the morning had become dim and dark and 'close' – the hills seemed to draw near. My blue lochan had lost its twinkle and lay flat and grey. A few flashes of lightning lit the gathering gloom, followed some time later by the rumble of distant thunder. It was time to get out of here and seek shelter. A few miles away lay the bothy where I had arranged to meet Nicholas that evening, an obvious haven in the gathering storm. I speeded on my way. As I approached I noticed the dark figure of Nicholas coming fast up the track from the other direction. We reached the bothy together as the rain started.

'We're only just in time,' he said. 'This is going to be one hell of a storm.'

'Well, you should know about such things if anyone should.'

We entered the musty gloom of our haven, lit a candle and got a fire going. Soon we had created a nook of comfort from the halliracket storm that was gathering its strength in the outside darkness. Between us we had enough simple food for a convivial meal.

Nicholas set the table and we sat down in golden candle light to a supper of bacon and beans, smoked sausage and crusty bread while the Sturm and Drang and Darkness performed boisterously outside.

'We are indeed fortunate,' said my diabolical companion, 'not many restaurants are as exclusive as this. No over-sophisticated people would gain admission here. They would be unable to afford the extortionate entrance fee of a ten mile walk. Even if they arrived, I suspect, they would be improperly dressed and in this weather we could hardly ask them to leave. So let's make the most of this moment of high privilege and enjoy each other's company and have a little intellectual joust. Let's make the most of this candle-lit corner of security while the storm outside roars and rustles.'

---

[1] This tale is an amalgam of two chapters (pp.133–43) of the late Iain Smart's book *Whatever Title*, Papyngay Press, 2016. Reproduced here by kind permission of the publisher Phil Todd. (Hon. Ed.)

Usually I had to take the initiative, this time Nicholas seemed keen to embark on a discussion.

'Okay there is a lot I would like to ask you. Last time we met you said that the human brain is one of the most dangerous things that has ever evolved on earth.'

'Yes indeed, our brain has the capacity to understand how the world actually works,' he enunciated, as if that explained everything.

I wasn't going to let him away with such a glib oversimplification:

'What's dangerous about that? To me understanding how things work is an advantage. It means that instead of having to adapt to our environment we can adapt our environment to suit us, to suit our priorities. That sounds like avoiding danger to me; successful adaptation gives us power to improve our lot. Civilisation is based on our control of the environment.'

'Yes, that is the conventional view, but it is only half the story. Stop and think for a moment, my friend. Adapting to our environment is one thing – it is essential for evolution but adapting our environment to suit us is quite another. Being able to control our environment rather than our environment controlling us puts the human race in the position of the Sorcerer's Apprentice – we have interfered with the complexities of an immensely powerful, dynamic universe without a full understanding of the nature of the forces we can release, still less how to control them. In our case, alas, there is no wise sorcerer to take over and come to our rescue; we are carried away by the powers we have released.'

'I think I see dimly what you are getting at. Please fill in the details.'

'The devil, as you correctly point out, is in the details and there is none better than myself to be Devil's Advocate in this matter.'

'Agreed, please proceed.'

'Let me take you back to the original creation myth you learned at Sunday School. The myth shows that the danger of what we were doing was anticipated by the ancients. You remember Adam and Eve were induced to eat of the fruit of the Tree of the Knowledge of Good and Evil?'

'I remember the story well.'

'Knowledge by itself is neither good nor evil; it is understanding how to put knowledge to use that led to what we now call good and evil. We have gradually understood how to adapt our environment to make our life easier. We started to live in a world created by us and not by nature's changing course untrimmed. This is the fact that turned us out of the Garden of Eden; we ceased to remain part of the Garden and began to adapt the Garden to suit us. Instead of the environment changing us we started to change the environment. The change led eventually to the Atom Bomb – or, more generally, we eventually gained access to the immense power immanent in the universe.'

This left me out of my depth. For a moment I had to tread water.

'Wasn't there a serpent involved who master-minded the project and used Eve as his patsy?'

'Yes indeed, Eve is the natural world and the serpent is a metaphor for our problem-solving superabundant circuitry; its inherent property is to understand cause and effect: that is what gave us our drive to understand how the world works. If we didn't have superabundant circuitry configured in the way it is we wouldn't be bothered with understanding what is going on around us. We would have remained happily with Mother Eve in the Garden of Eden impervious to the wiles of the serpent. We wouldn't have had the processing power to know what it was talking about. The apple would have been tasteless.'

'Even so, why did the ancients produce myths warning about the knowledge of good and evil? They weren't aware of the coming of industrial overproduction and desolation, still less, of atom bombs.'

'It wasn't "the ancients" who produced the unease. It was the superabundant circuitry inside their heads; deep down in its inner workings it had the capacity to assess various outcomes. It was intimidated by the environment and generated warning signals. Their superabundant circuitries did not come out with a specific theory of environmental conservation but their computations expressed a deep emotional unease about interfering with the powers behind nature which they saw as something supernatural with a mind similar to, but greater, more unpredictable than their own; the ambient world was something both benevolent and malevolent that had to be propitiated as if behind it was a mind similar to our own.'

At this point there was a flash of lightning of superlative brightness and an appalling prolonged basso-profundo rumble of thunder. Wind and rain battered the bothy making it shudder. Even I, a sceptic who knew this was all explainable in terms of thermodynamics, felt intimidated. I crouched at the table. I felt something was trying to burst in. The door blew open. 'Good God', I uttered involuntarily activating a primitive subroutine somewhere deep down in the interface between my core program and superabundant circuitry. I was momentarily overcome with primitive visceral fear and involuntarily made an appeal to a supernatural power. I looked at Nicholas to see how he was faring; he sat there calmly in the flickering candlelight cutting a piece of sausage and looking quizzically at me. He raised an eyebrow.

'I think we'd better close that door,' he was always practical and matter of fact.

We heaved the door shut with some difficulty and secured it with the back of a chair under the handle; the sneck had been broken.

We went back to the table and finished our supper.

'Considering the subject of our conversation, I think it would be appropriate if we ended by sharing this apple,' he said, quietly cutting it in two and handing me half. 'It goes well with that Gruyère cheese you brought.'

As I accepted the apple there was another thunder clap of intimidating loudness and a bolt of lightning struck the ground outside, close enough to make the bothy shudder. Nicholas sat unmoved enjoying his half apple.

'Aren't you overdoing things a bit?' I asked. 'Don't you find this all a bit over the top? Even the director of a Wagner opera would find all this Sturm and Drang a bit excessive.'

'The wild weather has nothing to do with me. I am only a poor devil. I have no power to order the universe about. Thunderstorms do happen. This one was predicted in last night's forecast. It's just that it's coinciding with the heavy discussion we are having. Do you really think there is an angry deity outside stage managing the collision of two masses of air of different temperatures and humidity just to terrify with his power a couple of poor souls for thinking impious thoughts?'

'No,' I conceded, 'we are too intellectually sophisticated to accept that explanation; we understand atmospheric physics. Nevertheless, a moment ago I did accept that interpretation; a few tens of thousands of years ago when I was a hunter-gatherer I no doubt would have accepted the commotion as the response of an angry deity to some transgression.'

Nicholas made a pot of coffee and we shifted our chairs to the fireside. We spent the rest of the evening sipping moderately from my flask of whisky and discussing the apparently trivial problem of picking up a stick; it is no easy task deciding which is the right and which the wrong end, a lot depends on which end we choose.

Nicholas ended the lesson by saying, 'You do realise that there never was such a place as a Garden of Eden. The whole concept of an original perfect paradise is in the same category as cloud cuckoo land. Even as a working hypothesis it leads up a blind alley. Like it or not we are and always have been subject to the laws of a universe indifferent to our desires and are cursed with the drive to understand them. But cheer up; we – bearers of a superabundant circuitry – may have been cruel to each other but we have on many occasions been kind. We have also produced beautifully ordered things, a feat impossible without breaking the Second Law.'

On this happy note the storm started to subside. We rolled out our sleeping bags on the floor. I slept a deep dreamless sleep, released from the burden of consciousness and all its complications.

I awoke the next morning with sunbeams from the open door lighting up the dust in the air. I thought at first that Nicholas had done his usual disappearing act but his sleeping bag was still there and I could hear him moving about outside. I emerged into a brilliant summer morning. The rain had refreshed the land and everything was new and bright. A slate or two had come off the roof, and a nearby tree felled by last night's thunderbolt, bowed gracefully towards the rising sun. Otherwise the storm had rendered all things bright and beautiful. Nicholas had a stove going and the rich aroma of freshly brewed coffee filled the air.

I brought out a couple of chairs and the rest of our food. We spent a relaxing hour breakfasting at our leisure in companionable silence. The beauty of the morning needed our full attention. The grass and leaves around us were silvered with raindrops reflecting the sunlight. The receding horizons of the surrounding hills were sharp and clear. The ambience was kind and benevolent in contrast to the violence of the previous night. The energy of yesterday's buildup of heat had dissipated and the air was cool.

It was a morning for being at one with the environment – one of my favourite clichés.

However I wasn't sure how long Nicholas would be around for questioning and I ruined the ambience by returning to last night's conversation.

'So have we picked up the right or wrong end of the stick? Have we brought our troubles on our own heads by interfering intelligently with the universe? The myth of the serpent influencing Eve to violate Adam's happy ignorance is just a way of shifting responsibility? If it had not been for them, we would still be living happily in the Garden?'

Nicholas looked pained at this inappropriate attempt to intellectualise a morning of such perfect tranquility.

'You have just demonstrated again that for us the stick has only one end. You obviously can't enjoy the version of the Garden of Eden we are in at the moment,' he said irritably, gesticulating at the smiling landscape. 'For people with brains like ours, letting even a generous environment, supposing there was one, mould us in its own way and in its own good time wasn't an option, our brains wouldn't have allowed it, neither would our unstable environment. As we concluded last night there never was a golden age when we humans lived harmoniously together in sweetness and light. The neural processing power with which we are over-endowed has always driven us to understand what was going on. In a world full of living things all of us are competing for the energy necessary to maintain our integrity. Organisms which we regard as agents of infectious disease are only doing their best to survive. We are to them merely accessible sources of energy which they are adapted to exploit, they are still in the garden; we are their paradise.'

He ended even more irritably by saying, 'Anyway as far as we humans are concerned competition is the ineradicable mark of Cain. If it comes to the bitter bit in the struggle for survival we will kill our own brothers – there is no shortage of civil wars and among the criminal fraternity the lives of competitors or informers are cheap whatever the degree of consanguinity. And Abel wasn't the last brother of the children of Adam to be done in by an ambitious sibling for getting in the way. More to the point there are circumstances when I could have induced you to do something similar. Be thankful they have never occurred.'

With this disturbing utterance he got up and began packing up his gear; he seemed in a hurry to leave.

'Don't go, the discussion is getting interesting.'

'You may think so, but I have better things to do on a fine morning, fresh after rain than wallow around in dark alleys of dismal theology.'

'But you say you are affecting to be the Devil. It's your job to lead me astray; you are doing a good job destabilising my belief systems.'

'Yes, but there are limits. I've done enough for the moment. I'm off to the east to explore Sgòrr Ruadh. You can come with me if you shut up about theology. But first we have to put the slates back on the roof and leave enough firewood for the next people.'

Thus admonished I dutifully cleared up the remains of breakfast. With some difficulty I replaced three slates on the roof. Nick found a bushman's saw in the bothy and cut up the dead branches of the fallen tree, leaving a neat pile of logs and kindling by the hearth for the next visitors.

We left in the warmth of the mid-morning sun and walked into a colourful landscape of near and far. I resolved to make the most of the high privilege of my temporary residence in the Garden of Eden that presently surrounded us. For the rest of the day I didn't ruin it by thinking. I just applied the undivided attention of my superabundant circuitry to being aware of the superabundant beauty of the landscape.

We climbed over the high pass to the foot of the east side of Sgòrr Ruadh and spent the warm summer day joyously scrambling on the two great buttresses that flank the summit. Some of the situations we got into were potentially dangerous but were not so because we took care to remain within our envelope of competence. The exposure merely added an agreeable frisson to our enjoyment, like lemon juice on an oyster.

In the evening we descended exuberantly southwards to Glen Carron where Nicholas had left his car.

LE MIROIR

By Ann MacDonald and Colwyn Jones

THE MIROIR D'ARGENTINE in the Vaud region of Western Switzerland is a must for every middle grade rock climber, but perhaps not at weekends. We recommend that you make a plan for a visit to climb on this awesome crag.

Evening sunlight bathes the Miroir d'Argentine.   Photo: Colwyn Jones.

The Miroir dominates the tiny hamlet of Solalex at the head of a long remote glen. It is a beautiful place to visit, whether to walk, climb, enjoy a heavy stultifying lunch of traditional Paysanne fare (ham, cheese and potatoes) or simply drink cold beer in the warm sunshine. Being slightly more than an hour by fast car from Geneva (witnessed by two speed cameras flashing, but not at us!) close to the eastern shore of Lac Leman it is a popular spot. However, they even have a park-n-ride to cater for those busy weekends.

We arrived late on a July Sunday afternoon and were driving uphill against the flow of tourist traffic on the very narrow country road so the journey was slow, but at least we found parking wasn't a problem when we arrived. Describing the area as rustic would be a cliché ('...sayings only become clichés because they're true.' – M Domovitch).

The Miroir is a perfect limestone slab and wall of substantial proportions. Perhaps the smooth surface of Le Miroir could have been created by a single stroke from the battle axe of a mighty ancient giant, or the sweep of the tail of the devil or a mighty northern fire dragon as they flew too low over this craggy mountain range. But the truth is more prosaic. It was in fact formed from ancient shells during the Mesozoic epoch when it was the bed of a vast enclosed sea. The resulting sedimentary limestone is of excellent quality for climbing with waterworn cracks and fissures. Geologically speaking, it has been pushed up and folded by the subducting African tectonic plate pushing under the European plate at a convergent zone deep under the rock of the bed of the Mediterranean sea. Which is why, again geologically speaking, the Alps are apparently getting higher through the resultant orogenesis (mountain building).

I believe Le Miroir got its name from when the huge face becomes a mirror immediately after a heavy summer shower soaks the slab and for a short time the sun is reflected back off the wet limestone. Argent translates as silver or money, but it can also mean rock, giving Mirror of Silver or perhaps less bling and bejewelled, Mirror of Rock.

The Jurassic (or Jurassique in the original tongue) was recognised and named by Alexander von Humboldt (1795) exploring in the Jura Mountains over on the other side of Lake Geneva. The result is that there are many fossils found on the surface of the slab, perhaps with the present company included.

The routes we have now climbed on this memorable venue are between 13 and 15 pitches, although we inadvertently added a few more on the Voie Normale this year! It was re-bolted in 1992, par Les Guides Vaudois, avec le soutien du CAS et de Mammut-Sport. There are large reassuring double ring fixed bolt belays pretty much every 50m so don't thread too much of your climbing rope through the belay rings if using 50m ropes. The intervening bolts for running belays were all sound, but sometimes seem quite widely spaced.

There are four buses to Solalex each day in summer and, having driven up there, I applaud the skill of the bus drivers, so efficient Swiss public transport to the venue is possible. It costs 5 CHF a day to park a car at Solalex, and we stayed in a rudimentary dortoir at the refuge de Solalex which was 23 CHF per person per night. They also have a rustic restaurant which seemed very charming, even alluring.

Our arrival so late in the day meant that the entire Miroir was bathed in evening sunshine. Owing to the north western orientation of the slab and the angle of the higher Arête d'Argentine, timing is important to allow climbing in either the sunshine (late start) or shade (early start). However, for us, the length of the route dictated an early start, regardless of our preference for insolation. In August 2016 we had climbed the Directe route (French grade 5a, 13 pitches) and our 2017 return match to scale the Voie Normale did not disappoint.

It takes about an hour to cross the river and walk up the steep talus slope from Solalex to the foot of the slab. The path is initially wooded then grass covered, allowing you to avoid the scree until the last few metres of the approach. On that day we had the pleasure of the company of a Swiss couple planning to climb Zygofolis (6a+). Once we realised we were not competing for the same route they chatted amiably while we just tried to follow, our perverse northern heavy breathing punctuated by affirmative or negative grunts as seemed appropriate to their polite questions. They specifically commented on whether we, adherents of the Scottish climbing tradition, should be spending time on bolted routes? They were gently taking the piss out of us, and the exchange allowed us to confirm our national characteristic of adaptability. We breathlessly replied that, as visitors, we would adopt the local Swiss climbing traditions and probably manage just fine!

Small metal plaques riveted to the rock announce the titles of the popular routes, so both they and the less popular (and harder) intervening routes are easy to find, at least at the start.

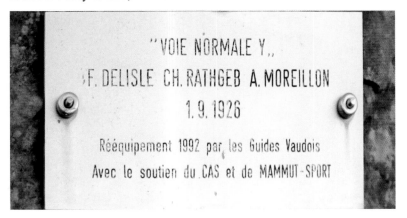

Route plaque at the foot of the Voie Normale.   Photo: Colwyn Jones.

The Voie Normale (or Voie de l'Y) was first climbed in 1926 according to the relevant plaque. There is a large Y-shaped fissure pretty much up the middle of the slab to guide you. The route follows two easy pitches graded 2b & 3b in the *Swiss Plaisir WEST* guidebook, although there is also a harder direct start. One then arrives on the vire inférieure where there is a scramble up easy ground for an indicated 40 metres. Colwyn thought he had found the belay, but closer inspection showed it was for Bal des Mutants (graded 6b+ on UKC) and with the title helpfully painted close to the slightly different belay bolts, suggesting that using the wrong belay may be a common error. Bobbing back down and in consultation with three Belgian lads following us, we finally found the correct ring bolts at the top of a blocky pinnacle above a big shallow bay. Once installed on the correct stance, the crux pitch loomed but was easily overcome if you have spent the winter climbing the thuggy overhangs at

Ann MacDonald leading pitch 6.   Photo: Colwyn Jones.

Ratho; the three bolts to protect the moves left onto the main slab may also have, ahem ...helped.

Moving confidently past the crux, the next pitch starts on the upper slab proper. However, Colwyn found he was suddenly teetering 15 to 20 feet above the last bolt on tenuous wrinkles and scoops. He did use a couple of intervening wires placed in traditional style on the pitch. It is graded 5a and on reaching the next belay bolts Colwyn found, that despite no direct sunshine, the chill of the morning air had clearly gone; he mentioned that he was perspiring somewhat.

Colwyn stuffed his lightweight jacket into the rucksack he was given, then Ann led onward on the superb surface of the upper slab. It continues for seven glorious pitches, never too hard, but never so easy as to be classed as carefree, exposed enough to be exhilarating. Superb, absorbing, slab climbing.

Having climbed Directe route the year before, we tried to follow the complete Voie Normale, rather than the option of the final few pitches of the Directe route. However, the bolts seemed to disappear and Ann was forced to downclimb, after threading a pegged maillion, presumably left by someone who had also found themselves in the same predicament.

Back at the junction of the Normale/Directe routes we changed option and finished up to the brèche in three fine pitches. They all had sketchy moves, similar to pitch 5 (after the crux), but the excellent rock and our earlier success on the first 12 pitches now made them familiar and attractive. Colwyn found that there was some damp rock at the top on the final pitch under the large overhang. An early traverse leftwards on pitch 15 avoids any unpleasant moistness and obviates the need for a short nerve-racking downclimb.

The two big ring bolts on the ridge at the top were a welcome sight, although the 14 other admirable pairs of bolts had been no less pleasing. We had taken 6.5 hours to climb the 15 pitches, plus the two extra we had added, not particularly by choice.

We sat at the brèche, having a late lunch looking down the slab as it curved away to infinity, or seemed to. The fertile green forest sat more than 500m below! Then the white helmet of one of the Belgian lads floated into view, perhaps on pitch 7 or 8. They were smoking tobacco with both the delaying effects of direct tobacco damage to the sensitive gas exchange membranes of their lungs, and the indirect delay caused by the time taken to smoke a cigarette on each belay. They spoke excellent English and on questioning had earlier assured Colwyn that they did know about the deleterious health effects of a tobacco addiction habit!

From the brèche there is an exposed scramble eastwards back along the Arête d'Argentine ridge, occasionally on a well-defined path, finally to meet the Col des Essets path, back to Anxeindax; our advice is to stick to the high ground where a choice presents itself. Around the summer pasture at Anxeindax there are at least two refuges where a pleasant overnight stay could be enjoyed. There is an option to follow a more direct

Ann belayed at the top of pitch 8. Photo: Colwyn Jones.

descent path from point 2044m (Col de la Poreyrette), down past a small lochan. We had used this shorter direct descent the year before. It was unpleasant, steep and loose, hence the choice of the longer, easier walk via Anxeindax back to Solalex.

Both of our routes to date, the Voie Normale and the Directe route would introduce debutants to the pleasures of climbing on this delightful limestone feature. Perhaps the letterbox on pitch 3 of Directe route and the traverse left onto the main slab on the fourth pitch mean Directe is the harder of the two, but on these occasions there was bolt protection reassuringly close, just as we found on the third pitch of the Voie Normale. A small rack of trad gear came in handy on the slab when the bolts suddenly appeared a long way off and smearing was required when holds mysteriously diminished.

There are about a dozen routes graded from 5a to 6c, so on reflection further visits to Le Miroir d'Argentine are probable, even likely.

Sadly the Voie Normale has now suffered the indignity of a winter ascent judging by the crampon scratches; the soft limestone displaying some deep scars. It looks like only one ascent by a pair of mixed climbers, ruining a classic rock route. We kept quiet about this on reaching the bar in Solalex. Perhaps a couple of other SMC members had been there previously!

THE LATE START

By Neil Quinn

FRIDAY EVENING, MID FEBRUARY 1966, the weather was foul with driving rain turning to sleet then snow as Doug Lang and I crossed Drumochter heading west to Fort William. We had been enticed away from the flesh pots of Dundee by a good weather forecast for the Saturday. The fish suppers we had bought in Hell's Kitchen were inedible and had been binned, we would have been better spending our money on a pie and a pint in the Jacobite.

By now the heavy rain had eased to a light drizzle as we drove up Glen Nevis to camp at the riverside beyond the youth hostel. A quick brew and into our sleeping bags. An alarm call at 5 a.m. showed the weather had not improved so we settled back down into our sleeping bags with mixed feelings. A call of nature took Doug out at 7 a.m. and whoops of joy announced the good weather had arrived. After a hurried breakfast we collected our gear from the car – a short axe each, a peg hammer, a few soft Stubai pegs and a couple of drive in ice pegs that were virtually useless, 300 feet of three-quarter weight rope and off we went just after 8 a.m. – not exactly an Alpine start but at least it was now daylight.

We crossed the river by the metal bridge at the hostel and climbed up to meet the tourist path and the new snow. At first the snow was just a dusting but as we climbed higher it got deeper and by the time we reached the half way lochan it was about a foot deep. We plodded round the lochan to the Allt a' Mhuilinn and headed down diagonally towards the CIC hut.

We stopped at the hut to decide what to do. The Ben was like an iced cake, plastered with snow and very little rock showing. Eventually we decided on Zero Gully, the theory being that it was so steep all the new snow would have fallen off it. At this time Zero had probably not had more than half a dozen ascents. I had dragged Doug to the foot of it the previous winter but he had decided it was a bit out of our league. However, an ascent earlier that winter of Eagle Ridge on Lochnagar had boosted Doug's confidence and he was agreeable. Unfortunately we had not thought where all the snow from Zero and the surrounding cliffs would be. From the CIC to the foot of Zero is not very far, however as we headed up hill the snow went from knee deep to thigh deep, and for the final section we were ploughing a trench waist deep to the foot of the cliff. Why the slope didn't avalanche I have no idea. In our naivety we didn't even consider the possibility, and had no knowledge or experience of avalanches and never thought of them happening in Scotland.

The climb looked in excellent condition but thanks to the deep snow it had taken five hours to reach the foot of it. It was now 1p.m. After gearing up I started up the first pitch, which was concave and allowed me to cut steps into the sides and keep in balance on the steep ice by bridging out. In places the ice was hollow and a few good blows of the axe cut a good

Zero Gully from Càrn Mòr Dearg. Photo: Roger Robb.

foot and hand hold. The snow was solid and I belayed on an ice axe, which in those days was considered adequate. No one had done loading tests and proved how useless these belays were. Doug disposed of the next section without much trouble but I found the traverse pitch on the section above a bit tricky. I couldn't get a belay and the snow was loose powder. I spent 45 minutes hunting for a peg crack before bringing Doug up on an ice axe driven into powder snow. Doug climbed the next small ice bulge and belayed below the last small steep section. Darkness had now fallen so head torches were donned, not an unusual occurrence in the pre-front pointing days. Fortunately for my tired arms the ice was hollow like parts of the first pitch and it made it fairly easy.

The ice in the upper gully was near perfect névé – ideal for climbing on and taking an ice axe belay. Both Doug and I carried MacInnes gully hammers as peg hammers. They were like North Wall hammers but had a short metal shaft and no spike. We decided to dispense with cutting steps and, other than for belays, climb like the modern system with our straight picks and front points. The upper 600 feet or so is about 56 degrees according to Dr Bell, but to our tired legs it was a long crawl to the top and it was a great relief to see the uncorniced rim of the plateau picked out in the torchlight.

The summit of the Ben was magical – everything pure white and, unusually, not a breath of wind. I remember dropping a sweet paper and it fluttered straight down to the snow. The sky was cloudless with a half moon and the stars blazing like lights in the sky. All the surrounding whitened hills were standing out above the gloom of the valleys. It was the sort of night that only happens very rarely in a lifetime of climbing. Magnificent. No matter how great the surroundings they do not keep you warm when the temperature is below freezing and we were forced to head down into the gloom of Glen Nevis. All the previous night's snow had been blown off the summit into Observatory Gully, as we knew to our cost earlier. The plateau was hard snow with lots of tracks showing us the way down. We kept our crampons on until we reached the end of the old hard snow and then a problem arose. Every time I bent down to take off my crampons my legs cramped up and I couldn't move. However, Doug did the decent thing and took off my crampons for me and we were able to proceed slowly back to our tent arriving just after 1 a.m.

A few good brews, our first liquid for 17 hours other than snow, and into our Fairy Down to lie and dream of Point Five. But that's another story.

REALITY AND IMAGE:
Three Scottish Artists

By Donald Orr

MOUNTAINS, AS SUBJECT MATTER for painters, are exposed to all the theories and philosophies prevalent at the time of their conception as artworks. They are never accurate accounts of geology or topography nor are they simply artistic records of structure and scale, form and colour, and while they may occasionally be peopled to assist scale, emphasise vista or aid a narrative aspect, it has always been the mountain's sheer bulk and dominance of the landscape that invited their inclusion in the world of fine art. While the Romantic tradition broke with the fixed views of the Classical School that demanded an idealised landscape based on the Italian aesthetic of the perfection of the Roman countryside, and moved into a more naturalistic sense of colour, with emotional content and an occasional foray into the exotic, the nineteenth century mountains and wilderness were seen as the work of the Divine, and an area of research, meditation and contemplation. Mountains were Ruskin's 'great cathedrals of the earth' and as such he believed they had a powerful influence on the human spirit.

Mountains also have an impact upon our senses whether it is the roughness of granite on our hands or the tether of an axe round our wrist, touch is important. Hearing too, especially the silence at altitude, and smell and taste add to the mountain experience, but sight has an extraordinary effect on our awareness. Within the mountain environment there exists an enormous variety of scene, a great diversity of features in rock and snow, and an endless permutation of light and weather impressions that can make our mountain days precious and our memories of them enduring. The few paintings discussed here are a point of departure – not a final word as there can be no conclusive statements about the mountain world. We continue to explore it seeking again what we have known and hoping for new revelations.

'So on we marched. That awful loneliness
Received our souls as air receives the smoke.
Then larger breath we drew, felt years gone by
And in a new dimension turned and spoke.'[1]

The three paintings by Scottish artists briefly examined here stand only as a reminder of a great collection of Scottish painting produced by the desire for scenes of wilderness and mountain grandeur that was generated by public taste for the views of 'Caledonia stern and wild' that pervaded

---

[1] Shepherd N. 'Above loch Avon', *In the Cairngorms*, Galileo, Cambridge, 2014, p.2.

'North Western View from Ben Lomond,' John Knox, 1778–1845.
Reproduced by kind permission of the Glasgow Museum Collection.

the Victorian era and was itself enhanced when Prince Albert purchased Balmoral castle for Queen Victoria in 1852 and thereafter popularised all things Highland.

John Knox was one of the most significant and original landscape painters of his day. Unfortunately many aspects of his life are uncertain, but it is known that he was born in Paisley and his family moved to Glasgow in 1799 where he may have trained under Alexander Nasmyth (1758–1840). Whatever the case he is undoubtedly considered to be Nasmyth's closest successor in terms of rural and urban landscape. From his studio in Glasgow, where he reputedly taught McCulloch, Macnee and Leitch, Knox moved in 1828 to London where he remained until 1836. He returned to Glasgow for some years before settling in Keswick where he spent the last five years of his life.

Knox's landscapes were in demand by 1821, at the time of the inaugural exhibition of the Glasgow Institute, where his movement away from the Italian Neo-Classicism of the eighteenth century towards a more Romantic treatment and realistic colour schemes had caught the public eye. His views of the Clyde valley around Lanark, the busy lower Clyde and his paintings of the Trossachs were all produced within that transition period between the Classical tradition that endorsed the notion of idealised landscape and the concept of the Picturesque in which the new Romantic movement strove for accuracy of colour and atmosphere. By far his most striking works were the dramatic panoramas often taken from mountain tops.

'North Western View from Ben Lomond'[2] is one of a pair of panoramic paintings produced in 1834; the grander and more imposing partner to 'South Western View of Ben Lomond', not that the latter is in any way a minor picture as its sweeping depiction from the summit stretches far into the distant Firth of Clyde and contains a hazy reference to the Paps of Jura. The North Western panoramic view is taken from above the steep north face of the peak whose summit is depicted on the left. Beyond can be seen the upper reaches of Loch Lomond with Loch Katrine on the right

---

[2] 'North Western View from Ben Lomond,' 1834, oil on canvas, 62.2 x 157.5cms. Kelvingrove Art Gallery and Museum. Bequeathed in 1874.

beyond which rise the distinctive peaks of Ben More and Stob Binnein. In the centre, almost lost in the haze, is the white cone of Ben Lui. Knox may well have been influenced by Edmund Burke's Philosophical Enquiry of 1757 and his concept of the 'Sublime' in which an awareness of the emotional aspects of landscape is revealed in notions of simultaneous fear and attraction. Knox's heightened viewpoint and the enhanced sweeping verticality of the north face add to the terror and majesty that was central to the Romantic philosophy. This impressive perspective is further enriched by either smoke or low cloud far below, and the inclusion of some wild goats which, while naturally occurring in that area, are surely a reference to the chamois of the Alps, placing the Scottish mountains on a par with anything in Europe. The diminutive figures on either side intensify the plunging verticality and the challenge of travelling in this landscape. A small group stand on the summit beneath what appears to be an obelisk. It is doubtful if this existed, but it swells the idea that Knox was proclaiming this area as a rival to the alpine ascents and experiments going on across the Channel. Only those aspiring to the contest with and contemplation of the heights should attempt this ascent. The group on the lower left appear to be hunters accompanied by a kilted guide which again encourages the impression of remoteness and the alien quality of the Highlands at that time. Luss is an area that is now easily accessible but only one hundred years ago was still a remote Gaelic speaking community.

Knox made an important and unique contribution to the development of the Romantic tradition in Scotland in the 19th Century that sought out the dramatic features of the Highland landscape to record for posterity. While his painting may contain ambitious emotional effects, his images are strengthened by his stunning visual accuracy.

Horatio McCulloch became the foremost landscape painter in Scotland during the nineteenth century Romantic period. Born in Glasgow he moved between his home city and Edinburgh throughout his life and made many painting expeditions to the West Highlands and Skye.[3] His paintings exhibit a clarity and naturalness of handling that were highly innovative in the nineteenth century. His ability to render a mountain massif in all its folds and contours and move smoothly from the fawns and ochres of the foreground to the light and air of the sky was matured and enhanced by his many trips to Glen Coe, Loch Maree, Skye and the Trossachs. This allowed him to produce canvases with an authenticity that maintained the landscapes' grandeur without the cloying sentimentality displayed by many of his contemporaries. His work relied on a realism and faithfulness to the scene in front of him. Genuineness of representation coupled with an ability to render atmospheric effects accurately, became the hallmarks of his work.

---

[3] Fuller details are available in 'The Enduring Image', *SMCJ*. No. 178. 1987, pp.397– 400.

'Glencoe, Argyllshire,' Horatio McCulloch, 1805–1867.
Reproduced by kind permission of the National Gallery of Scotland.

'Glencoe, Argyllshire'[4] is unique in its presentation of Am Buachaille
Etive Mòr – The Great Herdsman of Etive. The modern view of the
'Buachaille' is characterized in many images taken from the main road
to the south as it rises over the Blackmount and reveals the peak of Stob
Dearg rising sharply and the mountain ridge from that summit running
south west forming the northern side of Glen Etive. By contrast
McCulloch's observation is clearly taken from the area around the
Kingshouse Hotel. Built in the seventeenth century for travellers across
Rannoch Moor it was used as a barracks from 1746 but by the late
eighteenth century had reverted to its role as a coaching inn. This water
colour sketch is less well known than the large canvas of the same year
and title exhibited in the Kelvingrove Museum, Glasgow.[5]

This eastern viewpoint was well known to McCulloch as his earlier
'The Entrance to Glencoe From Rannoch Moor' of 1846[6] suggests more
than one visit to this area. In the latter study, he captures the bleak
ruggedness of the mountain and its dominance of the landscape. While
the sky is rendered freshly, the clouds shredding themselves over the
ridges to enhance the clarity of the blue sky beyond, the weather
overshadows the landscape heightening the sense of wildness and
desolation and hinting that the cloud filled Glen Etive is to be avoided.

---

[4] 'Glencoe, Argyllshire' – water colour and body colour over pencil on paper,
13.60 x 21.60cm. 1864. National Gallery of Scotland, Edinburgh.

[5] 'Glencoe', oil on canvas, 1105 x 1829mm. 1864. Kelvingrove Museum and Art
Galleries.

[6] 'The Entrance to Glencoe From Rannoch Moor,' oil on canvas, 34.6 x 60.6cm,
1846, private collection.

The small figures in the middle ground, one on horseback, are dominated by the landscape yet travel on using the mountain as a beacon or signpost on their journey. The treatment of the mountain is vague, in part due to the weather and changing light but also, one senses as a simplification of the many gullies and buttresses that seam the north face of the mountain. The painting is not just about the mountain but about being in the mountains of the West Highlands where changeable weather systems still make conditions difficult for the traveller on foot or the mountaineer. This image is at once an invitation to explore this wild environment and a warning that it is no easy tourist experience. Glen Coe is open and approachable but the traveller must always be well prepared.

Whatever influences there may have been in his work his highly individual approach to Scottish landscape painting, especially in his Highland and mountain scenery, displays a truth and understanding that hitherto had been absent in painting in Scotland. During his lifetime 'he was fortunate that his fondness for painting the wilder parts of his country coincided with public taste'[7] but his mountain landscapes, so thoroughly explored, still exhibit the clear, cold, blustery freshness any climber may meet in Glen Coe.

Born in Haddington, William Beattie-Brown was raised in Edinburgh, educated at Leith High School and apprenticed as a glass stainer in the city, however his artistic development was so rapid that on the strength of his own maturity he was sent to the Trustees' Art Academy then under the guidance of Robert Scott Lauder (1803–69). It was at this institution that he first met Horatio McCulloch and Daniel McNee amongst others. On leaving the Academy his early work was created in Edinburgh and the Borders, but he also worked successfully in England and Belgium. However, it was painting Scottish Highland landscapes en plein air (his chief delight) which allowed the vigour and realism of his work to come to the fore. An Associate of the Royal Scottish Academy by 1871 'Coire na Faireamh'[8] is his diploma picture donated to the Royal Scottish Academy on the occasion of his election as a full Academician in 1884.

The Giant's Coire, Coir' an Fhamair, as it appears on the current O.S. map, is the third of six coires situated against the long northern ridge of Beinn Bhàn in Applecross. Some four kilometres on the track north from the road bridge over the River Kishorn will land you in the vicinity of Lochan Coire na Poite which, with a bit of artistic licence, would serve as the area of standing water in the foreground of the canvas. The hollow of the mountain fastness is depicted in a low, raking light that catches the natural features of the mountainsides and allows a detailed appreciation of the scene. Crags, buttresses and gullies are delineated in a vast corried alcove that leads the eye into the recesses of the cauldron-like feature.

---

[7] Smith S, *Horatio McCulloch, 1805–1867*, Glasgow Museums and Galleries, Glasgow, 1988, p. 22.

[8] 'Coire Na Faireamh', oil on canvas, 1883/4. 67.8 x 114.6cm. Royal Scottish Academy of Art and Architecture, Edinburgh.

'Coire na Faireamh, Applecross.' William Beattie Brown, 1831–1909.
By kind permission of the Royal Scottish Academy of Art and Architecture.

The sense of verticality is enhanced by the flattened foreground where the undulations of the moor meet the upthrust of the mountains at a seeming right angle. While certain angles and aspects may be enriched to create the impact of the majesty of the corrie there is an attention to detail and a technical excellence in the dusting of cloud cover across the summits and the light of Applecross streaming through the high valley. The foreground colour and tone set the reality of the scene while the soaring ruggedness of the vertical walls lined with ledges and scored by gullies allows the mountaineer's eye to consider route after route.

His work is held in the municipal galleries of Liverpool, Manchester, Oldham and Bolton. He exhibited regularly at the RSA in Edinburgh, the Royal Academy in London, in Glasgow and in many exhibitions throughout Scotland where his realistic line and tone, his technical dynamism, and his ability to render accurately the passing atmospheric effects in the mountains delighted and continue to enchant many.

What is significant about these three works, and many others like them in the municipal galleries of the country, is that in many respects they still represent an image of the Highlands that is held by countless people. Despite the rise in cine-tourism, hillwalking and mountain 'experiences', Highland safaris or marine wildlife cruises, the mental picture of the North of Scotland is still that encased in the depictions of Victorian painters: the cottage nestling against the hillside, the soaring majesty of the high hills, sheep on the track, cattle in the water and stags at bay. While the nation has changed – we seem to have moved away from the 'tartantry' of The White Heather Club and the recordings of the Alexander Brothers – the image of the land held in many minds is still that reflected in Victorian landscapes whose enduring illustrations have been portrayed on decades of shortbread tins and in a continuing notion of 'grannie's hielan hame'.

We may appreciate the naturalness of Victorian paintings produced by men whose whole experience was different from ours, but it is not the world we see. It is not that our response to certain landscapes has changed but that new technologies, greater access, and a higher endeavour compel us all to think and see in new ways not expressible in the old language at all. A new generation, moving away from all this, will encounter a freshness of experience and the challenge of wild places, in much the same way as McCulloch and his contemporaries. It is sensed in the continuing excitement of coming over the Blackmount and that first glimpse of the 'Buachaille', that initial note of awe as we look upon the Cuillin Ridge or enter the lonely fastness of Torridon, and that exhilaration, if anything, is worth preserving.

A raw, misty day
that separated hill features
– turned boulders to peaks.

Hamish Brown

TO KEATS ON BEN NEVIS, 2 AUGUST, 1818[1]

By Graeme Morrison

You came by Windermere and Stock Ghyll force,
Cold-calling Wordsworth's door at Rydal Mount,
Surmounting Skiddaw in a morning's course,
And watering grog at its cool upland fount;
Tramped through the land of Lockhart's acid pen[2]
(No feeble Cockney now, could he but see
Your daily score of miles on muddy ways!),
Paying zigzag homage then
At Burns's tomb, high-domed so recently,
And old Iona's lichened effigies.

No little grist to a poetic mill,
Perhaps; but sit now on this giddy ledge,
And swing those bog-tanned bauchles, if you will,
Above the clouds that lap the summit's edge;
And count it wholesome if your senses fail
To quite digest such beauty manifest —
Far cry from Hampstead and so high above
That dark soul-making vale,
Where foul bacilli blight a youthful breast,
Devouring all despite a brother's love.

'Read me a lesson, Muse, and speak it loud',
You fondly ask.[3] So pause a while and hear
The Allt a' Mhuilinn plash beneath the cloud,
Or cawing ravens circling very near:
These are the germ of verses still unsung;
And those stupendous ridges wreathed in mist
Will conjure music from the sentient
In ages not yet sprung.
Now downwards, Master Keats, I must insist!
That tickling cough entails a swift descent.

---

[1] In 1818 John Keats (1795–1821) and his friend Charles Brown covered some 640 miles in 43 days of walking, starting at Lancaster in June and finishing at Inverness. On 1 August they walked north from Ballachulish, and after a night in an unknown location started their ascent from Glen Nevis around 5 a.m., accompanied by a tartan-clad guide and his dog. Fortified by whisky at Lochan Meall an t-Suidhe, they reached the summit by a route approximating the pony track. In a letter written the next day at Letterfinlay, Keats mentions 'chasms glutted with snow, 1500 feet in depth … the most tremendous places I have ever

seen', and despite swirling 'cloud veils' he was struck by the near and distant views. He goes on to describe a 'vile descent' in which he felt shaken 'all to pieces', though Brown elsewhere wrote how the poet 'scrambled down lightly and quickly'. By the time Keats reached Inverness on 6 August, he was suffering badly with an ulcerated throat that had started on their boggy crossing of Mull, and a local doctor pronounced him 'too thin and fevered to proceed on a journey'. He therefore cut short his walking tour and returned by sea to London, where he found that the health of his consumptive youngest brother – 'poor Tom' – had further deteriorated. As a qualified apothecary and surgeon, Keats nursed the youngster until his death in December. Within a couple of years Keats himself would die of tuberculosis, and yet this period saw his finest poetry, including the achingly beautiful Odes written in the spring of 1819.

[2] J G Lockhart, Sir Walter Scott's son-in-law, attacked Keats harshly in the Edinburgh publication *Blackwood's Magazine*. His Tory hostility was aroused by Keats's closeness to the radical politics of Leigh Hunt, but found its vent in a snobbish attack on his 'vulgar Cockney' upbringing & 'effeminate' poetry. Oddly enough, Lockhart was remembered as a kind man.

[3] Keats drafted his sonnet *Read me a lesson, Muse* while on the Ben, though its image of mist frustrating our exploration of heaven and hell may owe as much to his reading of Dante. The only books he took on the tour were the three volumes of *La Divina Commedia*. To cheer up Tom he also wrote a bawdy piece, peopled by Mrs Cameron (a fat lady), Red Crag, presumably his guide's rendering of Càrn Dearg, and Ben Nevis himself. These poems together with Keats's letter of 3 August can be found in *SMCJ*, 21/126 (Nov 1938), 407–13, or as an eBook at <http://www.gutenberg.org/files/35698/35698-h/35698-h.htm>, [retrieved 16 August 2018].

Beyond that, and perhaps a brief passage in *Hyperion*, it is hard to detect in Keats's verse any echoes of his day on the Ben.

MOUNTAIN RESCUE – THEN AND NOW

By Bob Sharp[1]

READERS WILL BE WELL AWARE that the mountains of Scotland have attracted walkers and climbers for a very long time. In the case of those who worked the land the period extends to many centuries. In the latter part of the eighteenth century drovers brought their cattle from the Hebrides to the Falkirk Tryst. They would follow the glens and climb high ground often for several days at a time. Gillies and gamekeepers who served the landowners worked in and explored the mountains on a daily basis. Some were employed to guide 'tourists' who wished to climb big hills for pleasure and they would take advantage of the stalkers' paths carved into the hillsides. In those days of course, there were no roads, vehicle tracks or OS maps. Ponies would convey many people, but others chose to tackle the mountains on foot and they did this for intrinsic motives – pleasure, enjoyment and exploration.

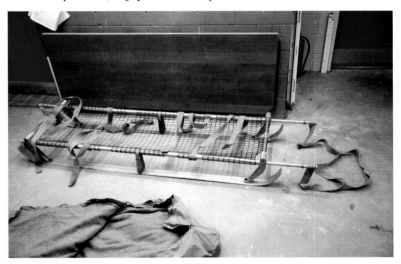

The original Thomas Stretcher. Photo: Patterdale MRT.

It is reasonable to assume that some of those who ventured into the mountains, whatever the purpose, occasionally came to grief. Indeed, the SMC published incident figures from early on in the last century. Local newspapers also provided documentary evidence of incidents that took

---

[1] Research carried out by Alfie Ingram (former Chair of the Mountain Rescue Committee of Scotland) and Judy Whiteside (Specialist Adviser to Mountain Rescue England and Wales) was significant in helping shape this article. Their work is gratefully acknowledged.

An original stretcher box at Styhead Tarn in the Lake District. Photo: Dave Sharp.

place in their area, often in great detail. For example, in 1874 the Dundee Advertiser reported one incident in which a man slipped on hard névé and fell to his death during a winter ascent of Ben More (Crianlarich). The article described how the man's friend ran down to Ben More farm to raise the alarm. A number of shepherds, accompanied by several sheepdogs climbed back up the hill and following a brief search located the man's body. Without a suitable stretcher to remove the man from the icy slope the shepherds placed his body beside a rock, marked the location, and returned to base for help. The following day a large number of local people returned and recovered the man's body by strapping him to a wooden ladder. With extreme difficulty – and great care – they carried the body down the icy slope to the farm. Here, the man's body was placed in a cart and taken to Crianlarich hotel. The numbers of incidents in those days were low compared to today. For example, in the period 1925–1945, the average number of recorded accidents in Scotland was just five each year. From 1945 to 1960, the average rose to 20 per year. By comparison, the average number of incidents over the five-year period up to 2015 was 563. It should be noted that about one third of these were 'non-mountaineering' incidents.

The rescue operation that took place on Ben More typified the approach taken in those days. Anyone who was injured or lost couldn't call upon help from a formalised mountain rescue service. If someone had an accident it was left to the resident constable or the casualty's companions to organise local people such as farmers, shepherds, climbers and local

RAF winter training in the Cairngorms 1953. Photo: RAF Kinloss MRT.

GPs into a makeshift rescue party. The procedures for calling in relevant agencies or personnel were non-existent or very crude. The deployment of personnel was typically ad hoc, complicated by poor communication systems and lack of specific expertise. Rescues often took a very long time to organise and initiate (sometimes several days) and rescuers invariably travelled great distances before they arrived on scene. The position was the same across the whole of the UK. A comment in 1966 by Ben Humble who was an early stalwart of mountain rescue and mountain safety in Scotland highlights some of the difficulties:

> I am old enough to remember an accident on the hills north of Bridge of Orchy. The survivor contacted the police, who sent a wire to the Scottish Mountaineering Club headquarters in Edinburgh. The telegram was put through the letterbox of the clubrooms. Two days later a member who happened to call found it.

Not only was communication a challenge but also there wasn't any specialised rescue equipment. The nearest five-bar gate, ladder or bed from a local bothy often doubled as a handy stretcher. Similarly, there weren't any dedicated rescue bases or special training for those who volunteered to help the cause.

It wasn't until the early 1930s that a more systematic and better co-ordinated approach to mountain rescue began to take shape. In 1933 two established mountaineering clubs of the time (the Rucksack Club and the Fell & Rock Climbing Club) formed the 'Joint Stretcher Committee' (now considered to represent the formal beginning of mountain rescue in the UK). A specific remit of the committee was to consider the most efficient way of transporting casualties off the mountain. Specifically, it was tasked to design a stretcher especially adapted for mountainous terrain. Two key

Body Recovery from the Grey Mare's Tail. Photo: Moffat MRT.

members of the committee were Eustace Thomas and Manchester surgeon
Wilson Hey. Hey was later instrumental in persuading the Home Office
to supply morphia for use in rescue posts. Thomas ran an engineering
company, which played a major part in the development and eventual
production of the first ever purpose-built mountain rescue stretcher – the
Thomas Sledge stretcher. In those early days, many trials and experiments
with various stretchers were proceeding.

In 1939, Donald Duff who was a surgeon at the Belford Hospital in Fort
William produced his first stretcher for mountain rescue. Affectionately
known as the Duff Stretcher, it was actually taken on the 1953 Everest
expedition. Dr Duff brought to mountain rescue a unique impetus with
his innovative training on both the technical and medical fronts. In
addition to developing one of the very first mountain stretchers, he was
involved in the legal battles with the Home Office concerning the
administration of morphia to casualties. Many others have made
outstanding contributions to the development of mountain rescue in
Scotland, none more so than Hamish MacInnes. Hamish founded the
Glencoe MRT in the early 1960s and established the Search and Rescue
Dog Association as well as the Scottish Avalanche Information Service.
His contributions to the development of climbing and rescue equipment
and methods for managing technical rescue are known worldwide. The
Mk VI version of his famous stretcher is the stretcher of choice for most
Scottish Mountain Rescue Teams (MRTs) and many others south of the
border.

The Joint Stretcher Committee was also tasked to report more generally on the kinds of equipment which should be available for use in accidents on the hills – a full list of medical supplies, stretchers and means of keeping casualties warm. It was suggested this equipment should be left at designated rescue posts, for use by climbers and local volunteers. A couple of years later in 1936, the Joint Stretcher Committee decided that to maintain and equip the posts and to administer the funds required, a permanent structure was required. To this end, the First Aid Committee of the British Mountaineering Clubs was formed with a remit to oversee these responsibilities.

Less than a year later the First Aid Committee of the SMC was established and it was tasked to 'exercise a general control' over the first aid posts in Scotland. The posts in Scotland were established in some of the popular climbing areas. The first three were set up in Glencoe (Clachaig Hotel), Fort William (Belford Hospital) and at Glen Brittle House in Skye. These were installed and paid for by the SMC. In 1938 the Grampian Club established a post at Derry Lodge and in 1939 a second stretcher was installed at the CIC hut. The Scottish Ski Club set up a post in Corrie Odhar on Beinn Ghlas in Perthshire. At the end of 1939 there were six posts in Scotland under the general control of the SMC's First Aid Committee. During the 1950s, further posts were sited at Loch Morlich, Glen Doll, Lagangarbh and Garve and these were paid for by the Ministry of Health. Others were installed at Gordonstoun School, Glenmore Lodge and Jean's Hut in Coire Cas. By the end of 1955 there were 17 authorised posts in Scotland and by 1966 the number had risen to 22.

As mountaineering participation expanded and accident numbers began to increase, more rescue posts were established and mountaineering clubs across the UK (in Scotland the Association of Scottish Climbing Clubs – ASCC) were asked to raise funds to provide and maintain equipment at the posts. But the financial commitment grew beyond the finances of the mountaineering clubs. As a result in 1950 the Ministry of Health and the Scottish Board of Health took responsibility and agreed to provide medical equipment (funded by the NHS) for all official posts. At the same time, individual mountaineering clubs were tasked to take responsibility for one or more posts and for arranging personnel for rescues. The ASCC established a number of 'regional panels', to provide personnel for rescue work. By 1955, panels had been established in Aberdeen, Dundee, Inverness, Fort William and Glasgow. All this was sound in theory, but it didn't work well in practice as many clubs were based in the cities. This often meant that it took a long time to alert and then mobilise personnel. As a consequence, by the time they made their way to the incident location it was often too late. It was quickly recognised that the best way forwards was to establish teams comprising local people who could act immediately.

If we go back a few years, it should be noted that mountain rescue

Lomond MRT on a technical rescue; a young Fergus Ewing on right. Photo: Bob Sharp.

changed rapidly in 1943 when the RAF Mountain Rescue Service (MRS) was established. This was a specific response to the large number of aircrew who died during training sorties in mountainous regions of the UK. In fact, in one year almost 600 aircrew lost their lives in air crashes in the mountains and upland areas of the UK. The service was formalised in 1947 when the Allied powers (now NATO/UN) signed the Chicago Convention. This stated that each member country should be responsible for the rescue and recovery of all military and missing civil aircrew and military personnel of all the other signatory countries should they come to grief in that member's country. This holds true today but in addition RAF MRTs may be requested by the police to assist civilian teams in search and rescue operations. There have been a large number of RAF teams over the years, many of which have ceased to exist or changed location. Today, the RAF MR Service comprises three teams, based at RAF Valley in Wales, RAF Leeming in England and RAF Lossiemouth in Scotland.

By 1960 it was realised that the work of the First Aid Committee and the mountaineering clubs needed support from some kind of overseeing or co-ordinating body. A start was made when, in 1962, the First Aid Committee of the British Mountaineering Clubs changed its name to the Mountain Rescue Committee. In Scotland, following a meeting of the ASCC and other bodies, two organisations were formed – one was a sub-committee of the Mountain Rescue Committee with Jack Arthur of the Red Cross as its Chair. It was responsible to the First Aid Committee for Scottish affairs including responsibility for running the posts and rescue organisation and for guiding and assisting the Committee in accident prevention. The other organisation was the Scottish Council for Mountain Rescue chaired by Donald Duff. It was regarded as a key branch of the ASCC and its functions were to form and train regional rescue teams, look after the posts and more widely provide publicity and education on accident prevention.

Writing in the 1961 issue of the SMC Journal, Ian Maitland expressed the hope that these two organisations would not only realise the aspirations of those who had laid the foundations so soundly in the past, but also improve search and rescue facilities and reduce the need for those services. It didn't quite work out like this. There was an obvious duplication of provision and the resulting amalgam of almost 30 representatives from organisations as diverse as Youth Hostels and Tourist Boards resulted in massive bureaucracy and very little was achieved. Very quickly, Bill Murray who was then President of the SMC took a lead role in reorganising the whole system. This took place in June 1965 when, in the Red Cross rooms in Bath Street Glasgow, the Mountain Rescue Committee of Scotland (MRCofS) was formed. This committee was established as an independent organisation with nine representative organisations and five regional representatives. Some of the organisations involved in the early days are no longer members, viz: the Scottish Youth Hostels Association and the British Red Cross Society, whilst teams such as the Dounreay MRT, the Ayrshire Hill Group, Lammermuir Search and Rescue Group and Moffat Hill Rescue Group were incorporated into teams currently affiliated to the national body (now called Scottish Mountain Rescue).

With a national body in place and a realisation that the provision of an effective mountain rescue service needed reliance on local people, MRTs as we know them today began to emerge and the fledgling rescue groups began to take shape. Simultaneously, the need for the existing rescue posts declined. The RAF teams played a big part in the early growth and evolution of several civilian teams. This came about essentially through the provision of equipment and training expertise. Civilian teams across the country started up at different times and for reasons specific to each team. Although in many cases, there was a common catalyst such as an increasing number of incidents, the need for better co-ordination or the occurrence of a tragic incident. For example, the Borders Search and Rescue Unit was formed (in 1963) mainly because of an increase in incidents in the Cheviot Hills, involving young and inexperienced people. The tragic death of two shepherds in a snowstorm was a further spur. Lochaber MRT had its beginnings in the 1950s and 60s through the Lochaber section of the Junior Mountaineering Club of Scotland. The team was formally established in 1969 in order to promote a more professional approach to mountain rescue. Torridon MRT had an early start in the 1960s,[2] where volunteers were 'rounded up' and deployed

[2] See 'Torridon Mountain Rescue Team', Charlie Rose et al, *SMCJ*, 44/207 (2016), 56–65. (Hon. Ed.)

under the direction of the local Police Officer. The team was formally established in 1971 following the deaths of five children and a student teacher in what is now referred to as the 'Cairngorm Tragedy'. Following this incident, the Scottish Office recognised the need for a formal network of rescue teams. It consulted with Hamish MacInnes and the police and concluded there should be additional rescue teams established in areas not covered at the time. Torridon was one of these teams and the youth hostel in Torridon became its base. In Central Scotland, the increasing number of people climbing accessible hills such as Ben Lomond, Conic Hill and Ben A'an (and the attendant likelihood of an increase in incidents), prompted a number of local people to form the Lomond MRT. Its establishment was not the result of a particular tragic incident or upsurge in incidents, but a perceived need to prepare for future incidents. Initially the team was called out infrequently but today it is one of Scotland's busier teams.

As the 1960s unfolded, mountain rescue provision advanced across Scotland in all the upland areas and became the business of people who were, by and large, not members of mountaineering clubs. Teams established a formal footing, gained recognition by the local police authorities, developed training programmes, operational procedures, fundraising strategies and established a niche in terms of their capability and locus within a prescribed geographical area. It must have been a very challenging time for the fledgling teams for there were many unanswered questions. Who would fund their operation? What kind of equipment would be needed? How would the team's area of operation be defined? Where would the team store its equipment? What kind of training was required? Who would take responsibility for the operation and how should it be organised? What kind of people would make up the team and what skills should they have? How would new members be recruited? Today, there are clear answers to all of these questions, but in the early days, it must have been daunting to face so many uncertainties.

The mid 1960s was a very prolific period with over one third of all Scottish MRTs starting up during this period. The first civilian team was Glencoe in 1961. Today there are 113 recognised teams operating in England, Wales, Scotland, Northern Ireland and the Republic of Ireland See Table 1. The core is the civilian operation. Table 2 shows the start-up date of each Scottish team.

	ENGLAND	WALES	SCOTLAND	IRELAND
Police	-	-	3	1
RAF	1	1	1	-0
Civilian	45	12	25	12
SARDA	6	2	2	2

Table 1: The number of rescue teams in each country
(Ireland includes both NI and the ROI)

NAME OF TEAM	YEAR FORMED
Police Scotland (Grampian) MRT	1960
Glencoe MRT	1961
Skye MRT	1962
Borders SAR Unit	1963
Cairngorm MRT	1963
Aberdeen MRT	1964
Arran MRT	1964
Braemar MRA	1965
Kintail MRT	1965
Scottish Cave Rescue Organisation	1966
Killin MRT	1967
Lomond MRT	1967
Tweed Valley MRT	1968
Lochaber MRT	1969
Moffat MRT	1969
Ochils MRT	1971
Police Scotland (Tayside) MRT	1971
Torridon MRT	1971
Dundonnell MRT	1972
Glenmore Lodge MRT	1972
Glenelg MRT	1973
Galloway MRT	1975
Police Scotland (Strathclyde) MRT	1975
Tayside MRT	1976
Assynt MRT	1977
Arrochar MRT	1978
SARDA (Southern Scotland)*	1984
SARDA (Scotland)*	1999
Oban MRT	2001
Hebrides MRT	2010
RAF Lossiemouth MRT**	2012

Table 2: The starting year for each of Scotland's current rescue teams

*   SARDA was established in 1965 but split in 1983. Both renamed themselves
     in the years indicated.
**   RAF Lossiemouth was founded as RAF Kinloss in 1944 but renamed when
     it moved to Lossiemouth in 2012.

The MRCofS remains the national body although it was recently rebranded as *Scottish Mountain Rescue* (SMR). It continues to provide a national support structure for mountain rescue in Scotland. It is an independent charity with a voluntary board and presently employs a full-time Manager and a part-time Administrator. It has three focal areas of work. Firstly, it provides a structure for teams to meet, share ideas and discuss best practice on common challenges. With help from the UKSAR[3] Training Fund it delivers national training courses run by team members for team members. Secondly, it provides a platform for the collective view of the individual teams to be heard at national level. Here SMR works regularly with its primary partners – Police Scotland, Scottish Government, UKSAR, Maritime and Coastguard Agency, Bristow Helicopters and Mountaineering Scotland, as well as mountain rescue colleagues in England, Wales, Ireland and the ROI. Thirdly, SMR provides collective access to funding at national level that might be difficult for individual MRTs to reach. Working alongside individual teams, it is able to develop national funding sources (e.g. from the Scottish Government, St. John Scotland and commercial companies) that complement the fundraising initiatives of individual teams. It should be noted that four teams: Glencoe, Lochaber, Cairngorm and Tayside are not members of SMR. As of 2016, they decided to operate outside the national framework.

It is clear that mountain rescue in Scotland has a long history of development and diversification, which is mirrored across the UK. Currently, there are around 4,500 team members with almost 1000 in Scotland. Over the years, teams have developed expertise and resources to cope with incidents in a wide range of challenging and hostile environments including mountains, forests, moorland, urban, underground and coastal settings. All teams operate in close harmony with the statutory emergency services and in addition to their regular work, teams are asked to assist with civil emergencies (e.g. flooding, extremely cold weather) and large-scale searches, sometimes where criminality may be a factor. On these occasions, teams play an operational role but also bring to bear immeasurable expertise in control, communication and casualty care.

The pioneers of mountain rescue back in the 1920s and 1930s, who saw a need for some kind of customised service, would probably be astounded to see how their initiatives and ideas have developed and expanded. Today's organisation is regarded as a world-class service, and continues at team, national and international levels to develop and adapt to changing needs, especially the unrelenting rise in mountain incidents year on year.

---

[3] UKSAR is the Department for Transport's overarching body which has responsibility for maritime, aeronautical and land search and rescue.

THE SEAM, THE SEAM

By Roger Webb

THE SEAM IS A modest route in a modest corrie with a striking line and marvellous climbing. It is a dichotomy of a route or perhaps it is the epitome of Scottish Winter, to misquote Marko Prezelj 'small route, big adventure'.

Anyway it saw me off for a decade or two.

I first went to Sneachda at New Year in 1982. We had been dossing under a bridge in Aviemore, wandered in and climbed The Runnel. We didn't bother looking at Fiacaill Buttress as there was nothing in the guidebook. I forgot about it and sought out bigger things further away. Others were more perceptive, amongst them James Grosset and John Lyall who at New Year 1986 climbed The Seam.

The eighties and the nineties passed as did my youth, short days became more attractive and one day Fiona and I found ourselves on Invernookie. The plan had been good, start late to avoid the queues. The plan failed because others had the same plan so I was slowly freezing on the second belay. I waited and watched in mute jealousy as a young boy cruised up to a belay on my right, produced a large duvet jacket and settled down in comfort to bring up his friend. Only then did I properly notice the immaculate line above him. His friend came up, took the lead then swarmed, udged[1] and stylishly grovelled past chockstones, clipping threads, thwacking turf and placing immaculate runners. The route had everything, I was smitten. It was The Seam.

The way ahead cleared and with a new ambition I set off up the current one. My right crampon promptly disintegrated and I hopped my way to the top. This juxtaposition set the tone for years ahead.

Each winter I made arrangements to get The Seam done. It never happened. Sometimes I never got past the front door. The phone would ring, 'can't make it the children are ill', 'Mr Webb one of your clients is in custody...', that kind of thing. Twice we got past the front door to find the A9 blocked by accidents at Slochd, once the ski road was blocked, occasionally the Sirens of Aviemore with proper coffee and cake were too tempting. Time rolled by, straight axes changed to curved, leashes went the way of dinosaurs, people had whole climbing careers, I still hadn't done the Seam.

On rare occasions we made it to the car park, but these days you can't escape the mobile phone. The school called to say my daughter was ill, James Edwards's boys' school called, Gary Kinsey's boy's school called, I started to get paranoid. Deviously Will Wilkinson, Andy Wardle and I went in pretending to do Stirling Bomber and definitely not The Seam as well. We did the former but there was an accident nearby and we got

---

[1] Udging: a version of thrutching, I believe. Hon. Ed.

diverted. I went back with James, he turned green on the walk in and revisited his breakfast, we went home. Paranoia stepped up. The Seam invaded my sleep. I left one morning with Gary, Aviemore had a strange seventies feel about it, the NAAFI from Osnabrück had replaced the petrol station, the streets were full of squaddies, something wasn't right. At the ski car park an officer warned us not to go further. We ignored him. The weather was good, the sky blue and the crags were white, so were the ski equipped troops of the 3rd Soviet Shock Army that blocked our way. Gary remarked that this was unusual. Somewhere a siren wailed, I woke up. Not good. I still hadn't done The Seam.

I couldn't even do it in my dreams.

I revisited the diversion tactic, and stacked the deck by recruiting Murdoch Jamieson. A man with six grades in hand should do the trick. We snuck in with an approach from above, abseiling to belay below the main pitch. Murdoch to lead Watch Out, me to do The Seam. Murdoch cruised his route but I couldn't understand the sudden outbreak of cursing as he finished. After a brutal lesson in the disparity between his skills and mine I got the answer, the abseil gear and Murdoch's spare gloves had gone. I still hadn't done The Seam.

Years passed. In late 2016 Gary was brave enough to try again. As in the dream the sky was blue and the crag was white, everything was perfect right up to the point when Gary stepped on ground that wasn't. I turned to see him swim a stroke or two before heaving himself onto ground that was. He was soaked, I was cruel. Ambition drove me on to the foot of The Seam and to the queue waiting there. These kinder, gentler souls offered to let us go first but by now Gary was chattering, I took pity, shamed by their looks of reproach. I still hadn't done The Seam.

Gary moved to New Zealand.

I sought inspiration, hippy stuff, karma, anything. Foreign intervention was a path worth trying. The French wanted to go at night as they were too busy doing grade 7s in the day. The Americans only did good weather which was unlikely. The answer should have been obvious, German efficiency, and by happy chance it arrived.

In 2017 the SMC dinner was in Carrbridge and Henning Wackerhage, SMC member, possibly the keenest German Scottish winter climber there has ever been, was coming across from Munich for the event. A mutual friend asked if I was free to climb with Henning. His fate and route choice were sealed in an instant.

We spoke on the phone, he came straight to the point. 'You wish to climb the Seam?' I hadn't realised that my absurd saga was public knowledge in Germany. I pretended to consider the question and, after the kind of pause the other person doesn't notice, admitted it.

The morning of 2 December we arrived in the Coire Cas car park. No one was ill. There were no phone calls from school as during this epic my daughter had finished primary school, secondary school, a year out and was now in second year at university. There were no crashes. The 3rd

At last! Roger Webb gets to grips with the Seam. Photo: Henning Wackerhage.

Soviet Shock Army had gone home and the Germans were on my side which, as events were to show, was a very good thing.

Conditions were not ideal, poor visibility, damp air, fresh snow and a biting wind. On the plus side my companion was. Henning turned out to be about 6' 4" of super fit canned morale, apparently impervious to doubt, cold or my whingeing. He strode into the corrie, I trotted behind. At the rescue box after a dispiriting flounder through the boulders we, or rather Henning, assessed the situation. I cowered in its lee while Henning surveyed the scene. The coffee shop was insinuating itself into my mind when Henning stated 'We do the Seam'. A small spark of spirit left in me agreed with him and followed on as he set off into the blank cloud. The rest of me had no choice but to go as well.

The angle steepened, ice became more apparent. We stopped to put on more clothes and crampons. The wind was wicked, powering down in random directions and unexpected gusts. A gust hit my freshly opened rucksack. In a moment my crampons were gone, my gloves, helmet and gear strewn down the slope. I looked up, the cloud cleared and The Seam leered at me. My spirit flickered and died. That was it, enough was enough, too much wasted life, I was off. I looked up at Henning with defeat in my face. He didn't notice but walked down gathering my possessions. I joined him.

At the bottom of the slope we found my crampons, turned and set off up again.

There was now no way I wasn't going to do it.

Despite the delay we were still first to the route. Henning with great generosity declined to lead any of it. The big pitch when it came was worth the wait. I swarmed and udged, stylishly grovelled past chockstones, clipped threads, thwacked turf and placed immaculate runners. I took my time, I saw Fiona shivering on the belay, James and Will constant in their enthusiasm, Andy's calm common sense, Gary dripping wet, Murdoch ranting at fate, Henning's imperturbability and thought of all the good times this ridiculous obsession had given me, the laughter, black humour and unadulterated fun. I wished all were still alive to share it. Pausing below the final moves, I thought once more of Will and James, then pulled through to the cheers of none, placed a nut, clipped a thread, and turned to shout to Henning, 'Belayed!'

At the SMC dinner that evening I was the satisfied one. I have done harder routes, longer routes, newer routes and more remote routes but for simple pleasure no better route. The line is immaculate, the moves robust but as I slowly drank too much I realised the old truth, it isn't what you do, it's who you do it with that counts. I had been more lucky than I deserved with all my companions and I thank them all.

Climb; but from the top
acknowledge the brief living
– and the long route down.

Hamish Brown

OUT OF DARKNESS ... INTO THE LIGHT

By Chris Dickinson

IS REALITY WHAT WE SEE or is it what we feel? The five senses are windows on the world we live in, but we don't always need all of them to understand what we are experiencing. Our lives are finite, yet we are in some senses immortal. We existed before and will exist long after we are apparently gone, if only as dust. Indeed, for some of us, even when we are alive there can be times when we are not. Sometimes it takes the reality of nature itself, most sublimely represented by the very rocks we stand on and touch, to bring us alive, to help us move away from those times when we are not.

A shaft of light was shining from the narrow gap in the bathroom door. Sliding out of bed to answer the insistent call I gazed out of the velux window in the bathroom at a clear and bright sky. Looking to the west, my eye rested briefly on the cemetery with its ancient yew trees and then lifted to the soaring peak beyond. Fresh snow was blanketing the upper hills above five hundred metres and a line of light and shade picked out the east ridge, at first a wide and complex buttress riven by a gully on its right side and rising finally to a fine windblown arête of snow leading directly to the summit. More than eleven hundred metres of stark reality, presenting a robust and enduring sentinel standing guard over the long glen stretching out to the east. The river flowing gently on its way to the deep loch and ultimately the sea. The snow from that arête would melt, and follow that course, perhaps as a rivulet becoming a stream, yet more likely as throughflow and re-emergence into that same stream. In any case it would go to that sea, to that ocean, to that sky and return again to perhaps fall on that peak, be moulded again by the wind and complete the cycle. Surely this was a day to go to that peak? Quietly, I began to pick out suitable clothes for the hill.

I was asleep and in a bizarre and unlikely, but reassuring, setting. I felt called and gradually the setting faded and the dream was history. I made the oft repeated pilgrimage and gained some comfort from that but felt a rising despair when I realised on my return to the bed, glancing at my phone, that it was ten to three in the morning. My partner was sleeping soundly, her rhythmical breathing like a metronome that I knew would now haunt me. I settled into the soft mattress and pulled the quilt around my neck, counting down from one thousand as I closed my eyes. Oh... not again! This had been going on for more than a month. Trying to mentally recite the numbers and thereby keep my mind clear of dark thoughts. Gradually, like clouds on a westerly wind, they began to gather, becoming progressively lower until a veil covered my entire consciousness and drops of despair began to fall. 'Rain' was back, falling from a grey and gloomy sky!

After gathering my socks, trousers, thermals and fleece I made my way downstairs, treading lightly so as not to disturb that sweet sleeping form. With a coffee in hand, easing open the door, the towel dropped from my waist, and I stepped outside into a crisp morning. Five seconds later I was engulfed in warm therapeutic water and lay back to take in the surroundings. A robin flitted from the fence. He was joined at the bird table by a pair of eager chaffinches, cleaning up yesterday's fare. A pheasant stalked across the grass below me and over by the river was a gaggle of sheep, working through a long and ever repeating breakfast, joined this morning by a pair of wild red deer. Looking west, my gaze passed the giant yew trees to the peak. There was a glow on the snowy arête and the great windmills to the south were still, as if taking a well-earned rest. The birdsong was sweet and uninterrupted. Two hooded crows looked on from the top of the aspens, surveying their patch and then answering a neighbour's call with a throaty caw-caw. As it called, the bird's whole body appeared to convulse. Thoroughly warmed through, joints feeling supple again, I slipped out of the hot tub and inside and proceeded to get dressed for the hill.

The 'rain' fell steadily and I could find no cover. Soon I was soaked in the coldness of it, unable to keep it out. The numbers started to fade and I tried again in vain. Thoughts came crowding in, so jumbled that it was impossible to decide which to address first. The 'voice' was back. It elaborated the thoughts that centred on the great significance of being unable to fall asleep. The voice was loud, so loud that sleep would again be impossible. Repeatedly turning over, readjusting the pillows again and again, I was conscious that even after a few minutes the pressure on my hip or shoulder would compel me to turn again…and again…and again. A sombre place crept out of the darkness. The path along the cliff, the pine tree on the lip of the gorge, the roar of the river below, the water inky black and jumbled boulders of schist littering the channel. Why had I gone there and why was I there now?

Bread was buttered and some peanut butter and jam added. Snapped into a box with two bars and an apple, they joined a flask of scented tea in my rucksack and for the first time this winter they were joined by a pair of crampons and a torch. I gave the stirring form in my bed a peck on the cheek and bade her farewell. Reaching out the old faithful curver, pocketing my phone, I went outside to relieve the car of its frosty regalia. The map showed that there was in fact a footpath winding to and fro all the way from the loch to the west ridge of the southernmost Munro. Having previously visited the peak at least three times, twice on skis, these visits had followed other lines that promised long snowfields. It was mid-November, and although surprisingly snowy for the time of year, there would be no base and so the skis stayed firmly in the cupboard. I felt a sense of satisfaction easing on the leather boots and fitting the freshly mended gaiters. I had felt inspired to polish and wax the boots and sew new straps on the rarely used gaiters. I must be coming alive.

Leaving the car, the loch was mirror calm, the southern mountains appearing twice before me. Shouldering my sack, I set out along the military road as it climbed steadily towards the mobile mast. From there the path set off in a northerly direction, picking first one way and then the other through the crags that barred the way directly ahead. A small posse of deer, startled by my appearance, hustled off across the mountainside. The footpath passed through a small marshy basin before climbing again onto better drained ground with sheets of shining bedrock interspersed with patches of snow and glistening streams of ice. Three figures laden with big packs teetered down over the largest of the slabs of rock. We exchanged greetings.

'You are coming down early?' I ventured, wondering if in fact the conditions higher up had led them to turn back.

'No, we have been camping up on the ridge and it was certainly pretty windy earlier in the night', explained the older fellow. Duly impressed that they would carry heavy packs all the way up there in November we went our separate ways, they downwards and myself ever upwards, like my mood.

The receptionist greeted me cheerfully, as ever, and invited me to sit down. I'd had two weeks to think about what to say and yet with just a few minutes before my appointment was due I still really had no idea what to say. On a crumpled note in my pocket were written a list of things to mention but it stayed right there, like a paper monument to my distress. Three weeks had now passed since re-starting the medication. It felt as if it might as well have been three years. I felt little different, that the sky was still grey, almost black in fact and that the voice was in charge. Listening to the voice was so incredibly tiring, exhausting in fact, and utterly frustrating as it had nothing positive to report. The voice had dissected every aspect of my life past and present and when that was complete it had started the whole thing over again...and then again. After my appointment I solemnly crossed the road and waited at the pharmacy to collect another month of pills and seven sleeping tablets, an insurance policy against exhaustion. The beautiful east European lady pharmacist who handed them over so cheerfully seemed, to me, to be in another world from my own.

On the way home I stopped and walked through the beechwoods to the folly. The tumbling water of the river ignored me and I made my way along the path that follows the rim of the defile. There, leaning precariously out over the void, was the pine tree. Vibrantly alive and solid, a large branch stretched outwards, with the rapids some fifty feet below. It would be too far to reach without falling but surely one could throw a weighted rope over it and then retrieve the end and tie it off on a tree behind the path? Yes, that would work and peering over the edge I was pleased to see that the cliff was overhanging below, streaming wet in places and mossy so there would be little or no chance of gaining any purchase to come back. A quick step out would be all that was needed, but of course I hadn't brought a rope with me today, although I had located

'The rocks were so reassuring and solid, so self-evidently real and long lasting, that they gave me a wonderful perspective of longevity, ...'   Photo: Chris Dickinson.

it, a pre-stretched and rather stiff white static rope.

It was a pleasure to linger at the slabs. The metamorphism had woven patterns in the rock that hinted at its origins and antiquity. The mica schist was probably in the region of 600 million years old, but of course the material had had more than one previous incarnation, one as a sedimentary rock, a mudstone, a life as a deposit and one as a solid rock eroded to become that deposit. The sunlight shone on the foliations: and the sheen and smoothness suggested the work of glacial ice and there, clearly at odds with the crinkled layering, were the tell-tale striations. These were perfectly aligned with the glen and revisiting my previous deliberations on ice direction I concluded once again that here the ice had definitely gone east and thence to Inverness. The rocks were so reassuring and solid, so self evidently real and long lasting, that they gave me a wonderful perspective of longevity, something which was so drastically missing during the dark period I had come through, where everything seemed transient, pointless and about to disappear. The path switchbacked through increasingly rocky terrain and was by now all covered with fresh snow. The view west was beginning to expand and as the path approached a huge area of massive boulders it neatly zigzagged up the steepening slopes to my left, threading its way quite ingeniously through small crags. Finally, it crested the west ridge and turned sharp right along the crest. Patches of ice adorned the pathway that could be missed by stepping off to the side into ever deepening snow. Time to take the trusty ice axe off my sack so that if needs be I could steady myself. The first summit could not be too far away now and I felt unexpectedly fresh, buoyed by the windless day, the decoration of the fresh snow and the variety in the route.

The pile of wood, covered by the tarpaulin, and the copious quantity of logs stacked haphazardly in my sheds had been irking me. My chain saw had stopped working more than two years ago and the attempt to resolve this by having it serviced had backfired. It was clearly unwell when started. The thing became blazing hot. Yet the wood stove in the house was hungry for more seasoned timber. It made its final journey to the recycling centre and I went to look at a higher quality machine. Worried about the same thing happening to an expensive Stihl machine, the salesman filled me with despondency as he described in detail all the actions that would result in ruining a chainsaw! It was left on the counter and we went home. Maybe I wouldn't be needing one anyway, or the wood!

The first summit arrived and a vista opened up into the corries beyond. Nourished by hot tea and a snack I set out along the rim, through patches of snow-ice and rock, at each step the corrie perspective changing slightly. Clouds were clearing fast, as if a gift, a perfect interlude to visit the highest summit. Skirting an intermediate top, with fine views westwards now, the final slopes beckoned me upward. First paying the usual respects to the cairn, then I was there: looking down the windblown arête of snow at the top of the east ridge, the very same one that had drawn my attention

Sgùrr nan Conbhairean from Càrn a' Mhadaidh-ruaidh. Photo: Chris Dickinson.

that morning from the bathroom window. Perhaps it could be ascended another day? The panorama took in the hills of Affric, Shiel, Nevis, the Aonachs and Meagaidh, gleaming in their fresh winter coats. I felt renewed, released, alive again.

So many times in the previous three months my brotherly friend had called from USA. Mostly I listened, unable to say much of value. It all made sense to him, to anybody sane in fact, but it didn't make sense to me. Sometimes when the phone would ring I could not bring myself to answer, partly out of fear, partly out of embarrassment. Mostly though, answering was a gesture of thanks for keeping me challenged and cared for. Truly I could not say that I felt any change in myself, the world was still dark. Pills had dutifully been taken. I had been barely able to engage with anything or anyone. Food appeared uninteresting, almost unthinkable in the past, and so the weight was falling off me. Trying to be patient, I read books as best I could, taking on minor tasks and sleeping a lot. Patience was all I had left. One day I pushed myself outside and climbed a new Munro in cloud, rain, wet snow and wind and returned surprised at physically managing it. Yet it felt like a door was slightly ajar, that behind those clouds would be the light.

This day, gazing down the windblown ridge of snow from the peak, I knew that the door had opened. The climb there had captivated me, refreshed me and, although alone on the mountains that day, I left my fears behind and saw that my world was familiar once again. Faintly I recalled something I once read in Walter Bonatti's book. It went something like this, 'The mountain is high, the way is difficult, but the route goes.'

A STARRY, STARRY NIGHT

By Gordon Ross

LOCHNAGAR IS ONE OF the most desirable mountains to climb in Scotland. Being a Munro at 1,155 metres or 3,811 feet it has the added incentive of some of the most challenging rock and ice climbs. So it was with anticipation that we set off one Friday night from Dumbarton after a hard day's work. It's a long drive up with busy roads as people escape from their offices to relax for the weekend, but not so for the climber. We arrived in good time near the village of Crathie and Lochnagar Distillery, where we would leave the car and make the walk in to the ancient pinewoods of the Ballochbuie Forest, en-route to a bothy for a night's kip.[1]

There is something magical about walking through these Caledonian forests, the trees rearing up like giants, the smell of the pine and if you are lucky the croak of a Capercaillie. However all was quiet that night, just the soft crunch of our boots on the pine needles. After walking for a good half hour or so, and not being familiar with the route, we arrived at the front grass of Balmoral Castle, not the place to be tonight, so off we trudged back on track towards the Gelder Shiel bothy. Unfortunately the bothy was full, however next to the bothy is one of the Queen's private country houses and as the door had been left open by some opportunists it seemed a good idea to have a more comfortable sleep.

It's a long walk in from the Gelder bothy but very rewarding with views of Lochnagar as you approach the lochan. The moor had plenty of hard firm snow, like the kind you get when you open the freezer, with a lovely crunch as you make your way towards the foreboding cliffs. The words of George Gordon, aka Lord Byron came into my mind:

> *Ah! there my young footsteps in infancy wandered,*
> *... As daily I strayed through the pine-covered glade.*

The temperature was below freezing and we had the pleasure of fairy dust; when the cold freezes the moisture in the air and sprinkles it around you. By the time you get to the bottom of the face you feel like it's already been a long day. A decision had to be made which route to go for, either Raeburn's Gully or Parallel A. Parallel B was a step too difficult for us and it had only had a few ascents by the crème de la crème of winter climbers. Our friends Brian Sprunt and Peter Hodgkiss decided on Raeburn's, so it would be Parallel A for us.

From the bottom it looks very impressive shooting straight up between the dark cliffs of the buttresses on either side. The route looked to be in great condition with plenty of hard névé and tumbling ice cataracts. After a quick bite and chocolate bar, it was on with the crampons, Whillans

---

[1] This article is an expanded version of a brief account in *SMCJ*, 42/204 (2013) pp. 365–6. (Hon. Ed.)

This photo of a print of a painting by Neil J. Barlow gives the feel of the article. Parallel A is the longer of the thin white strips on either side of Parallel Buttress just left of centre. Photo: Gordon Ross.

Harness, ice pegs double ropes and a measure of courage. And so off we shot onto the first pitch, which was fairly straightforward.

The névé was lovely; as you sunk the pick of your axe in, it was like going into wood; you knew it was a good placement; crampon points were similar, biting in and holding firm. We continued up various pitches to the crux pitch. It was here that we met two other young climbers. They seemed to be stuck and were having doubts. They had a good belay but it was obvious that they were inexperienced and kindly let us through. I had the pleasure of watching my partner Hamish Henderson wend his way up the steep ice; thankfully he got some protection in at various places. However I kept getting showered with splinters of snow and ice as I stood in the direct firing line. This is quite normal of course at the bottom of an ice pitch, unfortunately we don't carry umbrellas for such occasions. Eventually the call came to follow. So it was out with the belay and ready to go. It was at this point I probably made a wrong decision and offered to leave in our protection on the crux to make life a little easier for them. After I got to the top of the pitch I then dropped a rope down to assist them over the vertical ice cataract. The reason it was the wrong decision was that it made the route a little easier for them for which they probably weren't ready.

However all this started to take a lot of time and with the short days it was obvious that the light was beginning fail. By the time we got to the final pitches it was getting quite dark. We dug in to a comfortable belay like the entrance to a small cave and placed a classic deadman for protection. It was time to get out the head torches as it was now totally dark, with a few stars twinkling above us. The snow near the top for some reason was a bit softer, a bit like stiff porridge.

It was my turn to take the lead. I had to descend slightly to get round a bollard of snow and then ascend up past my partner. The glow from the torch lit the way and blanked out everything else, I was like a glow worm snaking my way up towards the cornice, deep kicks into the snow and ice axe in up to the adze. It felt perfectly safe, but now the cornice reared up ahead of me. My partner shouted 'I wish I had a camera! That looked amazing with the torchlight as you made your way upwards.' At that moment I wasn't too bothered about a photograph, but I was concerned by the cornice which towered above me. Lochnagar is infamous for its large cornices and with it being a pitch black night and having only a torch, I didn't fancy digging a hole through it, but luckily over to the right of my line was a perfect section for getting through without too much trouble. A few final kicks into the harder cornice, a couple of steps cut into folding hard snow, it was like a large ice cream that had started to melt and had frozen into waves.

As I was reaching the cornice the two other guys were arriving at the final belay. Apparently they looked exhausted but were glad to be at the final pitch. As I clambered out over the cornice I gave a shout that I was up.

I switched off the torch for a moment to appreciate the scene. The sky was a wonderful sight, with lots of stars. It reminded me of Don MacLean's song about Vincent Van Gogh, *Starry, Starry Night.*

We had arranged that when I had got up and found a belay I would tighten the rope and give three strong tugs to get my partner to come on as he would never hear me. A bit of a breeze had started which would make it even more difficult to communicate. I managed to get in a good deadman placement and my ice axe up to the hilt as well. It was not a technically difficult pitch so I was not concerned about Hamish coming off. I gave the tugs and waited to feel the slack on the rope as he started to climb the pitch, but of course he had to descend slightly to get round the bollard. At last the rope started to slacken and he made his way up to the cornice and finally up the last steeper section and onto the plateau. You would think you had just landed on the moon, everything was white and windswept with two torches illuminating the landing spot. It was one of those magical moments that you savour all too seldom.

We shook hands then started packing our gear away; just one problem, the rest of our gear that we left on the crux for the other two guys to use. So another wait of 20 minutes or so before the first of them came over and then another 20 minutes for the last man. A short discussion followed as they didn't remember having our gear; however after emptying out their sack we found the appropriate slings and karabiners.

Gelder Shiel Bothy undergoing internal renovation by members of the Mountain Bothies Association in 2016: it is now wood lined and has a stove – a far cry from its former status as a 'cauld hole'. Photo: Peter Biggar.

There was no time for small talk, so we left the two lads to pack up and make their own way down. It was a long way back to Gelder Shiel in the dark and we still had to find our way off the mountain. By good fortune Peter and Brian had completed Raeburn's Gully and were just ahead of us. We spied their torchlight in the distance and followed them down by the Meikle Pap and so down the long glen to our final destination. Our friends had enjoyed an equally good day on Raeburn's and savoured the summit moon landing as well. It was late in the evening before we got back to the Gelder but after a good brew-up and a bite to eat we were all ready for a night's sleep, but no Queen's cottage tonight, just a nice cosy bunk down on the floor. As I drifted off to sleep Byron's words kept repeating in my mind.

Now, a little older, but probably not much wiser, I still sigh for the valley of Dark Lochnagar.

CARNIVORE

By Richard McHardy

SOME PEOPLE CAN CLIMB rocks with ease. Then again some people become steel erectors. Others cringe with fear at the thought of either. I once belonged to the latter group. Over the years I have met and climbed with other climbers who started with a similar disadvantage. People with a natural ability seem to be able to perform well without the need for undue effort. More average people have to climb on a regular basis to keep from letting fear creep back in. A run of bad weather at weekends, a lack of climbing partners, work and later on, family life can all conspire to eat time. After a lay off or a winter spent ice climbing, the best way to get on form is to start slowly on the rock knowing that confidence and desire will return. The weather in late May of 1977 was too good to follow that formula. Glen Coe was in the sun and had been for a few weeks. Slime Wall was light gray, even the warm air wafting in from Rannoch Moor had a dry smell. A couple of years before, Dave Jenkins had remarked to me that in Scotland, unlike Wales or Derbyshire, letting a really good spell of weather pass by might be the last one you see for years.

Eleven years before, I had abseiled off after the first pitch of Carnivore, when my friend had sensibly refused to follow the traverse on the first pitch. (For the leader this traverse is protected; it starts with some downward moves but for the second a fall might see them brush the floor.) I should have had a day climbing some easier routes but since failing on Carnivore eleven years before it had sat festering in my wish list.

A much later, roped ascent: Ken Crocket traversing on Carnivore.
Photo: Crocket collection.

I think it is true to say that a lack of care on easy ground, especially soloing, has killed more people than being roped up on any climb hard or easy. I would be climbing solo, however I concluded that the above statistic had more to do with carelessness than anything else and to push myself to near my limit would prevent careless over-confidence. Not very logical but that was the plan, and anyway it was a short walk.

I set off in shorts and T-shirt with a 9mm rope and three or four slings, harness, rock shoes and trainers. I took the rope primarily to back rope the beginning of the traverse on the first pitch of Carnivore after which it would be a fairly useless weight.

The main feature of Creag a' Bhancair is an overhanging wall. The line of Carnivore weaves its way from the left to the right, then straight up and finally hard right, all the time ascending above this wall. Abseil retreat with one rope is soon impossible. Beyond the first pitch the rock looked a bit smooth and greenish. On such smooth rock you use what comes to hand and if you have a short reach the grade of a move can double, a bit like climbing on slate. On the rough rock of a dry Slime Wall or Clogwyn du'r Arddu you can creep your fingers across the rock like a pianist, often finding an intermediate rugosity.

In our abortive attempt in 1966 I had found the first part of the first pitch hard and a long reach: it still seemed hard. With a loop of rope clipped into in situ gear I made some precarious moves down and across right. Half way across the traverse I was able to untie and pull the rope out of the gear. I was now committed. The smooth rock went ok but I felt relief when after 40 metres I came to a stance.

The Whillans finish was above. It was bone dry and looked good but bold. I was very tempted but it looked difficult to move back down if you got the moves wrong. I wrongly thought that Don Whillans had got one up on John Cunningham when he found this alternative finish. Coming from Manchester and not Glasgow I had the chauvinistic idea that Whillans was the better climber and therefore the Cunningham finish must be easier: a mistake, as the original finish traverses right.

The climbing was soon hard but I was still thinking I had made the right choice when a long, wet, brown streak barred the way. I hoped it would be narrow enough to step over. The wet came oozing out from beneath an overhang. There were several very old rusty pitons which must have been there since the first ascent in 1958. Down amongst the slime was the odd small foot hold. Even if I could leave go to make a loop with the rope and clip all three pitons it would be pointless as any kind of fall would rip the pitons. I clipped my three slings one to each piton. I had nothing long enough to make a foot sling and anyway that would mean putting my weight on one peg. I just had to hope my feet would not slip off the wet footholds. By trying to pull evenly on two pegs at once, they held. The really dodgy move came when I had to use the third peg on its own while I unclipped the slings from the other two. Then, still with weight on the last piton I reached for a hold with my right hand.

Creag a' Bhancair: 'The great, smooth red wall at its steepest section has been likened to the side of a railway tunnel...' – Ken Crocket, Rock and Ice Climbs Glencoe and Glen Etive, (SMT, 1980), p103.
Photo: Cubby Images.

Eight years before I had been in a similar near death position when soloing the overhanging finish to The Grooves on Cyrn Las, in Wales. Back then 400ft above the ground I had to keep the lid on the panic as my arms began to tire. The Grooves are E2 5b and at that time I was climbing at the very top of my form. Now, with that form a distant memory, I was on rock graded E2 5c. Scared witless I tried to think. I had three slings and a wire but I could see no runner placements that would be good enough to hang on whilst I had a rest. The climbing was still hard. Trying to use my brain just made me more aware of my position. I cannot remember the rest of that pitch. I have never even had a nightmare about it. Marvellous: in order to survive the mind had totally blocked out any thought of where I was. Once on the easier ground above, I stopped on a grassy ledge for what seemed ages.

When it came to moving again I was frightened. Six years ago I had broken a femur soloing on Gritstone, since then I had never really pushed the boat out too far, until now. Creag a' Bhancair is low down on the hill; the sun was covering the Buachaille and particularly Slime Wall which looked like Shangri-la: five hundred feet of bone dry rhyolite.

Should I finish the day now or carry on? If I did go down I would look up from my van and probably regret not carrying on with my plan. I could only hope that my nervous energy would recover. At length caution flew the nest and enthusiasm returned so I carried on.

Great Gully was in the shade. Shivering in my shorts and t-shirt I was cold and apprehensive when I started up Apparition 145m E1 5b. Some way up the second pitch the way ahead looked hard and it was not exactly obvious where the line went. I was standing on a good foothold and so, unlike the crux on Carnivore, I had time to think. I had one wire and I found a good placement for it. A good sized loop in the rope clipped into the wire made me imagine I was in with a chance if I fell. In truth there was no way that it would have held a fall. The way ahead proved possible and, although always out of sight, a decent hold would appear every time I moved up. When I gained another decent foothold I unclipped the loop pulled it through, said goodbye to the wire and crab and carried on into the sun and the top of the hill.

The next day I was climbing a route called Scansor on Stob Coire nan Lochain with Ian Nicholson. On the top of the crag we sat and watched the traffic down in Glen Coe. Ian remarked on the different view and perspective the people in the tin and glass bubbles were experiencing. It was said with no hint of superiority but instead with some empathy for those who were missing out on this view and a genuine gratitude to fate for giving us both this experience. It goes to show even the hard men of the Creagh Dhu have a sensitive side. We had both escaped from the inner city and but for chance we could well have been sitting on a bus tour ourselves.

FIGURES ON ICE

By Mike Jacob

BETWEEN ROUGHLY 1300 and 1850 the northern hemisphere experienced a relatively cold period commonly referred to as the Little Ice Age, despite the fact that it included an interval of slight warming in the 1500s. The coldest years occurred between 1645 and 1715 with average temperatures at least 1°C lower than those of the following industrial period and excluding the more recent global warming effects caused by greenhouse gases. This figure may seem modest to the uninformed but even a small fluctuation can have a major impact on natural processes, leading to significant environmental changes – loss of sea ice, for example. Europe experienced particularly severe winters so it is not surprising that skating on ice became an efficient means of travel in countries with long, cold winters, such as Norway, Finland and, especially, Holland. There are many theories as to what caused these bitter years; ideas include fluctuations in solar radiation, ocean circulation and volcanic activity.

Samuel Pepys was one diarist to record *people sliding with their skeates* on a frozen River Thames in 1662. In Scotland, prolonged, harsh winters, often with considerable accumulations of snow, meant thickly frozen lochs, perfect for bonspiels – curling tournaments and revelry that would last all weekend. The traditional Grand Match between North and South Scotland on the Lake of Menteith in Perthshire requires the ice to be at least 7 inches thick. As a result, it has only been played 33 times in the last 150 years and only 3 times since 1945.

The first skating club in Britain was founded in Edinburgh, probably in the mid-eighteenth century, with the motto *Ocior Euro* (Swifter than the East Wind) and its formation was yet another example of the proliferation of congenial societies during the Scottish Enlightenment. From the start, the club membership was dominated by the local aristocracy and, although not socially exclusive, nearly all the members were the sons or relatives of landed families. The real criterion, however, was personal acceptability and, by the end of the nineteenth century, the club membership was drawn almost totally from a cross-section of wealthy merchants and professionals, with a preponderance of lawyers most of whom were Writers to the Signet[1], reflecting changes in the composition of Edinburgh society.

Primitive skates were crudely made from animal bone but evolved over time into metal blades with double edges which enabled accurate control of direction. The object of the club was not about skating at speed but *to*

---

[1] Originally, the Signet was the private seal of the early Scottish Kings, and the Writers to the Signet were those authorised to supervise its use. The oldest legal body in the world, it then became the preserve of Scottish solicitors who had, at one time, the exclusive privilege of practising in the Supreme Courts and whose privileges are now limited to the preparation of Crown writs.

enable the members to skate together in concert in precisely prescribed figures in *slow and graceful motion rather than by rapid and wonderful execution*. The club devised its own intricate patterns, such as *The Wild Goose* and *The Screw*, sometimes carried out by several skaters in combination, like a *corps de ballet*.

It is clear that a good sense of balance was required to master these skills and the club rule book might have been describing traditional rock climbing when it stated that *the requisites for fine skating in concert are a good attitude, correct time, perfect ease, close contact, and freedom from perceptible effort*. Under scrutiny, prospective members were expected to skate a perfect circle on each foot consecutively, to form a figure-of eight on the ice and then jump over one top-hat, then two, and finally three, placed one on top of the other. There was then a ballot among the council members and, if successful, the candidate had to pay for a silver medallion which had crossed skates and club motto on one side and their name and the name of the club on the other. What has all this to do with Scottish mountaineering? Read on.

It may come as a surprise to members to learn that Harold Raeburn was admitted to the Edinburgh Skating Club on 18 December 1901, member number 254 and described as a *mountaineer* in later Minutes, which inaccurately recorded his death as 1922 (actually, 1926). Although some examples of medallions still exist in the National Museum of Scotland, unfortunately they do not include Raeburn's, which possibly still languishes, unrecognised, at the back of a drawer somewhere.

The usual winter skating venues in Edinburgh were the lochs at Lochend and Duddingston and it was the duty of the Club Secretary to arrange for the ice to be swept of any snow and debris, keep boys and other nuisances off and send word to members when all was ready. This was done by posting notices early in the morning at a number of stated places around the city. The club held an annual dinner where the standard dish served was sheep's head and trotters perhaps in deference to the Sheep Heid Inn in Duddingston. Harold must already have been a proficient skater when he joined the club, the same year that the new Raeburn brewery opened in nearby Craigmillar, so perhaps he was looking for the opportunity for some convenient spare-time winter sport. Perhaps the most relevant image featuring a Scottish skater is that reproduced.

The painting shows the Reverend Robert Walker, who joined the Skating Club in 1780, practising figures on the translucent ice, a threatening winter sky beyond the snowy Salisbury Crags as daylight fades. The portrait is attributed[2] to Sir Henry Raeburn and it is tempting

---

[2] Stephen Lloyd, a curator at the National Portrait Gallery in Edinburgh, has recently reattributed the painting to Henri-Pierre Danloux, an obscure French artist who made lengthy visits to the Scottish capital in the 1790s to paint portraits of members of the French royal family in exile. Speculation continues!

Note: *Italics* indicates quotation from the Edinburgh Skating Club archive,

Reverend Robert Walker (1755–1808) skating on Duddingston Loch, Edinburgh, by Sir Henry Raeburn. By kind permission of National Galleries of Scotland.

to speculate that a young Harold may have been inspired by the evocative nature of the scene. In fact, however, he never saw the painting for it disappeared into the Walker family archives long before he was born (in 1865) and it did not reappear for public viewing until after 1949, when it was purchased for 500 guineas by the National Gallery of Scotland, where it now resides. The two Edinburgh Raeburn families of Sir Henry and Harold were not related although it is not possible to exclude some very distant ancestral link.

Lest it be thought that figure-skating seems a rather genteel activity for a budding mountaineer, it was actually a fairly hazardous pastime with numerous accidents and fatalities over the years when the ice gave way. Eventually, the simple expedient of fixing a long rope around the circumference of the loch was introduced, grappling-irons and brass buoyancy-rings having proved less than adequate as life-saving aids. When a skater ended up in the numbing water, the rope could be drawn across the ice by pulling on its loose ends, warning being given to other skaters by means of a loud rattle. They then had to make a rapid escape before the rope tripped them up and dragged them, like a purse-net harvesting a shoal of fish, to join the drowning victim in the freezing water.

The number of participating skaters at any one time was usually quite small. Harold's attendance is recorded at several meetings but usually there were no more than half-a-dozen skaters altogether on the ice. He seems to have remained an active member for only a year or two after election but, in any event, the club was already experiencing difficulty due to the declining popularity of figure-skating and insufficient winter ice, the last recorded gathering at Duddingston Loch being in 1903.

It is likely that, for Harold Raeburn, skating was an activity that merely complemented what had become his true passion – mountaineering – but one which surely helped to develop his poise and balance as he transferred his interest in ice from the horizontal to the vertical.

INEXORABLE DECLINE

By Noel Williams

IT IS A SAD FACT of life that once we pass the age of thirty our physical performance starts to decline – slowly at first but with increasing speed as the years go by. Many SMC members are already on the slippery slope by the time they join the Club. We can try to slow the process by remaining active, so what's the best we can hope for? Tables of age-related performance for a variety of athletic activities are available online. These are based on world record times and so strictly speaking they relate to elite athletes only, but they probably give a reasonable indication of how performance drops off for the general population.

I did quite a bit of hillrunning in my youth though my times were nothing special. I suppose I would have been described as on the fun-running fringe. It was uncanny how often I finished around the winner's time plus 50%. In the early years I was also quite often the 'second woman' home, though I gradually slipped down the ladies field as more women started to take up the sport. (The first official Ladies Ben Nevis Race was in 1981.)

Last year I notched up three score years and ten and I started to notice for the first time that it was becoming harder to keep up with my daughter on the hill. So I examined a number of age-related performance tables. I chose the male records for 10km road races as approximately equivalent to a hillwalking day. I discovered that the best a 71 year old man can expect is that he performs at 73% of his prime. In other words he will take at least 36% longer to complete a 10km road race than he did in the full flush of youth.

The drop off in performance for the marathon distance is more or less identical for male runners. So a four hour hillwalking trip for a youngster would probably take nearly five and a half hours for a 71 year old.

The figures for female runners differ slightly at different distances. In their prime elite females perform in 10km road races at about 88% of the level of elite male runners. This means they take 13% longer to complete this distance. For the marathon distance the gap closes slightly and elite females perform at nearly 91% of the level of elite males. The phenomenal records held in the UK by Nicky Spinks and Jasmin Paris suggest that females may even outperform males at ultra distance hillrunning.

My daughter happens to be 40 years younger than me, so out of interest I adjusted the female curve accordingly. The intersection of the two curves suggest that elite 16 year old females perform at exactly the same level for 10km road races as elite 56 year old males. The decline in performance at 10km seems to drop off slightly more sharply for women in middle age but then not so steeply for very elderly females.

It is dangerous to read too much into these curves, but, taking a ballpark figure of 150% of the winner's time, my peak performance corresponds to 66% of the elite male level. I would guess that my daughter has about the same sort of performance level as myself (i.e. 66% of the elite female level), so adding our curves to the elite performance curves probably won't alter the point at which our curves cross. Although my daughter is getting near the end of her peak performance level, I've little chance of beating her on the hill again.

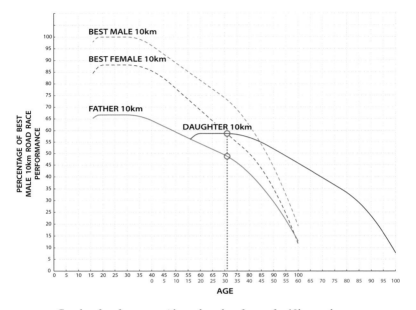

Graphs of performance with age based on figures for 10km road races.
Created from 2015 data for male and female road races downloaded from
<http://www.runscore.com/Alan/AgeGrade.html>. Retrieved 29 April 2018.

How does climbing fit into all this? Climbing is a bit of a specialist activity and the mental aspect of it is certainly important, so it's difficult to relate it to simple aerobic performance. However, the fall off in performance at the elite level is possibly similar to other athletic pursuits. But what about the masses? I find it interesting that a number of my elderly climbing friends still seem to operate at close to their peak level of climbing ability, while others – although remaining active – have slipped down a couple of grades. This is in part related to how strongly the 'passion' remains. I no longer get quite the buzz I used to get from climbing, and although I enjoy the social aspect of indoor walls I can't get very excited about them either. This may explain why I've joined the 'dropped a couple of grades' group.

Which brings me in a very roundabout way to the new *Outer Hebrides* guide… Maybe it's because I'm a complete non-swimmer, but I've always enjoyed the thrill of climbing by the sea. My first experience of sea cliff climbing was at Bosigran in Cornwall. Although it was February and quite chilly I found the whole atmosphere invigorating. Returning to Bosigran in June the same year the conditions were idyllic, and I was intoxicated by the sun-kissed rock and the turquoise colour of the water below.

For my third experience of sea cliff climbing I travelled up to Gogarth from Bristol with my friend Chris Reed on the back of my Honda 175. We did *Dream of White Horses*. It was November and only three years after the first ascent, so it wasn't common knowledge then that it's a soft touch at HVS. It got dark as we tackled the amazing last pitch, with the beam from South Stack lighthouse sweeping at regular intervals across the zawn behind us. I was hooked…

When I was teaching it was very frustrating to be stuck in school when the weather was fine in May. By the time the summer holidays came round the weather always seemed to be wet or unsettled at best. Since I've been retired I've been visiting a different Scottish island for a week each spring with some old climbing pals. Most of them have lost the climbing passion and are happy to just hillwalk, scramble or explore. Two years ago we had a pleasant week in a cottage in Miabhaig on Lewis. On the afternoon of the first day we wandered from Cliobh in a north-westerly direction along the cliff top. It was a bit up and down though quite scenic. We were thinking of heading back to base when I decided to press on just a little bit further. I got excited when a large bay came into view. Although it had a steep back wall it didn't seem very attractive from a climbing point of view. However, I thought I'd climb up leftwards to the highpoint overlooking the bay. When I looked back down I was astonished to see an impressive slab forming the eastern wall of the bay, just as my friend Gordon appeared on the cliff top above it. The slab appeared to be formed from a conspicuous vein of pink granite and it looked like it ought to be climbable, whereas the gneiss either side of it was very vegetated. At the foot of the slab a vertical wall plunged into the sea.

We hadn't any climbing gear with us on that visit so I couldn't think about checking it out. However that slab kept gnawing away at me. I eventually managed to persuade Paul Brian to return with me during a fine spell in October. Accommodation isn't easy to find for short visits in the Uig area so we stayed in a B&B at Aird Uig. This former military base is a bit of an eyesore, but it's conveniently placed for visiting the slab in the bay which by then I'd discovered was called Geòdha Gorm.

Simon Fraser had put me in touch with a couple of equally ancient locals who very kindly volunteered to help cart some of our ropes and climbing gear out to the cliff top for us. (Our combined age we discovered was over 280.) I'd brought out 80 metres of pre-stretched rope – a cast-off from Lochaber MRT. The plan was to abseil straight down the middle of the slab, check out the rock and clean the best looking line. Paul fed out the abseil rope as I set off down. The top section of wall was rather steep, but it started to ease about 5m down. It soon became apparent that the rock wasn't as good as we'd hoped. It would be an enormous job to

Paul Brian (left) with our two helpers, Alistair Pratt and John Glenesk, on the summit of Rubha Mòr, 10 October 2016. The top of the slab is visible in the background.
Photo: Noel Williams.

clean it properly. Looking down it seemed to improve below me but this was illusionary. After I'd abseiled about 30m I decided it was too much of a job. This wasn't going to be another Devil's Slide. Our helpers had not hung around and we had to make two trips to lug all the gear back to the car.

Over the winter for some reason that slab still kept gnawing away at me. Had I really given it a good shot? Spring came round again and I had a wonderful week on Islay with my 'Island' pals. From there I headed back to Lewis again, but this time for a week. My wife Carolyn booked a delightful house in Crowlista which we shared with my old climbing pal Andrew Wielochowski and his wife Fay.

I'd mentioned to Rab Anderson that I was going to Lewis for a week and hoping to climb. He asked me to take a photograph of a sea cliff for the new *Outer Hebrides* guide. He also offered to send me a draft copy of the Uig section of the manuscript, which I was thrilled to receive. I was hugely impressed by how much work he'd put into the guide and how many new routes he'd been responsible for. No wonder it had taken him so long to pull it all together. But more importantly there was no mention of any routes in Geòdha Gorm.

The weather was glorious and, for the first few days, Andrew and I did some pleasant easy new routes in Geòdha Ruadh near Gallan Head. One evening I mentioned to Andrew my visit to the slab the previous autumn. I still couldn't decide if it was worth spending time on. We agreed that Andrew would abseil down the next day to get a second opinion.

This time between us we managed to carry everything out in a oner to the cliff top above Geòdha Gorm. I was pleasantly surprised to find that I'd left a couple of stakes behind on my previous visit, so we had plenty of anchors. I tried to set up the rope so that Andrew could abseil straight down the centre of the slab as before, but he point blank refused to do that. He moved along the cliff edge about 5 metres and found a corner near the edge of the granite vein which he was much happier to descend. I paid out the rope as he set off down. He's a slightly impatient character and can't be bothered to clean routes properly so I wasn't surprised when the rope went out quite quickly. I used the climbing rope to lower the end of the abseil rope to him. The next thing I knew Andrew was standing in a slight alcove at the bottom left-hand side of the slab.

I thought he was then going to jumar straight back up again, but he shouted up that he was going to try climbing out instead. He made steady progress heading diagonally across the slab. At one point he disappeared from sight on the right-hand arête but it wasn't long before he reappeared again. He didn't seem to be pulling off too much loose rock and continued to make steady progress. In due course he finished up the corner he'd insisted on descending.

So he'd managed to climb it, albeit on a top rope. I was impressed, but what was it like?

Andrew was a bit non-committal, so we sat around on the cliff top and had a bite to eat. He's maintained his climbing standard into old age better than I have but he didn't seem to be in a huge hurry to lead it. However, after we'd used up all the delaying tactics, he eventually said, 'Well I suppose we've got to lead it or we'll never forgive ourselves.'

We each took a climbing rope and Andrew again abseiled all the way down to near the bottom of the slab. When it was my turn I was surprised to find there was quite a distinct arête on the right-hand edge of the slab looking down. This was the key to the route. I then had to work my way diagonally leftwards to reach the alcove where Andrew was waiting. This was a comfortable place to stand though the belays were poor.

Andrew thought the first pitch was probably the crux and so it proved. The rock was a bit suspect and the protection was fairly sparse. On the second pitch the rock was not as worrying and the climbing more enjoyable, though again there wasn't a lot of protection. For the third pitch I suggested that instead of following the steep corner he'd climbed on the top rope, Andrew might find it easier to move out onto the slab on the right. This turned out to be quite straightforward, though again the rock was not the best. The final corner though poorly protected also proved not too bad. It had been an inspired discovery by Andrew and not an option that I'd considered at all.

GEÒDHA GORM
East Face

1. Sunset Boulevard E1 4c

'Well I suppose we've got to lead it or we'll never forgive ourselves.'
Photo: Noel Williams.

As we headed back up to the top of Rubha Mòr the sun was moving round to the west and lighting up the slab. The name *Sunset Boulevard* seemed appropriate, more so when I read the blurb for this old Hollywood film – 'sensational...daring...unforgettable'.

The *Outer Hebrides* guide should be out by the time the Journal appears. It will be more or less comprehensive and have a hugely increased number of routes compared with half of the two-volume *Skye and the Hebrides* guide it replaces. Although a lot of the routes in it are way beyond my reach, I feel fortunate to be climbing at a time when new lines of a modest grade are still waiting to be done – inexorable decline or not.

PATAGONIA STERN AND WILD

By Rob Lovell

IT'S 3 A.M. AND WE'RE at the foot of the glacier less than half an hour away from our advanced camp…or are we? We've reached the sound of running water which we've been following on the assumption it's the point at which we joined the glacier this morning, but we don't see what we expect. Immediately our confidence is floored. Sleep deprivation is causing our minds to play tricks on us. I'm starting to hear voices in the sound of running water. Not coherent sentences, but snippets of words. 'Are we at the right lake?', asks Andy, all reference points from this morning forgotten. Andy, whom I thought was my brother Tom about half an hour earlier. I try to piece together our journey off the hill, the camp has got to be around here somewhere. The question is…where?

Five weeks earlier, as the Fitz Roy massif crept up over the horizon it was becoming clear that I was going to spend a significant proportion of my time in Patagonia feeling very intimidated. Confidence was evaporating quickly and I was secretly hoping that the notoriously poor weather would keep us from the mountains. Not so lucky. I'm here with my good friend Andy Hein, a regular climbing partner in the UK with whom I've spent many a day in the perfect alpine training grounds of Almscliff and Back Bowden, and climbed a few other routes here and there.

Four weeks on, and despite an initial lack of optimism, we've had a successful trip. An aborted first foray yielded to success on the second, and we climb Aguja Guillaumet via the Amy-Vidailhet. Even so, there is a desire left unsatisfied; we haven't had a true Patagonian adventure. Fortuitously a final weather window is forecast, so we have another chance. Our eyes are drawn to one of the most striking points on the Fitz Roy skyline – Aguja Poincenot. We plan to climb via the Whillans-Cochrane. 2000m of ascent crossing two glaciers, then a 550m route on steep snow-ice, mixed climbing up to Scottish VI and rock climbing at Hard Very Severe to the knife edge summit at 3002m.

We're at the bivi at Laguna de los Tres, the night before our planned ascent, and true to form my overactive imagination gets to work: exactly what you need when you're trying your hardest to sleep. I can't get the words of local climbing legend Rolo Garibotti, providing advice and support, but encouraging caution, out of my head:

'If you fall off from that approach slope you'll go for 1000m, no? But it's OK, you Brits are fast, so will be down before the wind gets up.'

A few Argentinians have said that. I thought our reputation was for the opposite? It gets me wondering which Brits he's met; a scan of the guidebook offers some suggestions: Carrington and Rouse, Parkin or Cave, Houlding or Kirkpatrick. A different league entirely.

Two friends have just spent four weeks trying to get up this route

The Fitz Roy range from the approach to Laguna de los Tres. Aguja Poincenot is the peak left of centre with the obvious snow ramp half way up. Photo: Rob Lovell.

without success, why is it going to be any different for us? I decide not to dwell on my conclusions, or any other scenarios running through my mind, as it's adding fuel to my doubts. And I'm still very much awake.

00:30 time to get up. We've calculated the time we think it will take us to get to the base of the route in time for sunrise (an extra hour added on to Rolo's suggestion). Getting up is easier than I thought it would be after one and a half hours sleep. A nice strong coffee and porridge with a good dose of highly sugared condensed milk helps.

The snow conditions underfoot mean we've been able to get across the approach slopes quickly and safely. The horizon first glows yellow, igniting the underside of the morning cloud, and a deep orange hue spreads across the sky. With every second that passes the colours grow in intensity. The silhouetted figures of Fitz Roy and Poincenot creep from the darkness, definition increasing until they are in plain sight. The burning orange sky sets the glacier and granite alight. Rays of sun penetrate the perfect alpine scene bringing warmth and optimism. We hear whoops of joy from across the Massif as each climbing team is brought into daylight. We've got our first belay in, it feels good to be attached to the mountain and to be starting our route.

Running the first 300m as two pitches we make quick progress up the diagonal snow ramp to the base of the mixed section which is the technical crux of the route. Careful and deliberate placement of picks and front points provides upward travel. Panting hard I bring Andy up to the belay. He presses on to the shoulder between the east and south faces, ready to commence the rock section of the route.

Spirits are high on reaching the south face and the upper section of the route. Laguna de los Tres is the left-hand lake behind the author. Photo: Andy Hein.

The south face brings with it views of the Torres, a view that I've dreamed of many times: Cerro Torre, Torre Egger and Aguja Standhardt. Spires of granite standing proud in front of the ice field, walls infinitely steep and rime plastered across the summits. Climbing Cerro Torre is a lifetime ambition, but I'm still on my Patagonian apprenticeship and the view from across the valley is enough.

The south face also brings the wind; we are no longer sheltered from the Patagonian westerlies. We knew the wind was forecast to increase throughout the day but shouldn't ever reach speeds that we need to worry about. That said, the temperature has dropped so we climb with gloved hands, often one hand and one axe. Route finding isn't always obvious, the direction of travel being determined by the path of least resistance, rather than a diagram. Andy does a great job making steady upward progress toward the summit with only mild complaint (it turns out that the auto-belays at Ratho or 7c roof routes in Kalymnos aren't the best training for awkward off-width cracks and squeeze-chimneys).

At some point near the top of this section, both of us independently glance west and notice the same thing. Clouds are pouring over Cerro Torre and hurtling towards us. Wind speeds are rising. The weather window is closing early, and the intimidation that I'd been able to hold in check all day starts to grip.

A pitch and a half from the summit we agree that if we find an abseil point we'll begin our descent. With tomorrow's storm arriving now, we don't want to be up here. As it happens we find the descent route virtually at the top so we take turns to dash, belayed from below, onto the

17 hours into the day the descent from the summit of Aguja Poincenot commences with the first of many abseils, the peaks of Aguja Rafael Juárez and Aguja Saint-Exupéry on the ridge line below. Photo: Rob Lovell.

precarious knife edge summit. I look up to Fitz Roy: what a view! I grab my camera but I've not even started opening the case and it's gone, obscured by a freight train of swirling mist.

Going up, one is focused on the immediate goal. The summit obscures the other task in hand, getting down. Sixteen hours into our day we're feeling fatigued. We're 3000m up, the weather is closing in. and no one else is on the mountain. The enormity of the situation hits home. There's no margin for error, no chance of help and plenty of opportunity for things to go wrong. My mind is working overtime, fuelled by the situation, energy gels and adrenaline.

We throw the ropes to begin abseiling the south face; they hover for a second then rise like a pair of angry vipers. A tangle of ropes, more tangled than should be possible, needing to be coaxed inch-by-inch into a usable state. Ropes untangled and abseil complete we find the next anchor and restart the process, throwing them down the face below. This time the ropes shoot sideways, lodging themselves around a horn of rock. Andy sets off, untangling as he goes. The rhythm one hopes for in descent is a far away dream; tangled ropes and re-climbed pitches playing loud instead.

I glance over to Aguja Saint-Exupéry as we abseil to the snow ramp. Clouds billow up on the lee-side of the mountain, capped by a swirling vortex where wind accelerates up and over the westerly face, roaring like a jet engine. Andy tells me he's just seen a volley of basketball size rocks rake the slope below. Stress levels go up again. Darkness falls. A fragment from Charles Darwin flits across my tired mind: Here mankind does not look like the lord at all.

We've been on the go for hours. I make myself safe in the bergschrund after traversing 120m across a steep slushy convex slope. Sitting on my bag I watch the lights of El Chaltén twinkle in the distance, unaware of the concerned hikers gathered in the valley to watch our head torches edge across the mountain. I'm so tired. My mind converses with itself, 'Are you sure we can't have a quick nap here?' Sadly not a realistic option. We'd soon be wet through and the weather is forecast to be worse. Time to move on. Andy heads out into the night.

Just after midnight we drop onto our bags in the middle of the glacier and rest our weary legs; the first meaningful break of the day so far. It's the first time since leaving the top of Aguja Poincenot that we feel like the objective danger has reduced enough for us to rest. The stress doesn't let up as we posthole our way down a steep ridge, which now has the consistency of mashed potato and is at the perfect angle for a wet snow avalanche. Onward to the lower glacier following a boot track left on our morning ascent. We hear the sound of water, which must be the river we crossed this morning. Immediately we set our course for the sound, the hard ice of the glacier pummelling our weary feet.

Finally we reach the source of the sound, but it's not where we should be. Immediately our confidence is floored. 'Are we at the right lake?', asks Andy, all reference points from this morning forgotten. Navigationally, I'm on my own and I'm desperately trying to find a feature I recognise, anything that will give me confidence that we are on the right track. Stumbling on, we finally reach a point where we can safely exit the ice. Traversing around the lake I'm still unsure of myself but finally I see something I know from before. The top of the tent emerges from the darkness, but the sense of relief is dampened by exhaustion. We collapse on the floor at 3.30 a.m. 26 hours after setting out.

SOUTH GLEN SHIEL RIDGE SKI TRAVERSE

By Finlay Wild

MANY TIMES I HAVE PASSED through Glen Shiel, looked up to the South Cluanie Ridge and wondered what it would be like as a ski traverse. Having run it once many years ago my memory was of grassy amenable slopes, and with this in mind it was certainly on my radar for a ski traverse on lightweight 'skimo' gear. But would I ever manage to get there when it was in condition?

On 16 December 2017 I found myself in a position to put this question to the test. The snowline had been low for a week and I'd had some days out in the east with my skis on straight from the car. But Glen Shiel is awfully near the sea, so I didn't know how low the snowline would be, or how consolidated the early season snowpack was.

Setting off from near the Cluanie Inn a little before sunrise I skinned along the old Fort William road right from the car. Firm snow crunched as I wove a line between the compressed vehicle tracks left by an estate truck in the previous days. Heading south and up into Coirean an Eich Bhric I came over a rise and was bathed in deep orange light rising from out east in the direction of Ben Alder. Behind me and across the quiet, frozen glen the snowy hills reflected this early morning light, taking on an extra clarity in its yellow luminosity. I was amazed by how close the Lochaber hills looked: the prominent Grey Corries' skyline merging with the Aonachs before ending in the distinctive dark hulk of Ben Nevis's

Early morning on the Cluanie to Tomdoun road. All photos: Finlay Wild.

Sunrise in Coirean an Eich Bhric of Creag a' Mhàim.

north face. A short section on foot took me up the north ridge to summit Creag a' Mhàim, the first of the nine Munros I hoped to visit.

Heading west along the broad ridge I ascended into the mist, managing to keep the skis on past some narrow rocky sections. After Aonach air Chrith I ran a short distance as again the ridge was narrow, rocky and scoured. Snow showers would blow through making me cinch my hood tighter as my muffled hearing gave in to the elemental sounds of transient gusts, the pelt of snow on my jacket, and the rhythmic efforts of my breathing. Mercifully these blasts would recede as quickly as they arrived, leaving me alone again with the silent untracked snow.

Further along the weather improved and I had more expansive views down to Glen Quoich, fully blanketed in snow. Following the old fenceline for a lot of the route made for mostly easy navigation through the intermittent cloud, although some careful contouring used the skis to advantage in enabling a more direct line that avoided several sub-summits. The snow cover was good although the base was variable. In practice this meant for quick uphill skinning but required careful descending to avoid rocks, fenceposts and unconsolidated drifts. Due to the nature of the undulating ridge it was quicker and more efficient to leave skis in uphill mode for some of the short, gentler descents. As anyone who has free-heeled downhill with skins on will know, this can be pretty ungainly!

By Creag nan Damh the sun was out and I had expanding winter vistas south and west, as well as glimpses through the cloud of a pristine looking snowy Saileag to the north. Following the fenceline down to Bealach Duibh Leac was undulating and made for exciting progress which was

Old fence posts point the way towards Sgùrr na Sgine.

not straightforward on skis. Here was the option of an obvious descent route down northwards to the road. With an enjoyable traverse of seven Munros behind me, was I hoping for too much if I went on traversing into the lengthening afternoon shadows?

Committing to finding out I headed upwards to cross the rocky summit of Sgùrr a' Bhac Chaolais, which gave access to the two remaining peaks beyond. Sgùrr na Sgine was a beauty, its steep eastern cliffs a barrier that I would have to go around. Taking my skis off briefly for a steep rocky descent, I then followed a lovely gentle slope traversing south-west under the cliffs. I spotted two climbers doing one of the chimney lines on the cliff, and then startled a fox from its snow-covered hideout in an old wall. I watched with primitive delight as it shot up the wide white slope, helter skelter, disappearing over the horizon. Following it more slowly I arrived at Sgùrr na Sgine and looked across to The Saddle, which was still capped in cloud. The snow was less consolidated here, closer to the sea, and the hills seemed rockier too. An awkward traverse down to Bealach Coire Mhàlagain was not free of rocky scrapes, but certainly would have been more arduous on foot, sinking deep in the soft snow.

Heading up The Saddle I felt tired. I had only taken a litre of water and not enough food, so I needed to concentrate. The cloud lifted as I got to the 1010m summit and I had welcome evening views to Loch Duich and Skye. This peak is complex and knowing I had only about half an hour of daylight left in which to descend focused my mind, adding feelings of urgency to those already engendered by the lonely harshness of the land. Skiing down the featured corrie heading east did not look totally

The author on the traverse.

straightforward, but walking off by any route would have been slow and exhausting in these conditions. Carefully avoiding rocks I skied the corrie and then traversed back to the base of the Forcan Ridge.

Ascending a final time I passed Meallan Odhar and joined the stalkers' track before jogging out the final 2km on foot, just as it became fully dark, some 8.5 hours after setting off. Thumb out hopefully, walking along the road in the darkness, I was a lucky boy as the first vehicle passing stopped for me! Thanks to Helen and Neil from Cioch Outdoor Clothing who gave me a lift back to my car for some celebratory food and rehydration. Skis made this journey possible in these conditions, but the window was brief: mild weather arrived the following day.

THREE AVALANCHE ADVENTURES ... AND MORE

By Tim Pettifer

CIRCULATING CHAMONIX for a few winter seasons were two unusual methods of avalanche avoidance. The first was *if in doubt let your best friend go first* and the second if you wanted to check the stability of a slope was *chuck in a Swede* referring to that excellent race of mountaineers and skiers well known for fearless bravery.

I have never let the truth get in the way of a good story but the following three accounts of avalanches here and across the Channel are the truth and I swear that not another drop of duty free will pass my lips while I go tappety-tap on the keyboard. These three incidents can be told without regret and only a little recrimination because the only serious injury was a man's pulverized pride, accentuating the basic teaching of Vajrayana Buddhism: ego is the enemy of all people.

It was clear, even desperate as I was to get the shots needed for an advertisement for a technical mountaineering fabric, that the snow conditions were about as bad as they could be. This was confirmed by the Chamonix Meteo, even though the next day's forecast was wall to wall sunshine and negligible wind. We had passed the time out there in blizzards trying to find our way around low level ski tours when even the lower lifts were closed. However, a famous and very expert mountaineer who was sponsored by the client thought otherwise and said 'I beg to differ' in the typical style of such people, leaving no room for discussion from common people who only understand plain language: 'Yera huge cam short o' a full rack, yer big eejit!'

In reality the expert wanted the money even more than the fame, so an opinion coming from Scotland where the mountains are mere pimples was laughable. For him the snow in Chamonix was always wonderful and after I was publicly ridiculed it is quite possible he left to give a lecture on environmental ice climbing, barefoot without crampons. (Please forgive me! This is the only bit I have made up but it helps place his character.)

Skiing and carrying our skis to the top of the planned gully overlooking Le Tour I was pleased it was not me that had made the decision to go and I was enjoying the morning. I went into a Zen state, not thinking about the far objective, creating a steady rhythm of sound from the skis brushing through the powder snow, the quiet almost imperceptible hiss enhanced in the dark and the cone of white light from the LED head torch. Paul Horth, normally a sergeant in the RAF pursued his usual approach 'travel slow and you travel well, travel well and you go far' but is always there in the pack. Always observant, noticing changes in the snow structures or watching out for potential avalanche traps from above, we had been on many assignments together and he was my insurance policy so I could concentrate on photography. A good grade five ice man and the hero of many practice extreme ski descents in Scotland and the full boonas over in the Alps. Bringing up the tail was the client from Geneva. A true Swiss she moved with an easy, natural grace. Up above, far up above was the lead role bouncing around spreading his ego over the snow, the mountain, the stars in a still dark sky and me in particular, the man with the cheque book. He was vain to the last but I was clicking away making sure a big head did not spoil the photos. Sure enough he looked good and must have been born wearing skis!

Photos over, job done, skis back on we headed down, firstly a chute, not extreme but steep enough to warrant some careful jump turns. Then the terrain opened out and we should have enjoyed the perks of the job: fun in the sun and home for a magnificent second breakfast. The expert was good for a least a few turns before a 1.5 crown wall 50m wide cut the slope and the expert was on the bad luck side of tumbling chaos of breaking slab.

It's not often you can watch an avalanche at close quarters, even rarer to witness a victim in its grasp. The avalanche was a jolly giant having a bit of a laugh! It had a funny, vertical revolving motion that threw up in nice parabolas, firstly an attractive but characterful ski hat, then a ski, then a rucksack and then its victim upside down, wearing the jacket we had given him (now that would have been a publicity shot and a half), followed by his rucksack and the victim up again, diving back after the rucksack that was followed by a ski.

Very lucky for us we were on the up side but only just. With two waiting above the crown wall keeping an eye on the *never to be believed again expert*, appearing and disappearing in the general melee I jumped down and followed behind and it's surprising how slow it moved. At length it stopped and directions to the likely burial chamber were given from above, being Paul and Lisa, and not actually from *The* Above. He comes into the story in the next paragraph.

The transceiver was switched to search. Fearing the worst, but very relieved and happy the shots were in the bag, I passed bits and pieces of clothing and equipment. Below, thanks be to God, the *very lucky to be alive, never to be believed again expert* had a hand sticking out and was soon brought to the surface from what could easily have been a deep burial.

We now faced a dilemma because the most likely avalanche areas, some infamous, were still ahead in the full glare of a warm sun on a south facing slope. Prudence took over, we made the decisions and carefully plotted a route down giving the expert, the option to follow us, which he meekly did, after we told him to 'go and take a hike' in French which is not my strong subject but he got the meaning. We used every trick in the book, keeping to the ridges, skiing one at a time and at an unavoidable chute, we used the rope and made some heavy jumps in the snow to give bad slopes some encouragement. Out at the bottom we headed to a restaurant and there the *lying, very lucky to be alive, never to believed again and thanking God expert* stripping off his wet gear unconsciously revealed he had not brought a transceiver. He said he would but how could we Scotch (it is not so strange they get confused between a man in a kilt and whisky) even have dared ask for a transceiver check? Had his hand not been out, we would have had a confusing search, looking for a skier with a transceiver who did not actually have one...as the clock ticked on. And if the situation had been the other way round how would he have found us...as the clock ticked on? Outside the restaurant it was time for a good hanging, followed by slow drawing, quartering and quartering again.

Back here in God's own country two brave boys are huddled in bivvy bags round the back of the CIC. They had become part of the snow drifts accumulating while we were walking in and very glad we were to shut the door of the hut, shake off the snow and get the heating on. The morning came with the forecast high wind, snow showers and powder avalanches pouring off the plateau in endless torrents. The cornices over 3, 4 and 5 were growing as you watched with curled, fragile feathered edges miraculously hanging in the swirling eddies. I have to admit I was not happy but peer pressure proved me wrong. And glad I am about it. Brian Shackleton quietly said Green Gully would be a safe and worthy route for a day that would see cornice collapses and quite possibly devastating avalanches. The objective decided, leaving the comfortable hut the only other team on the mountain were the brave, bivvy boys with full packs just ahead of us. How did they manage a bacon roll? Why did their sleeping bags not fill with snow? Being in touch with the mountain is one thing but this was stern stuff and I was full of admiration.

We kept to a higher line under Tower Ridge and they went into North Gully. The leader made a belay of sorts inside the first S bend and even as I watched, a section of cornice, maybe 6m wide came away just as the previous day's avalanche warnings had predicted. Its huge bulk dropped into the wide reach of the upper gully and the whole lot went, right up to the scarp slope under the remaining cornicing. Pouring through the narrow neck it plucked the first man off his stance, swept to the second and rolled them down. All that left was a yellow camper mat floating off, swirling in the wind and going up, up towards Càrn Mòr Dearg. Fearing the worst, we plotted a route across expecting a lot of digging just as the boys very nicely popped up, shaking themselves down.

One avalanche a day and a brush with the Other Side is more than enough for most people. Not these tough boys! They charged back into the gully in a furious attack, with the determination to attack again, again and again until they came out on the top. Ho hum, this is the stuff of men and made the great English bull dog with a stiff upper lip such a feared beast!

The most interesting aspect of avalanche prediction is the unpredictability of avalanches. The forecasters make a very good a job of it then its over to you to apply the forecast to your current very localised, very sun blessed or very cold position. In those situations I have

Tim Pettifer's party ski-touring in the Dachstein during the period of the third incident described. Photo: Tim Pettifer.

been heard to say 'this slope might go' meaning I might take an express route to destruction, but luckily my avalanche prediction is not all it could be. But only once have I heard 'this slope *will* avalanche.' An eyebrow raising, unequivocal, no compromise statement that forecasts interesting adventures immediately at hand. This came from a modest, quiet Austrian guide named Reiser Herbert. There was no test skiing and no test snow pits, just a long considered look at the surface. This was more than technical expertise. This was intuition that comes from intimate contact with local mountains where Herbert's relatives had been farmers, guides and gem hunters for generations, spending whole years on the alps.

It was the only gully down through a wide band of crags up in the Dachstein. Return was not an option because to get into this magnificent powder bowl we had skied from the Simmony Hut and then carried our skis almost to the top of the Hoher Dachstein and then descended by sometimes overhanging ladders, the remains of wartime defences. Unfortunately the last 5m had been blown away by shell blast and we had finished the descent by jumping into the powder.

Knowing that the slope would avalanche what was the alternative? Easy! Just ski it because knowing what will happen is more than half the battle. But then you have to be a very good skier.

It was a north facing fold in the mountains that would see no sun until the spring. A cold, dark, steep slope, 40m across and 75m down, hemmed in at the opposite side and the top by a line of steep crags and on our side, a steep gully and a snow arête hiding probably loose boulders. We were perched across this snow arête one above the other with skis sticking into space fore and aft.

Everyone wanted to see the impending action and in the jockeying, fencing of elbows, arguing and pushing for a good view, our hero was forgotten and was being shoved into space. He put up a textbook ski-pole defence and got in a few good whacks. Given no alternative to jumping before he was pushed he landed in a downwards traverse to soften the impact, but the slope wakened from its winter long stupor and filled with spite went with a menacing hiss, leaving no headwall taking the whole slope from top to bottom and right across. Turning to avoid the bigger lumps and keeping upright, Herbert kept in a steep traverse until it slowed towards the runout and then put his foot down to schuss beyond the final build up of deep debris. Now how easy was that? Well actually very easy *for us* because all that was left was a typically hard, icy, Scottish slope so we were well at home, cheers and thank you very much!

A year later we heard of Herbert's death in Switzerland. Many of his friends in Scotland wanted to know what had happened so Dr Joan Harvey and I travelled across to Windischarten, Herbert's home village in Austria and had a week skiing and ski touring with his friends and family. We learnt that he was killed helping to rescue another guide's client on the Zinal Rothorn. In appreciation of our visit his father gave us a marvellous cut stone, the size and shape of half a melon with double agates of exactly the same size, each an inch across and three inches apart.

Looking back on these events if the slope above Le Tour had split a few metres further back I would have been infamous as the first photographer to kill a client, as the blame was only mine for not following on from what I knew was right. But she wanted the photography in a hurry, paid well, wanted to have a dinner story to beat all others and would not have missed the adventure for a pension. Now that really was peer pressure on a grand scale.

Brian Shackleton's expertise and persuasion pulled off a route against the odds when almost all climbers were well away from the mountains, and coming to Herbert, a potentially very dangerous scenario was made harmless by vast knowledge and superior skills *without braggadocio*.

As a safety essential next time you are walking in to a route make an avalanche risk assessment of your comrades in arms. The neurotic who asks if they will be safe on the summit of Glas Maol rates Grade One; the partner who thinks he is safe because he has all the rescue kit a shop can throw into a rucksacks is Grade Two; anyone who thinks avalanches don't happen in Scotland is a monkey and if they propose a quick crossing of the Great Slab they are Four and the expert who is not really expert at all and therefore more dangerous than avalanches rates Grade Five.

You can probe into the deep unknown of the snow pack to gain what knowledge you can but what about the unknown party up above you? As the mountains become busier, there are more climbers and skiers buying skill. Ski instructing in Courmayeur I have seen them day after day going up on the first lifts with skis wide enough for virtual beginners to tackle difficult off piste snow. They have avalanche flotation packs loaded with

Massive avalanche debris at the Saddle, Cairngorm. Photo by kind permission of SAIS Northern Cairngorm.

snow shovel, probe and somewhere about them a complicated transceiver only used in the apartment. The technical goodies boost their confidence beyond their experience; they often ignore the golden rule of waiting 24 hours after the last big snowfall, racing to be the first to get to the untracked slopes, even in a white out.

The problem with working in those conditions is not giving in to reverse peer pressure and convincing your clients that you are not an old fuddy-duddy and that the worst might happen as it often does. But I am not going to write ill of the dead and tell you about the big, multiple burials that happen right next to the piste that never get into the press unless they involve UK nationals. Incidents involving Brits are few and far between.

Interestingly, much of the fame of Chamonix as the extreme climbing and skiing citadel of the world was created by three boys from Scotland. Roger Lambert from Aviemore and John Vaikus from Fife, having cut their teeth skiing the gullies of the Northern Corries and Loch Avon (in the sixties and seventies considered extremes) moved to Chamonix and were regular photographic fixtures in magazines, videos and equipment catalogues, photographed by Jess Stock who was well connected to the freestyle skiing scene on Cairngorm. The rest is history and 'extreme' is now measured by the dictum 'one slip and you're dead or very badly injured'. I got a chance to see an 'extreme' ski when Paul Horth, Ian Mills (on telemark!) and I shared the winter room of the Requin Hut with Pierre Tardival. We thought we were skiing extreme coming down from the

Aiguille du Tacul until we saw Pierre Tardival ski the TD gully, directly opposite across the Mer du Glace.

I have not seen John Vaikus in person for a few years but regularly see him still taking big air in the best photos adding to Chamonix's aura. Personally I think Chamonix is a bit like flying: even upgraded to First Class you have to convince yourself it's enjoyable!

———————•———————

They are wounded rocks,
these Cuillin; a good place though
for healing humans.

Hamish Brown

CRAIGLUG LOST IN TRANSLATION

By Phil Gribbon

I WANDERED UP OVER the stubble looking for a way through the fence and dropped down beside a rubbishy little quarry. There was no way through the rusting wire and tumbled sheets of corrugated iron littering the ground, so it was back and onward until a devious way got me into the scrap'n stack farmyard with its gate of sorts that led into the field sloping up towards the crag.

I hadn't been there for ages and my inquisitive nature had to know how this playground for besporting oneself upon those long past summer evenings had fared through my absence. The last visit had been with my semi-jetlagged son on the afternoon that he and his family had arrived in Fife from western Canada. We had pushed up through tussocky grass clumps to the base of the cliff to sample a few easy problems. There was not much sign of other recent visitors but this could be excusable because the popularity of this Fife outcrop had been greatest when the early summer rock creepers began to venture on to its various distinctive nameless miniscule routes.

Nevertheless it was strange how raggedy-ill-frequented looked the climbing lines with even a well established prickly gorse bush thrusting its roots into the unsuspecting crack of a standard descent route. No one was coming down, if no one was going up. Next time the use of a saw or clippers would be a public-spirited gesture, if I was coming back again.

Today it was enjoyable to feel the smooth warm planes of the tinged green lichened rock, get the fingertips round a sharp edge, and scan the panorama of the distant mountains. When we went home, we were well

Craiglug Crag near the village of Dairsie on the Cupar–St. Andrews road in Fife. Photo: Phil Gribbon.

satisfied with our brief visit to Craiglug. However his copybook had been blotted by dashing off and leaving his partner to manage two tired fractious boys installed with his mother-in-law: perhaps, it was all my fault, who knows?

Craiglug boasts not the most blissful of names, its origin being lost in dubious antiquity. Its meaning as 'bell shaped and steep' is implausible for a swollen lump with a belt of breaking dolerite arcing round below a spreading mass of overgrowing furze. I can't but associate it with my friend known in his school days as Lugs McCall whom we had tried to persuade to complete his Munros and although he came close to that final magic number (whatever it was in those days) the powers that be on these matters decided wisely to award it to the Unknown Munroist, of whom there are a lot around these days. Incidentally his lugs were not in any way too eye-catching, and to call this nice wee hill Rocky Ears is wholly inappropriate.

I walked up the field scanning the familiar rock band. Cursory inspection was my aim for the day. I saw the great gorse blobs lumping themselves indiscriminately across the weaknesses in the rock structure. She was hiding herself with living botany. Enclosing the tussocky slope up to the straggly elder trees under the crag was the pride and long lasting joy of the farmer: a well constructed partially mortar strengthened field boundary wall, except that nature's abrading onslaughts aided by gravity's willing help (and not forgetting cow behinds relieving their anal itches) had punched several gaps along its length.

This had been the once perfect wall over which Dougie Lang and pal, plus myself and two insignificant minor youths had struggled to hoist my companion Peter Riedi suspended on my car carpet with his well-broken thigh, and into the back of my estate car en route for a prolonged stay in Dundee Royal Infirmary.1 Poor Peter was always an enthusiastic hill walker, although he never could remember if he had done a given hill before.

I selected a gap and strolled through searching for the vestige of a path but there was no sign of anyone having stomped up the slope. I made for the near end where a scuffed dry stony scar had been the path through to the rock face but it had disappeared under ubiquitous gorse. Here was a blocky undercut little buttress flanked by a wall topped with unhelpful upside down holds that had foiled the very competent Brian McMillan who tediously pretended its difficulties just had to be climbable with persistence. Much easier to sidle in to the main crack splitting the crag, ignoring the chunky rusted peg battered in for direct aid, surmount the once-resident perched block without contact, and squeeze up towards the blue sky.

My inspection tour was not the time to brood on past endeavours. There was war to be waged, the bramble invaders loved the warm seclusion and shot exploratory barbed strands across every gap, so out with my wife's secateurs, to snip, clip, snip. Progress seemed slow, but then I was lined

*'Scarecrow': the image gives some idea of the quality of this largely forgotten outcrop.
Photo: Phil Gribbon.*

up with Scarecrow, on which, thrust out with all one's weight on the lip of a hanging shelf, one had to trust the treacherous holds to stay put for a bit longer, or so I've been told. I scare easily, especially when I see a smooth inviting surface and its brown buff scar marks where handy holds have exfoliated themselves at the wrong time. Strange to see that someone has neatly painted in its scary name and its number –17, leaving all the remainder of the crag devoid of human graffiti: no recent white paint, no defining green Roman numerals executed by the Leuchars Mountain Rescue brigade in their glory days. Go online, see the Craiglug numbers with grades, the unfathomable route notes, no pics, no sketches, no diagrams, and just no point in going there when there are indoor climbing gyms, fashionable outdoor venues, hidden walls in hollows and blatant buttresses for strutting the flight fantastic.

Here was the once obvious descent line, now thoroughly blocked by blossoming cumulonimbus wadges of gorse prickles. Next, the little infant pinnacle protrusion with its fingerhold that called for extendable arms when making the frictional step of commitment, and where once I had waited holding the rope for my son's pal to make the move while round the corner ahead came the groans of my companion with his newly shattered thighbone.

Ahead was the big wall, just high enough to let an abseiling novice hang back on the rope threaded round the stunted dwarf hawthorn living on its eyrie feel the air all around, and then with a few cautious steps walk the wall down to terra firma. This wall held steep if limited challenge: a toe plonked in a minimal scoop that just had to stay there, or the delicate striding step moving towards the reassuring ledge at eyeball level with the joyous pleasure of crux-over and feeling the sense of freedom. Once there was a stout elder tree trunk where backing-up-chimney action aided the initial attachment to the wall but the vandals came and flattened it. Next was the crack with the threatening rock coffin blocking progress, careful straddling recommended, but it fell (or was it pushed?) to vanish into undergrowth, a good move sequence obliterated.

This was base camp arena where the grass shrank to mown golf course height. Visiting climbers littered the ground with their gear and donned their fancy footwear while the assembled hordes of ill shod scouts on their annual outing to the Craiglug cliffs waited for a free rope-end to exhibit their prowess and inborn talent. Once on a spring evening there were thirty six folk climbing and spread along the crag; oh, how popular it was in those days. Today the arena grass is rankly damply dominant and there is nowhere nice to sit lazing and gazing at climbers doing their thing.

Everyone liked to try and get off the ground in an attempt on the big rock belly bulge, a test piece of character for those sure of success and not sensible for those unable to accept failure. Do it once and keep repeating it with the impetuousness of youth until strength fails and in the dimming light of the gloaming retreat to the transport. Everyone with any savvy liked to emulate the RAF rescue teams doing their local training exercise by sneaking up from Dairsie along the private road towards the Big Hoose, whipping past it and parking by the gardener's cottage to flit swiftly under the sycamores to the tussocky field and its well trampled serpentine path to the crag.

More features appeared: an inviting open ladder-way capped by a protruding tiny roof where access leftwards needed a big effort to gain a platform. At the roof an over confident student lost it, became cragfast: his fate beyond comprehension at one of the most docile places on the crag. Gorse now hid the roof and standing there promised prickly pain. The platform had been created when those nameless vandals used a car jack to lever off a genuine pinnacle that toppled downhill and with a puff of rock dust demolished a length of the field wall. Much diplomatic apology was offered but the farmer still wanted the large rocky intruder removed. Those who felt morally responsible proceeded to batter it with sledgehammers but to no avail, and it stayed there until the farmer turned his tractor on it and shifted it back a few feet to form a huge part of the replacement wall.

Beyond was a cleft stuffed with gorse. It had been an obvious sluice-like gutter of descent, the open-faced eroded chimney alternative to the zigzagging walk down a slab now overwhelmed by the spiny stuff. Here the last buttress was clamped between the advancing gorse but its pride of cracks still remained unclaimed by rampant nature and up there was the sweet traverse, fingers over the top and the step up on to drought dried grass and a turn around to face the sweeping northern fringe of homely highland hills.

I went down, sorely tested. The massive long stone with its blunt crest, like the blade of a splitting axe, lay where it had fallen aeons ago. It seemed only yesterday to me that my friend like a sacrificial victim had tumbled off the rocks above, perhaps holding still a broken fragment of dolerite shed from his virgin line before he landed crushingly across the waiting blade. We tried to get him moving to hop down to the field wall but one hop was sufficient to show this was madness.

I returned along the crag walkway but diverted to the shorter route round to the private road. It was sad and salutary to see my local crag so demoted, it had had its day, the climbing game has moved on, all translated to greater things. Craiglug was lost forgotten ground, merely now a place to remember the past.

BEN HOPE

By Andy Nisbet

BEN HOPE IS SCOTLAND'S second biggest cliff, at around 500m high and 2.5km long. So which is the biggest? No, it's not Ben Nevis but actually Beinn Lair at a similar height and 3km long. Not only that, but Ben Hope's west face is eroded into ridges and gullies to make fine lines. And an hour from the road. So why has it only been developed recently?

It's a bit of a mystery really, with the only answer being that it's not easy to see and also that it's in the far far north, not easy to get to in the depths of winter. Especially as the Hope road from Altnaharra is often blocked and you have to go via Tongue. The north end of the cliff is clearly seen from the main road along the north coast but that's not the most impressive part, while the 2km west wall stays largely hidden from the road below, and you have to walk close underneath to assess that it might give good climbing. Unless you take a helicopter, like the photographer of the topo picture.

Early summer visits to the mountain explored that more visible area at the north end. First on the scene were Glover and Ling in May 1910. They took a somewhat roundabout route which seems to have started up Tower Ridge and finished up Petticoat Ridge. There was then a long gap before J.H.B. Bell and D. Myles each climbed a ridge on opposite sides of a

W.N. Ling on the first recorded climb on Ben Hope, 14 May 1910.
Photo: G.T. Glover (SMCJ 1911).

prominent funnel in August 1933. After a further gap Scott and Molly Johnstone did Petticoat Ridge in April 1956.

The first recorded winter route was not done until December 1969 when Hamish Brown and D. Macnab fought their way up Myles' Ridge in a howling gale. The ridge has subsequently become known as Brown's Ridge but not named by Brown so I'm sure he won't mind the correction. Walter Taylor made a winter ascent of one of the gullies in the 1970s when he worked at Dounreay, but without remembering which one, except that it was long and had ice pitches. The locals in those days didn't record routes so who knows what was done, although the gullies may have been easier in the days of heavier snow. Neil Wilson and Ian Stewart climbed Bell's Ridge in 1985 while local climbers Jim Hall, Bob Tosh and S. Comrie climbed Petticoat Ridge in 1999, but it would seem that none of them visited the west face.

The early visits were in summer, so you can see why the vegetated schist didn't become popular. In fact J.H.B. Bell climbing his eponymous ridge might even have put future climbers off, especially those who know that vegetation wasn't a negative point for Bell. But why a winter visit took so long, and then at least three different groups did a route but didn't go back, is definitely puzzling because I only had to go once and I was hooked.

I was always aware that Ben Hope had some steep ground but my visits were a rush up the walkers' route to bag the Munro (in the afternoon after doing Klibreck in the morning), although I did climb it as a schoolboy with my parents long before I was interested in winter climbing. And probably many other potential climbers did similar. I do remember looking at the face in the distance on Foinaven trips, but curiosity wasn't enough when Foinaven had so much scope. Later, Dave McGimpsey watched a TV programme about flying round the Highlands and it contained some brief shots of impressive ridges on Ben Hope. But again we didn't go there. So I didn't go until 2013, after I'd met Bettyhill resident Steve Perry on an SMC aspirant meet, and he lived near enough to Ben Hope to be aware of an unclimbed icefall. He persuaded me that climbing on Ben Hope (tomorrow!) was worthwhile, so the two of us, with his wife Katie, climbed Hopefall (Grade III), up the 'prominent funnel' mentioned above, and were immediately hopeful of more routes.

Steve was the driving force in the early days, with local contacts to report on snow conditions (at least on the roads), and we would stay in the independent hostel in Tongue, very handy when you can see Ben Hope from its front door. He walked under the west face in April 2013 and took photos, although we didn't make it back till 2015. Tower Ridge had been identified in the 2010 scrambles guide, *Highland Scrambles North*, though it was only crossed over as a way of approaching Petticoat Ridge. Steve decided that we should climb Tower Ridge with a long lower extension right down to the cliff base. This turned out to be harder and better than either of us expected (in fact harder than anything done since) and a photo

Steve Perry on Turf Factor (IV,4). Photo: Andy Nisbet.

The Bad Step on the North Ridge. The three figures are about to start up the easy left-hand gully (Grade I). Taken direct it is Grade III. Photo: Noel Williams.

which appeared in *SMC Journal* 2015 (p543) kept reminding us that 2016 would be a Ben Hope year.

We were aware that good planning (and luck) had meant that the start of Tower Ridge Integral was frozen (and needed to be), so we were back in mid-January when the weather seemed cold enough. In those days, we started from the North Ridge parking place (NC 4593 5067, start of the Moine Path) and descended back down the North Ridge. It gave an extra challenge the first time, working out how to avoid the Bad Step at about 850m by a gully on the right (facing down), but lower boulder fields made it a long day even though you returned to the car.

Then we began working our way southwards along the cliff. Each ridge gave a good view of the next one along, so that tended to be the future target. But each was slightly further to walk, so Steve came up with a plan to try a direct approach. Parking at the start of a track (NC 4588 4925), we headed up beside a stream and breached the low cliffs with surprising ease to reach the south end of the cliffs in some 45 minutes, maybe an hour for most starts. This was a bit of a revelation, 600m routes as accessible as Sneachda, although conditions were hardly as reliable.

We climbed seven routes in 2016, a mixture of ridges and gullies, just picking what we fancied in the conditions. The advantage of the new approach was that the descent was down the easy south flank and fortunately, the old guy wasn't expected to do the 1.7km walk along the road for the car. The first route and first ridge right of Tower Ridge was called Viking Ridge and only Grade II, a bit of a surprise considering how steep it looked, but we were discovering that the routes were mostly on

Steve Perry on Valkyrie (IV,3). Photo: Andy Nisbet.

BEN HOPE
West Face

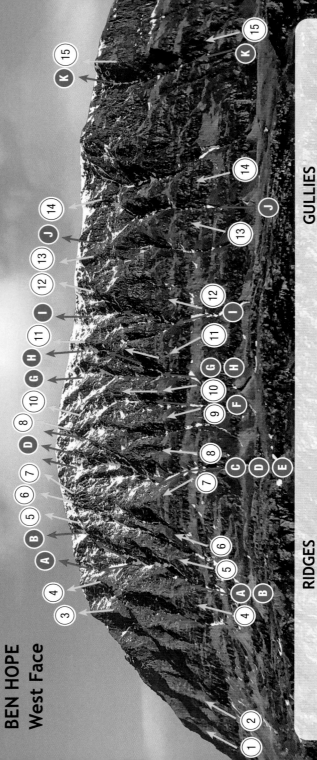

RIDGES

1. Myles' Ridge II
2. Bell's Ridge III
3. Petticoat Ridge III
4. Tower Ridge Integral ..V,6
5. Viking Ridge II
6. I Spy III
7. Notos III,4
8. Valhalla III,4
9. Scandi High IV,4
10. The Turf Factor IV,4
11. South Tower Ridge III
12. Ketosis III
13. Harpie III,4
14. Bobsled Buttress III
15. Valentine's Ridge IV,5

GULLIES

A. Longphort Left III
B. Longphort III
C. Odin IV,4
D. Odin Right IV,4
E. Loki III
F. Blue River IV,4

G. Valkyrie IV,3
H. Thor's Gully II
I. Freya III,4
J. Skeleton Gully IV,4
K. Polar Express IV,4

Photo (from a helicopter): Andrew Adamson

the easy side and that if you were happy soloing Grade II, then you could do them fairly quickly and only roping up for occasional pitches. And we also discovered that the starts were quite heathery, making them much less likely to freeze (only around 400m altitude), but that didn't really matter when you reached frozen ground fairly soon.

There were so many ridges and gullies that it was hard to describe them other than as a list, but a ridge with a tower made life easier. We called it the South Tower (as against the Tower on Tower Ridge) but you can't win as it's quite central on the face. The gullies either side of the South Tower are the deepest on the face but freeze slower than the ridges, especially when snow insulates the water. But the sun also comes round on to the face in the afternoon and hits the ridges more than the recessed gullies, so a very rough rule is ridges early season, gullies mid season and go to a higher mountain late season.

It was a poor winter in 2017 and we only did four routes, but we discovered that the climbs were still fun in poor conditions. The one exception was the first route of the season, after a major storm came in from the north-west and provided heavy rain quickly turning to a cold gale. The last and lowest gully on the face had clearly been given a fierce sub-zero updraught and was not only ice from bottom to top (no snow) but the freezing water had been plastered across its walls, giving the most continuous ice I've ever climbed in Scotland (Polar Express, 500m IV,4). And in a winter which seemed like one of the poorest ever. It only lasted a day but fortunately we were there.

This past winter has been cold for a long time, ideal for Ben Hope, so we've made the effort to complete the major lines, including many of the easier gullies. After another 10 routes, we rather ran out of steam for the long journey up north, but it had been great fun. The short walk-in had been great for me with a bad knee and Steve with a bad ankle, while Sandy Allan and Jonathan Preston have been happy with shorter days when they are guiding most of the time. And Dave McGimpsey has come out of retirement, inspired by Ben Hope and then ice elsewhere in what has been a great winter. The 'we' used above throughout the years refers to various combinations of the five members and we've enjoyed every day.

But we like long mountaineering routes as a change from technical climbs and that won't please everyone. We've really failed to decide on stars and will just have to see what you readers think.

NEW ROUTES

The deadline for sending route descriptions to the New Routes Editor is 30 June each year.

OUTER HEBRIDES

The following just missed the new guide.

ISLE OF LEWIS, Tobha Mòr, Valtos:
The broad headland to the north of Valtos is split in two by Geodha Maladail. In the new Outer Hebrides guide a number of routes are described on Tobha Beag, the eastern part of the headland. The routes below all lie on the western half of this headland which is called Tobha Mòr. They are described in a clockwise direction around the headland.

The first and most impressive crag lies on the west side of Tobha Mòr. It is very difficult to see from above though a distant view of it can be had from the cliff-top on the western side of Camas na Clibhe.

Park as for the Tobha Beag routes (NB 0878 3666). Head west at first before contouring northwards along the western flank of Seuchaval on pleasant grassy ground. Some minor amusement can be found on a boss of delightful rock on the shore at Stac a' Ruta. There is also a fun low level scramble on the south side of Camas Shannageadh – best done in a southerly direction.

Turn a corner after 500m and head in a north-westerly direction to a point overlooking the most westerly part of the headland. A slabby ramp runs out in a south-westerly direction from the base of the cliff. This ramp borders a narrow inlet called Geodha Staca nan Gall.

In order to inspect the face and identify the best place to abseil, it is worth scrambling down a little to the north of the ramp by a zigzag route on good rock starting from NB 08466 37713.

Since the top of the crag overhangs the base, it is important not to arrange the abseil too far north. A conspicuous boulder lies on the cliff-top above the middle of the crag. Place the rope further south opposite the southern tip of the ramp where there is a small south-facing shield of rock at the top of the crag (NB 08461 37646).

Stranger on the Shore 75m HVS 5a **. Andrew Wielochowski, Noel Williams. 16 May 2018.
This route follows a conspicuous break which traverses the whole face from south to north. Fine climbing on good rock with adequate protection. Most atmospheric at mid to high tide. Abseil directly to a ledge at the southern end of the traverse line. Move a few metres left along the ledge to where it is possible to arrange a belay with a view of the climb ahead.
1. 35m 5a Follow the natural break line leftwards. Hand-traverse a short section past guano-covered rock, and continue traversing till a fine Cam slot is reached. Step down and swing boldly left to a good foothold. Climb steeply leftwards to gain a commodious ledge. The second can remove the Cam and place it at foot level to protect the precarious move down.
2. 30m Continue traversing more easily to near the end of the ledge.
3. 10m 4a From the left end of the ledge, step down and cross a corner to gain the finishing slab.

Geodha Staca nan Gall: Stranger on the Shore (HVS, 5a) traverses the face by the obvious crackline. Photo: Noel Williams.

The scramble route down to the ramp can also be followed northwards along the base of the cliff to where two Diff corners were ascended. Eventually a wide rift stops further progress. The next three routes lie to the east of this rift on an area of excellent north-west-facing slabs. Although they start some distance above the sea, breaking waves can make things exciting at high tide. Approach by abseil from the vicinity of NB 08505 37766.

Ocean Edge 50m   Severe. Andrew Wielochowski, Noel Williams. 16 May 2018. A varied climb, which overlooks the rift on the right. Protection is spaced initially. Best split into two pitches. From a ledge overlooking the rift, climb the obvious arete with an awkward step followed by a small bulge. Continue on slightly easier ground to a stance. A black slabby wall leads to the top.

The Angry Sea 45m   Severe *. Noel Williams, Andrew Wielochowski. 17 May 2018.
Start a few metres left of the previous route. Climb up steps of excellent black rock with little protection at first. Continue up pleasant slabs and cracks to easy ground.

Breaking the Waves 40m   V.Diff. Andrew Wielochowski, Noel Williams. 17 May 2018.
Start from a big black ledge near the left (east) end of the slabby face. Climb a black corner via a hard step. Continue more easily above keeping left where possible.

To the east of the previous three routes, the headland is split by Geodha Dubh. On the eastern side of this geo there is a slanting cave. Situated above this is a broad band of pink pegmatite with a rift to its north. The next two routes are approached by an easy abseil down this band of pegmatite.

A Little Bit of Everything 25m   Severe *. Noel Williams, Andrew Wielochowski. 13 May 2018.
A pleasantly varied climb on very good rock. Traverse round leftwards into the rift just above where it seals. Climb up a steep corner and step right to gain a short slabby wall. Continue up this on the right, then step left to finish up a left-trending crack.

Rest Easy 15m   V.Diff. Andrew Wielochowski, Noel Williams. 13 May 2018.
Another well protected climb on good rock. Start on a good ledge 5m up and left of the rift. Climb a steep corner, then step left below a roof. Continue leftwards more easily.

LIANAMUIL (112m):
Lost Shepherds   70m   VS 4c. Daniel Grammatica, Rick Salter, Rob Woodall, Alan Whatley, Colin Crawford. 29 Jun 2018.
Land on a big platform on the west side of the stack, at the foot of four sea caves bounded by a rock terrace. Aim for swell forecast 0.5m or less, as it will likely be at least twice that at the stack. Best after mid August as a few razorbills on route, and fulmars on the top slopes. Start 10m to the right of the large roofless cave at the base of a large rounded buttress.

1. 20m 4b Climb a sloping ramp rightwards with increasing difficulty to a small stance.
2. 10m 4b Climb an open groove, then keep right to gain the end of a ledge, passing an overhung corner to a small stance.
3. 15m 4c Ascend the left wall passing a bulge. Exit the corner rightwards to cross a bird ledge and through quartzite bands.
4. 25m Scramble to grassy ground above.
Descent: From a block and platform directly above the big cave, using stake, block and peg anchors. A spectacular free hanging 50m abseil to sea-level slabs.

ST KILDA, Soay:

Wet Foot West 230m VS. Sam Tolhurst, Steven Van Dijck, Bob Harrison. 1 Jun 2018.
Located on the western tip of Soay, this route is a contender for the UK's most westerly climb. Arrival was via dinghy, landing on a platform with a small groove 20m left of the large sea cave.
1. 45m Climb a small chimney to a corner-crack and climb this for 4m to a prominent ramp which runs from right to left across the crag. Traverse the ramp for 30m.
2. 55m Continue along the ramp for 50m to below green walls.
3. 20m Climb up the green wall for 4m, then traverse left and climb down a prominent gully for 8m to its base above a large platform. Could be straightened.
4. 50m Traverse down left, then go up a left-trending ramp. Continue until below a large gully leading up the crag. From here it is possible to traverse left and up to a defined pinnacle that marks the end of the climb. The first ascentionists took a groove on the right.
5. 30m 4b Climb up a groove and subsequent corner to a large ledge, overlooking slabs to its left, cracking pitch.
6. 30m An exposed climb down the prominent slab gains the base of the pinnacle. Climb the pinnacle.
Descent back down the route.

Ruaival Slabs:

Walk towards Ruaival peak from the town. Descend at the end of the grass into the scree at the start of the sea cut between Hirta and Dun. Continue along the shore of the sea cut until below the large grey buttress of steepening slabs, with a large roof above the sea to the left.

The Last and Outmaist Ile 140m HVS. Sam Tolhurst, Steven Van Dijck, Bob Harrison. 2 Jun 2018.
A similar line may have been climbed in 1987 (*Soay*, see SMCJ 1998), but the description and route length varies.
1. 30m Climb the easiest way up the slab, onto the right of the large ledge that runs horizontally across the whole Ruaival slabs about one-third up.
2. 25m Follow the grey slabby ridge up to a ledge underneath the steeper wall.
3. 35m 4c Climb straight up the headwall to a large rock next to the obvious platform.
4. 50m A scramble leads over the ridge to the grass.

Cowboys From Hell 230m E1. Sam Tolhurst, Steven Van Dijck. 3 Jun 2018.
1. 30m As for *The Last and Outmaist Ile*.

2. 45m Traverse leftwards across the slab. Down-climb the obvious gully (mid-way across the slab) until possible to step across. Climb up leftwards in the cracks towards a small ledge on the arete.
3. 25m Continue around the corner of the buttress, traversing left until able to down-climb towards the obvious black platform. Belay with small roofs high above and sea below.
4. 20m 5b Continue the traverse blindly to the left, around the corner. Down-climb the steep overlaps to join the ledge which crosses the entire face. Belay below a roof with the ledge continuing left.
5. 50m 5b Follow the ledge leftwards to a sloping boulder. Traverse the lip of the boulder and mantel onto it. Climb up a fine corner and continue up to the slabs above.
6. 60m Scramble up the slopes to the top.

The Swallow over the Sea   165m   E1. Sam Tolhurst, Steven Van Dijck, Bob Harrison. 4 Jun 2018.
1. 30m As for *The Last and Outmaist Ile / Cowboys From Hell*.
2. 25m As for *Cowboys From Hell* but descend the gully to its base.
3. 25m 5b Traverse left and make an exposed traverse around the obvious bulge (over the bulge is easier). Climb straight up and belay underneath the cracks as for *Cowboys From Hell*.
4. 45m Climb just to the right of the left arete and through the bigger blocks at the top.
5. 40m Scramble to the top.

Jesus and the Leper   160m   VS. Sam Tolhurst, Bob Harrison. 9 Jun 2018.
1. 30m As for *The Last and Outmaist Ile / Cowboys From Hell*.
2. 30m Traverse out left as for *The Swallow over the Sea* to the top of the gully, then traverse left to the arete.
3. 50m 4b Step right and follow a right-trending crack-line to the mid-way ledge. Continue right along the mid-way ledge, to climb the steep headwall in a right-rising line, crossing and finishing right of *The Last and Outmaist Ile*.
4. 50m Scramble to the top.

Walk on Water   50m   E2 5b. Sam Tolhurst, Bob Harrison. 9 Jun 2018.
A harder variation to pitch 4 of *Jesus and the Leper*, climbing the blank slab right of its crack. Climb directly up the slabs to the halfway ledge.

The Ferry Man   50m   E4 5c. Sam Tolhurst, Steven Van Dijck. 3 Jun 2018.
A technical and bold climb, possibly E5 due to suspect rock and poor protection. Climbs the two steep black slabs to the right of the main Ruaival slabs. Start on a large vegetated ledge below the full height left slab. Climb the slab direct for 20m until possible to step right on grass to the base of the steeper darker second slab. Arrange poor brass offsets, then climb the centre of the slab trending slightly left to a small recess of micro blocks. Continue trending leftwards to join a small foot ledge between the right and left slabs. Step left and down onto the left slab. Traverse left across the slab to the arete, then climb it to top out in a loose gully. Belay on the large boulder as for *The Last and Outmaist Ile*. Scramble out 50m.

Ruaival Face:
The Dead Travel Fast   35m   E5 6b. Sam Tolhurst. 8 Jun 2018.

Sam Tolhurst on FA of The Kraken, E3 6a, The Ile of Dun, St Kilda.
Photo: Bob Harrison.

Access is gained by walking to the Mistress Stone from Harbour Village; pass under the Mistress Stone and scramble down to an abseil point. Abseil access as for *Boat Race* (SMCJ 2011).

Belay from slabs at the base of the face, just above the sea. Climb up trending leftwards through cracks until below the left end of the distinct horizontal roof. Climb up to below the left end of this roof, then climb over it into laybacks up the left side of the distinct upside down V feature (highly visible from below or sea). Make hard barn door moves up the layback to strenuous undercuts and poor side pulls. Leave the upside down V and continue straight up the face to large ledges below large roofs. A tricky right traverse with a sting in the tail mantel allows access to the ledges below the abseil; climb up and out.

The Ile of Dun (Giomach Sgòr):

The Kraken   120m   E3. Sam Tolhurst, Steven Van Dijck, Bob Harrison. 6 Jun 2018.

An instant classic on the south side of Dun, needing a double set of Cams. The obvious corner-crack on the west side of Giomach Sgor (pitch 4). Use a hanging belay, either in the obvious pod or just above on the slab. A challenge remains to climb the entire corner from the sea.

1. 50m From the east side of Giomach Sgor, land in the quiet bay below the obvious right to left ramp. Climb the ramp, then the dark vertical gully.
2. 20m Continue left below the ridge into the gap between two pinnacles.
3. 15m An airy traverse over an abyss and up to a large block that marks the access down into the corner. Abseil down into the corner to the hanging belay.
4. 35m 6a Climb the obvious corner through the roof.

INNER HEBRIDES AND ARRAN

RUM, Askival, Pineapple Crag:

Left of Big Blank Slab (SMCJ 2017) is a shorter wall.

Pineapple Juice   16m   VS 4c *. Colin Moody, Donette Swain, Billy Hood, Cynthia Grindley, Todd Swain. 2 Jun 2018.

Climb the left-facing corner-crack in the middle of the wall to the ledge. Step right and continue up the fault.

Pineapple Rings   18m   E2 5c *. Billy Hood, Cynthia Grindley, Colin Moody, Todd Swain. 2 Jun 2018.

Start at the right side of the wall below an overlap. Climb up and climb the overlap at the left-hand end; move up right to climb a bulge.

MULL:

A large number of routes on crags in Mull and on nearby islands are on the SMC website.

ARRAN, Cir Mhor:

Absolute Zero   80m   E6 ***. Jules Lines (on-sight). 13 Jul 2017.

This is an excellent direct line through *Vanishing Point*, low in the grade.

1. 50m 6a Climb the topless crack which leads directly up via very bold padding

into the flake of Vanishing Point. Follow the flake and at its top, veer up leftwards
to gain an intermittent pocketed crack and follow it to belay under the large roof
at its right side.
2. 30m 5c Pull directly over the roof and go up to join *West Flank Route*. Follow
toe pockets up and right to gain the flying arete and layback boldly up this to join
Vanishing Point where it traverses in from the right. Follow it up the bold slab to
finish.

Note: Pitch 3 of *The Sickle* doesn't seem possible as described (at 4c anyway).
The only suggestion is that the FAists followed the microgranite vein round the
corner and finished up *South Ridge Direct*. Going up direct to join Sou-Wester
Slabs is easy and logical.

SKYE

GLEN SLIGACHAN CRAGS:
Damselflies 70m V.Diff *. Colin Moody, Cynthia Grindley. 26 May 2018.
The ridge between *Runaway Slabs* and *Luke's Climb* (p33 Cuillin guide). Walk
up right below white overhanging walls to start. Climb up left, then up to the
overlap (45m). Move up right under the overlap, then step left over it and continue
up (25m).

SGÙRR NAN GILLEAN, Pinnacle Ridge:
Third-Fourth Gully 85m V,5 **. Donald MacLachlan, Mike Lates, Jeannie
Sherwood. 17 Mar 2018.
An ice route finally climbed in perfect conditions.
1. 35m Climb the prominent right-hand ice groove to a hanging belay where it
broadens.
2. 50m Climb up leftward until possible to break through the overlap. Traverse
the lip (crux) to a continuation and to the crest.

Note: *Second-Third Pinnacle Ridge*. The guide says 'Grade II if banked out' but
Mike Lates has failed on it twice and it looks at least Grade IV.
The rock routes on the Second Pinnacle have a very loose 20m band of rock low
down and Mike wonders if the original route started up *First-Second Gully*.

Knight's Peak:
Subsidiary Gully 210m III. Steve Kennedy, Andy MacDonald. 4 Mar 2018.
Mostly easy apart from the top pitch leading to *Pinnacle Ridge*. The initial section
is taken by *West Face* (right-hand start). Follow the gully easily on snow to a wall
which blocks access to the upper slopes. The wall is breached by a short ice filled
groove which provides access to the upper slopes and ridge above, finishing a
short distance right of the summit of Knight's Peak.

AM BASTEIR, North Face
Head Crusher 95m III *. Steve Kennedy, Stan Pearson. 24 Feb 2018.
Starts about 80m up and left from the start of *The Deadline*. Follows the most
prominent disjointed system of ramps running diagonally right across the upper
left side of the face.

1. 60m   Start up a short icefall leading onto the lower ramp. Move slightly leftwards at the top and continue to reach the buttress edge and large block (crossing the finishing gully of *The Breadline*).
2. 35m   Continue out rightwards following the upper right-trending ramp, via a short step, to reach the east ridge of Am Basteir.

SGÙRR A' BHASTEIR:
Norman's Conquest   80m   III. Mark Francis, David Bowdler, Murdo Nicolson. 12 Feb 2017.
Well to the right of *Broad Gully* and 150m to the left of the NW ridge is a dogleg gully with a narrow start.

SGÙRR THUILM, North Face:
The Mincing Link   300m   III. Mark Francis, David Bowdler. 13 Jan 2017.
The face is split by two gullies, most obvious lower down. This route starts 100m left of these and follows a series of short icefalls, trending left eventually to join the left gully and finishing up turfy chimneys ending on the ridge 150m from the summit.

Woman Friday   400m   III,4. Mark Francis, David Bowdler. 11 Feb 2017.
At the toe of the obvious buttress is a narrow gully running right to left. This route follows this for three pitches, then dog-legs to the right. Easier ground leads to various exit gullies which finish on the summit.

COIRE A' GHREADAIDH, An Diallaid:
Mother Tongue   150m   II/III. Mark Francis, David Bowdler, Murdo Nicolson. 14 Jan 2017.
To the right of *Footrot*, the buttress is split by a narrow chimney dyke. The route follows this in two pitches.

COIRE NA BANACHDAICH:
Calcutta Gully   55m   III,4. Donald McLachlan, Mike Lates, Lucy Spark. 25 Feb 2018.
This is the right-hand of the two obvious faults on the final tier below the summit slopes of Sgurr Dearg, the left-hand being *Bard's Gully* (2013?). Approach by the normal Coire na Banachdaich path and head straight up where the path leads left to Bealach na Banachdaich.
1. 25m   Neve led to a series of short ice steps and rock belay before the prominent steep ice-fall.
2. 30m   Good ice led up to a steep finish before easy slopes above.

Note: *Kibby's Route* gave a good 30m pitch of ice at Grade IV.

INACCESSIBLE PINNACLE:
South Crack   30m   VI,6. Douglas Sutton, Andrew Campbell, Matt Barratt. 7 Jan 2018.
The summer line gives sustained and quality climbing.

SGÙRR DEARG, North Face:
The Un Pin   250m   I. Andy Nisbet. 13 Mar 2018.
A surprisingly easy ramp-line immediately under the steep Coruisk sidewall of

An Stac and the Inaccessible Pinnacle. Just left of *Inaccessible Icefall* (SMCJ 2016). It was reached by descending from Bealach na Banachdaich but could also be reached by descending from the base of An Stac. Climbed under heavy snow conditions and might often be Grade II.

AN STAC:
North Wall Route 75m E1 **. Mike Lates, Malcolm Airey. 12 Jun 2018.
A wild adventure climbing a hidden chimney line on the steep north wall.
Approach by descending the scree and slabs on the north side of the In Pinn (presumably reversing the above route?). Descend a final 20m open chimney to reach a blocky bay.
1. 25m 4a Gain the shattered shelf line that leads easily but airily onto the face to an undercut corner-line. Hanging stance.
2. 25m 5b Above initial steep moves the angle eases to a large ledge.
3. 15m 5b Tackle the narrow pod with a well-protected wild exit to another recess. Exit this.
4. 10m 4b Finish more easily up to join *An Stac Direct*.

SGÙRR DEARG, Practise Buttress:
Tea and Talisker 55m HVS **. Al Phizacklea, Dennis Lee, John Holden. 19 May 2018.
Climbs the smooth wall left of *Western Drainpipe Ridge*. Perhaps E1. Scramble to the ledge above pitch 1 of *Western Drainpipe Ridge*.
1. 15m 4c Climb the crack left of pitch 2 of *Western Drainpipe Ridge* to reach a ledge out left.
2. 40m 5a Follow a shallow crease which peters out into a fine crack-line (old peg runner). Step left to a small ledge, and continue trending diagonally left across the slabs to reach a shallow corner which leads easily to a ledge with a block. Abseil off.

SGÙRR MHICCOINNICH, West Buttress:
Mackenzie's Fledgling Groove 95m VS 4c. Mike Lates, Malcolm Airey. 2 Jul 2018.
Takes the parallel line left of *Mackenzie's Flying Groove* from the grassy bay in *Bomb Alley*.
1. 50m 4b Start up the orange recess heading leftwards for 20m. Bear back more steeply rightward up blocky holds in an exposed position. Belay on Collie's Ledge.
2. 45m 4c Move 5m right and climb the vertical fault common to *Mackenzie's Flying Groove* for 15m. Traverse the horizontal fault leftwards for 10m until it is possible to climb more steeply into the upper flying groove. Follow this easily leftward to blocks immediately below the summit.

Mackenzie's Flying Groove 95m E1 **. Lucy Spark, Mike Lates. 9 Jun 2018.
Start at the back of the grassy bay in *Bomb Alley*.
1. 50m 5a Climb the central line with a crux at 5m. Belay on Collie's Ledge.
2. 45m 5b The fault continues vertically for 15m to a small overhung ledge. Committing moves give access to a flying groove that rises rightwards to finish above the left wall of *King's Chimney*. Good climbing in a superb position.

Cannon and Wall 20m E1 5c **. Mike Lates, Malcolm Airey. 2 Jul 2018.

Takes the right wall of *King's Chimney* before tackling the cannon directly to finish. Start at the upper ledge in *King's Chimney*. Climb *King's Chimney* for 5m and place a high side runner before foot traversing the obvious break to the right edge. Gain good holds on the very edge to make a short steep sequence. Continue easily to the final steepening where it is easy to finish by the normal route. Step round right and tackle the overhang by long fierce moves.

SRÒN NA CÌCHE:

Note: The slab and its right-bounding arete under *Rib of Doom* have been climbed but linking into an independent route has not been achieved. In June 2005, Alex Glasgow & Jamie Bankhead climbed the slab via a thin vertical crack (HVS 4c). Near the top of the slab, they escaped right on to *Rib of Doom*. In 2017, Rich Parker & Lucy Spark climbed the arete (15m 4c), then a strenuous overhanging corner. They moved up left and climbed an awkward wall (5a, crux). Easier climbing led to a belay at junction with *Wallwork's Route*, which they finished up.

COIRE A' GHRUNNDA, Sròn na Cìche, South Crag:

Thrice Brewed 105m HVS **. Al Phizacklea, John Holden. 23 May 2018.
Climbs the cleanest of the slabs left of *White Slab Direct*. Lovely delicate climbing on excellent rock. Start just left of *White Slab* and its graffiti.
1. 20m 4b Climb the shallow flake in the right side of the rounded rib just left of *White Slab*, to below a long slender groove.
2. 35m 5a Traverse left onto a blunt rib, go up this, then back right into the slender groove where it opens into a wide V. Trend left onto a rounded rib and follow this delicately to a ledge.
3. 50m 5a Start just right of two yellow flashes in the wall above. Pull directly onto the slab with a thin crack which leads to ledges. Use a vague scoop up the cleanest slabs above to gain a flake, step right and follow the slab which leads to a vague rib and the left side of a long horizontal roof. Climb out left to belay (level with the base of the White Slab).
The line becomes very broken and much easier above, so two abseils gains the base of the crag.

LOCH CORUISK CRAG:

This route is on the left-hand slabby buttress (Cuillin guide p224).

Mrs Merton 55m E1 *. Robert Middleton, Helen Fairclough. 30 Mar 2018.
1. 35m 5a Climb up at a niche towards the left of the main face and traverse leftwards for 5m above an overhang on an obvious ledge towards the left arete. Arrange good but fiddly protection at ledge level before committing boldly to the left-slanting crack above. Pass two jammed blocks to a slight rest at a downwards pointing flake, then go directly up where the crack peters out past a tiny triangular niche to a ledge. Continue up the easier wall above to a larger ledge and belay.
2. 20m 4b Climb the layback crack above.

Freda and Barry 50m Severe *. Helen Fairclough, Robert Middleton. 30 Mar 2018.
Start from the right end of the obvious ledge on *Mrs Merton*.
1. 30m 4b Climb directly up a vertical crack for 6m to join a left-slanting crack which is followed to a niche. Climb just left of a grassy groove to a large ledge.

2. 20m 4a Gain and follow the higher of two right-sloping cracks.

Note: *Mrs Beaton* was thought VS 4c ** and a good left to right diagonal route on the JMCS hut crag was climbed at about VS 4b **.

GLAMAIG, Sgurr Mhairi:
Obvious ice forms frequently on cliffs immediately above the sheep fanks in Sconser, but usually thin.

Mhairi's Christening 50m IV,5. Mike Lates. Lucy Spark. 7 Mar 2018.
Climbs the 2nd line from the left with a steep finish.

Mhairi's Wedding Cake 180m IV,5. Mike Lates. Lucy Spark. 7 Mar 2018.
Climbs the longest and most prominent line. A 25m vertical tier leads to easier ground for 50m. Climb two higher tiers more easily.

SGÙRR NAN EACH, Bealach Buttresses:
Trundle Chimney 60m III *. Nathan Adam, Gary Campbell. 12 Feb 2018.
The obvious and atmospheric chimney on the right side of the buttress, right of the summer route *Trundle Buttress*. Two well protected steps between snow leads to a small col and belay from where it is possible to either continue to the top of the crag via the summer line of *Trundle Buttress* or descend easily into a large snow gully on the right. A 40m pitch of ice and snow low down was omitted and would make a good start, but the base of the chimney can be gained from the right along a snowy ledge. Likely to be harder under thin conditions.

BLABHEINN, South Buttress
Note: *Canopy* is well worth a star or two when dry (Mike Lates).

CÀRN LIATH:
Western Arete Direct E1 5a. Dan Moore, Serge Gomez. 30 May 2016.
Climbs the left-hand groove all the way (rather than moving into the right-hand groove). Great but bold climbing, some suspect rock but not just here, all over the crag!

BALMACQUIEN:
Pinch Punch 18m Severe. Mark Hudson, Flora Hudson. 1 Apr 2018.
Takes a direct line up the wall 5m left of *Secret Weapon*. At half tide and below, scramble to a wide barnacle platform just left of that route. Climb towards a left-facing corner in the cliff-top forming the left end of the tower with *Secret Weapon* as its right end. Easy climbing leads past a reachy middle steepening (can be sidestepped to the left) and then takes fine airy steps up the final corner.

BORNESKETAIG, Organ Pipes:
Scull & Coxswain 12m E2 5c *. Todd Swain, Colin Moody. 13 May 2018.
Up and right from *Skull and Jawbone* is a small buttress. Climb the central crack-line in the buttress.

Cat Food 22m HVS 5a **. Colin Moody, Cynthia Grindley. 20 Aug 2017.
Twin cracks right of *Power to Believe*; finish up the right-hand crack.

Gully Walls:
These are wrongly marked as B on the map on p123 Skye Sea-Cliffs; they are mid-way between B and 9.

Tornado   12m   HVS 5a **. Todd Swain, Cynthia Grindley, Colin Moody. 13 May 2018.
The twin cracks right of *Twister*.

Cyclone   14m   HVS 5a *. Todd Swain, Cynthia Grindley, Colin Moody. 13 May 2018.
To the right are two cracks finishing on a ledge at about 5m. Climb the left crack to the ledge, then step up left and continue.

Whirlpool   14m   E2 5c *. Todd Swain, Donette Swain, Cynthia Grindley, Colin Moody. 14 May 2018.
Climb the desperate right crack to the ledge. Move up right to a higher ledge, step left and climb twin cracks.

Waterspout   14m   HVS 5a *. Todd Swain, Donette Swain, Cynthia Grindley, Colin Moody. 14 May 2018.
To the right are two more short cracks. Climb the left-hand crack to a ledge, twin cracks above, then the right-facing corner-crack.

Waterlogged   14m   HVS 5a *. Todd Swain, Donette Swain, Cynthia Grindley, Colin Moody. 14 May 2018.
Right of the second set of short cracks is a crack with a jammed log. Climb past the log, climb a corner-crack, then twin cracks. Step left and finish up *Waterspout*.

NA HURANAN:
A large number of routes on various new sectors are on the SMC website.

NEIST, Financial Sector:
Gammy's Link   E2 5b **. Michael Barnard, Adrian Crofton. 30 Jun 2017.
Good independent climbing. From the starting ledge of *Gammy's Purse*, climb the steep corner on the left (crux, micro-cams required). Step right around the arete (as for *Lottery Live Start*) to join and continue up *Gammy's Purse*.

Wall Street, Direct Finish   E3 6a. Michael Barnard, Adrian Crofton. 30 Jun 2017.
A brutal finish up the obvious thin crack.

South of the Steps, Sonamara Area:
Pretentious Neighbour   25m   HVS 5a. Al Phizacklea, John Holden. 22 May 2018.
Start on left side of the prow containing *Transitive Nightfall of Diamonds*. Pull out left to a cracked block on the arete and climb up to a ledge. Climb the centre of a short smooth face to enter a small V-groove and pull directly over the capping roof.

RAASAY, Fladda Walls:
A large number of routes on these walls are on the SMC website.

NORTHERN HIGHLANDS NORTH

ALLADALE SLABS, West Wing:
Grumble 150m Severe **. Dave Allan, Duncan McGavin. 7 Jun 2018.
Between *Bang* and *Tane*. Start at a grassy hollow 20m down and left of the rib
where *Tane* starts.
1. 45m Climb a tongue of rock, move left a little at its top and climb a left-facing
corner. At its top go 6m right to belay.
2. 35m Go back left to the top of the corner and climb a shallow scoop, then
continue up to the left of the twin overhangs and blocks under the overhang just
above.
3. 25m Traverse right under the overhang then climb up to beneath the upper
overhang.
4. 45m Traverse left under the overhang, then go up and climb a prominent 6m
right-facing corner to easier ground.

ARDMAIR Note:
The small abused rowan at the start of *Dangerous Dancer* is no more, making the
route slightly bolder and harder, but not enough to change the grade.

BEINN MOR COIGACH:
Eagle Gully 250m II. Dave Allan. 2 Mar 2001.
The leftmost gully line on the face a few hundred metres north-west of Sgurr an
Fhidleir. Take the right fork at the start and the left fork high up.

CUL BEAG, Lurgainn Slabs, West Face, Gully Wall:
This takes a deep corner on the approach, on the closest of the crags, 20mins. This
is the steep sidewall of the grassy gully used on the approach and two-thirds of
the way along this is a deep corner giving the following route.

Apex Corner 25m VS 5a **. John Mackenzie, Andrew James. 12 Jun 2018.
An interesting route with elegant moves, protected by medium to large gear. Climb
the corner to exit up left to finish by an easy slab to good belays.

Lower Tier:
Tip-Toe Slab 35m VS 4b. John Mackenzie, Andrew James. 12 Jun 2018.
To the right of *Forgotten Groove* (SMCJ 2010) is a slab, reached via a recess with
a juniper bush. Climb the slab tongue above the bush and keep mainly to the slab
on the left using a heathery crack for protection. A large heather bay above has a
short undercut slab which is taken on the right by a protruding hold to move up
left to finish.

Top Tier:
Towards the right-hand end of this tier, best approached via the 'normal' gully
right of the Lower Tier of slabs, is a fine looking pink slab topped by a headwall
split by a crack. To the left of this slab is another with an obvious corner bounding
its left side and taken by the following route.

Papier Mache 25m Severe 4b. John Mackenzie, Andrew James. 18 Jul 2017.
Climb the slab just right of the corner to reach a grass patch. Avoid this on the
right and climb a short wall and overhang on good holds to the top.

John Mackenzie on pitch 2 FA of Breakthrough, HVS 5a, Cul Beag. Photo: Andrew James.

Paper Tiger   30m   VS 4c ***. John Mackenzie, Andrew James. 18 Jul 2017.
A fine contrasting climb, easier than it looks, taking the pink slab and cracked headwall. Start at the lowest point of the slab below a short wall, climb the wall to reach the slab and follow a left-trending crack-line to below the headwall. Climb the steep crack to a platform. Finish by an easy short slab.

To reach the next route is more difficult. There is a deer trod running below the Middle Tier that runs below the highest part of the Top Tier below a shorter line of aretes and grooves that lie to the west, avoiding the cliff edge that drops off just beyond *G.F.C.* (SMCJ 2010). Though there are several other ways to reach the broad platform below the next section of crag the deer trod is the best. Another way would be to climb the first two pitches of *Pebbledash*, then to traverse left.

The WSW section of the crag has more lichen than the other areas, but the following route is very clean.

Breakthrough   85m   HVS 5a ***. Andrew James, John Mackenzie. 30 May 2018.
This very fine climb takes a central line well left of *G.F.C.* following a lower slab, then a chimney-crack and finally corners to the top. It is well protected, exposed and strenuous in places but delicate in others.
1. 30m 4a Start at the lowest rock rib before the platform drops away leftwards to a gully. Climb the rib to a large block, then up the fine slab above to a horizontal crack. Move left to a very narrow ledge with one crack.
2. 20m 5a A short traverse left along the ledge leads to the chimney crack. This is undercut to start and leads strenuously up over a variety of problems to arrive at large chockstones.
3. 20m 5a Step right onto the slab edge avoiding a dirty groove above and up this pleasantly to below the corners on the right. Climb the steep corner to a sloping stance below the top corner.
4. 15m 4c Climb the corner and a rib above to a large boulder at the top.

STAC POLLAIDH, West Buttress, North Face:
Note: Iain Young & John Higham repeated *Pollaidhstyrene* (V,6) in Jan 2018 but missed out the wide crack by traversing away to the right (IV,5 overall).

No.2 Buttress:
Sweaty Betty   45m   E4 **. Tess Fryer, Ian Taylor. 25 May 2018.
Lies to the left of *The Orifice* in the recess with the rockfall scar. Sustained well protected climbing, needs a few days to dry after a wet spell.
1. 25m 6a Scramble 5m to a ledge left of a small rowan, then climb the arching crack-line, passing the left side of the first big roof by awkward manoeuvres. One metre below the next small roof, go hard right to gain a crack-line on the right wall and follow this to a V shaped roof. Go round the left side of this and the right side of another roof to the ledge above.
2. 20m 5c Move a couple of metres left along the ledge until below a corner (best to re-belay here). Climb the deceptive corner, with a couple of hollow blocks which wouldn't move on abseil.

Upper No.2 Buttress:
The following route was climbed thinking it was *Bats in the Belfry*, but it was a lot harder. Whether it is new or not is uncertain.

Tess Fryer on the FA of Sweaty Betty, E4 6a, Stac Pollaidh. Photo: Ian Taylor.

Going Batty   35m   E1 5b *. Jonathan Preston, Sarah Atkinson. 5 Jul 2017.
Climb easily onto the concave slab at the right end of the buttress (sounds like *Bats in the Belfry* but didn't lead to a cave). Climb incipient cracks up the middle of the slab to a steepening. Using a rounded flake on the right, make steep moves up the groove above to a tricky exit. Easier ground leads up a crack and short gully to the top.

No.3 Buttress:
Half Axe Chimney   120m   III. Roger Webb, Neil Wilson. 20 Jan 2018.
The chimney line immediately left of *Summer Isle Arete*. Well shaded by the arete, it keeps condition better than other south facing lines on Stac Pollaidh and gives two good pitches before easy ground.

Note: *Slovo* is misplaced in Northern Highlands North (p125) and it actually takes a chimney set into 'the slender fin about 40m right of *Summer Isles Arete*', next to the route *Consider the Lillies*.

The Keep:
The following two routes lie on the lower left-hand buttress which overlooks the broad gully descending from the main col (where the walkers' path joins the ridge). Ascend directly from the road. One of the main features visible is a corner running up the crest of the buttress; this is the line of *Finders Keepers*. The routes can be approached by scrambling up from the left to reach good ledges near the crest.

The Grafter   20m   E1 5b *. Michael Barnard, Alan Hill. 10 Jun 2018.
Climbs a line of steep cracks immediately left of the crest.

Finders Keepers   20m   HVS 5a. Michael Barnard, Alan Hill. 10 Jun 2018.
Start as for the above, then move right to gain the corner which is followed to the top. Some blocks require care.

The next two routes lie on the same section of crag as the existing climbs and can be gained the same way, or alternatively by traversing round from the top of the above routes (passing a short awkward step), or by abseiling in from the ridge. Some blocks require care. Belay at the left end of the terrace, at the base of an obvious left-trending groove (*Coigach's Burning*).

Pollaidh Wants a Cracker   30m   HVS 5a. Michael Barnard, Alan Hill. 10 Jun 2018.
Climb the groove to the heather ledge. Instead of its leftward continuation, climb the vertical crack to its right via a series of steps, finishing directly.

Playing for Keeps   30m   HVS. Michael Barnard, Alan Hill. 10 Jun 2018.
An entertaining route with a traditional feel. Immediately right of the left-trending groove is a steep corner-crack; right again is a wide crack.
1. 15m 5b Climb the wide crack up to the roof, traverse left under this and pull onto a ledge. Ascend the short off-width crack above (crux) and move up to a large grassy ledge.
2. 15m 5a Start up the corner above, then take a slanting break to gain the left

arete. Continue up the crack just left of the arete, pulling through the bulge for an exposed finish.

REIFF, Seal Song Area:
Madness   12m   H.Severe 4b. Ewan Lyons. 9 Apr 2018.
Climbs the bulges on the wall between *Deep Chimney* and *Reiffer*.

Minch Walls:
The Year of the Ski   10m   E1 5b. Ian Taylor, Tess Fryer. Mar 2018.
Climb straight up between *Slip Jig* and *Polka*.

Bay of Pigs:
The peg on *Making Bacon* is no more, so it will now be solid E5.

Hidden Rock:
Bobby Shafto   8m   HVS 5b. Tess Fryer, Ian Taylor. Mar 2018.
Start as for *Storm in a Teacup* but climb the crack directly above.

Spaced Out Rockers Cliff:
Misha Direct   35m   E7 6b **. Ian Taylor, Tess Fryer. 24 Jul 2017.
Follow *Misha* to the top of the vague crack where it rejoins *Headlong*. Move right and up to a shallow incut break near a round pocket (poor F2 and RP in the break). From a good incut above, make a big move to a shallow break, then up to the *Spaced Out Rockers* break. Move slightly left and climb a hard thin seam using a shallow finger pocket. Finish direct. Low in the grade.

Leaning Block:
The Screamer Direct   15m   E5 6b *. Ian Taylor, Tess Fryer. Jul 2017.
Start mid-way between *The Screamer* and *The Gift* and climb direct to join *The Screamer*. Finish direct where the original moves right at the top.

CUL MOR:
North-East Ridge   350m   III,4. John Higham, Iain Young. 7 Jan 2018.
On this ascent a line was followed far to the right of the one depicted in the Highland Scrambles North guide. Approaching from the floor of Coire Gorm and traverse west until on the broad junction between the north and west faces of the lower buttress. Climb by short steep steps, turfy ledges and chimneys to gain the top of the pinnacle below Biod a' Mhioltait. Descend the gully to the west, regain the ridge, pass Biod a' Mhioltait itself to the east then climb grooves cutting through the final steep section of the ridge. Easy ground leads to the summit of Sròn Garbh. Escapable climbing, but very fine situations.

TARBET CRAGS, Brown Crag:
Gordon   12m   VS 4c *. Simon Needham, Denise Forster. 25 May 2018.
Start at the base of *Raw Sienna*, but follow the slabby scoop leftwards. Pull left across the overlap of *Distinctly Ochreish*, then climb directly to the top.

FAR NORTH-WEST CRAGS, Upstream Crag:
Michael Barnard notes that his route *In the Land of Grey and Pink* (SMCJ 2017 p150) is the best route on the crag and should be **.

RUHBA A' MHILL BHAIN (NC 2055 2155):

This small peninsula on the south side of the seaward end of Loch Inchard is home to some fine short sea-cliffs. These include:
Fisherman's Crag (NC 212 555), nearby Pinnacle Crag, Twin Walls, Dark Crag, The Grand Slabs and Eilean Dubh. Many new routes on these crags are on the SMC website.

ARKLE:

South Rib   280m   III. Neil Wilson, Roger Webb, Simon Richardson. 10 Dec 2017.
Follow the summer line over several steps to the top.

FOINAVEN:

Note: On a winter ascent of *Pobble* on 20 Jan 2018, Helen Rennard & Ben Silvestre went closer to the summer line on pitch one whereas the original ascent traversed in from the right on ledges.

CRANSTACKIE, Pink Slab:

Pegmatite Perfection 60m   VS 4b. Dave Allan, Duncan McGavin. 24 Jul 2017.
Start at the lowest rocks at the left side of the slab and climb a thin crack to a large patch of grass. Avoid the grass by climbing along an edge on the right. Gain the big crack above and follow it to a large ledge (40m). Continue up the crack, then rightwards to finish.

PORT MOR SEA-STACK (NC 19588 64170):

Seaward Edge   16m   H.Severe 4b *. Sam Wainwright, Caelan Barnes. 5 Nov 2017.
From the seaward toe, move up a wall and make a mantelshelf move onto a ledge (optional belay). Climb the steep slab on the left arete passing a thread to the summit.

BEN HOPE:

See article and topo on pp.109–15.
North-West Rib   350m   I/II. Iain Easingwood. 28 Dec 2017.
A narrow rib on the NW face running left to right starting at a small wedge shaped buttress , climbing the left side of the buttress initially, then continue along the crest of the rib taking the small steps direct without much difficulty, joining the North Ridge. This ridge is the second ridge left of *Miles' Ridge*.

Longphort   400m   III. Andy Nisbet, Jonathan Preston. 25 Jan 2018.
The big gully between *Tower Ridge* and *Viking Ridge*. Low in the grade. The lower section of the gully was not in condition, so this was passed by a zigzag line on the left side of *Viking Ridge* (not included in the length) before the gully could be gained. Climb snow and short ice steps to a fork. The main branch heads up slightly right. Follow this on snow to a 60m ice pitch, not steep. More snow and small steps lead up and easily left to the top. A steep groove on the right was taken as a 50m finish with more interest.

Longphort Left   400m   III. Andy Nisbet. 26 Jan 2018.
Start as for the main gully, but take the left fork at about half-height. This starts with an ice pitch, then snow leading to a steeper finish. Take an icy groove on the

Michael Barnard on FA of Direct Bombardment, HVS 5a, Ruhba a' Mhill Bhain, near Kinlochbervie.   Photo: Alan Hill.

right, but which leads fairly straight up to near the finish of North Ridge. Finish along its narrow crest.

I Spy   600m   III. Dave McGimpsey, Andy Nisbet. 16 Feb 2018.
A less prominent ridge right of *Viking Ridge*, but still independent climbing to the cliff-top. The easiest start is off to the right to gain the ridge proper. The first steep tier was climbed from the right and crossing the crest. The crest was then followed to a very steep section. Climb an iced corner on the right (needs good ice to be Grade III). Further ice leads to a right-slanting gully which leads more easily to the top.

Odin   400m   IV,4. Sandy Allan, Andy Nisbet. 13 Jan 2018.
A big depression between *Notos* and *Valhalla*. It has the advantage of easy access via *Notos* when there is no ice low down (as on this occasion). The easy start is not included in the length. Gain snow in the base of depression and follow this with increasing amounts of ice as it bends right into a gully. Continue up to a fork. The bigger left branch was taken leading to another fork high up where the right branch was taken.

Odin Right   400m   IV,4. Sandy Allan, Dave McGimpsey, Andy Nisbet. 21 Feb 2018.
Follow *Odin* to the fork. Take the right side of the big ice pitch and which leads into the right branch (not obvious as a branch as the right side of the ice pitch is convex) and follow this up three further ice pitches to a crest. Continue as a right rising traverse into a finishing snow gully (actually a branch of the following route).

Loki   400m   III. Dave McGimpsey, Andy Nisbet, Jonathan Preston. 9 Feb 2018.
A big gully which curves out of the big depression of *Odin* and runs parallel to the next ridge (*Valhalla*). Start as for *Odin* but when it begins to steepen, take an ice line out right (not obvious). It leads up into the big gully on the right and which starts with a steep but short ice pitch. Climb the gully with short ice pitches but mostly snow to the top. Low in the grade.

Blue River   600m   IV,4. Dave McGimpsey, Andy Nisbet. 13 Feb 2018.
The gully between *Scandi High* and the next ridge (*The Turf Factor*). Start up a small left-slanting gully to continue up the watercourse over small steps. A larger step was bypassed on the right, then another step climbed on ice. A barrier wall was passed on the left before the main gully was followed up over two bigger ice pitches. After the second, the gully turns left and heads up towards *Scandi High*. At the top, either go left via a through route or climb another ice pitch and go left. Go up into a snow bay, cross this rightwards and go up a ramp to a crest (*The Turf Factor*), which is close to the top.

The Turf Factor   600m   IV,4. Andy Nisbet, Steve Perry, Jonathan Preston. 4 Jan 2018.
The next ridge right of *Scandi High*, first left of *South Tower Ridge*. A line close to the crest was followed through the lower tiers to reach a steep band. This was climbed by a wide chimney on the left leading to a steep turfy corner in the next tier. The ridge turns left to an undercut tier. Pull up left at the left end of the undercut section and return immediately right to the crest. Follow this to another

steep section, again passed by moving left and immediately back right. Finish more easily.
Note: JP measured the vertical height as 500m, which would make the rope length an underestimate.

Skeleton Gully   500m   IV,4. Dave McGimpsey, Andy Nisbet. 17 Feb 2018.
A gully between *Harpie* and *Bobsled Buttress*. Only the initial step on the lower tier wasn't formed so this was passed on the left and the gully joined above. The gully was followed through the lower tier and more easily above to a junction. The right fork leads on to *Bobsled Buttress* so the left was taken. It steepens to a large icefall. This was gained from the left and followed to the top slopes, finishing on the right.

Bobsled Buttress   500m   III. Andy Nisbet, Steve Perry. 1 Jan 2018.
The next ridge to the right of *Harpie*. A short first tier was climbed centrally. The next and largest tier was started on its right edge and a ramp followed leftwards, then up steeply (crux). The crest was then followed apart from a steep tier high up, where a wide groove on the right led to easier ground.

BEN HEE, Coire Leacach:
Hopalong   120m   II. Andy Nisbet, Steve Perry. 10 Mar 2018.
A frozen stream at the exit of Coire Leacach (NC 446 348). A deep, narrow V-gully leads to easier ice and snow.

CREAG NA H-IOLAIRE (near Klibreck):
Easan Fheidh   90m   VI,6 ****. Steve Perry, Sophie Grace Chappell. 5 Mar 2018.
This spectacular waterfall at NC 5857 2528 forms only rarely, but is really worth seeking out when it does. Given its low altitude, it is unlikely to be in condition unless the burn beside the bridge at the Crask Inn is frozen. The climbing is steep and sustained, plus with added commitment due to the remote location.
Approach: Follow the track leading east from the Crask Inn, up into the Bealach Easach and descend the other side. The waterfall will come into view 1km before you reach Loch a' Bhealaich. Descend from the track and scramble up the gulch. The waterfall base is accessed easily from a magnificent amphitheatre at the top of the gulch.
1. 35m Climb the right side through a steep section at 10m, then traverse right on small rising foot ledges to a snow scoop right of an ice pillar.
2. 40m Move left around the ice pillar and climb a vertical section of chandeliered ice (crux) to hanging icicles. Move left under these into steadily easier ground trending right and reaching turf. Continue rightwards onto a turfy ramp and a block belay.
3. 15m Climb a turfy groove at the end of the short ramp to the top.

Sideshow Gully   70m   II/III. Davy Moy, Dave Allan. 24 Dec 2010.
This is 15m left of *Easan Fheidh*.

CARN AN TIONAIL, Creag na h-Uidhe:
Gully 3   200m   II. Dave Allan. 10 Apr 2013.
The third gully from the left.

Andy Wilby on Friend or Foe, 6c+, Creag Dubh (Loch Loyal). Photo: Simon Nadin.

CREAG DHUBH (Loch Loyal):
Macular Generator 7a+ *. Simon Nadin. 25 Jun 2018.
Start at the right side of the toe of the buttress. Follow the line of bolts trending rightwards to join Friend or Foe at the big pocket below the flake. Step left from the top of the flake and climb diagonally leftwards by a sustained and thin sequence across the slab to reach a break. Slightly easier climbing follows between breaks to the top of the crag.

Vision On 7b+ *. Simon Nadin. 23 Jul 2017.
The slab to the right of *Friend or Foe*, 12 bolts. Pull through the overlap 3m right and weave up the slab finishing just to the right of the obvious seam/crack on *Friend or Foe* by a technical and fingery sequence (crux). Sustained and very difficult to read.

NOSS HEAD, Castle Sinclair Stacks:
Castle Sinclair Girnigoe VS 4c. Steve Perry. 6 Jun 2018.
The larger stack north-east of the slender pinnacle. Climb the easy looking north-east end via a rightward traverse in (crux) on very friable rock. The tide will determine the length of this traverse.

ELLENS GEO (ND 327 407):
The Magical Red Line E4 5c. Simon Nadin, Ed Nind. 25 Aug 2017.
A direct line from a belay in a small corner to the large hanging corner right of *Nitty Gritty*. Move left from the top of the corner onto the arete, then climb a thin crack in the wall above (crux) to gain easier finishing cracks.
Note: Peter Herd added a new girdle. 4 pitches at E3 5c ***.

MID CLYTH, Shelf Area (NH North p369):
Rio Line 20m HVS 5a *. Mick Tighe. 17 Aug 2016.
Start 3m right of *Circle Line* and climb out of the right side of the little recess to a good ledge. Go up and right through the slate band to climb the steep headwall using a flake. Good rock and good protection.

Le Petit Balcon 20m HVS 5a **. Mick & Kathy Tighe. 13 Aug 2015.
There are some overhangs high up 10-15m right/north of *Rio Line*. Start below the left end of the overhangs beside some bright green weed. A good ledge runs along the cliff here at about 5m above sea-level. Climb up to the ledge or start from it. Climb a crack in the steep white wall until under the overhang. Go diagonally up and left across the slate band until under a smaller overhang. Step right onto the *Petit Balcon* and climb the fine crack to the top.

The Rite of Spring 20m VS 4b/c. Mick & Kathy Tighe. 13 Aug 2015.
Another 10m or so right a sinuous fault-line weaves up to the right of the overhangs. Can be wet after heavy rain, but fine climbing when dry.

Shades of Grey 20m HVS 5a (1PA). Mick & Kathy Tighe. 17 Aug 2016.
A shallow left/south facing corner in a grey area of rock in the middle of the main face. Excellent climbing up the corner to the much harder, short crack at the top (1PA).

There's a big cave where the shelf area ends with scope for adventurous routes.

Just before this (south) is a smaller shallow cave with a roof at half-height.

Mid Clyth Crisis   20m   VS 4c *. Mick & Kathy Tighe. 13 Aug 2015.
Start below the left end of the overhang emanating from the smaller cave. Balance up the fine black rock and climb a short wall just left of the overhang. Tricky moves up and left lead to the slate band and a hoodie groove to finish.

Tricky Issue   20m   E1 5b *. Mick & Kathy Tighe. 2015.
Start under the middle of the roof. Traverse up and left to the edge of the roof. A short wall leads to a crack. Climb this and find a way through the headwall.

Cave Issue   20m   E1 5b. Mick & Kathy Tighe. 2015.
Climb straight up 2m right of the cave via a short left-facing corner. There is a fragile steep headwall so go hard left or right.

CREAG BHEAG:
North Coast 500   50m   6a+. Dominic Oughton (unsec). 6 Aug 2017.
A left-to-right traverse of the whole crag following the obvious break near the top, clipping bolts on existing routes. Start up *Tied Up* to its 4th bolt and then make steep moves on under-clings to join the high level break around *Turbine Charged*. Head rightwards on generally good holds in the break clipping bolts just above, with a pumpy crux around *Fleet Street*. Beyond *Twin Track* the climbing becomes easier along a ledge system (slightly crumbly in places) to reach the lower-off of *The Bheaginning*. Lower off here (60m rope needed), or for the full 100m tick, reverse the route (as per the first ascent, or if your belayer doesn't fancy following).

MIGDALE ROCK:
A number of older routes on this crag near Bonar Bridge (NH 650 908) are on the SMC website.

THE BLACK SLAB:
A number of older routes on this crag near The Mound (NH 764 978) are on the SMC website.

ORKNEY, Tomb of the Eagles, Old Head:
Approach from the Tomb of the Eagles return path before taking the coastal path along the south side of the largest inlet of Ham Geo. Continue as far south as possible and after crossing a small stream, the area is visible to the left, marked by two triangular buttresses (skerries) flanked to the right (looking out) by a third square buttress. ND 470 835. The first route is tidal and best approached by descending behind the squarer southern buttress to reach a good ledge.

Old Head Route   25m   E2 ****. Simon Litchfield, Franco Cookson. 2 Aug 2017.
An excellent route, tackling the obvious groove. Start at the corner on the tidal ledge. Step right to climb the steep wall on big holds. Easy moves lead to a capping roof with a crack. Gain this with difficulty using a hanging rib to the left. The upper groove maintains technical interest, before a final layback up the flake.

The following route is non-tidal and is best approached by carefully scrambling down the north side of the most southern buttress.

The Overfall   8m   E6 6a **. Simon Litchfield, Franco Cookson. 2 Aug 2017.
The centre of the prominent, overhanging black wall provides a bold micro-route, tackling the face on crimps. The climbing is good and never technically desperate but the fall potential is double its length and almost certainly painful and wet.

Roseness:
A crag at ND 5218 9864. 6 routes on the SMC website.

SHETLAND, Foula:
Ultima Thule   353m   E7 6b ***. Dave MacLeod, Calum Muskett. 19 May 2018.
A big undertaking for an adventurous climbing team taking the central complex section of Nebbifjeld. To find the abseil point locate a large grassy corner that descends some 50m to the cliff-wide roof. Stakes would be useful although there is protection in a little hollow above the corner. The first ascentionists used a drone to locate the corner! A 250m abseil straight down with a few re-belays should take you to the foot of the route at the top of the grassy ledges and a left-facing corner with an off-width. Ropes were left in place. Most pitches are of E5 and above in difficulty and the rock varies from good quality sandstone to sand. There are also some bold pitches in the route's mid to upper half. Topo provided.
1. 35m 5a Up the initial sandy groove until several metres beneath an overhang, then traverse right on better rock to a ledge beneath the next short corner.
2. 40m 5c Up the chossy corner before moving right onto the wall to gain a sandy ledge and some good Cams. Traverse right along the bubbly soft sandstone just above the roof to gain the corner.
3. 45m 6a Follow the corner line up to the big roof. Awkwardly undercut beneath the roof with excellent protection to a rest at its end. Continue up the corner with excellent protection to a belay just beneath the final section of corner.
4. 30m 6b Continue to the top of the corner to a short blank wall above the final overlap. Make a big rock-over, then traverse up and right to a good belay on the large half-height ledge.
5. 68m 6a Traverse the break-line from the ledge with increasing difficulty (walk, crawl, heel-hook, slap!) and many Cams, until you're out of sight of your belayer and on a ledge with good Cams in a flake beneath a short wall capped by a 1m roof.
6. 15m 6b A bold undertaking climbing the wall with indifferent protection in sandy breaks ascending slightly leftwards to the roof. Gain good flat holds above the roof and a tricky mantel onto the ledge.
7. 20m 6b Traverse slightly up and right of the belay ledge with Cams in breaks for protection. Traverse slightly back to the left to a ledge. Make a surprisingly tough mantel to stand up on this ledge and find a belay in some good horizontal cracks almost immediately above the previous belay.
8. 15m 6b Climb the bold wall above the belay to a small jutting sloping ledge (possible RPs and pegs). Make a long reach up to gain another sloping ledge (micro-cams on right) and a further very long reach to gain better holds on a narrow ledge (small Cams out left). A few final tricky moves up a wall gains an awkward belay some 6m below the sandy groove beneath the roof.
9. 50m 6b Ascend the short wall above the belay and enter the sandy groove (pegs very useful) to move right onto the ledge beneath the roof. Traverse leftwards along this with big Cams for protection, until below the final corner. Powerful moves through the roof gain the upper corner and an easing in difficulties.
10. 35m 5a Finish up the grassy corner watching out for fulmars on your way!

Nebbifjeld

Photo: Dave MacLeod

NORTHERN HIGHLANDS CENTRAL

BEINN A' MHUINIDH, Waterfall Buttress:
La Voie Noire   80m   VS. Ewan Lyons. 9 Jun 2018.
Best climbed after a drought but may still be greasy near the top of pitch 1.
1. 40m 4c Start right of *Linea Nigra* and follow a ramp to steeper rock right of a big overhang. Exit left over small blocks to below a short, steep black wall.
2. 20m 4b Climb the wall rightwards to an easier angled slab to the lip of the watercourse.
3. 20m Scramble up the black rock left of the watercourse.

STONE VALLEY CRAGS, Stone Valley Crag:
The Time Warp, Stasis Leak Variation. Michael Barnard, Adrian Camm. 23 Sep 2017.
An independent upper section giving a more sustained route. From where the normal route moves up left to join the upper crack of *Beer Bottle*, instead pull out right, aiming for a large triangular hold above. Use this to gain ledges on the right, then step back left to pull onto easier ground. Grade is unchanged.

Creag nan Cadhag:
Andy Wilby notes two link ups.
Clip the first 2 bolts of *Game Over*, then climb straight up the wall to the *Game Over* first chain at 7c+. Continuing into the final boulder problem of Nuclear Nightmare and finishing up that is 8a+. Finishing up the *Game Over* extension will probably be 8b.

LOCH MAREE CRAG:
There are now 26 new sport routes.

Hyperlipid   50m   8c ****. Dave MacLeod. 12 May 2018.
Brilliant varied climbing with a fingery crux near the top. Start up *Testify* to the good rest below the headwall. Blast up the headwall, left of *Testify*'s groove, to gain a good resting jug. If you make it through the fingery boulder problem crux above, rejoin *Testify* at its last bolt.

Spring Voyage   8b/8b+ Dave MacLeod 24 April 2018
A variation on *Hyperlipid*. From the resting jug on the headwall, traverse hard left to the arete of the *Circus* and finish up this.

Testify   50m   8b ***. Dave MacLeod. Oct 2017.
Superb and varied climbing taking the full height of the crag. Start up the first three bolts of *Hafgufa*, then step right and attack a sustained sequence, eventually joining *Golgothic* at the overlap. Follow this to the no-hands rest below the headwall. Step right and follow a steep groove in the headwall to a sting in the tail moving left and up at the top.

Big Ballin'   30m   7b+. Dave MacLeod. 12 May 2018.
Climb the direct line through the bulge leading into the start of the groove on *Bling*.

Rainbow Warriors   35m   8b ***. Dave MacLeod. 2 May 2018.
A fingery direct/left finish to *Hafgufa*.

CARNMORE CRAG:
Wild Side   90m   E6 ****. Guy Robertson, Iain Small. 3 Jun 2018.
An outstanding voyage along the big diagonal crack crossing *Carnmore Corner*; brilliant, super-sustained and perfectly protected climbing. Climbed on-sight. Start at the obvious crack between *St George* and *Gob*.
1. 30m 5b Climb the crack past a block and over a small overhang to a junction with Gob, then follow this to where a ledge sneaks right towards the corner. Belay just round the edge at the start of the crack, as for *Wilderness*.
2. 25m 6c Climb the crack with sustained interest all the way to a good hold in the wall above and knee bar rest a few metres short of the corner. Power on along the crack (crux) to gain the corner and hanging belay.
3. 35m 6b Continue rightwards out into space on generally good handholds but poor feet to an in-situ thread, then plough on through much thinner but less steep terrain to join and finish up *The Orange Bow*.

GOAT CRAG:
Note from Ian Taylor: Lawrence Hughes has bolted a few new routes. On a buttress left just left of the main crag is 6b+, 6a, 6a (from left to right) and a route to the top of the crag. Climb *Teepee* or *Poster Boy* to belay on ledge above the lower-off, then 15m rising traverse at 4, then 20m pitch about 6a. 2 abseils to the ground.

AN TEALLACH:
Note: Brian Bathurst, Oliver Skeoch & Nigel Wombell climbed *1978 Face Route* on 3 Mar 2018 with a variation after the apex of the snowfield. Instead of making the crux move to gain the gully-ramp, they traversed right and climbed an icy chimney (reliant on a big build-up of ice) to rejoin the normal route higher up.

BEINN TARSUINN:
Tiresome Gully   300m   I. Michael Barnard. 25 Feb 2018.
The prominent gully on the NNE face. A fine line; would make a good ski descent.

FANNAICHS, Eag nam Fear-bogha, Icicle Works Buttress:
See SMCJ 2010. The upper left of the two major buttresses has a large rock pinnacle towards its left side (about 15m left of the start of *Icicle Works*).

Exit via the Gift Shop   50m   III,4 **. Colin Wells, Stephen Reid. 23 Feb 2018.
A fine climb at a reasonable grade with the hard moves well protected.
1. 15m Climb a narrow groove on the right of the pinnacle to its top. Continue up snow to a steepening and move up to a good rock belay on the right.
2. 35m Make a hard move up and out left. Climb straight up the left-hand of two lines until stopped by an overlap and traverse leftwards until it can be turned to finish up the shallow gully. A further 25m of snow attains a rock belay up on the left.

Only the Lonely   50m   IV,4 ***. Colin Wells, Stephen Reid. 25 Feb 2018.
A splendid climb with superb situations.
1. 15m As for *Exit via the Gift Shop*.

2. 35m Make a hard move up and out left. Climb the right-hand of two lines until it eases below a rock band. Traverse horizontally right to a break in the rock wall which allows the upper slope to be gained and go straight up this to an awkward exit.

Lone Star   55m   VI,6 ***. Stephen Reid, Colin Wells. 24 Feb 2018.
Steep strenuous climbing up the icefall right of the rock pinnacle. Start 10m right of the pinnacle at a short rock rib.
1. 20m Climb diagonally leftwards and up into an icy scoop. Traverse left onto good ice and climb strenuously to a break below the steep upper fall. Good rock belay hidden round on the left.
2. 35m Return right and climb the icefall with gusto. At its top, overcome a short rock wall and climb straight up to an awkward exit.

Isolation Buttress:
Solo Gully   40m   I/II. Stephen Reid, Colin Wells. 24 Feb 2018.
The easy gully splitting the buttress makes a good descent when banked out.

FANNAICHS, Creag Dubh a' Gorm Lochain (NH 237 693):
Note: For the routes in SMCJ 2010, *Wilkinson Sword* is an icefall on the east (left, not west) side of a low tier of the face and didn't look like 'a sword with a hilt' in 2018. *Just Another Thursday* is at the west end of the same tier (but still well left of *Gormless Gully*) and was the right of three icefalls on a slabby section of the tier. Topo available.

STRATHCONON, Creag Ruadh, 740m Top, North-East Face:
To the right of the routes climbed previously and set at a slightly lower level but accessed from the ramp that forms the base of the existing routes, is a further section of crag, reached by moving down and right along the ramp. This crag, split by shallow gullies and turfy ribs, is capped by a distinctive snow dome. The lines seem longer than first appearances would suggest.

Snow Dome   100m   II *. John Mackenzie. 23 Feb 2018.
This is the second and most prominent gully when moving right and steeper than it looks. Two or three steep turfy steps are followed by increasingly steep snow to crest just left of an outcrop.

Escape from Brexit   70m   III. John Mackenzie. 23 Feb 2018.
This lies on the right of the main face and was logically reached by moving down left from an upper ramp after climbing *Snow Dome*. A short icefall lies near the far right end of the main face but a longer and more prominent narrow one lies left again. This provided some awkward moves with 'Brexit-hard' ice over two bulges in a groove to reach snow which was followed to the top. Short lived but tricky.

CREAG A' GHLASTAIL (Glen Orrin):
Central Gully   150m   IV,4. Ewan Lyons. 10 Mar 2018.
Climb the initial 20m steep icefall in two steps. A further small step leads to easy ground and an amphitheatre. An easy angled 20m icefall ahead eases off into a big groove and the top. Two alternative steeper finishes are available on the left.

BEN WYVIS, An Cabar, West Face:

Hidden Corner   90m   I/II. John Mackenzie. 27 Feb 2018.
The left end of the crags has a rocky edge, well seen from the Garbat path. *Hidden Corner* is tucked away below this edge and follows close to the base of the rocks up steepening snow, turf and some rocky moves, all depending on conditions. It is in condition probably more often than anything else on this face. A purgatorial approach from below up 200m of steep heather could probably be avoided by walking up the Garbat path to the 'boulder', then descending slightly right to avoid the crags and traversing in.

Creag Coire na Feola:

Rapunzel   35m   V,5 *. Simon Tickle. 19 Mar 2018.
To the right of *True Blue* is a steep icefall. Climb the steep ice immediately to the right of a large free standing ice pillar.
Note: ST down-climbed the easy ramp line to the right of the icefall. This turned out to be Grade III.

Feola Falls Right-Hand   30m   V,5 ***. Simon Tickle. 19 Mar 2018.
Steep icefalls form on the left and right sides of the minor crag above the small lochan to the north of the main crag. This route climbs the right-hand icefall. Initially climb steep ice for 15m until the angle eases. The route now trends right on slightly less steep ice, but in an exhilarating position, before exiting left onto good turf. Traverse up and right on easy ground before descending to the corrie floor.
Another shorter icefall to the right of the minor crag was also climbed at IV,4.

Note: Simon Tickle's approach. Park at Heights of Docharty (NH 526 622). Follow a good track to Meall a' Ghuail, then cross the plantation, picking up a faint path over Meall na Speireig, ending at NH 491 665. Head NW over a spur to enter Coire na Feola. 6 miles and 2.5 to 3hrs depending on conditions underfoot.

BEN WYVIS AREA, STRUIE HILL CRAG:

The Whip Alternative Finish   Severe. Dave Allan, Duncan McGavin. Sep 2017.
Just above the first chockstone, traverse left into a niche above the nest. Climb out leftwards and up the arete.

The Long Nosed Lion   25m   VS 4c *. Dave Allan, Duncan McGavin. Sep 2017.
Starting at two tree stumps on the face and right of where the icefall forms, climb a crack to a large sloping ledge. Finish easily up a chimney.

MOY ROCK:

The Adder Stone   12m   6a+. Ian Taylor. 2 Nov 2017.
The line just right of *The Seer*. Continuing up *The Fear* gives a good 7a.

NORTHERN HIGHLANDS SOUTH

GLEN PEAN, Splitter Crag (NM 878 898):

This crag can be approached by boat along Loch Morar, or on foot from the west end of Loch Arkaig. It lies around 1km east of the end of Loch Morar and is the

Murdoch Jamieson on 2nd Ascent of The Crossing, Glen Pean.   Photo: Iain Small.

first and lowest crag reached when approaching from Loch Morar. It is recognisable by the huge left-facing roof and prow taken by *The Crossing*.

The Crossing   70m   E5 6a ****. Dave MacLeod, Natalie Berry. Apr 2018.
Many medium and large Cams are useful for this superb exposed and well protected line, taking the diagonal breaks and soaring flake that runs up the diagonal prow. Start at the leftmost vertical crack that comes down the lower wall.
1. 30m 5c Climb this for 10m to access the diagonal break. Follow the break leftwards with good hidden holds to reach a hanging belay on the arete.
2. 10m 6a Balance up to reach the wide, white diagonal crack in the arete and layback/jam along this until it is possible to reach the crack above which leads on jugs to a fine exposed belay as the crack goes around the corner into the roof. It would be possible to link pitches 1 and 2 with extra large Cams.
3. 25m 6a Follow the wild flake-line along the lip of the roof with good gear and huge holds but very strenuous climbing. An 'out there' pitch, as good as any in the country.

SGÙRR NA SGINE, East Face:
The attractive east face throws down a chaotic system of ribs, grooves and shallow gullies. Much variation is possible but there are some distinctive routes which are situated in a fine setting, finishing close to the summit cairn. The north ridge is also a fine route to the summit (Grade I). Routes are described from right to left.

Dirk   160m   II *. Steve Kennedy. 7 Jan 2018.
The deep gully on the right side of the face. Straightforward with some short steps. A finish was made up the middle of three corner lines but others are possible. The route ends on the exposed north ridge which leads to the summit cairn.

Sgian Dubh   150m   II/III *. Steve Kennedy, Bruce Taylor. 16 Dec 2017.
Takes a line well left of *Dirk*, just right of the centre of the face (right of an open gully), following a groove system in the upper part of the face. The grooves are quite distinct and run between some small pinnacles near the top to finish on what looks like (from the base) the highest point. A direct line was taken to reach the initial groove about halfway up the face, starting up open mixed ground.

Claymore   150m   II. Steve Kennedy, Bruce Taylor. 4 Feb 2018.
A mixed route up the left side of the face. Start just beyond (left) the highest point of the scree slopes at the foot and immediately left of a wide gully. Climb an open groove between two rock fins and follow the same line above to a more pronounced right-facing groove/corner in the upper half. From the top of the groove, open slopes lead to a cornice finish just left of the summit cairn.

AM BATHACH:
Beast from the East   400m   II. Andy Nisbet. 25 Feb 2018.
A gully on the north-east face and well seen from the track below. Normally there is an ice pitch but only steep snow on this occasion. The gully ends 20m south of the cairn. The length is a guess.

MULLACH FRAOCH-CHOIRE:
Meshugana   160m   II. Andy Nisbet. 24 Mar 2018.
Between the crests of *Meshuga* and *Frayed at the Edges* is this gully. It needs a

big build-up to be this grade and looked hard when *Meshuga* was first climbed. The gully starts more steeply (snow on this occasion), then eases and bends right to reach the col. Follow the gully until 20m below the col, then take a zigzag ramp up left to below the last pitch of *Meshuga*. Follow this to the top.

CREAG LUNDIE:
A miniguide with many new routes has been sent by Chris Dickinson. This will be on the SMC website, perhaps in the New Routes section.

BEINN FHADA, Sgurr a' Choire Ghairbh:
Note: *Left-Hand Gully* was climbed several times in 2018 and was reported as 250m II ***.

Far Right Gully   250m   I. Andy Nisbet. 5 Apr 2018.
The gully forming the right side of Summit Buttress and tucked in close to the buttress. It has a very short pitch in the narrows but could be Grade II without a good build-up.

Summit Ramps   140m   III. Andy Nisbet. 5 Apr 2018.
Climbed as a more interesting finish to the above route. Above the difficulties on the main gully is a left branch which ends in a steep groove. This finish takes a ramp-line overlooking the left branch. From the start of the left branch, traverse left and follow the ramp-line in three sections to an easy finish common to *Summit Buttress*.

Coire an Sgairne:
Attaboy   210m   V,6. Dave McGimpsey, Andy Nisbet. 7 Mar 2018.
Start up the right-hand and lower of the diagonal faults right of the big steep wall. Follow the fault to the first break left into an area of turf. Head up left to a steep sidewall and go up under this to reach a diagonal ramp breaking out left across the wall. Climb this and continue up left to a well defined crest. Follow the crest direct to the top, steep but very helpful sections on flakes.

Zeitgeist   210m   IV,5. Dave McGimpsey, Andy Nisbet. 26 Feb 2018.
Start up the right-hand and lower of the diagonal faults as for *Attaboy* but go up a little further, break left and go up to the top right side of the area of turf. Exit right over a short wall (about 120m total). Climb a groove above and move left into a gully which exits out of the top of the area of turf (50m). Finish up the gully (40m).

Bealach Buttress:
This is the buttress above Bealach an Sgairne. When standing on a knoll which sits on the bealach itself, a gully leads to the summit of Meall a' Bhealaich. This has been recorded as Grade II in an old district guide but missed from recent guides (it would be Grade I with a right finish and has perhaps been climbed several times by those making a winter traverse from A' Ghlas-bheinn to Beinn Fhada. The following route climbs the ridge on its right.

Bealach Buttress   150m   III,4. Andy Nisbet. 5 Apr 2018.
Easy turf leads to a prominent steep section with two distinct V-grooves. Climb just right of the crest between the grooves before traversing into and finishing up

the right groove. Further easy climbing leads to the final escapable buttress, climbed by a ramp on the right and leading left to the crest.

FUAR THOLL, Mainreachan Buttress:
Note: *Snoopy.* In March 2018, Keith Ball & Nick Bullock climbed pitch 5 direct, making it the technical crux of the route.

SGÒRR RUADH, North Face:
Surf 'n' Turf 110m V,6 *. Michael Barnard, Doug Bartholomew. 16 Dec 2017. Essentially a direct start and left variation to *Spanner in the Works*. Start between that route and *Sticky Fingers*, below an obvious right-facing, two stepped corner-groove. Climb this (crux) to the terrace (45m). Continue directly through *Spanner in the Works* and follow the left-hand groove to easier ground.

The American Way 100m IV,4. Simon Richardson, Kelly Cordes, Roger Webb. 5 Feb 2018.
A direct version of *Splintery Edge*. A useful alternative when spindrift is pouring down *Tango in the Night*.
1. 30m Take the left branch of the impasse of *Tango in the Night*, climb up to a ledge (as for *Splintery Edge*) and traverse 10m left to a break just left of a smooth triangular wall. Climb this to a terrace below a steep square-cut gully.
2. 50m Climb the gully passing an awkward bulge (crux), then trend slightly left up open grooves to easier ground.
3. 20m Finish easily up snow to the top.

GLAS BHEINN, East Coire:
To the west of Creag na h-Iolaire is a hanging corrie that forms the north aspect of the broad shoulder containing the 711m top of the mountain. The corrie takes the form of a right-slanting bowl that leads up to the col just south of the main summit. Left of this is the well-defined *Top Gully* that runs up to the top of the cliff. Approximately 200m left of this are two icy gullies. The hanging corrie can be accessed up heather slopes from the path leading to Bealach a'Ghlas-chnoic, although on this occasion a 50m stepped icefall (IV,4) formed from the outflow from the corrie at NG 411 440 was climbed.

Blackwood Gully 100m IV,4. Neil Wilson, Roger Webb, Simon Richardson, 4 Mar 2018.
Climb the better defined left-hand gully in two pitches to a broad terrace.

Tullich Gully 150m III. Simon Richardson. 4 Mar 2018.
The shallower right-hand gully is the longer of the two. It has a continuation pitch above the terrace that leads to a V-slot in the skyline.

Top Gully 160m III,4. Simon Richardson, Neil Wilson, Roger Webb, 4 Mar 2018.
Climb the gully in three long pitches with a steep section at mid-height.

BEINN BHAN, Coire an Fhamair:
Der Riesenwand Variation Finish VII,7. Nick Bullock, Murdo Jamieson. 24 Feb 2018.
Just before the 'memorable swing around a bulge' on the upper left-trending ramp

(near end of difficulties), make some mixed moves right to gain the hanging ice. Climb this and the gully above.

ARDHESLAIG, Right Half:

No Exception   35m   VS 4c. Barry & Kay Wright. 8 Jun 2018.
Follows a line between *Quite Gneiss* and *The Exception*. Climb the right edge of the rib. Step across above the overhangs and traverse slightly right. Move up on thin edges to the left of a black scoop. Follow a left-slanting crack above to the upper slab and finish leftwards.

BEINN DAMH, Creagan Dubh Toll nam Biast:

Adiona   200m   II. Sandy Allan, Andy Nisbet. 30 Nov 2017.
The right edge of the furthest right buttress (the buttress with *Fawn Gully*). Start up a curving gully on the very right edge (after its base has risen up), then trend left to follow a rounded rib which bounds the left branch of a Grade I gully.

Goulotte Damh   250m   V,6. Dave McGimpsey, Andy Nisbet. 4 Mar 2018.
A narrow gully towards the right side of the furthest right buttress and about 100m right of *Fawn Gully* is slow to ice up but good climbing when it does. Ice screw belays used. Climb the gully over several steps to a snow basin (80m). Climb this to its top and exit via a short chimney leading to easy upper slopes.

Stag Party   250m   III. Andy Nisbet, Jonathan Preston. 29 Dec 2017.
A line through steep and often icy ground just right of *Fawn Gully*. Start at the base of *Fawn Gully* and gain the widest of several right-slanting ramp-lines. Follow this to an icy steepening. This was incomplete so a traverse right gained turfy steps leading up to easier ground. Follow this left, then finish up by a choice of lines near a vague crest above.

Fawn Gully Right Branch   250m   III. Dave McGimpsey, Andy Nisbet. 2 Mar 2018.
Climb the first two pitches of *Fawn Gully*, then follow a gully on the right which gradually eases to snow. Much better than the original when fully iced.

Annex Gully   300m   III,4. Andy Nisbet, Jonathan Preston. 12 Dec 2017.
A parallel gully left of *Fawn Gully*, and which forms the edge of the buttress. Climb the gully until a steep right branch leads off. Follow this, with two steep ice bulges leading to the easier upper gully. Two more easy pitches lead to its end. Finish slightly leftwards to an obvious narrow break in the final tier.

Logoless   300m   II. Sandy Allan, Andy Nisbet, Jonathan Preston. 16 Dec 2017.
The next buttress left, climbed by turfy grooves near its left edge.

Bambi   350m   IV,4. Sandy Allan, Andy Nisbet, Jonathan Preston. 10 Jan 2018.
A big gully between the buttresses either side. The gully extends to the slopes below the cliff but this section rarely holds snow and the gully was gained by walking in from the right at the cliff base. A long easy section of snow with one steep step gained a fork. The right fork is barred by a short overhanging step so the left fork was taken on ice before traversing immediately back right above the step. Higher up, another short step was bypassed on the right. A narrowing high up proved the crux, but would get easier with a good build-up.

Bambi, Left Branch 350m III. Andy Nisbet, Jonathan Preston. 7 Jan 2018.
As above but continuing up the left fork on snow and turf until fairly near the crest, then take a right-trending gully (crux) to two easier pitches to finish.

Abeona 350m III,4. Andy Nisbet, Jonathan Preston. 14 Dec 2017.
The buttress between *Bambi* and *Stalker's Gully*. Make a rising traverse in from the right below slabby ground to below a steep initial band. Start on the crest quite close to *Stalker's Gully*. Start just left of a short corner, cross the top of the corner and gain a ledge. Move left and climb grooves just left of the crest (45m). Go straight up a groove just left of slabs (50m). Go diagonally right up a ramp above the slabs, then straight up (50m). Continue up (60m). Move right and climb a wide groove to a terrace, then continue up (100m). Finish up grooves near the left end of the final tier (55m).

LOCH DIABAIGAS AIRDE:
The south side of Loch Diabaigas Airde contains a selection of slabby buttresses giving good short climbs and boulder problems. The east end of this area is best reached either by walking round the east end of the loch on rough marshy ground or, more pleasantly, by following the track towards a phone mast. This starts some 50m east of the parking place at the Bealach a' Gaoithe. From just east of the mast, follow the high ground round to the west and drop down to the crags. The section of the Bluffs containing the following routes is at (NG 818 592). It is a short narrow defile with slabs on the west side and shorter steeper walls on the east.

Broadband 30m Severe. Roger Robb, Peter Biggar. 18 Aug 2016.
This takes the large shield-like slab. Climb the central crack to an overlap. Go R and up to a second overlap with a grassy ledge: climb the corner and slabs to finish.

Exchange Line 30m V.Diff. Peter MacDonald, Peter Biggar, Roger Robb. 24 Aug 2016.
Climb crack left of a grass moustache to an overlap. Traverse left and go up to and over small overlaps, then take a curving line to the right up the slab.

LIATHACH, Coire Dubh Beag:
Commutation 210m IV,4. Sophie Grace Chappell, Andy Nisbet. 17 Mar 2018.
A direct finish to *The Executioner* but the start of that route wasn't formed so a start was made up *Nil Can't* (50m, 30m) followed by a traverse left along a big terrace (60m) to reach and climb a gully system (60m) which leads up from an unclimbed direct second pitch of *The Executioner*. Finish to steep snow (10m).
Note: *Nil Can't* might be worth Grade III.

Coire Dubh Mor:
Late Forties Groove 60m III,4. Ewan Lyons. 30 Mar 2018.
An icy groove just up and left of *Over Sixties Icefall*. Start at a steep step below the groove or an easier small groove to the right. A further steep icy step leads to easier ground. Visible as a thin white line left of *Over Sixties Icefall* on the topo in NH South.

Coire na Caime:

Sweet Spot   250m   V,5. Dave McGimpsey, Andy Nisbet. 23 Feb 2017.
A line of grooves up the crest of the buttress right of *Valentine Buttress* (which is actually a gully). Good but thin icy conditions encountered. Start close to *Vanadium Couloir Direct Start* (although it may have started further right).
1. 60m Climb the left side of ice, then trend left over chockstones to the main groove line. Go up this to below a short narrow chimney.
2. 60m Climb the chimney and trend right to climb a big prominent groove and snow above.
3. 60m A long groove is the continuation. This was entered from the right at mid-height and climbed.
4. 70m Climb a snow crest and a final steepening to the cornice.
Note: A future ascent can try and climb a direct start up a groove in the lowest tier (which was bare) and the top tier groove direct.

LIATHACH, South Side:

Triceratops   70m   IV,5. Michael Barnard, Doug Bartholomew. 27 Dec 2017.
Gain the ridge at the gap after the first pinnacle (the summer line probably does this). The second pinnacle was passed on its right flank, with the top wall (third pinnacle) providing the crux.

BEINN EIGHE:

Note: Ewan Lyons thought the *Upper Girdle* was VS 4b.

Sail Mhor:

KerPlunk   90m   VII,7. Pete Davies, Ross Cowie. 31 Mar 2018.
An exciting alternative finish to *Jenga* following a steep chimney and corner in the upper headwall 10m to the left.
1. 35m Climb the first pitch of *Jenga* to a snow slope beneath the steep upper headwall. Belay beneath the chimney.
2. 25m Climb the chimney to a semi-hanging belay.
3. 30m Step left out of the chimney to a crack leading into the upper corner. Climb the corner (crux) exiting onto a snow ledge. An easier corner and its right wall lead to the crest and a junction with *Lawson, Ling & Glover's Route*. Follow this to the top.

CAIRNGORMS

HELL'S LUM CRAG:

The Devil's Alternative   130m   IV,4 **. Ewan Lyons. 18 Dec 2017.
Open to variation but basically follow the summer line starting at a bulge around the twin cracks on pitch 2. Iced slabs and bulges lead to the final headwall (crux).

Lost Souls   155m   E1 *. Michael Barnard, Alan Hill. 2 Jul 2018.
Variations on *The Devil's Alternative*. Low in the grade.
1. 45m 5a As for *The Devil's Alternative* (hardest move low down).
2. 40m 4c The slabby wall right of *The Devil's Alternative* pitch 2. Move up as for that route, but then initially using a crack on the right, climb the wall (much easier than it looks from below). Continue directly up a short crack, then an easy corner above (*Auld Nick*) to reach the glacis.

3. 25m 5a Start up the stepped wall as for *The Devil's Alternative*, but continue up the right side of the wall (at one point quite near to *Auld Nick*) to a ledge below the top bulge. Move up leftwards to take the obvious break in the bulge (as for *The Devil's Alternative*).

4. 45m 4c Step left and climb the next wall to exit onto the slab above. Follow *Auld Nick* to the top.

The Devil's Playground   30m   E3 5c *. Michael Barnard, Alan Hill. 2 Jul 2018.
This route lies on the upper buttress at the extreme right end of the crag and can be approached either by ascending *The Escalator* or by traversing easily in from the right. The route climbs a line of thin seams up the obvious blankest part of the buttress. Go easily up to a corner on the left, place a cam at the base of the wide crack, then step onto the line. Move up rightwards and climb the thin seam (crux, RPs protect) to gain a ledge on the left. Continue more easily to ledges (can walk off right from here).

Sooty's Revenge   180m   E2 **. Michael Barnard, Alan Hill. 27 Jun 2018.
Some good climbing right of *Clean Sweep*, with two contrasting crux pitches. The first of these takes the obvious thin right-left diagonal crack-line in the green whaleback. Start below a hairline crack which goes up to reach the main crack.

1. 35m 5b Go up the hairline crack to place a good high RP, then step back down and move right to traverse in under a slanting overlap, reaching the main crack at a small overlap. Pad up past the overlap to an actual hold and continue up the crack-line which gradually eases, to join *Clean Sweep*.

2. 45m 4a As for *Clean Sweep* to the huge block belay.

3. 40m 5b Follow *Clean Sweep* for a few metres, then traverse right via a flake and undercling to reach a line of two thin seams going up the wall above. Climb these (harder for the short), then step left to go more easily up a flake-crack. Step right into a fault-line (the continuation of *The Omen* crack) and ascend this to ledges, then step back left to climb a crack just right of *Clean Sweep*.

4. 25m 5a Move right and starting up a couple of flakes, climb the wall between two blind seams.

5. 35m 4b Continue in a similar line up the wall above, directly up a small tower, then more easily up a fault.

Hell Ain't a Bad Place to Be   40m   VS 4b. Michael Barnard, Alan Hill 27 Jun 2018.
Left of *Highway to Hell* is an area of dark pink rock, the most obvious line consisting of a prominent, short right-angled corner at half-height, with vertical cracks above. The corner is surprisingly bold.

The Exorcist   VIII,8. Greg Boswell, Guy Robertson. 24 Nov 2017.
Follow the summer route throughout. Thin and technical on the summer crux.

SHELTER STONE CRAG, Central Slabs:
Notes from Jules Lines: There is no longer a peg in *Cupid's Bow*; instead place a small Cam and IMP 1 in the flake on the left.

The peg runners on *Missing Link* have now gone. There is alternative protection including a Rock 2 on its side for the hard move to gain the flake.

The bolt and peg on *Thor* have gone, but there are good wires and a small Cam at the side pull next to where the bolt was. Also good small Cam at right end of alcove roof to bolster the belay.

The abseil points have been replaced. There are new ones above *Snipers* and *Cupid's Bow*. It is intended to replace *The Pin* abseil during 2018.

Quiver 95m E4 **. Jules Lines, Steve Perry (on-sight). 28 Jun 2018.
Good climbing based on the crack-line to the left of Run of the Arrow.
1. 40m 5a As for *Run of the Arrow*.
2. 30m 6a Climb round the rib as for *Run of the Arrow* to the RPs . Make a thin move left to a sloping foothold in the scoop. Continue on more positive holds until you can step left onto a sloping ledge. Continue up the vague crack-line in the rib until a step right reaches a small wire belay on *Run of the Arrow*.
3. 25m 6a Step back left into the line and continue up the blind flake-line via a difficult mantel and better holds to the top.

Cupid's Bow 80m E6 6b ****. Jules Lines, Caelan Barnes. 27 Jun 2018.
The route follows the bow feature in its entirety (hence no change in name), offering one of the best and most varied pitches on the central slabs.
1. 40m 5a/b As per the original line.
2. 40m 6b Follow the original line to the kink in the bow where the original steps delicately left onto the *Aphrodite* slab. Climb rightwards along the flake of the bow to near its end where an obvious hold provides access to the slab above. Continue thinly up the slab and into the groove. Pull out left onto a shelf and continue left for 5m to belay on Cams. The abseil point is 5m further to the left.

Sweet Granite Kiss 100m E7 ***. Jules Lines, Steve Perry. 13 Jul 2018.
A fantastic direct line up the slabs, amalgamating sections of older routes with new sections. Pitch 1 is *Cupid's Bow Variation Start*.
1. 20m 5c Scramble up to below the crack in the steep wall to its right. Climb it up into the corner and continue for 5m to a ledge on the left.
2. 30m 6b Go back into the corner, climb it to its top and continue over an overlap to follow a thin crack to join the diagonal of *Missing Link*. Follow *Missing Link* for 10m to a flake feature directly below the Thor belay. Place an assortment of Cams and RPs here before making hard moves directly to belay.
4) 50m 6b A superb slab pitch. Climb *Thor* to the crescent shaped crack and from its left end, climb thinly up onto a small foothold. A flake jug is agonisingly out of reach. Make a harrowing move, or jump, to gain it (crux). (Very tall people might reach the jug, making the route significantly easier). Continue up to the overlap on the new section of *Cupid's Bow*, gain the hold above the overlap and boldly climb the slab into the corner before stepping out left onto the shelf. Having arranged gear on the shelf, climb the rib above into the diagonal crack and slab above to reach a thin ledge (possible belay, 40m). Continue to the *Icon* belay at the apex of the slabs.

The Graduate 90m HVS. Caelan Barnes, Jules Lines. 27 Jun 2018.
A line which climbs to the cliff-top above the *Cupid's / Run of the Arrow* abseil point.
1. 25m 5a Climb the centre of the slab to reach the *Icon* belay at the apex of the slabs.
2. 45m 4c Scramble up and left to pull into a niche in the centre of the next slab.

Continue climbing diagonally left to reach the notch and block on the skyline arete.
3. 20m Scramble carefully to the plateau. Best to head right and then back left.

Meteor 60m E2 *. Jules Lines, Steve Perry. 13 Jul 2018.
This is a worthwhile finish to any of the slab routes below. Start at the *Icon* belay at the apex of the slabs. From *Cupid's Bow*, climb the first pitch of the previous route. From *The Pin*, scramble up left. The route involves some scrambling but escalates into a superb finale on the headwall. The top 20m headwall is *** in its own right if abseiled from the top and climbed.
1. 20m 5a Scramble up to an overhanging corner. Climb this and the crack in the slab above to a good ledge.
2. 40m 5b Climb rocks up and right heading for the base of the headwall. Step right onto a huge flake ledge with loose blocks. Climb the centre of the wall on good holds, moving left into a continuation crack when possible to reach a chokestone at the top. A superb sustained pitch at upper limit of its grade.

Main Bastion:
The Shard 280m E5 ***. Callum Johnson, Guy Robertson. 4 Jul 2018.
A superb route combining thin slabs low down with strenuous cracks high up. Well protected apart from a serious section near the start of the second pitch. Start at the very lowest point of the crag.
1. 35m 5a From just up and right, step left to gain and follow a crack-line which leads up slightly left to an overlap and hollow blocks. Pull over, move left, then climb the slab using the obvious thin curving crack. Head up left to the grass filled groove and belay by a huge block on the left.
2. 45m 6a Climb the groove, then go right and up to the overlap and good protection. Traverse delicately left to gain good holds, stand on the highest of these, then make thin moves directly (serious) to gain a horizontal break. Step left at the next overlap, then pull over with difficulty to gain and follow the flake-groove to the next overlap and the superb thin crack-line which is followed to a ledge.
3. 60m 4c Climb the easier continuation groove to join *Haystack* and follow this to its belay below the *Steeple* fault.
4. 50m 6a Start up *Haystack/Steeple*, but quickly step left onto the right rib of the *Citadel* fault, then up to gain and follow the overhanging groove and crack-line between big overhangs. Above the overhangs, continue up easier ground to join *Citadel* where it comes back right. Belay below the cracked nose with a chimney just up on the left.
5. 40m 6b Step up right then pull left into a slight groove to gain a sloping ledge. Pull up then steeply out right into the overhanging finger crack and follow this with hard moves near its top just before it lies back. Continue up the superbly-positioned crack to join *Citadel* where it comes in from the right. Climb over the bulge (as for *Citadel*) and belay at the foot on the long, right-trending shallow groove.
6. 50m 5c Climb the sustained groove, then move up slightly left into a final short corner.

CREAGAN COIRE A' CHA-NO, Blood Buttress:
Blue Blood 40m III. Roger Webb, Simon Richardson. 26 Nov 2017.
Start 10m up and left of the left edge of the buttress and follow a right-slanting

gully cutting across the wall. Pull over a jutting flake at 20m and step right to the wide crack of *True Blood* (possible belay). Finish up *True Blood* to the top. This section of the cliff cornices easily, but it can be avoided by moving right onto the right arete of the finishing depression.

Cutty Sark Area:
Cutty Ranks   35m   IV,6. Luke Davies, Georgia Drew. 25 Nov 2017.
The corner-crack immediately left of *Mainmast*. Features some thin moves lower down before getting to a good rest on a block. Continue up the crack and then easier ground to finish. Probably easier if the bottom of the route is banked out.

Duke's Wall:
Fast and Furry-ous   60m   IV,6. Simon Richardson, Roger Webb. 26 Nov 2017.
The line of cracks and grooves between *Wile-E-Coyote* and *Road Runner*.
1. 30m   Start up the initial gully of *Road Runner*, then trend left to climb two steep steps to below a vertical cracked wall. Climb the short corner on the right to a ledge and pull through the vertical crack above to a terrace.
2. 30m   Move up to the gully-slot above. Pull steeply through its left wall and continue up easier ground left of the final tower of *Kerplunk* to the top.

Road Runner   60m   IV,5. Simon Richardson, Roger Webb. 24 Nov 2017.
The left-facing corner 20m right of the prominent groove of *Wile-E-Coyote*.
1. 25m   Ascend a wide gully to a short cracked wall and climb it (crux) to good hooks on a ledge. Continue up a second awkward wall that leads through a wide slot to a terrace (junction with *Kerplunk*).
2. 35m   Climb the chimney just right of the short corner of *Kerplunk* and continue up the snowy groove right of the final tower to the top.

Reconnaissance Rib   60m   III. Simon Richardson. 2 Dec 2017.
The shallow rib between *Kerplunk* and *Hobnailers' Gully*. A steep start leads to easier climbing and a finish up an open right-facing corner.

Downtime   70m   II. Christopher Cookson, Neil Taylor. 4 Jan 2018.
Start at the base of *Hobnailers' Gully*. Pass the large block and head left towards the obvious corner. Follow the sequence of corners as they trend left before climbing a steep awkward block to the left. Potential cornice on the final slope. The finish is the same as *Reconnaissance Rib*.

Hobnailers' Gully   60m   I/II. Sarah Atkinson, Stephen Blackman, Richard Bott, Alison Coull, Ian Crofton, Andrew Hewison, Chris Huntley, Graeme Morrison, Donald Orr, Jonathan Preston, Fiona Reid, Simon Richardson, Kenny Robb, Alan Smith, Graham Tough, Henning Wackerhage, Mike Watson, Roger Webb. 3 Dec 2017.
The prominent gully to the left of *Duke's Rib*.

Jenga Buttress:
Note: Caelan Barnes & Alex Riley on 5 Jan 2017 started *Jenga Buttress* by the obvious chockstone capped chimney seen on the approach (IV,5).

Turf Factory   60m   II. Caelan Barnes. 8 Jan 2017.
The obvious turfy gully immediately right of *Once we were Alpinists*.

LURCHER'S CRAG:

Nan 150m III. Simon Yearsley, Malcolm Bass, Andy Nisbet, Steve Perry, Sarah Sigley. 20 Jan 2018.
An icy depression parallel and right of *Right-Hand Icefall*. Forms much less readily.

Hot Dog 250m IV,4. Sandy Allan, Andy Nisbet. 18 Dec 2017.
An ice line which sometimes forms right of *Ultramontane*, just before the buttress base starts to rise up right. Climb an iced slab straight up and over a steepening to a barrier wall. Pass this on the left and continue up to an iced chimney (40m). Climb this to a wall, passed on the left before returning right and up to rock (40m). Climb easily up to a bay right of *Ultramontane*'s ridge, then move right to a vague ridge (*Akita*), followed to join *Ultramontane* high up.

Soo True Start 100m III. Sandy Allan, Andy Nisbet. 22 Jan 2018.
A line of thick ice up the lower tier followed by an icy depression leads direct to the upper depression of the original route (SMCJ 2015).

Piggyback Gully 150m III,4. Sandy Allan, Andy Nisbet. 3 Dec 2017.
A gully between *Piggie in the Middle* and *Husky* is blocked by an overhanging step. Start as for *Perception Gully* but move right and up to the step. Climb a slabby ramp at its right end until possible to move into the easy upper gully. Follow this to the top.

Far South End:
Note: Greg Strange thinks *Deerhound Ridge* should be called *Southern Ridge* as this was its original name in summer. Andy Nisbet admits this is true but thought the original name was dull.

Drystane Ridge 120m III,4 *.
A new description and grade.
The ridge forming the left side of the amphitheatre is steep but helpful. Start on the front face (outside the amphitheatre) and climb a groove to the crest (20m). Follow the crest, often just on its right, with the crux being a steep blocky section with some good flakes at mid-height, to reach a ledge on the left (40m). Finish by the easier upper crest (60m).
Note: To make the route Grade II but not as good, start inside the amphitheatre and climb a turfy corner which forms the right side of the ridge to reach the easier upper crest.

Pegleg 80m III,4. Andy Nisbet, Steve Perry, Jonathan Preston. 19 Nov 2017.
A wide fault right of *Drystane Ridge*. Tucked in to the right side of *Drystane Ridge* is the turfy corner mentioned above. This route climbs a parallel fault just to the right until possible to traverse right to the opposite side of the fault. Make steep moves through a barrier wall, then trend up right to the top.

Wolf Whistle 75m VII,7. Kacper Tekiele, Sandy Allan, Andy Nisbet. 4 Feb 2018.
Based on a pillar which forms the left edge of the back wall of the amphitheatre. Start just left of its crest.
1. 25m Climb a steep corner formed left of its crest and step right to a big ledge.

2. 25m Climb a line of flakes and blocks right of the crest before moving left to the crest.
3. 25m Climb cracks left of the crest to finish up it.

Jaws 70m VII,8. Kacper Tekiele, Sandy Allan. 6 Feb 2018.
A direct line up the pillar gives a bouldery route, using the same belays. Start below the crest.
1. 25m Gain and follow a crack-line in a shallow groove to a big V-groove which leads to the ledge.
2. 25m Climb a cracked bulge on the left, step right and climb to a prominent overhanging groove with a wide crack. Go up this and left to the crest, followed to the third tier.
3. 20m Step up on to a big boulder as for *Wolf Whistle*, then make a strenuous traverse right and climb a steep crack-line to easy ground.

Rottweiler 100m VI,7 ***. Andy Nisbet, Jonathan Preston. 2 Feb 2018.
A more direct line up the amphitheatre face, crossing *Collie's Route*, gives sustained climbing and spectacular moves off a pinnacle. Start at a slabby ramp just left of *Quinn*.
1. 30m Climb the turfy lower part of the ramp before traversing left along a ledge to a narrow V-groove. Wriggle up the groove, then up a couple of bulges rightwards to climb a right-facing corner. At its top, trend left to reach the terrace. Move 5m left to a groove.
2. 35m Move left again and climb a ramp rightwards across the top of the groove and beyond to a pinnacle. Stand on top of the pinnacle and make a wild step up left (excellent protection). Climb a ramp leftwards before moving straight up to a ledge below a steep groove.
3. 15m Climb the groove and easier ground to the crest of *Collie's Ridge*.
4. 20m Finish up this.

BEINN BHROTAIN, Dee Face:
The following routes lie on a slab at the far left end of the cliff (*Brodan's Dyke* crosses this in its upper section). The main feature here is the fine central fault in the slab, obvious on the approach. A narrow line of heather separates this main slab from another slab on the left. Protection is limited and the first three routes are basically solos. Topo provided.

Absolutely Slabulous 55m VS 4a. Michael Barnard. 8 Jul 2017.
The left-hand slab.

Mastiff Slab 65m HVS 4b. Michael Barnard. 8 Jul 2017.
Start below a fault on the far left side of the main slab (just right of the line of heather). Climb the fault, moving rightwards higher up to join the central fault at a short steeper section. Climb this (crux), then move up and right to reach *Brodan's Dyke* (if leading, protection can be found up and right, at the left end of the upper juniper ledge). Follow the dyke out left to just before the grassy gully, then step up and go rightwards up a ramp (delicate). Finish easily.

The Paws 65m HVS 4b *. Michael Barnard. 8 Jul 2017.
Start a few metres up and left of the obvious direct entry to the central fault. Move up on flakes, then up and right to gain the fault. Go up the fault to below a short

steeper section (taken by *Mastiff Slab*); instead climb the knobbly wall on the right, then move up to reach *Brodan's Dyke* (if leading, protection can be found up and right, at the left end of the upper juniper ledge). Continue as for *Mastiff Slab*.

Granite Planet 90m E1 *. Michael Barnard, David Bird. 2 Sep 2017.
Down and right of the direct entry to the central fault is another slab which leads up to the right-hand side of the main slab.
1. 55m 5b Climb the obvious line of weakness in the slab, then move up and right to step left onto a heather ledge. Traverse the ledge until possible to gain the left end of a small higher ledge. Step right and surmount the bulge (unprotected 5a), then move up rightwards to arrange good gear below a small overlap (obvious from below). Step left and surmount the bulge (technical crux), then boldly to gain and continue up a thinner dyke below *Brodan's Dyke* to reach and belay on the right side of the heather ledge.
2. 35m 4b As for *Double Dyker*.

Granite Planet, True Finish 35m E3 5b *. Michael Barnard, David Bird. 2 Sep 2017.
An independent but very bold top pitch. From the belay, traverse left to place gear at the left end of the upper juniper ledge. Step down to *Brodan's Dyke* and follow this to a shallow vertical fault (the upper section of the central fault in the main slab). Go up the fault to where it steepens. Now either continue up the fault (crux) to easier ground, or pad up the thin ramp on the right (slightly easier but more delicate). Pre-practiced.

Double Dyker 90m HVS *. Michael Barnard. 8 July 2017.
Start just right of Granite Planet.
1. 55m 4c Climb directly up the fine slab (crux) to gain a heather ledge on the right. Move rightwards up the slab above, passing a single nobble, to gain *Brodan's Dyke* and follow this up and left to the next heather ledge (belay on the right).
2. 35m 4b Move up, initially via a flake, to a right-leaning corner. Go up this to gain the start of another dyke and follow this (protection) to the top.

BEINN A' BHUIRD, Dividing Buttress:
Outpost Route 120m IV,6. Malcolm Bass, Simon Yearsley. 26 Feb 2018.
Enjoyable climbing up the buttress between *Sentinel Route* and *Dividend Route*. Scramble up easy ground to belay at the toe of the flying buttress immediately left of the groove of *Sentinel Route*.
1. 50m Climb steep groves and flakes just right of the crest, then move more easily left to the base of a groove/corner which is climbed through a steep wall to a cracked slab onto easier ground.
2. 40m Easier climbing staying right of the fault of *Dividend Route* to the cul-de-sac of that fault. Climb a short corner at the top right of the cul-de-sac (just right of where *Dividend Route* goes steeply up), then step back left and climb easier slabs to belay.
3. 30m Move up ledges to the foot of the prominent squat tower on the skyline. Climb this with excellent moves across to and through the flake-crack.

BEN AVON, Meall Gaineimh:
Torniquet 10m   VS 5a. Alan Hill, Michael Barnard. 23 Jun 2018.
Left of the existing routes. Start at the base of an easy right-slanting ramp. Take a left-trending crack-line up the wall to its left.

Clach Mheadhoin:
(NJ 164 052)   East facing
This is the larger tor between Meall Gaineimh and Clach Bhan. On the right side of the tor is a large buttress with several horizontal breaks on its front face and a chimney-crack on its left side.

Grittier than Grit 20m   E1 5a *. Michael Barnard, Alan Hill. 23 Jun 2018.
Take at least one Friend 6. Climb the chimney-crack to its top, reach down to reclaim the cam, then make a tricky move up to gain the big break. Traverse left into the gully, ascend this then step back right to a natural thread belay.

East Meur Gorm Craig:
Exploding Weasles 30m   HVS 5b. Alan Hill, Michael Barnard. 23 Jun 2018.
Start as for *That's the Badger* (SMCJ 2016), but take the right fork of the crack up to a ledge below the steep top corner-crack (optional belay). Climb this (crux, large Cams useful).

The Tale of Mr Tod 30m   HVS 5b *. Michael Barnard, Alan Hill. 23 Jun 2018.
Start right of the above, below a wide flake-crack. Climb this, finishing as for the above.

The Candyman 25m   E2 5c **. Michael Barnard, Alan Hill. 23 Jun 2018.
Good sustained climbing up the steep vertical crack between *Wafer* and *99*, gained from the ledge on the right.

Leabaidh an Daimh Buidhe (Summit Tor):
Routes start on the steeper right-hand side of the SW face (the side seen when approaching from the Sneck). The first main line reached is a fine vertical stepped crack leading directly towards the south summit of the tor.

Bananas in Bandanas 10m   HVS 5a. Alan Hill, Michael Barnard. 24 Jun 2018.
A short distance left of the vertical stepped crack is a short hanging crack.

Jim Jams 30m   E1 5b **. Michael Barnard, Alan Hill. 24 Jun 2018.
The vertical stepped crack is the line of the crag. After the third step (crux), continue easily to the final tower. Move rightwards up slabby slanting cracks to reach a pedestal. Make the final move from this to gain the south summit.

Nightcap 15m   E1 5b **. Michael Barnard, Alan Hill. 24 Jun 2018.
Right of the above is a chimney-gully. Climb the flake-crack on the left wall to reach the horizontal break at its top. Hand-traverse left to gain the ledge below the upper crack of *Jim Jams* (can walk off from here).

Nice One, Cyril 20m   V.Diff. Alan Hill, Michael Barnard. 24 Jun 2018.
The chimney-gully.

Variation: *Seesaw Finish*   10m   HVS 5b *. Michael Barnard, Alan Hill. 24 Jun 2018.
From the belay above the chimney-gully, carefully stand on a block (the 'Seesaw') and reach up to gain the left-hand flake-crack in the top wall. Climb this to the pedestal of *Jim Jams*, finishing as for that route.

Sneering Crack   25m   HVS 5b. Michael Barnard, Alan Hill. 24 Jun 2018.
At the bottom right end of the face is a chimney-crack with large chockstones at half-height. Get established in the chimney with difficulty and continue to its top. Step right and go up a short wall to a thread belay.

The Aardvark   40m   HVS 5a. Michael Barnard, Alan Hill. 24 Jun 2018.
The upper part of the SE face of the tor is characterised by two parallel wide cracks; start below the right-hand one. Go up the groove to the base of this crack, then traverse left to climb the other one. Step left at the top of the crack and go up a short wall (as for *Sneering Crack*).

Rocky Raccoon   25m   HVS 5a *. Michael Barnard, Alan Hill. 24 Jun 2018.
The ENE face of the tor is split by an open gully. This route climbs a steep chimney-crack on its right wall (crux). Continue up the fine slanting crack in the wall above.

LOCHNAGAR, Southern Sector, Perseverance Wall:
Holdfast   80m   IV,6. Simon Richardson, Sophie Grace Chappell. 30 Jan 2018.
The rib and gable wall at the right end of the cliff.
1. 30m Start just right of *Windfall* and climb the well-defined arete to its right to where it eases.
2. 20m Cross the gully of *Windfall* and climb the vertical wall on the left via a large flake (crux) and the right-facing corner above.
3. 30m Continue up the right edge of the buttress above (to the right of the gully of *Athos*), to gain the top of the second exit chimney of *Windfall*. Finish easily up the snow slope above to the top.

Black Spout Pinnacle:
Early Bird Groove   35m   IV,6. Drew Stevenson, Stuart Cossar. 11 Nov 2017.
A groove immediately right of *Early Bird*.

West Buttress:
Gryphon Grooves   250m   VI,6. Forrest Templeton, Simon Richardson. 25 Mar 2018.
The gully line of *Gargoyle Direct* splits into two above an amphitheatre. This route follows the left branch. Pitches 4 and 5 comprise the new climbing, but the complete ascent is described.
1. and 2. 120m As for *Quasimodo*.
3. 40m Climb the initial ice gully of *Gargoyle Direct* to the amphitheatre.
4. 25m Climb snow up the left side of the amphitheatre to below a huge overhang of chockstones with a frieze of icicles. Climb a short corner on the right, then step left onto the icicle frieze and climb it over the chockstones to belay on *Bell's Pillar.*
5. 35m Step right and continue up the narrow continuation gully up the left branch to below Radar Wall.

6. 30m Finish as for *Quasimodo* by climbing underneath the Gargoyle and moving up and right to finish.

COIRE Kander:
The Committee 60m III. Will Attridge, Oli Jepsen. 10 Mar 2018.
On the first icefall to the right of the bastion approach slopes, climb a narrow iced gully and ascend a series of steeper bulges. Belay in the rocks to the right (60m). Trend rightwards in a broad gully to reach the ramp of The Bastion.

GLEN CLOVA, The Scorrie:
Corner Ahoy! 190m V,6. Forrest Templeton, Simon Richardson. 11 Feb 2018.
A route based on the prominent corner system on the right side of the conical front face of The Scorrie. Approximately 50m right of the start of *Ramp it up Ye*, a left-trending ramp leads up the lower section of the initial left-facing corner. Belay below a steep chimney where the corner steepens.
1. 20m Climb up to the chimney and wriggle up it to where the angle eases.
2. 50m Continue in the line of the corner up and left to where it fades. Trend up and right up a slab by a corner to reach a broad terrace with a 3m pinnacle-block.
3. 50m The right-facing corner defining the upper part of the route is up and right but hidden from this point. Trend diagonally right over a couple of ribs, then climb steeply to a good ledge at the foot of the corner.
4. 20m Climb the corner using the flake on its left wall to a good ledge (crux). A deceptively awkward pitch.
5. 50m Continue in the line of the corner (avoiding the initial chimney-crack on the right) to gain the flat top of the buttress.

The following routes are on the two tiered steep buttress high up just below the summit cairn of the Scorrie (topo provided). This is visible from the car park at the Ranger base. Follow the Scorrie path ridge until a large obvious boulder is encountered. Gear up here and sacks can be left as the descent comes down the same way. Descend steep snow below the buttress. *The Scorrie Romp* (now Grade II, SMCJ 2016) starts up where the dividing ledge (Gastric Band) reaches the ground.

One Man Gastric Band 160m II. Forrest Templeton. 25 Feb 2018.
Start at the same place as *The Scorrie Romp* but instead of going up the continuation corner, follow the Gastric Band leftwards until the next obvious chimney is reached. This peters into a shallow gully and comes out just above and to the left of the obvious tree on pitch 2 of *The Scorrie Romp*. Finish up this.

Catheter Corner 155m V,6. Kevin Murphy, Matt Smith, Forrest Templeton. 31 Mar 2018.
Three excellent pitches with quite sustained climbing. Descend from the ridge passing the start of *The Scorrie Romp* and contour round the toe of the buttress to below an inset rectangular slab leading up to a capping roofed corner.
1. 25m Climb small turfy protrusions with the occasional useful crack, cross a small overlap and pass a small tree to the obvious corner.
2. 30m Make awkward undercling moves rightwards under a roof until placements can be reached in a turfy groove. Follow this past another more substantial tree over small overlaps to reach the Gastric Band just below a left-facing slabby corner.

3. 30m Climb the left side of the slab until a move right into the corner can be made at about two-thirds height. Belay on a large obvious block which lies almost directly between where *The Scorrie Romp* and *One Man Gastric Band* converge.
4. 70m Share the same easy finish to the top.

The highest line up on the right with an icefall at its base is *Short Hearse* (25m III, Forrest Templeton, 25 Feb 2018)

Coire Farchal:
Silver Surfers   150m   IV,5. Euan Whittaker, Paul Warnock, Martin Holland. 7 Feb 2018.
Start between *Coffin Dodger* and *Over the Hill*.
1. 40m Climb straight up over a short step and easy ground to the base of an icicled wall with a protruding block right of the icefall of *Coffin Dodger*.
2. 40m Climb the icy wall past the block to easier ground and a cave formed by an ice shield and the undercut base of a wall.
3. 30m Climb steeply up the ice shield to gain the right-facing corner, which is left of the slot of *Over the Hill*. Easier ground leads to another cave belay under a large block.
4. 40m Easy ground on the left leads to a finish up the short steep groove of *Coffin Dodger* and easy ground above.

Winter Corrie note:
On 6 Feb 2018, the same team climbed *Sun Rock Blues* with a variation finish to pitch 3, by traversing right from the small cave.

Bassies:
Message in a Bottle   130m   II. George Allan, John Thomas. 29 Nov 2017.
Left of the buttress containing the grooves of *Flotsam and Jetsam* is a slab beyond which is a snowfield. Climb this, move left and follow a depression to a wall which was climbed up its left side followed by a right traverse above it (other options possible). Continue rightward to finish up short steps as for *Flotsam*.

Corrie of Clova:
Birthday Icefall   100m   III. Simon Richardson, Ben Richardson. 28 Dec 2017.
The enclosed frozen stream bed starting at NO 331 758 rises in four distinct steps to a prominent headwall that provides a superb 40m ice pitch to finish.

Carpe Diem   80m   III,4. Simon Richardson, Sophie Grace Chappell. 18 Dec 2017.
The furthest left buttress on the south face of the corrie. Start at a terrace at the right end of the first tier.
1. 40m Climb a right-slanting open gully and bear left at its top to reach a diagonal left-trending ledge.
2. 40m Continue up the steep left-facing corner (crux) and finish up the easier gully above.

YOLO   40m   III. Jeremy Windsor, Simon Richardson. 9 Feb 2018.
The S shaped depression right of *Carpe Diem* finishing just left of the prominent rock tower.

Wildcat Ridge   70m   IV,6. Simon Richardson, Jeremy Windsor. 9 Feb 2018.
A little gem taking the well-defined ridge to the right of *Carpe Diem* buttress.
1. 20m Start below the centre of the ridge and climb turfy cracks to below a prominent triangular wall guarding access to the upper ridge.
2. 20m Climb the left-hand of two vertical corner-cracks on surprisingly helpful holds to gain the crest above. Move up this to blocks.
3. 30m Finish along the well-defined upper ridge to the top.

Cat Gully   70m   I. Simon Richardson, Jeremy Windsor. 9 Feb 2018.
The well-defined gully to the right of *Wild Cat Ridge* provides a convenient descent.

Feline Crest   60m   IV,4. Simon Richardson, Jeremy Windsor. 9 Feb 2018.
The buttress right of *Cat Gully*.
1. 30m Start at the toe of the buttress and climb vegetated slabs to a vertical wall. Step left around the crest and climb a right-facing slot into a groove leading to the crest.
2. 30m Straightforward climbing along the crest leads to the top.

Mousehole Gully   60m   II. Jeremy Windsor, Simon Richardson. 9 Feb 2018.
The gully between *Feline Crest* and *Cat's Whiskers* is blocked by an impasse with a remarkable through route.

Cat's Whiskers   60m   V,7. Simon Richardson, Jeremy Windsor. 9 Feb 2018.
1. 30m The rightmost buttress and the narrowest of the four. Climb up and right past a large flake at the foot of the buttress and move up a vegetated crack to where the buttress steepens. Traverse 3m left (crux) and move up and right to rejoin the vegetated crack. Follow this up the crest to sloping shelves.
2. 30m Continue up the shelves followed by easier ground to the top.

Corrie Brandy:
VSOP   120m   V,5. Simon Richardson, Sophie Grace Chappell. 13 Jan 2018.
A surprisingly steep and technical line up the steep ground left of *Waterloo Gully*. Low down on the cliff, and approximately mid-way between the south end of the crag and *Waterloo Gully* is a prominent, inset, 5m high triangular spike. The route climbs just right of this and continues up mixed ground above exiting up a gully left of a vertical headwall.
1. 30m Climb up a short steep gully to below a V-groove formed on the right side of the inset triangular spike. Climb the groove, exit right at its top and climb delicately up a turfy slab to exit onto a terrace.
2. 35m Step left and climb up to a second terrace. Climb a 5m vertical corner and continue up to a left-trending ramp that leads under the headwall to an icy gully.
3. 15m Climb the gully to its top.
4. 40m Finish up easy snow slopes to the top.

Waterloo Gully   140m   III,4. Simon Richardson. 26 Dec 2017.
The prominent deep-cut gully splitting the upper half of the west wall is the most natural winter line in the corrie, but it is hidden from the approach on the west side of Loch Brandy. Start roughly in the centre of the face in a small bay at NO

336 755. Climb an icy gully for 50m to reach easier ground that leads up to the gully. Finish up the snow slope above to the top.

Napoleon 180m V,4. Simon Richardson, Sophie Grace Chappell. 1 Jan 2018.
A serious expedition up the wall to the right of *Waterloo Gully*.
1. 40m Start approx. 100m right of Waterloo Gully beneath a prominent icefall. Climb this and exit left below its final tier to a prominent 2m spike.
2. 30m Move left and climb steepening ground to below a steeper wall.
3. 30m Step left and move up awkward turf shelves to enter an open rocky gully. Climb awkwardly past a huge chokestone to exit onto easier ground leading to a clean vertical wall. Move left 10m to a corner-niche.
4. 40m Move left out of the niche and climb up to a well-defined hidden gully. Climb this to its top.
5. 40m Continue up open snow slopes to the cornice taking care to avoid the landslip crevasse just below the plateau.

First Footing 100m IV,5. Simon Richardson, Sophie Grace Chappell. 1 Jan 2018.
A direct line up the buttress taken by *The Brandy Pad*. Note that poor visibility on the first ascent meant that *The Brandy Pad* was incorrectly located in the 2007 edition of the SMC Cairngorms guidebook. The buttress is situated at NO 340 759 and is the next feature right of the buttress taken by *Smuggler*.
1. 40m Start on the right side of the gully dividing the buttresses taken by *Smuggler* and *The Brandy Pad*. Climb up and trend right over a couple of steep walls to an awkward stance on the left side of the crest.
2. 40m Climb boldly up mossy shelves to reach a clean-cut right-facing corner. Climb this with interest and then follow a turfy ramp to under a short steep wall. Climb that diagonally right to exit on the large terrace below the final tier. Above is the slanting shelf taken by *The Brandy Pad*.
3. 20m Move slightly left and climb the vegetated line of weakness on the left side of the headwall to the top.

Craigs of Loch Wharral:
Y-Gully, Right-Hand 120m II. Simon Richardson. 21 Dec 2017.
The gully defining the left side of the buttress taken by *Heather Boulevard* splits at two-thirds height. Take the right branch along a deep hanging slot (crux) and continue up the snow slope above to the top.

GLEN DOLL, Creag Maud:
Maud's Groove 120m IV,5 *. Pete Benson, Adrian Crofton. 30 Nov 2017.
Climb the left-bounding gully of *Pinnacle Ridge* to the steep walls high on the right. Here there is an obvious bay from which a left-slanting chimney groove starts.
1. 45m Climb the groove to a large stance below a steep wall.
2. 30m Move up right, then use turf blobs to cross a steep slab to step into a shallow chimney groove; climb this to a rocky band moving up and left to a good stance.
3. Easy ground to the summit of the crag.

GLEN PROSEN, South Craig:

Tequila Sunrise   130m   IV,4. Simon Richardson, Sophie Grace Chappell. 2 Feb 2018.

A pleasant climb up mixed ground left of *Spanish Dinner*.

1. 50m Start at the foot of *Summit Gully* and trend left across *Spanish Dinner*, to gain a left-slanting diagonal gully. Follow this to where it fades.
2. 50m Continue directly up the cliff, negotiate an awkward steep band by climbing right then left, and belay below the final headwall.
3. 30m Climb a short corner to gain the right-trending ramp leading through the headwall to the top.

WATER OF SAUGHS, Corrie na Berran:

Thales Cleft   80m   II. Simon Richardson. 22 Jan 2018.

High up on the left side of the cliff is a shallow-angled buttress cut by a right-slanting gully groove. Approach by easy ground and climb the groove to the top.

Aristotle's Groove   150m   III,4. Simon Richardson. 22 Jan 2018.

Approximately 40m right of *S Gully* is a right-facing curling corner-groove that sometimes fills with ice. Climb the groove, exiting left at its top and continue up easier ground to finish up the broad open buttress above, approximately mid-way between the open gully finishes of *S Gully* and *Isosceles*.

Euclid's Proof   150m   IV,4. Simon Richardson, Sophie Grace Chappell. 9 Mar 2018.

The well-defined right tending line of ice 50m to the right of *Aristotle's Groove*.

1. 40m Start at the foot of the ramp of *Isosceles* and climb a steep icefall to a terrace. Step right and surmount a second ice step to a left-facing corner.
2. 30m Continue up the corner to a second terrace and climb the steep ice step above on the right.
3. 80m Finish up the easy angled shallow crest right of the open gully of *Isosceles*.

To the right of the left-trending ramp of *Pythagoras* is a 40m wall steep wall that ices readily.

Archimedes' Screw   40m   III,4. Simon Richardson, Sophie Grace Chappell. 9 Mar 2018.

In the centre of the wall is a steep sweep of rock. This route follows the right-trending shallow gully to its left.

Plato's Cave   40m   IV,5. Simon Richardson, Sophie Grace Chappell. 9 Mar 2018.

The narrow gully to the right of the steep sweep of rock. An excellent pitch.

GLEN ESK, Earn Craig:

Note: Toby Burrell & Julie Black on 10 Dec 2017 climbed an alternate finish to *Earn Gully* (SMCJ 2010) when the ice pitch wasn't formed. Climb *Earn Gully* to the flat spot below the exit ice pitch. On the right wall, take a right-facing corner and wall to a prow (8m), then continue along the ridge to exit through heather bushes to the top (15m). IV,4 overall.

Craig Maskeldie:

Central Gully, Alternate Right Wall Finish 45m V,6 (1PA). Ruari Sheehan, Toby Burrell. 11 Feb 2018.
After climbing the centre gully of the trilogy (left of *Dochty Gully*), continue to easier ground below a left-facing corner system. Head slightly rightwards, then directly up steep heather wall into a steep open corner. Mantel this onto easier ground before the crux section. Bridge up a slightly overhanging corner for several metres, ending up on the broad ridge and easier ground (15m, 1PA).

Note: The obvious left-facing corner marking the top of the left edge of the buttress left of *Dochty Gully* is Grade III (George Allan, John Thomas, 6 Mar 2016). Short ice pitches can be climbed or avoided approaching this.
George Allan has noticed a mistake in SMC 2010, that *Shaula Ridge* is to the right of *Doughty Gully*, not *Lee Gully* (which is much further left).

NORTH-EAST OUTCROPS

LONGHAVEN, Red Wall Quarry:

Cesar 12m 7b+ **.
An easier alternative finish to *The King* provides one of the best routes in the quarry. A future classic! Climb *The King* to the 4th bolt, then continue up left past 2 more bolts to a lower-off. The hardest move is the start to *The King* and all the holds are pretty big so no excuses!!!

LONG HAVEN TO BODDAM, Buchan Walls:

This multi-pitch crag lies in the inlet south of Meackie Point, only about 100m from the road near a cliff-top house. Apparently only one route has been previously recorded here despite the crag's sunny aspect and generally good clean rock. There are a few Kittiwake and Cormorant nests on the left side. A couple of abseil stakes have been placed and these are also useful for belays. It is also possible to access the non-tidal base of the cliff via steep grass to the east, near Meakie Point. Routes by Keith Milne, Ian Milne & David Bird.

Gold Dust HVS (1977).
1. 45m 5a The exact line of this route is not certain. The guidebook description seems to fit the leftmost line, but possibly overlaps with the next route. 'In the centre of the walls is a steep right-sloping ramp. Start 8m along a ledge leading left from the foot of the ramp. Climb the grooves above and the wall to their left to reach a prominent corner. Climb this until below the overhang where a sand filled crack leads left across an undercut wall. When the crack runs out a short wall leads to easy slabs and the top.'

Gold Placer 40m E1 **. Mar 2017.
Takes the straight groove above the orange slab.
1. 25m 5b Climb directly up the lower wall using side pulls to gain the ramp (or bypass on the right). From the ramp, the first few moves are on the left wall, reaching right into the groove to a good wire placement. Above this there are some marginal runners with intricate climbing. After a small ledge, the line continues with solid runners in a wonderful clean granite corner. Belay below a small overhang.

2. 15m 5a Climb the overhang with difficulty using reachy sidepulls to an easy angled slab which finishes on the left.

Prospector   50m   VS *. Sep 2016.
Start just right of an overhanging wall.
1. 25m 4b/4c An interesting pitch. Climb a left-slanting ramp until it is possible to move up into a niche. Step left awkwardly and then up short cracks to a ledge. With a high runner on the right, climb the slab centre to the left and up to broken ledges.
2. 25m 4c Climb the corner-crack on the left. Move past a doubtful block by moves on the left wall and then a few moves back right, finishing up a clean slab with a thin crack.

End of the Rainbow   50m   E1 *. Apr 2017.
A few metres right is a steep wall with good holds.
1. 30m 5b Climb the wall and onto easier ground. Move left into a shallow groove and crack system which leads up to an overhanging wall. Climb this initially on the right using small ledges and move back right and finish on jugs. Belay at the bollard.
2. 20m 5b Move right around the nose and traverse to the base of the corner. Climb the short overhanging crack to a mantelshelf. Finish easily up a slab. Large Cam useful to protect the mantelshelf.

Nuggets   40m   E2 **. Mar 2017.
1. 30m 5a Climb the same initial wall and slab as the previous route. After a few metres, step left and mantelshelf onto the nose. A short crack leads to delicate moves onto a sloping shelf. Move up and left past a smooth nose to a good bollard stance. Excellent rock.
2. 10m 5c Step left to below a thin crack. Move left and up strenuously on rounded holds to reach a better crack. Continue steeply onto a final shelf just below the top.

Panning for Gold   55m   H.Severe **. Mar 2017.
Start from a broken ridge at the right side.
1. 30m 4b A few easy steps lead to an enjoyable clean corner-groove. Belay on a ledge 3m below the main overhang.
2. 25m 4b Step up left onto the slab and move around the nose (possible belay). Traverse left onto a slab. Take a wide crack to finish (or a strenuous alternative past a jutting block just to the right, 5a).

COVESEA:
Tusken Raider   30m   E3 5c *. Peter Herd, Russell Birkett. 1 May 2017.
A mid-height girdle of the main wall in Boulders Bay. Start up *Sandanista* and follow obvious flat holds across the wall, climbing above the roof and joining the following route. The middle section is bold and care should be taken to protect the second.

Fascist Republic   15m   E2 5b **. Steve Perry, Julian Lines. 19 Apr 2017.
Climb up *Banana Republic* past the roof. Now make an exhilarating traverse above the roof, all the way to the corner of *Fascist Octopus* using an obvious handrail and placing a good cam in the crack of *Banana Republic – Corbyn*

Variation. Once at the corner, make a couple of bold mantels to reach good protection in the upper corner.

Anchuria 15m E6 6c **. Jules Lines. 26 Mar 2017.
The roof and wall to the left of *Banana Republic*. Start off a boulder and climb the wall to the roof just right of a black weep. Make athletic moves through the roof and continue up the hairline in the wall above, shifting to its right side just below the top.

Prisoner of Conscience 15m E7 6b **. Jules Lines. 30 Apr 2017.
A direct line through the overhanging face to the right of *Bottle Dungeon*. Boulder up on crimps to a flat jug at 3m in the faint right-hand groove system. Follow the flying groove up and left to a hands-off rest at half-height. Launch up and right into a sequence of blind right-facing corners and pull wildly through the roof to get established on the leaning headwall. Finish up this more easily.

The Bear 15m E1 5a. Steve Perry. Michael Barnard. 24 Jun 2017.
Climb the corner beside *Honey Barrel*.

Typhoon 15m VS 5a. Steve Perry, Sarah Sigley. 21 Mar 2017.
An easier route on the wall (and easier still using a bunk-up at the start). Start as for *Celebrate the Bullet*, then step right and climb up to the roof directly beneath the upper crack of *Protection Racket*. Traverse rightwards under the roof to the base of a crack on the west face. Climb this on jugs to the top.
Note: A direct start from below has been climbed but only as a boulder problem. Doing this and the top would probably drop the grade.

I Live, I Die, I Live Again 15m E4 6a *. Steve Perry. 18 Apr 2017.
Starts in the corner left of *Creepie Crawlie* where a small seep in the bottom can be avoided. Make a boulder problem start and arrange gear in a thin vertical crack before a bold but easier traverse right along a rail. Welcome gear in another thin vertical crack and steady wall climbing leads to a second roof. Finish as for *Creepie Crawlie*.

PASS OF BALLATER:
Odorono 10m E1 5c. Michael Barnard (unsec). 13 Jun 2017.
Eliminate, but a good move. Climb *Stinker* to place gear under the overlap, then step down and left to join *Brut*. Now move up and pull directly through the overlap to finish easily.

Zapata 8m HVS 5a. Greg Strange, Rob Archbold. 14 Jul 2016.
Start 1m right of *Fungus Face* and climb the wall left of *Lime Chimney*, finishing at a small right-facing corner.

Poker's Rib E6 6b *. Jules Lines. Mar 2017.
Start on the boulder as for *Peel's Wall* and pull on at undercuts, then move left to gain a good pinch on the rib. Follow the rib to the horizontal. Using a mono, rock up to gain a set of tiny crimps that veer right, then slap for a very smooth pinch on the rib. Use this go for the top.

Slope Shoulders E4 6b *. Jules Lines, Richard Biggar. Summer 2016.

The direct finish to *Slope Arms* gives a fine and fierce micro pitch. Start up *Slope Arms* and at the break (small Cam), gain a pinch in the seam up and right. Finish direct.

Morphine Drip   E7 6c **. Jules Lines. 26 Oct 2017.
The central line following a hairline seam 2m to the right of *Private Parts*. Start at the diamond shaped block and gain a slot in the wall. Make a desperate move to gain a niche hold before sprinting up to a superb finishing sequence in the scoop at the highest part of the wall. Probably F7c and graded for gear placed on the lead as per FA.

IVF   E5 6b. Jules Lines. 2016.
Pull through the roof as per *Copulation* and then improvise right to a good hold on the arete. Finish up it in a fine position.

Sobriety   E5 6b **. Jules Lines. Jan 2017.
The parallel line to the left of *Larup Head* gives a good pitch at the upper limit of the grade. Make bouldery moves via an undercut and blind flake to reach a break. Continue direct via a sustained sequence to gain a narrow ledge. Continue on up the crack in the upper wall veering slightly left to finish on jugs.

GLEN CLOVA, Lower North-West Crag:
For a Handful of Beans   30m   HVS 5a **.
The route as described in SMCJ 2015 Journal was repeated. Following cleaning and removal of several large loose blocks, the undernoted description provides a more direct independent line.
   Good climbing up the centre of the wall. Climb direct up a cracked wall to a niche and arrange protection in the wide left-curving crack above. Step back right and climb the wall above on good positive holds, trending left to a large rowan. Finish up a crack above past a further rowan.

Fifties Crag:
Located above and right of the Upper Doonie, a short distance below and left of High Crag. Three routes by Simon Stewart are on the SMC website.

HIGHLAND OUTCROPS

TIGHNABRUAICH CRAG:
Note by Will Morris: Many of the bolts have been reported as corroded and no longer usable, May 2018.

APPIN, Dallen's Rock (NM 930 485):
The west facing quartzite crag at Lettershuna overlooking the A828, clearly visible from the road and about 20mins drive south from Ballachulish. The original trad routes here have never proved popular due to poor protection and snappy rock so, with local approval, those routes have been superseded by the following cleaned sport routes. A public parking area is situated adjacent to the A828 a few hundred yards to the north. The crag gets the benefit of any afternoon or evening sun. Most of the trees along the base were recently cleared by the Forestry Commission

(2016). The best approach is to come in slightly from the right through some remaining mature trees. The routes are described from right to left.

Power of the West   23m   6a+ **. Steve Kennedy, Chris Docherty, Cynthia Grindley. 5 Jul 2017.
The vague groove line starting from the tree stump on the right side of the crag. Pull steeply into the groove which is followed until steep moves lead left onto the edge of the slab. Move back up right onto the tricky final wall which leads to lower-offs.

The following routes share a lower-off situated under the main roof.

Waldrom   16m   6a **. Steve Kennedy, Chris Docherty, Cynthia Grindley. 5 Jul 2017.
The next line of bolts up the golden coloured slab starting 5m left of *Power of the West*. Climb the initial slab, surmount a bulge, then climb the steep slab, moving left at the finishing moves to gain the lower-off. The final moves may prove difficult for the short. The upper part is close to but always right of *Philomena*.

Philomena   16m   6a **. Cynthia Grindley, Steve Kennedy, Chris Docherty, Julie MacIntyre. 18 Jul 2017.
A sustained line up the left side of the slab, moving rightwards at the top to reach the lower-off.

ARDNAMURCHAN, Meall an Fhir-eoin, Hooded Wall:
Craters of the Moon   20m   E1 5a *. Steve Kennedy, Cynthia Grindley. 11 Mar 2018.
The bold slab near the left edge between *Vesuvius* and *Krakatoa*. Slightly eliminate. Start on the right as for *Etna* (or by *Krakatoa*) and traverse left along the lip to the base of the *Krakatoa* crack. Step left into a short left-facing corner, then climb the slab fairly directly above (small Cam in horizontal crack about halfway). Avoid the temptation to place gear in *Krakatoa*!

GLEN NEVIS, Scimitar Buttress:
The Pleasures of the Damned   35m   VS 4c. Oliver Barr-Skeoch. 25 Jul 2017.
Climb the steep triangular wall right of *Wanderlust* direct to finish where *Wanderlust* is wrongly marked on p249 of Highland Outcrops South (the correct finish is further left).
Note: The same line was repeated and recorded as E2 5b.

BINNEIN SHUAS:
Dun Briste   55m   E8 6c ***. Dave MacLeod. Jul 2017.
The obvious direct finish to *Siege Engine*, taking the large roof and headwall above its traverse. Follow *Siege Engine* to the thread. Arrange good Cams in the roof. Make a very powerful stretch across the roof to gain the short flake-crack on the lip (protection). From the top of the crack, make a hard lunge (crux) to reach the slabs. Climb easily up the slabs above to finish. Well protected and excellent 8a+ climbing.

Isinglas   40m   E7 6b ***. Iain Small. 2017.
An excellent varied climb taking the large flange feature in the centre of the wall,

left of *Ardanfreaky*. Climb a delicate slab to reach the roof at the base of the flange. Undercut rightwards to reach a welcome peg runner (crucial wire above). Make a hard move over the bulge and follow the corner/ramp with slightly less difficulty to its top. Move right, then up under the large roof, then step left with a technical move to reach a jug in the break at the left edge of the roof. Make hard technical moves to get established on the slab above (crux) and continue easily to a belay at a flake on the heathery ledge above.

The Braes of Balquither   50m   E7/8 6c ***. Iain Small. Jul 2017.
Excellent climbing taking the orange streak in the bulging wall above the start of *Wild Mountain Thyme*. Only just adequately protected. Climb the first 5m of *Wild Mountain Thyme* and arrange protection. Make a hard move up and blindly place a crucial small cam in an undercut. Continue directly with difficulty to reach less steep ground and a good break. Climb the featured wall directly above to reach a belay on the terraces at the top.

CREAGAN NAN NEAD:
Aenbharr   50m   E6 6a **. Jules Lines, Dave Cuthbertson. 24 Jun 2018.
An inescapable and very serious climb up the centre of the slab. Climb onto the ledge and from its centre stretch for a pocket and make a committing move to get stood in it. Pad dangerously up the slab to gain a grey incut, step right and up to the vein. Place a Camalot 0.4 and continue directly above this on good holds to the ledge. Continue up the rib as for *Niamh*.

Notes: Jules Lines has straightened several routes, also thought one or two stars at most (but still good).

Fionn: Climb to the nubbin, rock onto it and go up to the pocket, rejoining *Fionn* at the flake.

Niamh: Slightly straightened. From the three pockets, climb up to the break and get small Cams in the letterbox. Climb directly up to better pockets and the pegmatite vein.

Oisin: Go direct from the 2.5 Friend to the prominent flake at E5 6a.

HUNTLY'S CAVE:
The Otherside   12m   E2 5c. Ted Collins, Martin Collins. 9 May 2018.
On the other side of the stream from the main crag is a small buttress with an obvious crack and a small roof at half-height. Climb the crack with well protected crux moves past the roof. Traverse left just before the top to abseil off a pine. Some hollow rock at the start.

CREAG TIRIBEG:
The Black Throat   12m   Severe 4a. Iain Thow. 27 June 2018.
Climb the black streak up the middle of the crag. Only worthwhile in a drought.

DUNTELCHAIG, Seventy Foot Wall:
Elisha Grays   15m   E5 6b *. Steve Perry, Jules Lines. 17 Jun 2018.
Immediately right from the start of *Seventy Foot Wall*, follow a crack which continues through the overhanging headwall above. The headwall is climbed via

the crack and arete, and has nasty fall potential, although it can be protected by two RP zeros (crux placing).

BEN NEVIS, AONACHS, CREAG MEAGAIDH

BEN NEVIS, Tower Ridge, East Flank:
Optimists' Arete 150m V,6 *. Steve Holmes, Ken Applegate. 15 Nov 2017.
Start 3m right of the steep wall and blunt arete just left of *Upper Tower Cascade RH*.
1. 30m Climb cracked blocks and a large offwidth flake to steep walls interspersed with small ledges before belaying under a short left-trending fist crack jammed with chockstones.
2. 30m Make a very exposed step down and left regaining the arete. Climb sustained cracks for 20m to reach easier ground.
3. 50m Climb the faint fault-line to the right gaining a cracked wall.
4. 40m Finish up stepped chimneys to finish 10m left of *Tower Ridge*.

Frosty's Vigil VIII,8. Greg Boswell, Guy Robertson, Adam Russell. 6 Mar 2017.
Pitches 1 & 2 of *Angry Chair* (SMCJ 2013), finishing up the top pitch of *Piece Maker* (SMCJ 2015).

Pinnacle Buttress of the Tower:
Infinity Condition 110m IV,5. Robin Clothier, Simon Richardson. 29 Mar 2018.
A parallel line to an unnamed route (Small-Richardson, Mar 2013).
1. 60m Start 50m left of *Fatal Error* and climb an awkward right-slanting ramp to easier ground that leads up to the first terrace on Pinnacle Buttress of the Tower. Cross the terrace and climb a short left-trending gully to a belay on the right-slanting ramp of the Small-Richardson.
2. 50m Continue left then right, zigzagging through steep walls to gain a broad gully that exits on the left crest of the buttress (junction with *Pincer*). From here, follow *Pincer* to join *Tower Ridge* at the foot of the Great Tower in another three pitches.

Moulin Rouge 270m VI,6. Simon Richardson, Sophie Grace Chappell. 20 Mar 2018.
A good mixed route between *Pinnacle Buttress Direct* and *Pinnacle Buttress Right-Hand*. Low in the grade.
1. 50m Start as for *Pinnacle Buttress Direct* and climb an icy diagonal ramp to where the icefall steepens. Take the right branch (sometimes climbed on *Pinnacle Buttress Direct* but depends on how the ice has formed), then continue right along a diagonal terrace (hidden from below) to near its end.
2. 50m Climb straight up, cross the major horizontal terrace and climb the groove system in the well defined rib to the right of *Pinnacle Buttress Direct*. Pass two steep sections and belay below a steep wall with a left-trending corner on the left.
3. 50m Climb the corner to gain the crest and follow this to the terrace below the Great Tower.
4. 50m Move up to Great Tower headwall.
5. 40m Climb the lower section of *Rotten Chimney* and then follow the Western Traverse to a ledge.

6. 30m Step left, and climb the inset groove on the right side of the rib defining the right side of *Rotten Chimney* to the summit of The Great Tower.

The Comb:
Mr Fahrenheit   55m   E7 6b ***. Dave MacLeod, Iain Small (both led). 27 Jun 2018.
A pitch of contrast with a serious lower slab and sustained but well protected upper half. It takes the dark brown slab and wall at the left side of The Comb's front face, joining *Don't Die of Ignorance* near the end of its crux pitch. Start in the centre of the immaculate lower slab. Climb on edges to a welcome Cam slot at 8m. Continue boldly up and slightly left to the foot of a small ramp (poor wire and bat-hook runner). Go up and left to the rib, then back right and up to ledges and good protection. Step right into a small corner and climb this to just before the roof at its top. Swing right onto the vertical wall and make a hard move to access the excellent finger crack. Follow this with sustained interest to better holds pulling on the slab grooves above. Continue directly to join the last few metres of *Don't Die of Ignorance* and belay as for that route in a recess below a long chimney. Descend by abseil or continue via much easier terrain above to the plateau.

Don't Stop Me Now   55m   E6 6b. Iain Small, Murdo Jamieson (both led). 30 Jun 2018.
The impressive left-facing corner that bounds the right side of the wall taken by the previous route. Sustained technical bridging with the crux high up. From the sloping shelf, climb easier ground to the base of the corner. Climb the corner, pulling out left at a first roof to gain a good foot ledge. Continue up the increasingly technical corner to pull out left round a second small roof (gear strenuous to place) to a ledge. Finish up the awkward final corner to an in-situ abseil point.

South Trident Buttress:
Tempest Corners   320m   VI,6. Robin Clothier, Simon Richardson. 18 Mar 2018.
Good mixed climbing up the wall between *The Copenhagen Interpretation* and *Joyful Chimneys*. Start on the left side of the long narrow rib (the original line of *Joyful Chimneys* climbs the groove on the right side of the rib).
1. 50m Climb the groove to the left of the rib to join the initial snow bay of *The Copenhagen Interpretation*.
2. 20m Move round the top of rib on mixed ground to belay below a series of left-stepping corners that cut through the steep wall above.
3. 60m Climb the corners past two difficult steps to their end. Continue up a snow slope to steeper mixed ground that is cut by two parallel gully systems.
4. 60m   Move across to the left-hand gully system (*The Copenhagen Interpretation* follows the gully to the right) and follow it to a good platform below a steep right-facing corner to the right of the edge of *Pinnacle Arete*.
5. 30m Climb the corner and exit on easier ground at the top of the middle tier of South Trident Buttress (in the vicinity of the top of *The Clanger*).
6. 100m Finish up the top section of *Pinnacle Arete* to the plateau.

Càrn Dearg, North Wall:
Chasing the Ephemeral   60m   E6 6b. Iain Small. Martin McKenna. 2 Jul 2018.
Climbs the immaculate steep wall just left of *The Shroud*. A long pitch on

Iain Small on FA of Mr Fahrenheit, E7 6b, Comb Gully Buttress, Ben Nevis.
Photo: Dave MacLeod.

Iain Small on FA of Don't Stop Me Now, E6 6b, Comb Gully Buttress, Ben Nevis.
Photo: Murdoch Jamieson.

beautifully clean, water washed rock that was climbed on-sight. Probably best done during a protracted heat wave! Scramble up grassy ramps and walls to a good grassy ledge immediately below the wall and to the left of the wet gully that forms the start of *Harrison's Route*.

Climb up a short wall, move right and up to a spike and short corner. Take the corner and move out leftwards on sloping holds to gain a foot ledge. Head diagonally right to a large corner flake and climb this to a sloping ramp on top. Arrange Cams above and make hard moves up and left to gain the shallow right-facing corner system that leads to the left end of a long diagonal roof. Climb the finger-crack directly above, with increasing difficulty, to reach a niche. Pull steeply out of this and follow slabbier ground to the big grassy terrace and a large flake on the left. Abseil from this (in-situ cord and screwgate).

Raeburn's Buttress:
The Good Friday Agreement   320m   VII,7. Iain Small, Simon Richardson. 30 Mar 2018.
A direct line up the rib to the left of *Intermediate Gully*.
1. 40m As for pitch 1 of *Raeburn's Buttress/Boomer's Requiem* to the bifurcation. Belay on the left.
2. 50m Climb *Raeburn's Buttress Original Route* past the cave to the chockstone. Instead of traversing right continue up the steep chimney directly above to a good ledge.
3. 40m   Step left and pull into the chimney-gully splitting the left rib of *Intermediate Gully*. Climb up to where the gully steepens and continue up a steep chimney-line past three chockstones before exiting right up a right-slanting fist crack. Move up and left across the *Girdle Traverse* ledge to belay below a steep wide crack slicing through the buttress above.
4. 50m Climb the crack that rises in three distinct sections to more moderate ground and a belay on the crest.
5. 40m Continue up the crest on helpful blocky ground before skirting the final steepening by following a narrow shelf on the right.
6. and 7. 100m Continue up snow and short mixed sections to the summit of Carn Dearg NW.

North Wall of Castle Ridge:
Note: Guy Robertson & Adam Russell freed *Alchemist* at VII,8 on 1 Apr 2018.

Wanderings of Mr Sea   295m   IV,4. Robin Clothier, Stuart McFarlane. 3 Apr 2018.
1. 60m Climb pitch 1 of *Last Day in Purgatory*.
2. 55m Move up and right to gain a shelf beneath steep rock; traverse right towards a chimney.
3. 60m Climb the steep chimney to gain a ramp leading to the edge of the buttress (exposed). Move up to belay.
4. 60m Follow grooves above beneath a steep chimney.
5. 60m Traverse 20m right and climb a steep corner to gain snow slopes above.

MAMORES, Mullach nan Coirean (NN 135 656):
Disco Corner   80m   IV,5. Gary Campbell, Nathan Adam. 29 Nov 2017.
On the left side of the main crag, following a line close to *Captain Caveman* at

the start, before breaking left near the top. Good, well protected climbing on the upper section.

1. 20m Start as for *Captain Caveman* to the first cave, but move left and follow snow and turf before trending right to belay in the second cave.

2. 15m Step out onto a left-trending ramp via a short corner (bold/poorly protected) before reaching easier ground and moving right to a large ledge.

3. 45m Gain a higher ledge, move left and climb the obvious corner-crack to stand on top of a pinnacle. Pull onto the wall and follow turfy ledges leftwards to easier ground, which is climbed to the top.

Coire Dearg:

The principal crag in Coire Dearg faces north and has a very steep bottom section at 850m. On the approach from Glen Nevis the left side of this is masked by another more broken buttress to the north. Between the two and starting higher up is a short buttress with a large obvious gendarme feature near the top; this is called the *Gendarme Buttress of Coire Dearg* in Noel Williams' Scrambles in Lochaber. The route climbs the edge of the buttress in the foreground on the approach.

Mistaken Identity   120m   III,4. Jon Sanders, Alan Halewood. 28 Nov 2017.

From the toe of this buttress, scramble over bouldery terrain to where the crest steepens. Climb an awkward flake filled groove on the left and then step back onto a ledge on the crest. Step up right delicately or more positively left but regain the crest and easier angled ground. Follow short walls and corners as close to the crest as possible at about Grade II to descend a small tower near the top of the ridge.

CREAG MEAGAIDH, Coire Choille-rais, Aisre-chaim:

Eighties Rules   130m   V,7. Simon Richardson, Mark Robson, Roger Webb. 4 Jan 2018.

1. 30m Start up and left of *Cat Burglar* and climb turf left of a blunt rib. Step left below a roof after 15m and move up steps to the foot of a steep impending corner.

2. 30m Climb the corner (crux), then continue up the ramp to the right before taking the natural line left that leads to a terrace.

3. 30m Step left and climb the right-trending groove to the headwall. Move left under this and climb the bulging chimney-slot in the corner above to where the angle eases.

4. 40m Finish easily up the crest of the buttress as for the other routes.

CREAG MEAGAIDH, Coire Ardair, Pinnacle Buttress:

The Moth Direct   360m   VIII,8 **. Iain Small, Helen Rennard, Dave MacLeod. 4 Mar 2018.

A direct start and finish to *The Moth* making the overall route more sustained and more logical. Start 20m down and right of the parent route, below a left-facing corner capped by a roof.

1. 30m Climb the corner, then traverse left under the roof on thin ice to gain a useful incut block (good protection). Pull over the roof to join the turfy traverse of *The Moth* pitch 1 and move up to the belay.

2. 40m Climb the left-facing corner to a roof and span left using thin ice and continue to a short steep corner. Bridge up this and move out right to a difficult mantel. Move diagonally back left on steep turf to reach a cracked ledge.

3. 50m Move to the left end of the ledge and access a left-facing corner forming the edge of the huge flake. Move up this, then diagonally right on turf, before climbing the steep turfy wall above.
4. 80m Follow ice and turf (common with *The Midge Direct*) to eventually reach the large ledge system. Move slightly left to an in-situ peg under a small roof and belay. Split this pitch if ice is suitable for making an anchor.
5. 50m Step right, climb a steep turfy wall and continue to the next ledge system below the final barrier wall (*The Moth* escapes right from here).
6. 50m Climb the steep wall directly above the belay to gain an easier but poorly protected turfy groove that leads to a large shelf on the edge of the buttress. Walk right along this for about 10m to a left-facing spike.
7. 60m Mount the spike and climb easily above, just right of the arete to a small cairn on the summit of the Pinnacle.

Paradise Lost 170m VII,8 ***. Iain Small, Andy Inglis. 24 Feb 2018.
Excellent ice and mixed climbing on the buttress left of *Smith's Gully*, adjacent to *Last Day in Paradise*.
1. 50m Start up the first pitch of *Last Day in Paradise* (left-facing corner for 10m, then traverse right onto the large icy slab) then climb the icy slab direct for 15m to steep ice, before climbing up and leftwards for some 15m to a rocky rib and belay at the top of the slab.
2. 40m Step left and climb the helpful, overhanging left-facing corner and roof past an icicle to a mossy left-slanting corner and narrow ice smeared ramp-line. Climb the ramp-line and corner to easier ground, and continue up the snow slope to a belay below the final barrier wall.
3. 50m Traverse right (probably joining *Last Day in Paradise*) and climb the icy central fault to an overhung niche. Step left and forge straight up the steep ice to glory and the final snow slopes.
4. A further 20-30m of easy ground remains to the plateau.

Paradise Lost, Independent Finish 100m VI,7. Simon Richardson, Guy Robertson. 12 Mar 2018.
1. 50m From the belay on *Appolyon Ledge* where *Paradise Lost* rejoins *Last Day in Paradise*, traverse 10m left to gain a short steep gully-groove. Climb this with difficulty and exit onto an exposed crest overlooking *Ritchie's Gully*. Follow this to a snow slope and good belay.
2. 50m Finish up and left on the right flank of *Ritchie's Gully* to gain the plateau.

Note: *Eye Candy* – Pitch 2 is only 30m (not 40m as noted in existing description), so with a 70m rope pitches 2 and 3 can be run together.

GLEN COE

BUACHAILLE ETIVE MOR, The Chasm:
Note: Ewan Lyons has sent a pitch by pitch description of *The Chasm* with photos of each pitch.
Note: Lawrie Brand & Neil Kerr climbed the direct finish to *The Chasm* at VI,5 on 20 Mar 2018. Looking at their pictures, Andy Nisbet doubts it has ever been done at IV,4 and therefore whether it has ever been done.

Central Buttress, South Face:
Poker 85m HVS **. Michael Barnard, John MacLeod. 24 Jul 2017.
A fine companion to *Pegleg*. Start as for that route.
1. 45m 4c Go up the left-trending weakness, then move right to below a slight
rib in the wall above (6m right of the *Pegleg* belay). Start up the rib and climb
directly up the wall to eventually reach a left-trending line of flakes; follow these
more easily and continue up to belay at a small corner which is level with the
obvious undercut roof on the right (Friend 3 & 3.5). Excellent bold climbing.
2. 40m 4c Step right to gain the crack just left of the undercut roof (*Waterslide
Gully?*). Follow the crack until possible to traverse into the white groove on the
right. Climb the groove and continue directly up the corner and crack above.

Poker, Direct Start 20m E3 5b **. Michael Barnard (unsec). 24 Jul 2017.
Start just right of the left-trending weakness of *Pegleg* and climb clean water
washed rock leading directly to the slight rib on pitch 1 (unprotected after the first
metre or so).

Note: *Gravity and Grace* was thought to be one star, although starting up
Pontoon for 2 pitches, then stepping left, would be better. 50m E2 5b.

D Gully Buttress:
Marmalade 80m VI,6 *. Michael Barnard, John MacLeod. 7 Jan 2018.
As for summer (two 40m pitches, crux at the start).

Notes from Michael Barnard: *Alpen* – the cave belay can be reached in one
35m pitch.
The diagram on p56 of the Glen Coe guide is a bit misleading as it gives the
impression that *Alpen* goes straight up from where it's marked, when really it
comes up from the right. Also the routes on p62 are in the wrong order – though
the summer routes (*Toast*, *Marmalade*, *Cornflake*) all cross *Alpen* at mid-height,
they start to its left (as does *Special K*).

BUACHAILLE ETIVE MOR, Crowberry Ridge North-East Face:
Dingle VII,7. Tim Miller, Calum Hicks. 4 Feb 2018.
By the summer route.

The Orphan VII,8. Steve Holmes, Duncan Curry, Hannah Evans. 14 Dec 2017
By the summer route.

The Holy Grail 160m IX,11. Guy Robertson, Greg Boswell. 11 Jan 2018.
One of the best at Grade IX in Scotland – brilliant, very well protected hard
climbing and should be in condition most seasons.
1. and 2. 30m, 20m Climb *Raven's Gully* to above the first big chockstone, where
a crack-line breaks up on the left.
3. 30m Climb the sustained cracks to belay at an obvious spike and junction with
Guerdon Grooves (in-situ sling).
4. 30m Climb directly (as for *Guerdon Grooves*) over the steep bulge but where
that route goes right follow the obvious right-facing groove up into the base of
the Great Cave.
5. 20m An unlikely pitch! Climb delicately up to gain and climb the big off-width

crack through the roof of the Great Cave, to belay in a much smaller cave right on the very lip.
6. 30m Continue up the very steep crack-line (common with *Shibboleth True Finish*) to easier ground.

BUACHAILLE ETIVE BEAG:
Gully 2   II/III. Dean Roberts, Mike Kelly, Tunnell Morgan. 25 Jan 2008.
A winter ascent of a gully first named by T. Graham Brown & party after a summer ascent. The second gully from the left following a stream before climbing right to a snow field.

AONACH DUBH WEST FACE, E Buttress:
Prophets of Pragmatism   45m   E8 6b **. Iain Small, Dave MacLeod (both led). 12 Jun 2018.
A serious pitch with poor protection until high up, but good climbing, cutting through the long traverse of *Prophet of Purism*. Start up *Salome* for 7m and arrange runners. Climb rightwards across the wall with difficulty to a good hold and dubious runners. Move up the wall to gain large sidepull pockets and follow these (avoiding a loose flake) to reach jugs and assortment of runners (Cams in pockets and poor wires). Step up and left and make hard moves up the bulging wall (crux) to a welcome pocket that takes a good Camalot 3. Continue up to a further pocket (Camalot 4 and wire) and then move right, then up on small holds, then back left to a break (good wire). Move up and left on good holds to gain the ramp of *Big Top*. Follow *Big Top* to the belay ledge.

STOB COIRE NAN LOCHAIN:
En Garde   IX,9. Murdo Jamieson, Iain Small. 16 Dec 2017.
By the summer route, except pitch 1 was extended by continuing up the groove to a ledge below the off-width.

The following three routes start from a belay on the right side of *SC Gully* above its main difficulties. Alternatively, the same point can be reached by a 50m abseil down the upper right wall of *SC Gully*.

SC Chimney   50m   V,6. Peter Davies, Helen Rennard. 6 Mar 2017.
A prominent chimney high on the right wall of *SC Gully* easily seen from the corrie floor.
1. 40m Climb steep snow on the right wall of *SC Gully* for 15m to the bottom of a large right-facing corner. Climb the chimney in the corner's left wall and to a good ledge.
2. 10m Step down and left from the ledge into a square-cut recess that leads to the top.

Consolation Corner   45m   V,6. Peter Davies, Helen Rennard. 1 Jan 2018.
1. 15m Follow *SC Chimney* to the bottom of the large right-facing corner.
2. 30m On the right wall of the corner, a short thin crack leads to the bottom of a shallow chimney. Climb the chimney and continue direct up a right-facing corner above.

Dig for Victory   45m   VI,7. Peter Davies, Donie O'Sullivan. 7 Jan 2018.
The centre of the rib to the left of *SC Chimney*.

1. 35m Climb a steep crack, then a shallow right-facing corner in the centre of the rib to belay on the good ledge as for *SC Chimney*.
2. 10m As for *SC Chimney*. The short cracked wall directly above the ledge would give a good independent finish.

CHURCH DOOR BUTTRESS:
The Lost Arrow 100m X,10. Greg Boswell, Guy Robertson. 11 Dec 2017.
The first winter ascent of the main front face of the crag provides an unusually sustained and exacting climb. Protection is generally excellent, with the exception of the off-width chimney groove. High in the grade.
1. 25m Climb *Lost Arrow* pitch 1.
2. 15m Go up the summer line a short way, then break hard right under the roof crack to climb the precarious wall to its right, before traversing back left to belay on the summer line just above the lip.
3. 20m Step left again and climb the dirty left-hand crack to join the summer route where that swings right at the sloping ledge. Continue direct up cracks to a roof which is passed on the right to belay as for summer below the overhanging off-width at the base of the main corner.
4. 20m Climb the hideous off-width chimney-groove to rejoin the corner which is followed to a hanging belay at the end of the traverse right to the flake.
5. 20m Climb the summer line to the top.

Dark Angel VII,8. Matt Helliker, Nick Bullock, Pete Whittaker. 3 Feb 2018.
A fantastic route up the centre of the tower between *Crypt Route* and *Flake Route* to the top of the right-hand side of the Arch. Cross *West Chimney* and continue direct between *Un Poco Loco* and *Knights Templar* to the top of the buttress.
1. 20m Climb from the foot of the buttress up the left-hand facing off-width to a roof. Step left into a niche and a hanging belay.
2. 40m Follow the crack left for 5m, before stepping right through a overlap to enter the bottom of a splinter crack (crux). Continue up the flared crack to its end with poor feet to pull out left onto a ledge. Continue through the overlaps above to the right of the Arch and belay under an arching rightward line of weakness.
3. 50m Pull steeply up, trending right into the bottom of a hanging groove. Pull through the groove and continue up leftwards following a ramp and steep steps to the top.

AONACH EAGACH, Am Bodach:
At NN169 580 there are two buttresses. They can be accessed easily by approaching up Coire an Ruigh, then turning left (south-west) at the Bealach at 816m, and walking for 5mins to their base, 1hr 15mins.

Bodach Buttress 100m III,4. Andy Hogarth, Andy Nelson. 30 Dec 2017.
The obvious ridge, climbed in four pitches with good stances. Possible to include trickier steps.

Òganach Chimney 60m III,4. Andy Hogarth, Andy Nelson. 30 Dec 2017.
The obvious deep chimney on the buttress nearer the bealach. It has a tricky move under an enormous chockstone, that leads into a bomb bay. Step right to gain an easy groove that exits onto the other side of the buttress. Walk off or continue up scrambling terrain to the top.

CLACH LEATHAD, Summit Cliff:

Gelato 160m IV,5. Andy Nisbet, Ali Rose. 2 Apr 2018.
An ice line on the right side of the left buttress of the cliff. Start easily trending right up an obvious break to reach the side wall of a fault. Pull through a bulge, then go diagonally left to reach a ledge. Traverse back right to the right-hand of twin faults. Go up this to a steep wall on the right (55m). Move back left into the icy fault and climb this to a rock buttress in snow (40m). Climb steep snow to the top (65m).

Scarface 140m IV,5. Andy Nisbet, Jonathan Preston. 26 Mar 2018.
The left branch of the V ice lines (*Eclipse* is the right branch). A steep start leads to an easier groove and a belay on the left (35m). Return right and climb an iced corner to easier ground. Continue up an ice bulge, short groove and snow to a belay (45m). Steep snow to the top, the cornice being small at the top left of the face (60m).

Skyblind 150m V,6. Andy Nisbet, Sarah Sigley. 31 Mar 2018.
The buttress right of *Holme Moss*. Climb turfy ground centrally to below the steep section of the buttress (25m). Start steeply up the centre of this, then move left up steps to gain a ledge. Traverse back right and climb a recess to crux moves over a capping wide crack. Move up to a good belay in a corner below an overhang (45m). Step back down to move left on to easier ground. Go up and left to the isolated buttress (40m). A diagonal line left gained a break in the cornice (40m).

CLACH LEATHAD, Sròn nam Forsair:

Some 300m left (east) of the Summit Cliff and on the north side of Sron nam Forsair ridge is this section of cliff.

Maundy Buttress 120m IV,4. Sophie Grace Chappell, Andy Nisbet, Sarah Sigley. 29 Mar 2018.
At the left end of this section of cliff is this buttress. Start just inside the gully on its right and climb up on to a ramp which leads right into a shallow groove. Follow this to the crest and up to an easing in angle (60m). Follow the vague crest to the top (60m).

Maundy Gully 100m IV,5. Sophie Grace Chappell, Andy Nisbet, Sarah Sigley. 29 Mar 2018.
Close to the right end of this section of cliff is this long groove. Start just left of a steep ice step and mixed climb until above the step (or climb the step, harder). The subsequent groove curves left and steepens. Move right below the steepest section and climb a short ramp and steep mixed ground before returning to the groove above its steep section (60m). Climb steep snow to the top (40m).
Note: A direct ascent of the groove would require ice and good conditions.

CREACH BHEINN, Zeppelin Face (Ardgour):

No Quarter 110m IV,5 *. Steve Kennedy, Andy MacDonald. 7 Feb 2018.
The narrow gully immediately right of *Bring it on Home* (SMCJ 2015). Probably easier in a heavier build up. The description and length excludes the approach up the easy lower section of the gully.
1. 55m From the point where the gully deepens, climb to a small cave with a chockstone which is turned by a short wall on the left. Continue to a steep groove

with the assistance of an accommodating crack on the right wall (crux).
2. 55m Continue up easier slopes into a snow bowl. Move out rightwards to finish.

BEINN MHICCEDIDH, North-East Corrie (Moidart):
Arabian Nights   60m   III,4. Steve Kennedy, Andy MacDonald. 10 Dec 2017.
The open groove approximately 50m above and left of the lowest point of the
buttress and just left of a deep groove (*Perfumed Garden* starts right of the lowest
point – see SMCJ 2016). Easy ground leads to the base of a right-slanting groove
(10m). Follow the groove on thin ice and finish up easier mixed ground (50m).

Pink Pearl   55m   III. Steve Kennedy, Andy MacDonald. 10 Dec 2017.
The disjointed groove system starting about 10m left of *Arabian Nights*. A short
groove leads to a big spike at 10m. Climb the groove above to a steep wall, step
up left and continue to a large jammed block. Pull steeply over the block then
move right (behind the block) and climb a wide crack rightwards to an edge.
Finish up leftwards via a further groove.

SGÙRR GHIUBHSACHAIN, North Buttress (Loch Shiel):
Below and right (west) of the summit are a number of easy angled, north facing
buttresses split by wide gullies. The steepest rightmost buttress (north to north-
west facing) is bounded on the right by a wide slabby bowl. This route starts up
a prominent wide ramp running up the right side of the lower part of the buttress.

Bestial Devotion   110m   III **. Steve Kennedy, Andy MacDonald. 20 Jan 2018.
1. 60m Follow the ramp until it narrows and bends left to form a gully containing
a large chockstone. Move right onto the buttress edge, avoiding the chockstone,
and climb the gully above. At the top of the gully, a nice through route (may need
clearing of snow) leads to a belay on the buttress edge.
2. 50m Finish by the easy gully and mixed ground above.

SOUTHERN HIGHLANDS

THE COBBLER, South Peak:
Punters Crack   50m   E1 5b. Tim Miller, Hugh Simons, Martin McKenna. 10
May 2017.
The direct line to *Deadman's Groove*, probably rarely dry. Start as for *Deadman's
Groove*. After the initial corner climb up to the grotty roof, through this towards
a second roof and past some dodgy looking blocks. Finish up the corner back into
Deadman's Groove.

Winter: VIII,9. Martin McKenna, Tim Miller. 15 Dec 2017.
An obvious overhanging crack from the first pitch of *North Wall Groove* linking
into the top corner of *Deadman's Groove*.

Note: Dave MacLeod re-cleaned *Ruskoline* on 24 Jun 2018, and climbed it. Now
**.

Colander-head Corner   100m   V,6 *. Calum Hicks, Morna Baillie. 29 Dec 2017.
Located on the right side of the band of rock to the right of *Chockstone Gully*.

Topo provided. Best accessed by dropping down the small col off the north side of the north peak for 100m. Start below the short obvious open book corner.
1. 20m The difficult pitch. Climb the obvious corner with a hard start up to chockstones and easier climbing.
2. and 3. 80m Easy ground leads to the top of Great Gully Buttress.

Centre Peak:
Summit Gully 120m I/II *. Graham Uney, James Pierce. 29 Mar 2018.
The obvious snow gully that finishes at a rocky notch immediately left of the summit block. Climb the gully, go through the notch onto a rock ledge. Traverse the ledge beneath the summit block, and step down at its far end. Almost certainly climbed before, but unrecorded.

Sugar Walls:
Comical Corner 20m IV,5. Ole Kemi, Jeremy Morris. 6 Feb 2018.
Follow the summer line, an obvious corner to the top. Its low altitude means conditions can be tricky, but when in condition, it provides a good option for a short second route of the day or as an approach to the big terrace below North Peak and Great Gully Buttress.

No Pro Wall 15m Severe. Ole Kemi. 17 Jul 2017.
The wall right of *Comical Corner*. Sparse gear, but going left to *Comical Corner* for gear is possible low down. Climb up to a wide grass ledge, and then either walk off right or finish up *Comical Corner* on the left.

Some Pro Edge 15m V.Diff. Ole Kemi. 17 Jul 2017.
An edge and wide crack with a high chockstone right of *Comical Corner* and *No Pro Wall*. Not much gear low down.

BEINN AN LOCHAIN:
Black & White 60m V,5 *. Guy Robertson, Greg Boswell. Jan 2018.
The obvious well-defined arete right of *Back Alley*.
1. 30m Climb direct through the lower bulge right of *Back Alley*. Continue up slightly right by a short steep wall to gain the edge which is followed up and left to a belay by large blocks.
2. 30m Make an exposed traverse left then go back up onto the edge which is followed in a fine position to easier ground.

ARDVORLICH, Quarterdome:
Alan Cassidy & Rob Sutton climbed the *Quarterdome* project on p56 of the Sport guide in May 2018 and felt it to be 8a+ **. The 6b described doesn't seem to make a lot of sense, or at very least needs some more bolts to make it safe!

BEINN AN DOTHAIDH, North-East Corrie:
L'Apéritif 40m III,4/5. Ken Applegate, Ryan Ras. 7 Mar 2018.
The crest of the small cone-shaped hillock (p302 Arran, Arrochar and the Southern Highlands guide), was surprisingly good. Start at a small sapling and climb easy ground to gain a short steep groove. Climb this and trend right, then back left to climb a short steepening.

BEINN UDLAIDH:

Jump the Train   170m   IV,4. John Higham, Ruth Love. 11 Dec 2017.

This route provides a more direct start to *Sidestep* and an alternative finish to *Hobo*. Start 10m left of *Sidestep* on the left-hand edge of the bay which has the deep chimney approach to *Organ-Pipe Wall* on its right-hand side.

Climb with difficulty a short steep prow, turning small roofs and bulges until easier ground is reached. Trend leftwards for about 20m as the route converges with *Sidestep* to belay in a steep corner. Now trend diagonally rightwards to cross a snowfield and enter the wide gully of *Hobo* to belay where it steepens abruptly. Exit left (*Hobo* exits right) and follow an excellent left-trending groove to the summit snowfields.

BEINN CHUIRN, Coire na Saobhaidhe:

Prospectors   80m   IV,4. Martin Holland, Sharon Tinsley, Ian McIntosh. 30 Mar 2018.

To the left of the main central gully is another large gully. Left of this the crag is north facing and fairly continuous. About a third of the way along the crag left of the gully it changes in steepness at an obvious wall / right-facing corner. Start down from and just left of this.

1. 55m Move easily up to gain the bottom of the wall/corner and follow this before breaking right over turf to a ramp coming up from the right. Cross the ramp and make a steep move up to gain a turf groove continuing in the same line as the lower section. Follow the turf groove and corners moving slightly left higher up to near a wedged flake. An excellent long pitch, which could be split at optional belays.
2. 25m Move right from the wedged flake and back left up easy ground to the top.

Lucky Strike   115m   III. Martin W. Holland. 6 Mar 2018.

Start at the lowest rocks just left of the main gully. Climb easy ground over a couple of steps to reach the upper buttress between the main gully and the next gully left. Climb the centre of the buttress initially moving right then back left though a short chimney notch.

Gold Star Start   25m   III,4. Martin Holland, Sharon Tinsley, Ian McIntosh. 30 Mar 2018.

An ice line can form on the centre right of the lower tier directly below *Silver Star*. This is steeper than it looks and would make a good direct start to *Silver Star*.

BEN LOMOND:

Opinionator   120m   IV,5. Robin Clothier, Ian Dempster, Stuart McFarlane. 25 Feb 2018.

Starts between *Endrick Corner* and *Rowardennan Rib*.

1. 30m Climb turfy ground up and right to belay in recess on the square rib.
2. 50m Move left along a ledge to an overlap, then follow a groove above heading for a corner parallel with *Endrick Corner*. Where it steepens, belay on a ledge on the right.
3. 40m Step left onto slab and pull steeply into a groove above (crux). Follow the groove to the top.

Note: David Webster thinks *Solo Buttress* and *Lomond Delight* (Arran, Arrochar and the Southern Highlands guide p350) are the same route.

INVERARNAN:
Drover Falls II/III. Robert Giddy, David Webster. 12 Dec 2017.
On the Allt Arnan starting at NN 3125 1870. After a deep freeze a number of good slabby icefalls may form on the watercourse and can be viewed from the Drovers Inn car park. The first main pitch is 5mins walk from the road. If not fully formed, follow the river up for a further 10mins or so to a roughly 15m high steep ice slide which forms more readily and can be climbed by a number of lines. Between the two main pitches a number of smaller ice steps can also be climbed, and a scramble up the frozen river bed is fun in its own right. The crux of the route may be avoiding falling through thin ice into a plunge pool!
Note: The first pitch was later climbed direct by David Webster on 3 Mar 2018.

BEINN HEASGARNICH, Coire Heasgarnich:
White Lion 110m IV,4. George Allan, John Thomas. 20 Mar 2018.
Four icefalls form on the lower section of cliff right of *Cub Gully*. Climb the third icefall to the right of the gully to belay at the base of a groove in the upper buttress (40m). Climb this and continue directly via walls and corners (50m). Move up right and climb a corner to reach easy ground (20m). A good route.

Androcles 140m V,5. Roger Webb, Simon Richardson. 29 Nov 2017.
An exciting route through the headwall in the centre of the cliff.
1. 50m Follow the open gully system of *The Rambler* to the first terrace.
2. 40m Continue up the right-slanting gully of *The Rambler* to the second terrace beneath the headwall. Cross the terrace to the right then follow a slanting ramp system left to a shallow cave on the right.
3. 30m Make a difficult horizontal left traverse for 5m, then climb delicately up and back right to enter a groove directly above the belay. Climb this to where the angle eases and a small ledge on the left.
4. 20m Continue more easily up grooves to the top.

King of the Jungle 140m VI,5. Simon Richardson , Sophie Grace Chappell. 25 Jan 2018.
A serious and more direct version of *Androcles*.
1. 50m Climb the broad rib of *Simba* to the first terrace,
2. 30m Trend diagonally left and climb an undercut groove just right of an arete to reach the second terrace.
3. 50m Cross the terrace and climb thin ice to reach the end of the traverse of *Androcles*. Instead of trending back right, continue straight up the groove above to a belay where the angle eases.
4. 10m Finish up the groove to the top.

LOWLAND OUTCROPS AND GALLOWAY HILLS

BEN A'AN:
Park at the Ben A'an car park and walk up the path for about 20mins to a crossroads. Turn right and continue along the path for about 300m. Look up to

the left for a large slab. The slab is easy angled and faces south-east with a pleasant open outlook. Rock is a rough schist.

Lazy Fault 12m Diff *. Michael Limonci, Marco Limonci. 5 Jun 2018.
NN 5101 0787. Start at the lowest point on the slab. Climb the large crack on good holds straight to the top. A variation exists near the top to follow another short crack to the right.

Trad 11m V.Diff. Marco Limonci, Danny Flynn. 12 Jun 2018.
A V shaped slab 3m left of *Lazy Fault*. Climb a crack trending right. Continue straight up past an obvious triangular recess.

Givemepeace 11m Severe *. Marco Limonci, Danny Flynn. 12 Jun 2018.
On the same slab as *Trad*. Climb a thin crack up and left, then straight up the blank slab above on small holds.

Little Arete 25m V.Diff. Marco Limonci, Danny Flynn. 12 Jun 2018.
NN 5098 0790. The arete is the second crag from the left edge of the obvious large slab. Start at the lowest point, quite steep at first then easing to a small sloping ledge, then up another short and steep wall; the angle then easing off.

DUMBARTON ROCK:
Note: Alan Cassidy added a new 7a right-hand exit to *Persistence of Vision*, called *Eurovision*.

GALLOWAY HILLS, Cauldron of the Dungeon (NX 461 852):
The Vice Squad 65m V,5 **. Stephen Reid, Andrew Fraser (alt). 9 Feb 2018.
Excellent well protected climbing up the prominent left-trending corner in the Main Buttress. Start at a corner-crack with a vertical right wall, 2m left of a crack with a square hole at 3m and 2m right of a huge block on the terrace.
1. 20m Climb the crack to an awkward exit onto a narrow turf ledge. Climb a short crack on the right to a large heather ledge and flake.
2. 25m On the wall on the left is a massive flake with a body width crack (the Vice) separating it from the main crag. Traverse easily to its right end and start thrutching. Belay on the large second ledge.
3. 20m Climb up onto a small ledge and thence with difficulty to a larger ledge. The offwidth crack above is harder than anything else on the route but is mercifully well protected and brief. Easy ground leads to the end of difficulties.

The Clints of the Spout (NX 509 667):
The corrie to the left of the crag contains several short and broken icefalls, the longest of which, *Up the Spout* (100m, II/III, Andrew Fraser, Stephen Reid, Kev Callachan, 9 Mar 2018), lies towards its right-hand side and has a good top pitch that can be climbed on its left or right.

North-East Corrie of Milldown (NX 514 844):
Fridge Buttress is the broken buttress to the right of *Better Gully* which gives long routes consisting of short hard sections with much scrambling in between. It comes into condition quite quickly but the climbs are very run out in lean conditions. Its main identifying mark is a wide, low left-slanting wall towards its right side which marks the start of *Fridge Magnate* (2011).

Frigidare 205m IV,4. Ian Dempster, Stephen Reid (alt). 10 Dec 2017.
A broad iced slab lies 20m left of the left-slanting wall. Climb the centre of this and intermittent short steps to the left end of a rock buttress (45m). Move right 3m and climb a short icy groove. Easier ground leads up rightwards to the right side of an amphitheatre made of three low buttresses (30m). Traverse left on snow and climb the icy nose of the central buttress (35m). Climb up and left to a short icy slab with overhanging rock on its left. Climb the slab (possible belay) to a snow terrace and traverse left to a spike in amongst blocks 10m below the final buttress (55m). The steep icy groove and wall above towards the right side of this buttress provides a bold hard finish (30m). Alternatively the finish of *Fridge Magnate* lies up the easier angled groove just round to the left.
Note: Due to the sudden appearance of a falling dog and subsequent rescue of a crag-bound party of walkers and dogs, only the leader completed the final pitch. The dog was not badly injured.

Doggone Gully I. Linda Biggar, John Biggar. 10 Dec 2017.
This gully is hidden high up on the right, beyond the low left-slanting wall and an obvious, heathery left-slanting fault. It can be gained by various ways and makes a reasonable descent with care.

Clifton (NX 909 573):
D.I.Y. Low Variation 15m E1 5b *. Tommy Heron, Connor Henley.
9 Sep 2017.
Climb the thin crack flanking *Red Slab* on its right to its top, then traverse right under a bulge along a horizontal crack to the arete. Bold moves gain the huge break and a finish as for *D.I.Y.*

GALLOWAY SEA-CLIFFS, Laggantalluch Head:
Shadow of Intent 25m E3 5c **. Matthew Thompson, Lauren Purkuliar. 13 May 2018.
Another steep and exciting route on this wall. Climb the obvious crack 2m left of *First Touch* to beneath the roof. Style over this on a variety of jams, jugs and nubbins to gain a position of pumpy insecurity above. Move up to meet the ramp of *First Touch*, but swing due left to jugs in a niche and finish up the easier wide crack.

MISCELLANEOUS NOTES

THE W.H. MURRAY LITERARY PRIZE

As a tribute to the late Bill Murray, whose mountain and environment writings have been an inspiration to many a budding mountaineer, the SMC have set up a modest writing prize, to be run through the pages of the Journal. The basic rules are set out below, and will be reprinted each year. The prize is run with a deadline of midnight on the last day of April each year.

The Rules:
1. There shall be a competition for the best entry on Scottish Mountaineering published in the *Scottish Mountaineering Club Journal*. The competition shall be called the 'W.H. Murray Literary Prize', hereafter called the 'Prize'.
2. The judging panel shall consist of, in the first instance, the following: The current Editor of the *SMC Journal*; The current President of the SMC; and two or three lay members, who may be drawn from the membership of the SMC. The lay members of the panel will sit for three years after which they will be replaced.
3. If, in the view of the panel, there is in any year no entry suitable for the Prize, then there shall be no award that year.
4. Entries shall be writing on the general theme of 'Scottish Mountaineering', and may be prose articles of up to approximately 3000 words in length, or shorter verse. Entries may be fictional.
5. Panel members may not enter for the competition during the period of their membership.
6. Entries must be of original, previously unpublished material. Entries should be submitted to the Editor of the *SMC Journal* by the end of April for consideration that year. Electronic contributions are preferred and should be submitted via e-mail, although double-spaced typewritten hard copies will also be accepted by post. (See Office Bearers page at end of this Journal for address etc.) Any contributor to the *SMC Journal* is entitled to exclude their material from consideration for the Prize and should so notify the Editor of this wish in advance.
7. The Prize will be a cheque for the amount £250.
8. Contributors may make different submissions in different years.
9. The decision of the panel is final.
10. Any winning entry will be announced in the *SMC Journal*, and will be published in the *SMC Journal* and on the SMC Website. Thereafter, authors retain copyright.

THE WH MURRAY LITERARY PRIZE 2018

The four judges were in complete agreement that Roger Webb's article *The Seam, The Seam* was the winner of the prize. This witty and wise account of 'thwarted – and ultimately realised – ambition' was 'self-effacing', 'well constructed', and 'evoked a nearly visceral empathy with the situation'. It's always good when a long time contributor to the *Journal* really rises to the occasion and caps years of effort with a prize-winning piece.

Among the distinctively Scottish writing this year, winter activity was prominent. Murdoch Jamieson provided a 'gripping account of hard modern mixed climbing' on Beinn Eighe. Neil Quinn contributed an 'evocative memory of step-cutting days' on Zero Gully. Curly Ross provided a 'pleasant reminiscence' of times gone by on Lochnagar. Tim Pettifer and Finlay Wild both wrote in very different veins about skiing: Pettifer's piece on various avalanche incidents was 'as enjoyable as it is instructive'. Pity the skier who fails Tim's test of avalanche awareness. Finlay's piece by contrast, which recounted a pleasant but challenging traverse of the South Cluanie hills on ski, was thought 'fresh and inspiring' and captured 'the tension of a big undertaking'. To continue the snowy theme, Andy Nisbet's explorations of Ben Hope as a winter climbing venue revealed his 'deep understanding of Scottish mountains' and particularly of how the weather can affect the ephemeral conditions. As a footnote to winter, Mike Jacob went skating with Harold Raeburn on Duddingston Loch: a delightful 'historical snippet,' well referenced and researched, which adds a facet to our understanding of Raeburn and the times he inhabited.

Away from ice and snow Richard McHardy captured the 'drama of soloing' Carnivore on Creag a' Bhancair. Robin Campbell described the climbing scene in Edinburgh in the sixties. 'Good social history' this: 'makes you feel as if you were there' with 'engaging anecdotes and tart observations'. The judges were also impressed by Donald Orr's piece on three nineteenth century Scottish artists. It was felt that Orr made 'the art come alive'. It is very pleasing to find contributors to the Journal willing to tackle the cultural history of our mountains. Bob Sharp, veteran mountain rescue expert, contributed an authoritative account of the development of the service in Scotland. This was thought 'clear and concise' and, in the current climate, 'opportune and helpful'. Noel Williams entertained with his thoughts on ageing and provided an uplifting conclusion on the cliffs of Lewis.

Finally, mention must be made of Chris Dickinson's article on the positive role which the mountains play in his struggle with depression. It was felt that, despite taking 'a couple of re-reads ... to figure out', this was a 'brave and honest' attempt to tackle a difficult subject which might also help other sufferers.

Future contenders for the Prize are reminded that their entries **must have Scottish relevance and reach the Editor by 30 April.**

SCOTTISH WINTER NOTES 2017–18

THE 2018 SCOTTISH WINTER season was excellent. The weather was consistently cold from December through to March, and unlike recent seasons when snowfalls were decimated by major thaws, snow lay thick over the Highlands for many weeks.

It took time for this to consolidate, but once it did in late February, the ice climbing conditions were superb. Good ice democratises the Scottish winter game and it was pleasing to see that more new folk were involved in pioneering new routes than in recent years.

Paradoxically icy winters do not always produce the most innovative or technically demanding ascents, and this season was a case in point. There are so many outstanding icy lines waiting for early repeats that even the most hardened mixed climbers are only too happy to ascend rarely formed ice routes when they are in condition. There were exceptions to this rule of course, and Greg Boswell and Guy Robertson added two very difficult mixed climbs to Glen Coe. *The Holy Grail* (IX,11), which was hailed as 'one of the best grade IXs in Scotland', takes the very steep crack-line on the right side of Slime Wall on Buachaille Etive Mòr. Equally impressive was *The Lost Arrow* (X,10) on Church Door Buttress on Bidean, a direct ascent of the main front face of the crag that had previously been the preserve of high standard summer routes.

Iain Small and Murdoch Jamieson also had a productive time in Glen Coe with the first winter ascent of *En Garde* (IX,9) on Stob Coire nan Lochan and a winter version of the *Trapeze* on Aonach Dubh. This spectacular and as yet unnamed route, sits high up in the Grade VIII/IX category. The same pair also added a difficult Grade IX to the Rogue's Rib area in Coire na Ciste on Ben Nevis.

Northern Highlands

The irrepressible Andy Nisbet added a series of excellent climbs to the North-West Face of Ben Hope in the Far North. As Andy explains (see his article in this Journal), Ben Hope has Scotland's second biggest cliff, so it is surprising that only now is it being thoroughly explored. Six-hundred-metre-long routes such as *Blue River* (IV,4) climbed with Dave McGimpsey and *Turf Factor* (IV,4) with Steve Perry and Jonathan Preston will undoubtedly attract repeat ascents in the near future, especially when you factor in the colder weather at the northern tip of the country and the short approach.

Nearby on the flanks of Ben Klibreck, Steve Perry and Sophie Grace Chappell scored a notable coup with the first ascent of the 90m vertical waterfall *Easan Fheid* (VI,6). Continuing the icy theme, Colin Wells and Stephen Reid had a productive three days on Icicle Works Buttress on Eag nam Fear-bogha in the Fannaichs with ascents of the excellent *Only the Lonely* (IV,4) and the bold *Lone Star* (VI,6), Simon Tickle soloed two single pitch Grade V icefalls in Cire na Feola on Ben Wyvis and Ewan Lyons pioneered *Central Gully* (IV,4) on Creag a' Ghlastail in Glen Orrin.

Across in Torridon, Andy Nisbet, Dave McGimpsey and Jonathan Preston thoroughly explored the easily accessible Creagan Dubh Toll nam Biast on Beinn Damh. Their finest discoveries were *Bambi* (IV,4) the 350m-long prominent cleft near the centre of the cliff, and *Goulotte Damh* (V,6), the narrow gully on the

Stephen Reid on Lone Star (VI,6), Eag nam Fear-bogha, Fannaichs. Photo: Colin Wells.

Kacper Tekiele on Wolf Whistle (VII,7), Lurcher's Crag. Photo: Andy Nisbet.

furthest right buttress. Nearby on Liathach, Nisbet and McGimpsey found *Sweet Spot* (V,5) in Coire na Caime, and on the south side of the mountain, Michael Barnard and Doug Bartholomew climbed a winter version of *Triceratops* (IV,5). Next door on Beinn Eighe's Sail Mhòr, Pete Davies and Ross Cowie added *KerPlunk* (VII,7), a steep direct finish to Jenga. On Beinn Bhan, Nick Bullock and Murdoch Jamieson found a logical *Variation Finish* (VII,7) to *Der Riesenwand* that featured a section of very steep mixed climbing to gain a prominent hanging gully.

The Cairngorms

The most difficult new route added in the Cairngorms was the first winter ascent of *The Exorcist* (VIII,8) on Hell's Lum by Greg Boswell and Guy Robertson. Climbing alone, Ewan Lyons made the bold first winter ascent of the nearby *Devil's Alternative* (IV,4). Lurcher's Crag saw continued development and visiting Polish climber Kacper Tekiele added the testing *Wolf Whistle* (VII,7) and *Jaws* (VII,7) in the company of Andy Nisbet and Sandy Allan.

Creagan Cha-no saw several more additions, especially in Duke's Wall area between Anvil and Jenga buttresses. Somehow this part of the cliff was overlooked when the cliff was originally developed, but it yielded some good additions such as *Fast and Furry-ous* (IV,6) and *Road Runner* (IV,5). Most enjoyable of all was *Hobnailers' Gully* (I/II) climbed by an 18-strong team after the Dinner – never before have I seen so many happy faces at the top of a winter route!

The strong north-westerlies during the first half of the season favoured climbing in the sheltered corries of the Angus Glens, and over two dozen worthwhile new climbs were found. With many routes to choose from it is difficult to know which ones to highlight, but the pick of the bunch are probably the sustained *Catheter Corner* (V,6), the technical *Wildcat Ridge* (V,6), the prominent *Maud's Groove* (IV,5) and the bold *Napoleon* (V,4).

Glen Coe

There were some interesting ascents on Buachaille Etive Mor by those largely new to winter pioneering. In December, Steve Holmes, Duncan Curry and Hannah Evans made the first winter ascent of *The Orphan* (VII,8) on the north-east side of Crowberry Ridge. A few weeks later, Tim Miller and Calum Hicks climbed *Dingle* (VII,7), and across on D Gully Buttress, Michael Barnard and John MacLeod made a winter ascent of *Marmalade* (VI,6). In March Lawrie Brand and Neil Kerr climbed a spectacular *Direct Finish* (VI,5) to The Chasm, which is not thought to have been climbed before in winter. On the neighbouring Buachaille Etive Beag, Dean Roberts, Mike Kelly and Tunnell Morgan made a winter ascent of *Gully 2* (II/III) first climbed by Graham Brown and Parish in June 1950. (Both pictured in the photo which accompanies Parish's obituary in this edition. Hon. Ed.).

On Stob Coire nan Lochan, Pete Davies, Helen Rennard and Donie O'Sullivan discovered *Consolation Corner* (V,6) and *Dig for Victory* (VI,7) on the upper right side of SC Gully, and across on the Aonach Eagach, Andy Hogarth and Andy Nelson found two easily accessible Grade III mixed routes on Am Bodach. Similar to recent years, Clach Leathad continued to offer up late season possibilities, with *Skyblind* (V,6), possibly the finest of the five new routes, falling to Andy Nisbet and Sarah Sigley. Across the water on Creach Bheinn in Ardgour, Steve Kennedy, Andy MacDonald made the first ascent of *No Quarter* (IV,5), the narrow gully right of the 2015 addition Bring it on Home.

Guy Robertson on Holy Grail (IX,11), Buachaille Etive Mor.
Photo: Greg Boswell.

Murdoch Jamieson on the first winter ascent of En Garde (IX,9), Stob Coire nan Lochan.
Photo: Iain Small.

Southern Highlands

Tim Miller and Martin McKenna made a good technical addition to The Cobbler with the first winter ascent of *Punters Crack* (VIII,9), a route they had first climbed in summer (as *Davie Taenails*) with Hugh Simons a few months before. Also in Arrochar, Guy Robertson and Greg Boswell climbed *Black and White* (V,5), the well-defined arête bordering the right side of Back Alley. On Beinn Chuirn, Martin Holland found several new routes including *Prospectors* (IV,4) climbed with Sharon Tinsley and Ian McIntosh, and on Ben Lomond, Robin Clothier, Ian Dempster and Stuart McFarlane added *Opinionator* (IV,5).

Following on from recent seasons, Beinn Heasgarnich saw continued attention from Roger Webb, Sophie Grace Chappell and myself with *Androcles* (V,5) and *King of the Jungle* (VI,5) which both tackle the steep ground in the centre of the cliff. Later in the season, George Allan and John Thomas climbed *White Lion* (IV,4), an excellent ice route just to the right.

In the Galloway Hills, Ian Dempster and Stephen Reid found the 200m *Frigidaire* (IV,4) in the North-East Coire of Milldown. Later in the season, Reid teamed up with Andrew Fraser to climb *The Vice Squad* (V,5), which takes the prominent left-facing corner on the main buttress of the Cauldron of Buchan.

Ben Nevis and Central Highlands

In late February, Pinnacle Buttress on Creag Meagaidh came into its best condition since 2005. There were several ascents of the modern classic *The Fly Direct* (VII,7), but the first team to climb new ground were Iain Small and Andy Inglis who found the excellent *Paradise Lost* (VII,8) which takes steep icy ground up the centre of the buttress taken by Last Day in Paradise. The pair were so quick, that they had time to descend Raeburn's Gully and make the second ascent of *Eye Candy* (VII,7) that afternoon. A few days later, Iain Small returned with Helen Rennard and Dave MacLeod to add *The Moth Direct* (VIII,8). This comprises a difficult new start and finish to The Moth making the route more direct. Guy Robertson and I repeated Paradise Lost two weeks later (unaware of the first ascent) adding a *Variation Finish* (VI,7) in the process.

Early in the season on Ben Nevis, Steve Holmes and Ken Applegate made the long trek up Observatory Gully to climb *Optimists' Arête* (V,6) which lies just left of Upper Tower Cascade Right-Hand. Later in March in Coire na Ciste, Robin Clothier and I linked together grooves and corners between The Copenhagen Interpretation and Joyful Chimneys to give *Tempest Corners* (VI,6). Two days later, Sophie Grace Chappell and I climbed *Moulin Rouge* (VI,6), a good mixed route between Pinnacle Buttress Direct and Pinnacle Buttress Right-Hand finishing up the headwall on The Great Tower. At the beginning of the Easter weekend, Iain Small and I followed a direct line up the rib left of Intermediate Gully on Raeburn's Buttress to give *The Good Friday Agreement* (VII,7).

On the rarely visited North Wall of Castle Ridge, Guy Robertson and Adam Russell enjoyed some spectacular climbing during a free ascent of *Alchemist* (VI,7), and Robin Clothier and Stuart McFarlane found *Wanderings of Mr Sea* (IV,4), a new line near Last Day in Purgatory.

Hopes for late season ice on Orion Face and Indicator Wall were dashed when the weather began to warm up in early April. Cold temperatures throughout the winter meant that snow high on the Ben never consolidated and winter rapidly melted away. This gave rise to superb mountain rock climbing in the dry spring weather, but that of course, is another story.

Simon Richardson

100 YEARS AGO – THE CLUB IN 1918

(*Italics* indicates quotation from the Journal or other named source)

THE GREAT WAR CONTINUED to influence everyone's lives during 1918. To illustrate the point, in May, the Royal Navy wireless station on Hirta, St. Kilda (the population of which wasn't evacuated until 1930) was shelled by a German submarine. Seventy-two shells were fired and the wireless station was destroyed but there was no loss of human life although a lamb was killed. I'll try to summarise some of the other significant world events.

In an all-out bid for victory, Germany launched a series of Spring offensives on the Western Front and recaptured all the ground that they had lost in 1916 during the Battle of the Somme. It seems almost surreal that, amongst the wretched conditions and carnage of trench warfare, mundane routines still continued, as demonstrated by the following extract from the diary of Captain William Cuthbertson, a young officer from the King's Own Scottish Borderers:

A German postman two nights ago lost his way and ... jumped into the trenches quite unconcerned but hearing English voices took to his heels and was chased along the trench finally being captured. After his mail was inspected, it was dropped again last night in the enemy lines. A sporting action that could not be expected from the enemy. By this act the German soldiers were not deprived of the affectionate thoughts of their home people.

However, the German momentum faltered and soldiers from all sides began to succumb to a virulent strain of influenza with losses from the disease soon exceeding combat casualties. The pandemic lasted about a year, killing approximately 50 million people worldwide, before vanishing as mysteriously as it had appeared.

In July, Bolsheviks murdered the Russian royal family and civil war erupted with indiscriminate killings, disease and starvation being commonplace. In Britain, rationing was extended to foods such as meat, sugar and butter. Meanwhile, the German army became steadily weaker with declining discipline, food shortages, desertions and drunkenness. Confronted by the unstoppable strength of the Allies in all theatres of war and faced with the prospect of an outright military defeat on the Western Front, the Kaiser agreed to an armistice, which came into effect on the eleventh hour of the eleventh day of the eleventh month. The war was finally over but its expense left Britain in severe debt and destroyed its global pre-eminence; in reality, it was the industrial might of the United States that had swung the balance in favour of the Allies.

The contribution to the war effort by women made it impossible to maintain that they were unfit to vote and so the General Election in December was the first at which they were entitled to stand or vote, although they were still not given the same full rights as men. It was, however, a major advance in women's suffrage. This election was notable, too, for the rejection of government policy in Ireland and the start of the Irish War of Independence.

In Scotland, the death-rate rose as a result of the influenza epidemic, known as 'Spanish Flu', spread unwittingly by soldiers returning home. Although the war had given a boost to industry, the post-war decline in demand led to increasing unemployment and poverty. Many servicemen returned home with the belief that they had been promised property as a reward for fighting for their country. When this was not forthcoming, they occupied land without the owner's permission, citing an old law which they claimed gave them the right to work the land if they could build a wooden shelter and a hearth on which they could light a fire. The following year, the government passed the Land Settlement Act making land available for men who had served in the war. However, the debt-laden government could not afford to fulfil its promises and the land raids continued. By the end of the 1920s the problem of land ownership, overcrowding and poverty had still not been resolved in the Highlands and many people saw emigration as the only option.

So how did the SMC fit into all this social turmoil? Well, the President, W. Inglis Clark, compared progress in promoting the SMC's charter to *water-hens endeavouring to make headway against a driving gale* whilst, with a pre-war wind behind it, there was no great effort necessary to secure new members – *each one jostling to make new routes, new experiences*. Although it was necessary to bring younger, more-vibrant members into the governance of the Club, an ideal which had received a severe check *whilst members were serving their country to the utmost, he predicted that, with determination, the SMC will rise to greater heights in the future than ever in the past*. I think it fair to say that he was correct.

He made this point at an informal dinner (at which there were just 26 members present) following the 29th AGM at the North British Hotel, Glasgow on 7 December, 1917. At that point, the membership stood at 186 and it was proposed that the annual subscription be raised from 15 shillings (75p) to £1 as *the Club's expenditure last year had considerably exceeded its income*. The Treasurer stated that the Club did not have sufficient funds in hand to honour the motion (made at the previous AGM) to make a donation of £21 to the Scottish Red Cross and that, therefore, the payment had not been made.

It was decided to reduce the number of issues of the Journal from three to two annually (in April and October) and also to raise the price to the public from one shilling (5p) to one shilling and sixpence (7.5p). The cancellation of all formal Club Meets would continue.

The Journal

Several members queried the non-arrival of the February issue, not having been aware of the decision to cancel its publication. The Hon. Editor, F.S. Goggs, felt obliged to give an explanation: namely, the difficulty in obtaining suitable material and the cost of printing and postage. The April issue had several nostalgic items, the most interesting perhaps is an account by Scott Moncrieff Penney who used his bicycle to ride 35,600 miles during thirty years-worth of exploration. In a visit to Loch Arkaig, this truly exquisite piece of Scottish scenery, he describes how Cameron of Lochiel's orders for the planting of an avenue of beech trees at Achnacarry were interrupted by news of the landing of Bonny Prince Charlie in 1745. The Cameron men were called to arms and so the plan was changed:

> Then dig a trench upon the bank
> Where Arkaig rolls along,
> And set my beechen babes in rank
> To listen to her song.

Many of the original 'babes' remain as large trees today although some came to grief during the violent storm which contributed to the Tay Bridge disaster in December, 1879.

George Sang writes about 'Walks Near Edinburgh' (when there was a handy railway to Leadburn and Dolphinton) and W.W. Naismith and Gilbert Thomson give similar accounts about 'Saturday Hill Walks Near Glasgow'. I feel that G. E. Howard, however, captures the general mood of the time in 'The Rain Of Peace' which he starts with:

All day long the rain has teemed down on the grey roofs of the factory; all day the wind has moaned. Muddy roads, vistas of murky east London streets, a sodden feeling of dirt and endless work, and over all the dull pall of war, doubly drab on this drab day.

And yet when one thinks of other drab days, of rain to which this is but a faint dew, and of great winds roaring among the glens, one glories in the memory. Indeed it is just those memories which keep one alive and working nowadays – magic memories of the hills.

The news was announced of the death of Captain Charles Inglis Clark who died March 1918 in Mesopotamia from gunshot wounds in the head. F. S. Goggs wrote that *we had watched him grow up, we saw his character develop .... What I think endeared him to us all was the utter absence in his character of all swank or side. He was so sincere, simple, modest .... All who knew him could not fail but be attracted by his quietly winning personality.* In a longer obituary in the October issue of the Journal, George Sang echoed these heartfelt words – *he was a man whose charming personality, sunny nature and attractive modesty endeared him to all mountaineers with whom he came in contact. Somewhere north of Baghdad he met a soldier's death, giving his young life for all he held most sacred – love and home, freedom and peace ...*

Many mountaineers have had cause to be grateful for the subsequent building of the CIC hut on Ben Nevis,[1] a very fitting memorial to this fine man. Charles Clark was married and had a young son, and I wonder if there are any family descendants alive today? Another SMC member to lose his life was Captain George Almond who was killed instantly by an explosion on 9 August 1918. Both of his brothers had earlier been killed on active service. The third (and twelfth in total) SMC member to die in action was Lieutenant Charles Deards of the Royal Flying Corps who was a member of the Kite Balloon Section. At the end of September 1918 his balloon got adrift and he had perforce to land by means of a parachute from a height of some 5,000ft. He landed safely but in doing so probably grazed himself. A few days afterwards blood poisoning set in and he died in hospital at Rouen on 5 October, aged 37.

Elsewhere in the October issue there are items looking back to trips made when *there was the time and the heart to indulge in our favourite sport.* Sir Hugh Munro reflects on a solitary multi-day walk during which … *I was met by my boatman of the night before, who insisted on my going to his cottage and drinking milk, introducing me with 'This is my wife. Isn't she fat?' She was!* John Levack muses about 'A Week-End At Inchnadamph' with outings to various Sutherland hills. I have to admit to falling asleep whilst attempting to make progress with Green's 'Old Volumes of The Journal', Stott's 'A Chronicle Of The Old Men' and Goggs' treatise on 'Robert Browning'. Good luck if you want to have a go. Finally, J.A. Parker contributes a note about Creag An Dubh Loch … *these magnificent crags which rise up steeply … have recently been examined by some of the Aberdeen members …* and describes most of it as *manifestly hopeless.* It would be another ten years before the first rock-climb was recorded on what is now considered to

---

[1] Not least the author, see e.g. his 'Breaking the Ice', *SMCJ* (2013), 408–15. (Hon. Ed.)

have *more to offer the hard climber than any other Scottish mountain cliff;*[2] *it is considered by many as Britain's finest* (1995 SMC Guide 'The Cairngorms', Vol. 2).

Members excursions

Once again I have to rely on the diaries (Book 13) of W. Ling. He records no fewer than 25 days when he was out-and-about. The earlier months of the year were spent on extremely long hill-walks (for example, 42 miles and 51 miles) in the hill country near his home at Wetheral, near Carlisle. These were usually with his friend R.P. Bicknell. It would seem that, despite the cancellation of official Club Meets, some members decided to proceed with private get-togethers, staying at hotels at Killin (Easter) and Tyndrum (New Year). Again, long walk-ins were accepted as the norm; for example, on 29 March accompanied by G. Sang and Mrs. Sang, he walked from Killin to Ben Lawers and Beinn Ghlas return, a mere 22 miles plus ascent.

He managed to include several rock-climbing excursions; for example, a wet and slimy evening ascent of Raven Crag Gully (Combe Ghyll, Borrowdale), Bowfell Buttress and Jones' Route from Deep Ghyll, Scafell on three successive days in May. At the conclusion of the latter outing they had their usual swim in the beck before cycling from Rosthwaite to Keswick, catching the train to Penrith and then cycling home to Wetheral. His summer Alpine season was diverted to North Wales for more rock-climbing. The year was concluded at the end of December in Tyndrum, ascending the Central Gully of Ben Lui, where they kicked steps with the occasional use of the axe to the top, and traversing Beinn Oss on the final day of the year.

Mike Jacob

---

[2] For example Julian Lines's ascent of *Magrathea* (E9 7a) as described by Steve Perry in *SMCJ* (2017), 1–4. (Hon. Ed.)

200 YEARS AGO

ALTHOUGH 1818 IS NOT ASSOCIATED with any particular new ascents in the Highlands, it sits in the period when the Rev. Thomas Grierson, the geologist John MacCulloch, and the naturalist William McGillivray were exploring Highland hills. Ian Mitchell's admirable survey – *Scotland's Mountains before the Mountaineers* – gives some details of their wanderings. The only published tour of note was *Sketch of a tour in the Highlands of Scotland; through Perthshire, Argyleshire and Inverness-shire, in September and October, 1818.* (Baldwin, Cradock & Joy, 1819). This anonymous work was later given to an unspecified Mr Larkin. It is an engaging account, but the mountaineering interest is low. An ascent of Ben Nevis *via* the east flank of Meall an t-Suidhe (commonplace by this date) is described, and Larkin advises that 'The ascent can hardly be completed in less than four or five hours, and the descent will require nearly as much time. The temptation, resulting from the exhaustion produced by the fatigue of the ascent, to recruit by drinking wine or ardent spirits, ought to be entirely resisted, or yielded to with great caution; otherwise from the natural unsteadiness of the footing, and steepness of the stony declivity, the descent will be a work of considerable danger as well as difficulty.' One suspects that here we benefit from Larkin's own bitter experience.

The artists Joseph Turner and Joshua Cristall visited Scotland. Turner did not get beyond the Central Lowlands on this visit, but Cristall travelled at least as far as Killin via the Trossachs and Glen Falloch. Some of his lively sketches may be viewed in the Tate and British Museum collections, and there are several surviving finished watercolours. Here is a sketch of the 'Trosachs, with Benan in the distance' which I bought a few years ago. It demonstrates the fidelity of Cristall's work well.

'Trosachs, with Benan in the distance', sketch by Joshua Cristall. Campbell Collection.

One of his finished watercolours showed the paddle-steamer *Marion* in her first year of operation on Loch Lomond. Built for David Napier by Archibald McLachlan, Dumbarton, she was manoeuvred up the Leven into the Loch early in the year and sailed throughout the summer (see Alan Brown's *Loch Lomond*

Detail from Cristall's watercolour of Loch Lomond; the paddle steamer Marion is transferring passengers at Luss. Photo: Robin Campbell.

Passenger Steamers 1818–1989, Condie, 2000). In Cristall's watercolour she is transferring passengers at Luss.

Famously, the poet John Keats visited Scotland in 1818 – a long tour beginning in Lancaster and ending on the summit of Ben Nevis, where Keats wrote a bewildered sonnet, and became ill.

However, perhaps the most remarkable event of the year was Walter Scott's discovery of the hiding-place of the Honours of Scotland in Edinburgh Castle, a feat of historical ingenuity and persistence for which he would later receive his baronetcy.

Robin N.Campbell

'I FOUGHT THE LAW AND THE LAW WON'

THE WORDS OF SONNY CURTIS, amplified by The Clash ring in my ears, as the importance of the decision from the highest court in the land sinks home. Formality and format had served to emphasise the significance on the day. Wigs and robes, red and black, in a calm, wooden-box of a room, at the centre of the capital's courts complex. Standing to attention when the judge, Lord Boyd of Duncansby, arrived. Evidence and arguments and more evidence. Yet despite the trappings of seriousness it felt as though Scotland's mountains were somehow being treated casually – it was after all about them, not the law. Under scrutiny was a decision to allow one of the largest wind farms ever contemplated on land in Scotland. And it was a decision that had been taken by our Scottish Government – nominally by our Scottish Ministers. Suddenly it seemed normal, ordinary, even trivialised. Come back next week and I'll tell you my decision. Was that it? And what did it signify?

Contemplation eventually lasted much longer than a week. It took more than three months before a decision was reached. Suitable pause? No window dressing will hide the fact that the legal challenge was lost. No 'spin' is required. Twenty-two turbines were 'legitimately' approved. Each one 125 metres high – very nearly the height of the Old Man of Hoy, spread across the Crask Moors. On a clear day from the top of Ben Stack, Foinaven, Ben Hope, Ben Loyal and especially Ben Klibreck you could not fail to see this windfarm. Walkers and climbers are only there briefly, so will not mind – had been the original reasoning. The merits of this decision, whether lamentable or completely credible, were not in contention.

The Crask Moors from Ben Klibreck. Wind Turbines here will be visible from as far north as Foinaven and probably Ben More Assynt. Photo: Bob Reid.

But was the decision legal? Sadly, Lord Boyd's pronouncement says it was. And that was it. I say 'sadly', because Lord Boyd clearly had pause. I may be clutching at straws, but the good judge's language suggests legitimacy is one thing but the law could well be an ass.

An industrial scale development has been approved, using legislation put in place by the Westminster Parliament (the Electricity Act), which was designed to speed up the construction of power stations by the newly privatised utility industry. It doesn't even mention wind farms. Legitimate? It seems so. Incredible? Absolutely.

I fought the law but the law won.

Bob Reid

SCOTTISH MOUNTAINEERING TRUST – 2017
Scottish Charity Number SC009117

The Trustees met on 28 April and 14 October 2017. During the course of these meetings support was given to:
Mountain Aid – Mountain Safety Event 2017; Mountaineering Scotland – Winter Skills Students; APEX 5 – Medical Research; Ladies Scottish Climbing Club – Digital Projector; M Nicolson – Collie/Mackenzie Sculpture; R Crawford – Dundee Mountain Film Festival; Jonathan Conville Memorial Trust – Scottish Winter Courses 2018; K Lynch – Paraclimb; Ladies Scottish Climbing Club – Renovations to Hut in Aultbea; Scottish Mountaineering Club – Journal; DL Baird – Wide Mountain Path Project; AM Riddell – Scottish Rights of Way Society; G & J Surveys – Heights of Munros etc; Scottish Mountaineering Club – Database of Scottish Climbs; D Wright – Borders Walking Festival; A Nisbet – Re-bolting Black Rock; North-West Highlands Geopark – Accessible Mountain Top Exhibition; Mountaineering Scotland – Access and Conservation.

The present Trustees are DN Williams (Chairman) (*Ex Officio* Immediate Past President of the SMC), R Anderson (*Ex Officio* Convenor of the Publications Sub-Committee), PJ Biggar (*Ex Officio* Editor of the SMC Journal), SM Richardson (*Ex Officio* President of the SMC), JAP Hutchinson, JRG MacKenzie, SD Pearson, CR Ravey, E Riley and G Ross. JM Shaw is the Trust Treasurer and JD Hotchkis is the Trust Secretary. The Trustees wish to record their gratitude and appreciation for the valuable input of Dick Allan and Andrew James who have each served on the Trust for the last 3 years and have now retired by rotation.

CR Ravey (who is both a Director of the Publications Company and Trustee) provides valuable liaison between the Publications Company and the Trust.

The following grants have been committed by the Trustees during 2017:

Mountain Aid – Mountain Safety Event 2017	£500
Mountaineering Scotland – Winter Skills Students	£2,000
APEX 5 – Medical Research	£1,000
Ladies Scottish Climbing Club – Digital Projector	£450
M Nicolson – Collie/Mackenzie Sculpture	£2,000
R Crawford – Dundee Mountain Film Festival	£800
Jonathan Conville Memorial Trust – Scottish Winter Courses 2018	£1,000
K Lynch – Paraclimb	£1,000
Ladies Scottish Climbing Club – Renovations to Hut in Aultbea	£4,000
Scottish Mountaineering Club – Journal £5,000 per annum max for next 3 years	
DL Baird – Wide Mountain Path Project	£6,000
AM Riddell – Scottish Rights of Way Society	£2,000
G & J Surveys – Heights of Munros etc	£1,950
Scottish Mountaineering Club – Database of Scottish Climbs	£5,000
D Wright – Borders Walking Festival	£800
A Nisbet – Re-bolting Black Rock	£400
North-West Highlands Geopark – Accessible Mountain Top Exhibition	£8,000
Mountaineering Scotland – Access and Conservation	£13,600

James Hotchkis (Hon. Sec. SMT)

MUNRO MATTERS

by Dave Broadhead (Clerk of the List)

This report covers 1 January to 31 December 2017. The five columns below give number, name and year of Compleation of Munros, Tops and Furths as appropriate. *SMC member, **LSCC member.

No.	Name	M	T	F	No.	Name	M	T	F
6103	Jonny Rowan	2016			6153	Keith D. Johnston	2017		
6104	Chris H. Maingay	2010			6154	Margaret Johnstone	2017		
6105	Andrew Gibb	2016			6155	Johann Bolton	2017		
6106	Jennifer White	2014			6156	Peter Bolton	2017		
6107	Rab Mungall	2015			6157	Jean Whittaker	2017		
6108	Ed Fitzgibbon	2016			6158	Paul Spooner	2017		
6109	Malcolm H. Fitter	2016			6159	Richard Blair	2017		
6110	Huw Davies	2016			6160	Stuart Ferguson	2017		
6111	Gina Graham	2017			6161	Jon L. Edgar	2017	2017	2017
6112	Derek Graham	2017			6162	W. Nigel Taylor	2017		
6113	Edmond R. Mansion	1995			6163	Iain W. Fergusson	2017		
6114	Shaun Wallington	2016			6164	James Ogilvie	2017		
6115	Paul Prior	2017			6165	Matthew Fautley	2017	2017	
6116	Yvonne Calvert	2016			6166	David Armin	2017		
6117	Colin Sparling	2017			6167	Rosie Dawson	2017		
6118	Ian W. Downie	2017			6168	Richard Winsborrow	2017		
6119	Richard Helliwell	2017			6169	Jennifer Sessions	2017		
6120	Helen Webster	2017			6170	Keith Weston	2017		
6121	Graham Neish	2017			6171	Peter McCullock	2017		
6122	Tim Doyle	2017			6172	Sheena M. Hendrie	2017		
6123	Rab Walker	2017			6173	Jeremy Voaden	2017		
6124	Bill Rattray	2017			6174	Louise Arnison	2017		
6125	Ian Forrest	2013			6175	Chris Arnison	2017		
6126	Kenny Rowat	2017			6176	Alex J. Clark	2016		
6127	Ian Barr	2017			6177	Emmanuelle Tulle	2017		
6128	Pete Robertson	2017		2017	6178	Kristin Skrzypczak	2017		
6129	Ross Clark	2017			6179	Nick Young	2017		
6130	Tony Gladstone	2017			6180	Margaret Sweenie	2017		
6131	Rick Houghton	2017			6181	Joel Sylvester	2017		
6132	Anthony Brockway	2016			6182	Jean Adams	2017		
6133	Ian Magill	2017			6183	Ian McCullough	2017		
6134	David Raffe	2017			6184	Alan Stewart	2017		
6135	David Innes	2017			6185	Stuart Roxburgh	2007		
6136	David Powell	2017			6186	Andrew Smith	2017		
6137	Dave Valentine	2017			6187	Alison C. Stewart	2017		
6138	Jim Pennel	2017			6188	Pamela Lee	2017		
6139	Colin A. Roberts	2017			6189	Peter Mackenzie	2017		
6140	Robert W. Wight	2017			6190	Ivor L. Roberts	2017		
6141	Gill Sharples	2017			6191	Alastair Laing	2017		
6142	Steve Ingleby	2017			6192	Hannah Green	2017		
6143	William Paul	2017			6193	Jim Freer	2017		
6144	Tony Harden	2017			6194	David King	2017	2017	
6145	Malcolm Moir	2017			6195	Alan Hewitt-Dutton	2017		
6146	Nick Kelly	2017			6196	Alexander McMillan	2017		
6147	Gary Glencross	2016			6197	Stephen Heggie	2017		
6148	Wayne D. Cook	2017		2017	6198	Margaret M. Munro	2017		
6149	Frank Reed	2017			6199	John G. Munro	2017		
6150	Chris Mutter	2017			6200	Celia Watson	2017		
6151	Andy Bennett	2017			6201	Stuart Watson	2017		
6152	Roderick MacLean	2017			6202	Scott McCormick	2017		

No.	Name	M	T	F	No.	Name	M	T	F
6203	Norma Short	2017			6245	Claire Gordon	2017		2017
6204	Carl Sugden	2017			6246	Daniel Beckett	2017		
6205	Susan Lunn	2017			6247	Jim Foster	2017		
6206	David Lever	2017			6248	Andrew Maudsley	2017		
6207	Ewan Bayne	2017			6249	James Dowley	2017		
6208	Terry Leyland	2016			6250	Jane Stevens	2017		
6209	Celia Brady	2017			6251	Adrian Stevens	2017		
6210	Linda Kerr	2017			6252	David Thompson	2017		
6211	Phil Prescott	2017			6253	Fiona Ewen	2017		
6212	Elaine H. Smith	2017			6254	Graham White	2017		
6213	Garry J. Smith	2017			6255	Janet Reid	2010		
6214	David Cunningham	2017			6256	Walter Reid	2010		
6215	Nigel Williams	2017			6257	Sam Ferguson	2017		
6216	Peter Lodge	2017			6258	Peter W. Evans	2017		
6217	Andrew S. Orrock	2017			6259	June Manson	2017		
6218	Michael Thorpe	2017			6260	Christopher J. Reeve	2017		
6219	Clare Williams	2017			6261	David Comins	2017		2014
6220	William Gagie	2017			6262	Owain Bristow	2017		
6221	Mark Wade	2016			6263	Nigel Ashton	2017		
6222	Les Sutherland	2017			6264	Simon Johnston	2017		
6223	Neil McCann	2017			6265	Iain M. Forrest	2017		
6224	Cord Wischhofer	2017			6266	Michael B. Burrows	2017		
6225	Frank Muller	2017			6267	Stephen R. MacGrain	2017		
6226	Gavin Bowie	2017			6268	Lisa Trollope	2017		
6227	Miles Harrison	2017			6269	Libby Kerr	2017		
6228	John Ritchie	2017			6270	Dan Bodey	2017		
6229	Maja Staerke	2017			6271	Nigel Webber	2017		
6230	Kay Beechey	2017			6272	Marion Wood	2005		
6231	David Bingham	2017			6273	Michael Wood	2005		
6232	Brian Fenton	2017			6274	Graham J. Dolby	2017		
6233	Julie Garland	2017			6275	Sunny He Huang	2017		
6234	Steve Richardson	2017			6276	Tom Kerr	2017		
6235	Stan Hutchinson	2017			6277	Kelvin Palmer	2017		
6236	John M. Evans	2017			6278	Paula Rogers	2017		
6237	Bill Dryburgh	2017			6279	Derek Dougall	2017		
6238	Anne Brown	2017			6280	Anne Garsed	2017		
6239	Sarah O'Neil	2017			6281	Stephen Garsed	2017		
6240	Simon Morehead	2017			6282	Samantha Penn	2017		
6241	Ben Dipper	2017			6283	Dave Hoare	2017		
6242	Dianne Scolari	2017			6284	Matthew Burrows	2017		
6243	Susan Freebairn	2017			6285	Garry Wardrope	2017		
6244	Stephen J. Flynn	2017			6286	Catherine Gillespie	2016		

Comparing this year's data with last year (in brackets): New Munroists 184 (202); males 76% (77%); resident in Scotland 61% (66%); couples 13% (13%); average age 56 (55); size of Compleation summit party 12 (13); average Compleation time 26 (24) years; Golden Munroists 10 (10).

This is the first year since 2002–2003 that the annual total of new Munroists has fallen below 200. I can suggest no obvious reason for this, especially since the other figures have remained steady. It does however suggest a theme for this year's report:

MUNROISTS BY NUMBERS
86 Munro summits saw Compleations in 2017 and the TOP TEN were: Ben More (Mull) 19; Beinn na Lap 10; Gulvain, Meall nan Tarmachan 6; Ben Lomond, Bla Bheinn 5; Beinn Sgulaird, Ben Hope, Braeriach, Stob Dearg (Buachaille Etive Mor) 4.

One item of FAKE NEWS caused a few red faces over the summer. On a short visit to Edinburgh I nipped in to the National Library to see the excellent Enduring Eye exhibition featuring the familiar Frank Hurley images of Shackleton's ill-fated Endurance expedition, recently scanned and digitized, along with a few other artefacts and background details of members of the party. In the section about geologist James Wordie I was surprised by the caption claiming 'he had climbed all the Munros before he was 21.' A remarkable feat for a young student before the Great War which prompted some on-line research, spurred on by Hamish Brown (62) who dropped me a note expressing his surprise too. An enquiry to Archivist Robin Campbell produced a scan of Wordie's SMC application form, submitted in 1912, which confirmed that he had climbed some Munros, easily accessible by railway from Glasgow. Finally, the curator of the exhibition sent an apologetic email confirming 'the statement is a mistake. I meant to check the numbers, but it slipped through the edit.' Reassuring to know that it is not just your Clerk who makes the occasional error!

Two Scots have now Compleated both the Munros and the Seven Summits according to the second, James Ogilvie (6164). (The other is Vicky Jack who has not yet registered).

'18 years, two pairs of boots, two pairs of walking poles, five cameras (they seem to get bashed about a bit!) and lots of amazing experiences' summed up Jeremy Voaden's (6173) Round. He also mentioned that he only has four of the highest points in all the Scottish counties still to climb, having finished England and Wales.

1,345m 'did not seem like a serious mountaineering outing' to Emmanuelle Tulle (6177) a French woman who, on the day of the 1982 World Cup Final climbed Ben Nevis 'wearing only a tee-shirt, shorts and trainers. I never knew the enormity or foolishness of what I had done until many years later.' Older and wiser now, she has become the first French Munroist, though she does live in Falkirk. Jennifer White (6106) also remembered the hot sunny summer days of yore and noted 'my only claim to fame is soloing the Cuillins in a green bikini. Being booed for putting clothes on to abseil off the In. Pin. was a new experience.'

Three more Germans registered. Frank Muller (6225) started in 1991 with Beinn Alligin while Cord Wischhofer (6224) joined him in 1993 on The Saddle. Cord reported 'At that time we were completely oblivious of the rather compulsory nature the passion of hill-bagging can take in humans. Later we realized that there is a list of the highest hills in Scotland compiled and maintained by the SMC. An online documentation of our hill-climbing efforts is given on the website 'Bloody German Munro Baggers' <www.bgmb.de>. Maja Staerke (6229) 'was born in Germany but have lived longer in Scotland.' She described one of her favourite trips 'where I swam across Loch Quoich to climb Gairich – possibly the only lilo approach to a Munro?'

£1,000 was the cost to climb Gairich for Jennifer Sessions (6169) 'the most expensive Munro I did, the only one we managed in a hugely wet and windy week in September 2016.' She also remembered 'Raptor Day' on Carn a' Chlamain 'when we saw an Osprey, a Merlin, a Golden Eagle, a Peregrine Falcon and a Hen Harrier.'

£3,500 was raised by Carl Sugden (6204) 'for a local hospice, Martin House, in memory of my daughter, through a series of sporting challenges, of which completing the Munros was one.' Celia (6200) and Stuart Watson (6201) raised £1,600 'for the Calvert Trust, an outdoor centre in the Lake District that provides holidays for disabled people. We put a pound aside each time we climbed a Munro, so were able to start the pot off with £282.' They also supplied some numbers from their Round: '144 days on the hill, 2300km travelled, 144000m height gain 530km cycled, views from 222 summits.' Elaine H. (6212) and Garry J. Smith (6213) also 'did 144 walks to complete the list ranging from 3 to 18.75 hours' and reminded me 'our home town of Kirriemuir is where Munro lived at Lindertis Farm and the town has an engraved paving stone in honour of him so it feels good to have finished this journey here.' Stan Hutchinson (6235) also did some calculations and worked out that his Round 'involved 61 trips to Scotland and 139 days in the mountains. My accommodation was a tent for 181 Munros and our family caravan for 90.'

400 yards from the car, after his Compleation on Sgùrr na Banachdaich on Skye, Scott McCormick (6202) 'broke my leg in 2 places and had it operated on in Broadford hospital before being transferred to Paisley Royal Alexander Hospital for further treatment. The Mountain Rescue and Medical Team were amazing.'

88 years old, the father of Anne Brown (6238) was unable to join her Compleation on Beinn Fionnlaidh in Glen Etive, though 'he was there in spirit'. Grateful that he had started her on her way, back in 1968, aged 8, she went on to describe how 'the Munros have been a constant throughout my life, always a joy and a grounding experience, giving a real sense of space and time and putting life back into perspective.' Anne's 49 year Round means she just missed joining the GOLDEN MUNROISTS who were Malcolm H. Fitter (6109) 62 years; Tony Gladstone (6130) 60 years; Colin A. Roberts (6139) 52 years; Steve Ingleby (6142) 50 years; Roderick MacLean (6152) 56 years; Richard Winsborrow (6168); Alan Hewitt-Dutton (6195) 53 years; David Lever (6206) 52 years; Jim Foster (6247) 50 years; Stephen Garsed (6281) 52 years.

77 days after starting on Ben More (Mull), on 3 July, Lisa Trollope (6268) and Libby Kerr (6269) completed a continuous self-propelled Round on Ben Hope on 17 September. They believe this is a new female record and reported 'we had an absolutely fantastic trip and have fallen in love with the Scottish mountains. We hope our adventure will inspire more women to get out into the mountains and challenge themselves.'

131 Munros in 5 months was a challenge to another feisty female Sunny He Huang (6275) who became the first Chinese Munroist. She explained 'living in Scotland for over 13 years, currently working for NHS Lothian as a Cardiothoracic Theatre Nurse, I started walking in 2015 for Christian Aid 70 Munros Challenge. Once I completed 70 I took the 282 Challenge for charity fundraising.' Only two other Munroists gave their occupations, one a brickie, the other a postie. Sunny also explained 'I work 37.5 hours and have been picking up most of the on calls and overtime during weekdays to support the department because of staff shortage issues. I used all my days off and weekends in the mountains regardless of weather conditions.' Her future plan 'is to do some cracking Corbetts and Hadrian's Wall and other hills at a leisurely pace.'

Five attributes required by David Lever (6206) for future outings will be 'a summit of decent prominence, an OS trig point, a good walk in, a good view and the prospect of some peace and quiet. Since Compleating I have been on Dun Caan on Raasay, which ticks all these boxes.'

22 members of the Ochils Mountaineering Club accompanied Nigel Webber (6271) on his Compleation on Beinn Fhionlaidh from Glen Etive. He explained 'one's last Munro should be a bit special so we did it in dresses!' and enclosed a fine photo to prove it. 27 other clubs mentioned this year, whose members presumably favour more conventional attire include Aberdeen MC; Aberdeen

Grammar School HWC; Aberdeen Young Walkers; Bishopton Walking Group; Cairngorm Club; Calderglen Harriers; Castle MC; Corriemulzie MC; Edinburgh University MC; Forfar HWC; Friockheim HWC; Grampian HWC; Inverclyde Ramblers; Inverness MC; Karabiner MC; Lomond MC; Lylecraigs Walking Group; Moray MC; Milngavie MC; Nevis HWC; Nottingham University Munro Society; Ochils MC; Paisley HWC; Perth HWC; Peterborough MC; Reading MC; Starav MC.

No members of the SMC or LSCC registered in 2017. Come on ladies and gentlemen!

Two Contiguous Compleations were reported. David Raffe (6134) mopped up his final Munros, Corbetts and Grahams by traversing Belig, Garbh Bheinn and Bla Bheinn via Clach Glas on the Isle of Skye, where Jon L. Edgar (6161) managed Munros, Tops and Furths, Compleating on Am Basteir, followed by the Bastier Tooth and climbing Helvellyn on the way home to Surrey. He notes that 'a meeting with Malcolm Slesser started me on the Tops, to complicate matters.' Malcolm would have been particularly interested to learn that seven celebratory whiskies were mentioned this year, including Lagavulin 16; Glen Moray single cask; Highland Park; Cardhu; Glenmorangie; Talisker; Loch Lomond, Old Pulteney. Other whiskies are available – no sponsorship deals for the SMC yet!

AMENDMENTS

No.	Name	M	T	F	C	G	D
3776	Alex Thomson	2006		2012	2012		
1279	Nigel P. Morters	1994	2009	2016	1999	2015	
		2008					
2530	*Barry G. Hard	2001					
		2016					
3061	Nigel G. Thackrah	2003	2010	2006			2016
2199	Keith Gault	1999					
		2007					
		2016					
2803	Jamie Brogan	2002			2016		
		2009					
3497	Richard Knight	2005	2017		2010		2011
		2014					
4088	David McSporran	2008	2017		2011	2014	2017
1668	Lesley Barrie	1996			2003	2012	2017
580	John Green	1988	1989	1989	2010		2017
3839	Ray Hunter	2007		2014	2014		2017
2191	*Heather Morning	1999			2017		
3745	Jean Ramsay Smith	2006			2016		
4037	Sue Lyth	2008	2011	2011	2017		
		2015					
4883	David Williamson	2011	2011	2011	2017		
5318	M. Clair Bale	2010			2010	2017	2017
1029	Andrew Naylor	1992					
		2017					
2431	Carl Emery	2000		2000	2017		
6134	David Raffe	2017			2017	2017	
1952	Douglas Prentice	1998			2017		

No.	Name	M	T	F	C	G	D
2871	Peter Hamilton	1992	2017	2002	1997		
		2002			2011		
		2008					
		2015					
5485	Carol Oliver	2014	2017				
3075	Phil Hardy	2003			2017		
5066	Blair Cunningham	2012					2017
5506	Alistair Deering	2014	2015	2017	2015	2017	2016
4218	Gordon Nicoll	2008	2014				2017
3293	Paul Ormerod	2004	2004	2005			2017
1801	Lindsay Boyd	1997	2002		2004	2009	2010
		2000					
		2002					
		2008					
		2010					
		2017					
707	Robert F. Gibson	1989	1996	2017	2013		
3600	Ian J. Hawkes	2006	2006		2017		
2429	Graham C. Kelly	2000			2014		
3093	Leslie Shore	2003	2017				
1758	Steve Hinde	1997	1997		2017		
358	Michael B. Slater	1984	1987	1987			
		1988		2009			
		1990		2011			
		1993		2013			
		1996		2014			
		1999		2017			
		2003					
		2008					
3468	John Henderson	2005		2017	2010	2014	2015
3737	Hans Van Dijk	2008			2017		
3061	Nigel G. Thackrah	2003	2010	2006	2017		2016
876	Elsa Yates	1991		1991			
		1996					
		2017					
2371	Graeme Crowe	2000			2017		
5307	Eileen McLaren	2013		2017			
5308	John McLaren	2013		2017			
2991	Ewan J. Lyons	2003	2009	2012	2009	2016	2017
		2012					
1019	James I. R. Tees	1992			2017		
3366	Anne Butler	2005	2017	2017	2010		2017
		2010					
		2011					
		2012					
		2014					
3998	Linda Ross	2007			2017		
3999	William A. Ross	2007			2017		
3878	John McKechnie	2007			2014		
		2017					

No.	Name	M	T	F	C	G	D
4035	Stuart McKeggie	2008					
		2017					
2408	Donald Barnett	2000					
		2017					
5057	Robert Phillips	2012		2017	2013	2014	2015
2780	Colin Ballantyne	1991			2017		
		2002					
3041	Rebecca Trengrove	2003			2017		
2067	Julie A. Brown	1999			2017		
4006	Chris Pine	2007	2017	2015	2010	2013	2014
2982	George Gallacher	2003			2017		
3409	William Robertson	2005			2017		
4653	Arthur Greenwood	2010			2017		
4472	Alison Paterson	2009			2017		
778	John Ullock	1990			2017		
787	Neil Williams	1990					
		2017					
2597	Richard Hardaker	2001		1999	2017		2015
4151	Norman Wares	2008	2010	2011	2014	2017	2015
3990	Christine Gordon	1998	2000	2007	2017		2013
225	Alan L. Brook	1980	1980	1978	2004	2013	2010
		2002	2002				
		2017	2017				
5505	Allison Robertson	2014		2017	2015	2017	2017
3362	David Hallam	2005					
		2017					
3988	Janet Tyler	2007					
		2017					
5577	Neil A. Milloy	2014					2017
3438	Hazel Strachan	2005					2011
		2008					2012
		2010					2012
		2012					
		2013					
		2014					
		2015					
		2016					
		2017					
2535	William H. Ramsden	2001			2017		
4213	Trevor Carter	2008	2014		2017		
3249	Carmel Smith	2004		2012			
3250	Ian Smith	2004	2017	2012			
		2016					
1221	John F. Wilson	1993	1997		2017		
		1999					
		2007					
2818	Geoff Carson	2002					
		2017					
2511	George Hall	2000			2009	2017	
3112	Bert Barnett	2001	2002	2002	1998	2000	2012

No.	Name	M	T	F	C	G	D
		2001	2009	2007	2007	2009	2013
		2009					
		2012					
		2016					
5599	Robin G. Wallace	2014		2017			
660	Paul Gillies	1989	2005	2006			
		2017					
4038	Humphrey Mather	2008			2017		
182	William Steele	1978					
		1986					
		1991					
		1997					
		2000					
		2005					
		2010					
		2014					
		2016					
		2017					
2078	Marek Wilcojc	1999					2017
2079	Grant Wilson	1999					2017
4224	Roger Mitchell	2008			2017		
480	Andrew Finnimore	1986	1986	1986	2003	2013	
5361	Fiona Clark	2013		2015			
		2017					
5362	Stuart Clark	2013		2015			
		2017					
2060	Keith Foster	1996			2014	2014	

In 2017 I heard from 87 (75) Munroists requesting amendments to entries on our Lists (last year's figure in brackets) as follows: New Munro Rounds 20 (14); Tops 10 (6); Furths 13 (11); Corbetts 35 (40); Grahams 8 (11); Donalds 18 (12). Full House 4 (4) (total now 48).

Amendments are still a growth area, keeping your Clerk increasingly busy. The heighters, in particular Alan Dawson, have also been busy and in Spring 2017 announced the discovery of a new Top, Mullach nan Coirean East Top (NN137656) 916.6m (3007 feet).

Another lady remembering that we have not always had such bad summers, M. Clair Bale (5318) reported her Graham Compleation on Suilven at the second attempt. On the first, 'at least five years ago, the weather was too hot.' A few months later I received another letter from Clair, reporting 'my last Donald, New Donald, Donald Tops on Larg Hill, Newton Stewart. This was a second attempt (again!), the first being thwarted by 1) hummocky land 2) too many trees 3) no path 4) heavy rain.' These lower hills clearly present different challenges. This determined lady acknowledged 'I would not have been able to achieve this if I did not have such a supportive husband who has kept his counsel and been a superb 'Sherpa', keeping his pace at my plodding level and occasionally carrying my flask. OK, always carries my flask.' The gallant gentleman concerned is an active SMC member who will remain nameless, to save embarrassment! Reporting her record 9th Munro Round, Hazel Strachan (3438) also acknowledged her supportive husband Ian, 'chief driver and caterer.' She reported 110 days out on the hill, fitted around her full-time job!

Reporting Furth Round 6, Michael B. Slater (358) still remembers his first 3000-foot hill as Snowdon in August 1953, as a ten-year old. He is half way through his next Round already. Clearly lured over to the other side (the metric lists), Norman Wares (4151) informed me that his last Graham, Drum na Sgriodain was also his 1000th Marilyn (150m prominence), 1200th Tump (100m prominence) and 2000th Hump (30m prominence). 'In recognition of this eccentric behaviour several members of the Relative Hills Society also joined me on the climb, including three of only ten people to have climbed all the Marilyns.' George Hall (2511) sent me an interesting spreadsheet of distances, ascents and times of his various Rounds and concluded 'Corbetts are harder than Munros, both in terms of distance and ascent per hill and Grahams require the longest walks.' Fiona (5361) and Stuart Clark (5362) Compleated their second Munro Round on A' Mhaighdean via Ruadh Stac Mor on 25 December, reporting 'we had already celebrated Christmas with all the children and grandchildren together a couple of weeks earlier, leaving them free to be with others. That left just the 2 of us with no time pressures and a reasonable forecast for the day.' Nigel Morters (1279) reported finishing his Furths on Broad Crag in the English Lakes on St George's Day, having finished his Irish summits on St Patrick's Day. He was clearly upset at the circumstances which lead to finishing his Grahams the day before St Andrew's Day.

Five and a half years ago, Tony Stone took over as SMC Webmaster and his efficient support has been much appreciated over the years. At the end of 2017 he gave the website a major make-over before handing over to his successor, Mike Watson (4082). Many thanks to Tony and welcome to the team Mike. The new Keeper of Regalia, Chris Huntley (903) has also been kept busy satisfying the insatiable demand for ties and brooches.

Twenty-two years after Compleation, Edmund R. Mansion (6113) finally got around to registering. Remember it is never too late to add your achievements to our six Lists by writing to Dave Broadhead, 17 Drumdyre Road, Dingwall, IV15 9RW. For a Munro or Corbett Compleation certificate please enclose an A4 sae (with correct Large Letter postage please). Check <www.smc.org.uk> for further details and to view the popular picture galleries of Munroists and Corbetteers celebrating on their final summit.

Enjoy your hills.

Dave Broadhead (690)(Clerk of the List)

SCOTTISH MOUNTAIN ACCIDENTS 2017

MOUNTAIN RESCUE IN SCOTLAND is coordinated by Police Scotland. They receive the initial call through the 999 system and then usually task the local Mountain Rescue Team (MRT). There are 27 voluntary civilian MRTs and 3 Police Scotland MRTs in Scotland.

There is an unfortunate split in the affiliations of these MRTs. *Scottish Mountain Rescue* (a registered Scottish Charity, No. SC045003) is the representative body for most of the MRTs in Scotland. The statistics for 2017 listed below have been extracted from a report compiled by the SMR Statistician from information received from the 23 civilian and 3 Police teams that are members of SMR. They do not include incidents from the four civilian teams that are not members of SMR, except where the SMR teams have assisted those teams.

MRTs were involved in a significant number of non-mountaineering incidents, but only **mountaineering incidents** are described in detail here. The incidents for 2017 are compared with those in the 2016 SMR report.

TYPE	DESCRIPTION	NUMBER OF INCIDENTS	
		2017	2016
Rescue	the subject is at a known location and requires assistance	153	158
Search and rescue	the subject is unsure of their location and requires assistance	106	108
Search	little information exists to locate the subject	78	104
Medical emergency		17	Not Known
Police investigation		10	14
False alarm		14	10
Body recovery		13	9
Technical rescue	steep ground ropework is needed to access, treat or evacuate the subject	6	7
Other		4	7
Search – water	little information exists to locate the subject next to, or in, water	6	6
Animal rescue		8	6
Civil resilience	response to natural or man made disasters	2	4
Water rescue	the subject requires assistance in a water environment at a known location	3	3
Advice		1	0
Not recorded		2	0
TOTAL		423	436

ACTIVITY	2017		2016	
	Number	%	Number	%
Hillwalking (summer)	158	73.1	173	73.6
Hillwalking (winter)	47	21.8	41	17.4
Rock climbing	5	2.3	9	3.8
Scrambling	4	1.9	4	1.7
Snow/Ice climbing	1	0.5	6	2.6
MRT activity	1	0.5	2	0.9
TOTAL	216	100	235	100

GENDER	2017		2016	
	Number	%	Number	%
Female	138	40	124	31
Male	159	46	205	52
Unspecified	45	13	66	17
TOTAL	342	100	395	100

AGE	2017		2016	
	Number	%	Number	%
0–16		6		10
17–25		15		19
26–35		22		20
36–45		13		12
46–55		20		13
56–65		17		19
66–75		4		5
75+		3		2
TOTAL	232	100	242	100

In 2017, **July** was the busiest month. In previous years it was consistently August.

Saturday continues to be the busiest day of the week, but there was a slight % increase compared to previous years. Thursday is the quietest day.

CAUSE	2017		2016	
	Number	%	Number	%
Slip/Trip	74	34.3	72	30.6
Lost	49	22.7	38	16.2
Overdue	12	5.6	31	13.2
Cragfast	8	3.7	24	10.2
Navigational error	23	10.6	14	6.0
Fall	15	6.9	13	5.5
Separated	3	1.4	10	4.3
Benighted	3	1.4	8	3.4
Medical emergency	17	7.9	7	3.0
Other	2	0.9	5	2.1
River crossing	1	0.5	0	0
Exhaustion	0	0	2	0.9
Missing equipment	5	2.3	2	0.9
Technology reliance	0	0	2	0.9
Avalanche-natural	0	0	1	0.4
Flooding	0	0	1	0.4
Hoax call	0	0	1	0.4
Over extended	0	0	1	0.4
PLB activation	0	0	1	0.4
Rockfall	0	0	1	0.4
Weatherbound	4	1.9	1	0.4
TOTAL	216	100	235	100

CASUALTY CONDITION	2017		2016	
	Number	%	Number	%
Uninjured	212	62	256	65
Injured	130	38	139	35
TOTAL	342	100	395	100

INJURY TYPE	2017 (%)	2016 (%)
Fracture/Dislocation	50	29
Not recorded	9	21
Sprains	13	10
Minor	1	7
Fatal	3	6
Other	0	6
Hypothermia	3	5
Lacerations	6	0
Multiple	2	4
Illness	6	4
Bruising	1	1
Exhaustion	0	1
Internal	1	1
Pain	2	1
Dizziness	0	1
Heart	2	0
Seizure	2	0

INJURY LOCATION	2017		2016	
	Number	%	Number	%
Ankle	37	35.2	33	33.7
Lower leg	22	21.0	17	17.3
Head	13	12.4	12	12.2
Knee	9	8.6	10	10.2
Hand + wrist	4	3.8	2	2.0
Chest	3	2.9	6	6.1
Lower Arm	3	2.9	2	2.0
Back	2	1.9	0	0
Shoulder	2	1.9	0	0
Spinal	2	1.9	3	3.1
Upper arm + elbow	2	1.9	1	1.0
Leg	2	1.9	6	6.1
Neck	1	1.0	1	1.0
Pelvis	1	1.0	2	2.0
Thigh	1	1.0	0	0
Foot	1	1.0	0	0
Face	0	0	1	1.0
Upper body	0	0	1	1.0
Abdomen	0	0	0	0
Hip	0	0	1	1.0
TOTAL	105	100	98	100

NATIONALITY	2017		2016	
	Number	%	Number	%
United Kingdom	171	85.5	212	77.1
Netherlands	8	4.0	6	2.2
France	7	3.5	7	2.5
Belgium	3	1.5	2	0.7
Germany	3	1.5	14	5.1
New Zealand	2	1.0	1	0.4
Denmark	1	0.5	1	0.4
Ireland	1	0.5	0	0
Lithuania	1	0.5	0	0
Sweden	1	0.5	0	0
USA	1	0.5	6	2.2
Australia	1	0.5	4	1.5
Malaysia	0	0	10	3.6
Poland	0	0	4	1.5
Czech Republic	0	0	2	0.7
Spain	0	0	1	0.4
Norway	0	0	1	0.4
Italy	0	0	1	0.4
Colombia	0	0	1	0.4
China	0	0	1	0.4
Canada	0	0	1	0.4
TOTAL	200	100	275	100

HOME NATIONS	2017 (%)	2016 (%)
Scotland	59	64
England	18	15
Wales	0	0
Northern Ireland	0	0
Not Recorded	22	21

SMR AREA	2017		2016	
	CALLOUTS	HOURS	CALLOUTS	HOURS
Aberdeen	8	531	20	828.5
Arran	32	2,046.2	22	716.8
Arrochar	16	429.6	24	991.3
Assynt	11	132	9	198
Braemar	25	645.5	51	1,592
Borders	20	677.9	24	1,090.5
Dundonnell	30	1,138.5	30	1,387.5
Galloway	14	722.4	14	433
Glenelg	1	26	4	80.5
Glenmore Lodge	7	70	7	74
Hebrides	20	535.8	19	715
Killin	42	2,167.3	35	1,505.5
Kintail	12	296	10	393.5
Lomond	36	1,350.8	24	1,243.7
Moffat	11	520	13	748
Oban	14	684.8	23	1,225.7
Ochils	18	701.2	19	557.5
Skye	43	1,425	49	1,947.5
Torridon	12	326.5	22	522
Tweed Valley	32	1,275.5	32	1,519
SARDA (Scotland)	36	362.4	63	962.1
SARDA (Southern)	26	374.5	46	372.5
Scottish Cave Rescue	0	0	2	11
TOTAL	466	16,438	562	19,115

2017 Statistics for teams that are NOT members of SMR

OTHER AREA	2017	
	INCIDENTS	MANHOURS
Cairngorm	38	2,259
Glencoe	47	1,271
Lochaber	77	3,386.15
Tayside	44	1,122
TOTAL	206	8,038.15

Total Casualties: 185
Total Fatalities: 12

CAIRNGORM Mountain Accident Reports 2017

(I am most grateful to Willie Anderson, Leader of Cairngorm MRT, for submitting these reports. It is hoped that other teams will follow his example in due course. Hon. Ed.)

[R951 indicates a Rescue Helicopter]

Jan 1   Couple missing on plateau all night. Huge search with a great outcome considering weather. CMRT. 60 hrs.

Jan 2   Continued search for two folk missing from previous day. CMRT. 240 hours.

Jan 2   Rescue of a male who was found lying in the snow. Team got him back safely. Third life saved this year. CMRT. 88 hours.

Feb 13   Thirty-year old male took ill on approach to Carn Ban Mor. Stretchered off due to his general condition. CMRT. 42 hours.

Feb 18   Male with broken ankle in Coire an t-Sneachda. Arran outdoor centre along with Assynt MRT were in the area. Small group of CMRT sent to assist. CMRT. 10 hours

Feb 18   Climbers overdue on Spiral Gully. Advice given. CMRT. 8 hours.

Feb 19   Male overdue in Lairig Ghru. Huge rucksack and deep snow held him up. CMRT. 40 hours.

Feb 21   Male gets blown over the edge near Mess of Potage. Fatal head injuries. CMRT. 60 hours

Mar 28   Female calls in saying she is lost on Cairngorm. She was actually lost in Glen Coe! CMRT 24 hours

Mar 29   Male cragfast above Pools of Dee. Given a stern talking to by members of CMRT. He eventually jettisoned his rucksack and made his own way off the hill. CMRT. 24 hours.

Apr 29   Group from Malta overdue from walk on the plateau. CMRT gave advice to police. All resolved. CMRT. 1 hour.

May 25   Paraglider crashes into Meall a' Bhuachaille and breaks a leg. R951 airlifted him to Raigmore. CMRT. 50 hours.

Jun 2   Duke of Edinburgh group from Dyce Academy lost. Located by two CMRT and walked to safety. CMRT. 21 hours.

Jun 10   Injured climber on Fingers Ridge. Technical lower. A great team effort. CMRT. 160 hours.

Jun 10   Three walkers lost on Bynack More. Talked off by CMRT members. CMRT. 8 hours.

Jun 11   Climber was hit by rockfall on Pygmy Ridge. Compound fracture of thumb. He managed to walk to ski area and then asked for assistance from CMRT. CMRT. 8 hours.

Jun 14   Female cragfast at Foyers waterfall. It was resolved while team were en route. CMRT. 10 hours.

Jun 14   Female with injured leg near reindeer hut. CMRT on standby. Glenmore Lodge sorted it. CMRT. 5 hours.

Jun 15   Climber falls on Lurchers crag. Fractured pelvis and elbow. Packed by CMRT members and placed into R951. CMRT. 85 hours.

Jun 17   Fallen climber on Shelter Stone Crag. Braemar and CMRT both assist. Great effort by team members to get him down to safety. Broken pelvis. CMRT. 240 hours.

Jul 9   Two Americans got lost and called for assistance near Ryvoan. They
           turned up safe and well. CMRT. 3 hours.
Jul 21   Sixty-five year old male lost on Braeriach. Large search located him safe
           and well. CMRT. 144 hours.
Jul 24   Male separated from group on Macdui. Turned up safe and well. CMRT.
           3 hours.
Jul 31   Fallen Climber on Duntelchaig Crag. Team deployed; assisted to waiting
           ambulance. CMRT. 20 hours.
Aug 8   Two folk reported as being ill beside Loch Cuaich. It transpired to be
           Loch Quoich near Barrisdale!   CMRT. 2 hours.
Aug 10   Mountain biker crashed on Geal Charn above Tulchan. CMRT
           encouraged them to self- rescue. Broken Collar bone. CMRT. 15 hours.
Aug 10   Scouts missing at Sluggan Bridge. Located miles off route by R951. Then
           the two Scout leaders who went to search for them got lost! CMRT. 72
           hours.
Aug 19   Female in Duke of Edinburgh group with migraine. CMRT sorted it all
           out. CMRT. 15 hours.
Aug 19   Mountain bike accident at Wolftrax. CMRT and R951 got the casualty
           on board. CMRT. 27 hours.
Sep 3   Female breaks her ankle on Geal Charn. Airlifted off by R951. CMRT. 8
           hours.
Sep 3   A mountain biker incident. The biker fell off his bike injuring his
           shoulder. CMRT. 6 hours.
Sep 15   Two males overdue from Corrour bothy. Simply delayed by big wind.
           CMRT. 6 hours.
Oct 18   Female lost and overdue. As it turned out she was on route and made her
           way off the mountain. CMRT. 15 hours.
Oct 21   A party of three got lost whilst returning from Ben Macdui. Very
           inexperienced. Not able to give a grid ref. or read a map. From
           description it sounded like they were in Strath Nethy. R951 located them
           and dropped them off at Glenmore Lodge. CMRT. 12 hours
Oct 28   Male falls into burn in Coire Raibert. Compound fracture of leg. Carried
           to ski ground by CMRT. Big effort in difficult conditions. CMRT. 135
           hours.
Dec 16   Two males cragfast whilst soloing Jacob's ladder. Technical rescue. They
           were hauled to the top and flown off. CMRT. 162 hours.
Dec 27   Party of three lost on the plateau. No map. Recovered by CMRT safe and
           well. CMRT. 54 hours
Dec 31   Vulnerable male suspected to have gone into the river at Grantown. Later
           found deceased. CMRT on standby for first light. CMRT. 360 hours.

(I am grateful to Lisa Hutchison for helping to edit these reports. Hon. Ed.)

Extrapolating wildly between the two sources, the most likely Scottish mountain
incident in 2017 seemed to involve an uninjured 30-year-old Scottish male
hillwalker in Lochaber on Saturday in summer! If he was injured, it's likely to
have been a fracture/dislocation of the ankle caused by a simple slip or trip.

IN MEMORIAM

MICHAEL (MIKE) FLEMING j. 1962

MIKE WAS BORN ON 18 November 1936, brought-up in Linlithgow, and, after a year at university, he enlisted for National Service spending time in Aden. Having married Pat, they lived in Edinburgh while Mike completed his PhD in chemistry and biochemistry and then moved to Minnesota for Mike to complete a Post-Doctorate. They were in Minnesota for two years, and when they returned to Edinburgh, Mike achieved a lectureship at Heriot Watt University which was the beginning of his academic career at Heriot Watt which he pursued until his retirement.

Initially they lived in Currie but moved to Broughton in 1974 where Mike immersed himself in village life. He played badminton in the village hall, stewarded hill races, trod the boards with the local dramatic society, played the piano rather well and spent hours in his impressive two acre garden. Mike was a loving husband to Pat; a caring father to Morag and Donald and of course a friend to many. But I knew Mike principally through our love of climbing and mountaineering and we did many, many climbs together in the 1970s, '80s and '90s. Our last climb together was Whortleberry Wall on the Buachaille in 1994 and Mike led his pitches with ease.

Mike's climbing went back to the late 1950s when he was privileged to associate with folk who have become illustrious names in Scottish mountaineering such as Marshall, Moriarty, Smith and Haston. He climbed extensively all over the UK and although well-built and hugely strong, he was noted for his graceful style on climbs and his delicate footwork – 'good on his feet' as we say. He loved to tell the story of the introduction of PAs from France. No-one then understood Continental foot sizing so one would draw a template of one's foot on a sheet of paper and send this off to Paris ensuring a good fit!

He was a member of the Edinburgh JMCS from that time to the present and his calm style and quiet enthusiasm was a model for the way climbing should be done. In the JMCS he instigated the 'Week Meet' which always took place in May for the best weather. Carnmore was a favourite destination together with Skye, Applecross and Foinaven but we also travelled abroad to Ireland (and Cornwall). He became a member of the SMC in 1962, Smith and Leaver supported his application, and was General Editor of the guidebook series for a few years in the 1960s. He also served a term as a Trustee in the 1980s.

In 1961 he participated in an Edinburgh JMCS expedition to East Greenland led by Jim Clarkson to the Stauning Alps. This was a considerable venture in those days and they were rewarded with fine weather. The party of nine climbed some 24 virgin peaks and the most difficult mountain climbed, by Mike along with Keith Murray, was named Eilean Donan after the Scottish castle. This TD ascent involved twelve hours of rock climbing on the almost vertical north face, continuously IV and V with one pitch of V+ and the party was away from camp for a full 24 hours.

Tiso's 1967 climbing guide to Creag Dubh and The Eastern Outcrops was a classic of its time and the first plastic bound guidebook in Scotland. The credit page lists Graham as the 'Organiser' with the Squirrels et al 'Executing' the climbs. Tellingly it also states that the text was 'Reorganised' by M Fleming and I suspect he had a lot to do. Indeed Tiso later states 'Mike Fleming spent many hours making sure Campbell's left was the same as McKeith's and generally tidying up the various styles of various writers. He also receives my special thanks'.

Mike wasn't designed for speed but in other respects he was a natural sportsman who could play golf, cricket, badminton, throw a decent set of darts and play a pretty good game of pool. Cooking however was not his forte. Pat solved the problem by creating a sausage and liver casserole which Mike would bring every weekend and consume with great relish. So did a dog which got into the tent on an occasion in Arran. We had no tea that night!

It is unfortunate that Mike's climbing was stopped in the 1990s by increasing back problems as he missed out on extending his career like the rest of us by visiting the limestone of France and Spain. But as we left the humanist service to the Chopin Nocturne I reflected that in one's lifetime one acquires only a few real friends. Mike was certainly one of mine.

John Fowler

MILES HUTCHINSON j. 1955

MILES HUTCHINSON, who died in June 2017, aged 90, was one of the Club's longest serving members having been elected to membership in 1955. He was a committee member for a number of years and remained an enthusiastic participant in Club activities and missed very few of its annual dinners during his sixty two years as a member including his final one in 2016 despite the first signs of his debilitating illness.

Although latterly a dedicated hill walker in his younger days he was an accomplished rock and snow and ice climber with many fine routes, winter and summer, to his credit and creditable Alpine experience. He was also an active member of the Lochaber Mountaineering Club for many years.

As a fellow member of the Lochaber JMCS my first meeting with Miles was in February 1965 when he led me up what was my first winter climb, an ascent of Creag Meagaidh by Staghorn Gully. I was rather in awe of him then as a stalwart member of the SMC but went on to further climbs with him of similar nature and have valued his friendship and companionship on countless hills over the last fifty two years.

As a Scout Leader who has introduced several generations of Scouts to the hills I benefited enormously from Miles' help on many outings, winter and summer, and to many of these young people Miles was a living legend.

He was for many years the oldest living Munroist, having completed his first round of the Munros in 1955. He is number 23 on the list of 'compleaters'. He went on to complete a further three rounds of the Munros in 1992, 1998 and 2004, and added the successful completion of the Corbetts, the Grahams and the Donalds to his impressive climbing CV. He climbed his final Donald, Carrifran Gans above the Grey Mare's Tail, in 2014 when he was 87 and had climbed what was to be his last Munro, Schiehallion, two years earlier aged 85. Miles' knowledge of Scotland's mountains and glens was unrivalled and even in the latter days of his terminal illness he could remember the details of all his climbs and the names of even the most insignificant of Scotland's hills.

In 2004, at the age of 78, having finished the other lists he 'discovered' the Marilyns, the name given to every high point in the UK with a protuberance all round of 150 metres. There are 1556 of these and Miles was proud to be elected immediately to the Marilynists' role of honour having then climbed more than the required 600. This gave Miles a new lease of life and in his eighties he travelled far and wide from his home in Kirkcaldy 'ticking off' the Marilyns and in his 91st year he climbed ten of them bringing his final total to 1119. What impressed his climbing friends was not only his continuing commitment, energy and stamina but his enthusiasm and ability as a driver, thinking nothing of a 200 mile round trip to tick off another one or two Marilyns.

Never someone to take the easy way up a hill or along a ridge he would always opt for an 'interesting' route up the duller Munros and scramble over every pinnacle on mountain ridges such as Liathach in Torridon.

Miles owed his love of the hills to his parents. His father was a well respected GP in the village of Holme in Yorkshire where Miles was born in 1926. Family holidays were spent in Scotland where Miles and his younger sister Mary were introduced to some of the wilder parts of the country.

He gained his Natural Sciences degree at St John's College at Cambridge University and following his National Service as a Sergeant in the Royal Army Education Corps based in Egypt and further studies at Bradford University he took up a post with the British Aluminium Company in Fort William. Whether fortuitously or by design this move to Lochaber and the proximity of Ben Nevis and easy access to the Northern Highlands allowed him to pursue his love of the mountains.

There he met Margaret whom he married in 1954. They set up home in Kinlochleven where their first son, Miles, was born in 1956 followed by John, four years later. The family moved to Kirkcaldy in 1966 where Miles lived until January this year.

He remained with British Aluminium, latterly part of Alcan, for the rest of his career, working for fifteen years as a Manager at the Smelter in Kinlochleven before moving to the Burntisland Works in the role of Research Scientist/Technical Officer and retiring from there in 1988.

Miles' other great love, apart from his family was gardening. To this he applied the same dedication and pursuit of perfection which he gave to his hill climbing and he was undoubtedly an expert.

Miles was encouraged by Margaret in the pursuit of these two great passions and they enjoyed a long and happy life and celebrated their Golden Wedding in 2004.

Having cared for Margaret in the latter years of her own debilitating illness until her death in 2012, Miles continued to enjoy an active life, pursuing his hill walking and gardening with undiminished energy and enthusiasm and celebrated his 90th birthday in the Lake District with family members. Still climbing in the latter half of 2016 he was diagnosed with Motor Neurone Disease in January last year and passed away peacefully on 6 June.

He is survived by son John and his wife Sandra and by his two grandchildren, Andrew and Nicole.

Iain Park

POSTSCRIPT: In July last year a party of former members and leaders of the Strathaven Scouts spent a challenging weekend in Glen Etive where, with the help of the estate, they carried out the reconstruction of two bridges over a fast flowing stream on the path which takes climbers up from the glen to climb Beinn Fionnlaidh. It was decided to dedicate this work to Miles and a commemorative plaque was erected on the site.

THESE BRIDGES REFURBISHED BY
THE FRIENDS OF STRATHAVEN SCOUTS
IN MEMORY OF
"MAN OF THE MOUNTAINS"
MILES HUTCHINSON
WHO DIED.AGED 90
ON 6th JUNE 2017

IAIN A.T. McPHAIL j. 1948

I SHALL BE REFERRING TO Ian as The Old Man throughout this tribute as it was his preferred title. There is no doubt 'The Old Man' lived a very full and active life to the end. He was a high octane, adventurous and highly competitive person who has had a profound impact on so many people's lives.

He was born in Edinburgh in 1929, the son of Bobby and Jenny McPhail and big brother to his sister Sheena. Ian married his first wife, Lesley Greig, in 1955 and they had two sons Malcolm and Colin. Most of his schooling was at The Edinburgh Academy, followed by Edinburgh University where he graduated with an honours degree in Geography in 1950. He studied under Arthur Geddes, son of the pioneering conservationist Sir Patrick Geddes and he often credited his interest in land, farming and the wider environment from studying geography and the Geddes influence.

After two years National Service in the RAF, which included teaching mountaineering skills to other servicemen, he joined the family firm of James Macintyre & Co, Grain Merchants in Leith. He then decided to move away from the grain trade and worked for some time as Transport Manager for Russell of Bathgate haulage contractors. Ian then became a full time farmer for a number of years, before joining the Countryside Commission for Scotland, managing the planting and growing of trees throughout the Central Belt. His final job before retiring was Regional Cereals Officer for Scotland & Northern Ireland which meant his rather eclectic career had brought him full circle back to the grain trade where he had started out with his father.

In the early 1960s he bought a remote hill farm, Tavool, on Mull with no electricity and suitable only for sheep, goats and suckler cows before buying Hardiston in Kinross-shire. This was followed by the purchase of Parks of Aldie and then the Glenfeochan Estate just south of Oban. His final purchase was Culcharron, just north of Oban which he continued to farm until 1990. Retirement was not however in his nature and returning to Edinburgh, he set up an English language school from which he never retired and which still continues today.

He spent the last 22 years actively supporting the development of the school in many ways. His most memorable contributions were, as an extremely knowledgeable guide on afternoon excursions to distilleries, historic houses, monuments alongside many places of interest in and around Edinburgh. His geography degree and previous work experience had unwittingly prepared him, even for this. On the bus, microphone in hand he enthusiastically transmitted his passion for Scotland and the Scottish countryside, demonstrating his unparalleled knowledge of whisky, salmon, the deep mining of coal, and the current price of sheep at auction, to a captured audience of international students.

The Old Man was also passionate about fast cars, flying and sailing. He managed to find time in between his other activities to race cars and motorbikes, own three aircraft, race yachts on the Firth of Forth and the west coast. He also skied actively in Scotland and abroad, but had a special love for Glen Coe. His last skiing trip to the French Alps was in March 2017 less than a year after finally having a hip replacement. He chose France over other countries for the pensioners free lift pass which meant the excessive winter-sports insurance for pensioners would now work to within his budget.

He hoped that his enthusiasm for life and some of his interests would live on through his children in their businesses and in his grandchildren – Greig, Susan, Jen and Sally and his great-grandchildren Max, Abi and Sophie, all of whom he had great pride and affection for.

Colin McPhail

John Fowler writes: Iain McPhail joined the Club from the Edinburgh JMCS in 1948 at the age of nineteen. But this was no mistake as by that age he had done some remarkable climbing including around 100 Munros with some 20 ascents of the Ben by various routes. And at the age of fifteen he soloed the Cuillin Ridge in 8hrs 25mins – a good effort by any standards for one so young. He records that 'all food was carried and all pitches were climbed up and down'.

He climbed with many partners from the Club including Haworth, Slesser, Smart and Williams as well as with friends from the EUMC but when partners were not available he was happy to climb un-roped and these solos included Cioch Direct, Eagle's Nest Direct on The Napes and Innominate Crack on Kern Knotts – a stiff VS even today.

When he died on 13 December 2017 he was the father of the Club and while we had not seen so much of him in recent years, he leaves a remarkable story of climbing and adventure.

JAMES GORDON PARISH j. 1947

GORDON PARISH WAS OUR longest-standing member (70 years) when he died last September, aged 91. Gordon was born in Bromley, Kent in 1925. His parents were both scientists, working for the pharmaceutical business Burroughs Wellcome. Gordon attended Dauntsey's School in Wiltshire, and then Edinburgh University, where he studied medicine.

Gordon was one of the founders (or re-founders) of the Edinburgh University Mountaineering Club. Amongst its first officers we find a number of pillars of our Club: Gordon (President), Derek Haworth, Malcolm Slesser, John Berkeley, Donald McIntyre and Geoff Dutton, with Iain Smart joining the party a year or

Gordon Parish (left) with Tom Graham Brown (centre) at Lagangarbh, probably summer 1950. Photographer unknown. SMC Collection.

two later. EUMC began by attacking and describing the crags of Arthur's Seat. A comprehensive guide of 113 routes was prepared by Parish, Haworth and Slesser in 1946. It is doubtful whether this was ever published, but it was used by Dutton to prepare a short version of 50 routes, published in 1947. Dutton's typescript copy of the comprehensive guide is held in our Library. A second area of exploration were the Gullies of Glen Nevis: after many attempts by Parish and others, the formidable Surgeon's Gully – named for Donald Duff – was climbed as far as the fork by Derek Haworth. And a third effort was made on Rum in 1947, where a clandestine trip yielded a considerable number of routes. The Edinburgh group were aware of the 1946 guidebook to Rum produced by the Junior Mountaineering Club of Yorkshire – a considerable rarity then and now.

After graduation, discharging his National Service obligation, Gordon served for five years as a medical officer in the R.A.F. During this time he helped found the R.A.F. Mountaineering Association along with Johnny Lees and Michael Holton, and worked with Holton to ensure that experienced mountaineers were attached to all R.A.F. Mountain Rescue teams. During this time he met Tom Graham Brown, who was recruited to this cause as an advisor. At various R.A.F.M.A. meets at Lagangarbh Gordon and Graham Brown explored neglected corners of Glen Coe such as the Red Campion Gully of Buachaille Etive Beag, and later – aided by Graham Brown's yacht – the gullies of Beinn Trilleachan.

Gordon's first medical post was in Durham, and it was there that he first suffered the effects of what came to be known as ME – Myalgic Encephalomyelitis, or CFS – Chronic Fatigue Syndrome, an illness which came and went throughout his remaining life. Naturally, he studied it, mapping its epidemiology, and seeking its cause. There is a tribute to his work on ME at <meresearch.org.uk>. He moved to Edmonton in Alberta for a while, before returning to a consultant post in physical medicine at Colchester. He retired on health grounds in 1982, and moved to Stanley where he remained. Although he had moved back to Scotland in the hope of resuming his interests in mountaineering, this didn't prove possible. He devoted his retirement to support for ME research through his own eponymous charitable trust, and to working with the Possum Trust, a charity that develops and provides assistive technology for people with severe disabilities.

He is survived by his wife Shiona and by four children from a previous marriage. Shiona Parish very generously donated Gordon's mountaineering books and journals to the Club, and provided a great deal of the information presented here.

Robin N Campbell

ALASDAIR 'PLOD' ROSS j. 1989

IN TRUTH I DON'T remember Plod ever being called Alasdair and why he got that nickname varies according to who tells you, though most say it was related to his spade-like feet. Plod was a very active member of the North East climbing community in the early 1980s through to the '90s. He worked in the family fish business which involved early starts from home in Banchory to get to the fish market in Peterhead and then back to Aberdeen with many fast miles covered in his Silver MG Metro. Plod loved to drive and used this to explore far and wide. At the time the North East climbing scene was split between the Winers and

Plod at Dubh Loch, August 1984

Diners who frequented the Harriet Street bar and the Etchachan Club whose local was the Blue Lamp. Though his affiliation was more to the Harriet Street side of things, Plod managed the tricky political skill of associating with both and not falling out of favour with either group. His access to a car and generosity in providing lifts may have been a contributory factor! He was always on the lookout for partners to explore new venues or to further develop existing ones and I recall him driving from Banchory into Aberdeen to pick me up for a day at the Pass of Ballater and then returning me to Aberdeen at high speed on the South Deeside racetrack. He got his new route done though so it was well worth it.

His frequent journeys to the Blue Toon allowed him to explore the crags around Longhaven extensively and he developed a variety of routes. Across the area he added a number of routes with a variety of partners. His boldest offerings were at the lonely South End of Scimitar Ridge and his most technical was Shere Khan at The Escarpment. Some of these routes were the subject of doubt and controversy as others were unable to repeat them even years later. What is clear to me from my time climbing with Plod was that he was hugely strong, outstanding technically and had fully embraced the pre-inspection and practice of routes ethic that had developed at the time. He was also persistent –and maybe this is where the nickname really came from – he simply plodded away at routes until he got them.

Plod's richest vein of new-routing was on Deeside where he added many routes at the Pass of Ballater, Clachnaben and at the more esoteric venues of the Cadha Dubh and Crag X. The latter two were literally dug out from the hillside and nature has reclaimed most of the lines. Many of these developments were with a small group of friends that included Ian Davidson and Marion Sutherland. Plod's last major contribution on Deeside was in 1988 when he climbed Idiot Savant at E7 6c in Cambus O'May quarries. This was controversial as it was both chipped and yo-yoed from previous highpoints but it is crucial to understand that Plod was actually operating ahead of the curve and created a tremendous hard route for the rest of us to go at. I later retro bolted it while developing the rest of the quarry and after some thought Plod was happy that it should be bolted as the gear was in the way of the holds. However, he was adamant that his E6 beside it remain free of bolts as he saw it as a better achievement. On Deeside Plod left a legacy of hard routes but was also instrumental in encouraging others like Graham Livingston to put up new routes and he mentored younger climbers such as Colin Stewart.

Elsewhere he enjoyed exploring the Cairngorms and authored new routes on the Crimson Slabs of Creagan a' Choire Etchachan and explored the esoteric Dee face of Beinn Bhrotain though the details have been lost. He enjoyed trips furth of Scotland and I recall the trusty MG Metro taking Brian Lawrie, Colin MacLean and myself on a summer trip around the Peak and North Wales. He wasn't averse to a wee wind-up and after MacLean and I had complained about his driving we were left to walk the long hill out from Beeston Tor in scorching temperatures while Plod and Brian enjoyed a cooling beer. We didn't voice our complaints again!

Plod had a love of the hills, their flora and fauna, but particularly their history. This was always evident in his conversations and observations and his later choice to study History and Celtic Studies at the University of Aberdeen. When he applied to join the SMC his application form was both copious and meticulous showing a love of the hills way beyond the technicalities of rock climbing with Munros and Corbetts across Scotland snatched in fast raids over the Lecht or the Cairn O' Mount. A nasty finger injury hampered Plod's climbing for some time and took the edge off his harder explorations, then a move to Maud left him further from the hills and the climbing scene. His enrolment at the University of Aberdeen saw him become immersed in academia and gave a new focus to his life which ultimately led to Stirling University and a successful academic career though he still enjoyed the hills from that ideal base. My abiding memories are his enthusiasm for new- routing, particularly on Deeside, his generosity with his time and knowledge and happy times careering around the north east's roads in search of rock. Any drive up the South Deeside road brings Plod to mind.

Neil Morrison

Professor Richard Oram writes: It is painfully difficult to write a tribute to a someone who has been taken from us so suddenly and at such an early age, just as he was coming into the full maturity of his career and where the future held so much promise personally and professionally. With the death of Alasdair (Ally) Ross, the world has lost a flash of brilliance and warmth that touched the hearts of everyone who came into contact with him. For me, I have not simply lost a former student, one of the first whom I saw through the full degree track from pre-university to doctorate, but also a colleague whose skills, knowledge and experience I valued, welcomed and sought. But above all I have lost a friend whose passions and interests – Scotland's mountains and upland environments, history, musical tastes (from Duncan Chisholm to Smashing Pumpkins), Indian cooking, wine and whisky – matched so closely with my own (well, mostly, I loathed his taste in Punk bands with a passion and we shall draw a veil over his strange liking for Japanese boy-bands), and who was always there to keep me grounded with his dry but good-natured put-downs. I know that I have not even begun to understand how much I will miss him.

Dr Ross on the south top of Chno Dearg

Central to much of Ally's work over the last decade was Scotland's environment and he understood well how much impact environment had on individual experience and character-building. He was the exemplar of that truth. Although he would often label himself an Aberdonian to help the uninitiated understand his north-eastern roots, Ally was a Kincardine man, born and spending his early childhood in the coastal village of Newtonhill and then later in Banchory on Deeside. It was in this beautiful place, between the sea and the mountains, with the sandstones and conglomerates of the Mearns' sea-cliffs and the granites of the Cairngorms as his play-ground, that he found two of his enduring loves – the richness and diversity of Scotland's environment and the exhilarating risks of climbing. Those things informed so much of his later research.

Despite his early love of history and nature, Ally did not pursue an academic route after school but moved instead into business, eventually setting up a fish merchant company in Aberdeen. But, like many before and since, his growing interest in Scotland's past – and future – drew him back towards education and, aged 29, he decided to seek entry to university. Aberdeen University's Access Summer School introduced him to two of his deepest loves, medieval Scottish history and his future wife, Sonja, whom after a long time trying he eventually persuaded to come climbing with him on the sea-cliffs of the Kincardine coast. It was during one of those expeditions that he finally plucked up the courage to ask Sonja out on a date: she said she'd think about it and, several weeks later during another climb, eventually said yes.

But climbing and courtship were accompanied by hard graft and total commitment to his studies. He was an outstanding student who took to academic study with flare and brilliance. Having been talked out of his initial thoughts of studying archaeology, he immersed himself in Scottish History and Celtic Studies, securing a 1st Class degree. That interdisciplinary grounding provided him with the platform for his PhD research into the structures of lordship in early medieval Moray, delivering a ground-breaking thesis which overturned decades of scholarship and forced a wholesale re-evaluation of what we thought we understood about lordship, society and economies in the country north of the Tay.

From there, the only way was upwards and onwards, meeting new challenges just as he would have tackled a rock-face. In 2003 Ally joined the research staff at the University of Stirling as a member of a project exploring environmental change in the uplands around Loch Tay before becoming a permanent member of staff in the Division of History and Politics in 2007 as one of four environmental history lecturers. In the previous year, he had become Editor of History Scotland, taking on that role at a critical point in this magazine's development and using his growing network of professional contacts to reinvigorate and reorient its editorial style and content. Two years later, he became Director of the Centre for Environmental History and Policy.

It was during this period that Ally and I began to mesh work and pleasure, for our mutual research interests in upland environments and love for Scotland's mountains allowed us to undertake fieldtrips that were as much opportunities just to get into the hills as they were focused exercises of survey and sampling. Ally, of course, was a great rock-climber; I am most definitely not, having decided in my early twenties that I wanted to live to a ripe old age and not have arthritis in every digit and limb joint! After a lot of effort, I eventually managed to persuade him that enjoying climbing Munros was socially acceptable, especially when it meant stopping off at a pub on the way home to reflect on the day's achievements. But there was a serious side to this; it meant that we were able to penetrate remote country where the boundaries of the ancient land-units that he was researching could still be seen on the ground, following the march-cairns across the Cairngorm plateau and up to the summits, or down to distant bealachs where no modern routeways run. Research into settlement and environmental resources in 16th-century Stratha'an took us on extended trips to find on the ground shieling sites that he had discovered recorded in charters and estate records. Despite my best efforts, sadly, I never was able to persuade him to continue up the strath to Ben Avon. But it was on these expeditions that I first saw how his intimate knowledge of this landscape from his climbing days gave him a mental map; his new academic knowledge gave him understanding of where settlements and shieling sites might be located, where resources might be found, and how best to access them.

Few of us have the chance to blend work and pleasure together in this way. For Ally, it was an opportunity to cash-in on understanding that he had banked during his 'mis-spent youth', drawing down that experience to inform a series of academic projects on which he was engaged. As his research and publication output grew, across a range of topics from early Scottish kingship to grassland management regimes or wood-production in Highland Scotland, further promotion followed, first to Senior Lecturer and then to Reader in Environmental and Medieval Scottish History. A Chair surely lay just around the corner. But then fate, unexpected and cruelly quick, intervened.

Ally's illness and death came so fast that very few of us were able to say our good-byes. His calmness and dignity when confronted with his diagnosis was a comfort to those of us who were numbed by the news, and his concern for us and for what he saw as the inconvenience he was causing us was a humbling reflection of the warmth and care that he showed for everyone. Sadly, there is now a deeper poignancy to the toast he gave so often and which we gave to him at his funeral:

> Here's tae us
> Wha's like us?
> Damn few
> An' they're a' deid.

DREW SOMMERVILLE j. 1971

DREW WAS BORN AND brought up in Bearsden and started work at the Scottish Mutual in 1951. He worked there until he retired in 1991 apart from a small gap for National Service spent in Cyprus. His leaving present from the Scottish Mutual was a pair of ski touring boots.

He joined the Glasgow section of the JMCS in 1956 and following an initial active period, by his own admission had a short break for business and family

commitments before becoming active for the second time in 1964. Due to this short hiatus Drew's days on the hill thereafter were spent with two groups. The first was the old guard of active JMCS and SMC members he started climbing with when he initially joined the JMCS; the second being younger members of the JMCS who joined the club following his return in 1964. Drew easily fitted in to both groups.

During his latter active period with the Glasgow section of the JMCS which spanned nearly a decade Drew was a regular attender at meets becoming club secretary in 1967 a position he held until becoming president in 1970. At this time he was the proud owner of a 1965 split screen VW Dormobile which was used to good effect by the JMCS as a people carrier with several members travelling to and from meets in the van. The club on occasion hired a mini-bus and used this with Drew's van to allow parties to start from different locations crossing over mountainous terrain from one vehicle to the other. On one such occasion Drew drove to Kinlochewe whilst the hired van was driven to Dundonnell.

Over the following two days the parties made their way in small groups from one van to the other all with the strict instructions to be at their transport by 2 p.m. on the Sunday. Drew paired up with another member and on the Saturday evening camped along the route in a new tent which the other member had recently purchased. On the Sunday morning they left the tent to climb a A' Mhaighdean. On their return they were unable to find the tent which was made of camouflaged material. After finally locating the tent they completed the journey arriving well beyond the stipulated time. Drew then drove the hired vehicle to Garve where his own vehicle awaited with the second group who were becoming increasingly concerned, there being no mobile phones for instant communication at that time.

In the summer of 1968 The Glasgow JMCS held an Alpine meet with all the participants travelling in Drew's van to the Zillertal Alps in Austria. A report of the meet printed in the 1969 SMC Journal stated that the party enjoyed some of the worst alpine weather for many seasons whilst missing the best summer in Scotland for thirteen years. The report ended by giving two pieces of advice. It suggested not travelling on the autobahns over the weekend and if taking advantage of the seller's market in laid nylon rope to make sure you had the owner's permission first.

Despite the difficulties experienced on the autobahns and the entrepreneurial skills of his companions Drew continued to visit the Alps regularly, normally in the context of a family holiday but often meeting up with other JMCS and SMC members on his travels. On one occasion he arrived at Randa with Nancy and family and, meeting up with several SMC members who happened to be there, he was kitted out with some climbing gear and joined them on an ascent of the NE Face of the Lenzspitze. Following this he returned the borrowed gear and went off to continue his family holiday.

From the mid 1960s to the mid '70s the Glasgow JMCS were not only active climbing hills but also this was a decade when hut building and renovation was carried out enthusiastically by several club members and Drew was involved in much of this work. He was one of the stalwarts who carried a glass fibre igloo from Aberardair Farm to Coire Ardair on Creag Meaghaidh in December 1968, only for it to be carried away in the gales of January 1969. Along with others he then spent several weekends in the summer and autumn of the following year building a hut of local stone in Coire Ardair contributing to the design by suggesting the window in the sleeping area be constructed with jam jars. His theory being that the jars would reflect light better than the glass proposed. This theory was never proved.

Much work was done to renovate the CIC Hut and Lagangarbh through the late 1960s and early '70s and again Drew was a willing participant. During the renovation at Lagangarbh in 1972 he managed to mix family life with work on the hut as on this particular project, which lasted for several months, wives and children became a welcome feature.

Drew joined the SMC in 1971 and was club treasurer from 1997 to 2000. In 1993 he joined other SMC members on a trip to the Atlas Mountains in North Africa. He was a regular attender at club dinners until recently when poor health made travelling difficult. On the journey to and from the dinner there was always time to ascend a Munro or two. On one journey Drew suggested climbing Stob Coire Sgreamhach which had a short time earlier been promoted to Munro status. When his travelling companions stated that they had already climbed this mountain many times Drew defended his choice by declaring that it was not a Munro when climbed previously.

In the late 1960s Drew introduced his young family to skiing with regular trips to Glen Coe and the Cairngorms. After retiring he ventured further afield with regular piste bashing trips to the Alps (usually the Dolomites) with other SMC members.

Although Drew never lost his love of visiting the hills either on foot or ski he became a very keen orienteer in 1978, joining the sport in its earliest days in Scotland. This once again was a family affair with all members performing at different levels. Over many years Drew assisted in organising and competed in the Scottish Six Day International Orienteering event which scheduled a rest day midway through the competition. Whilst other competitors rested Drew often saw this as an opportunity to climb the nearest Munro.

Drew was an outdoor man and whether climbing, skiing, or orienteering he will be remembered as much for what he contributed to the sport as for his achievements which were many.

Andrew Sommerville and George Wilkinson

STAN THOMPSON j. 1959

STAN THOMPSON BEGAN CLIMBING as a young teenager, making trips before the war from Harrogate to the Lake District. When 14 he climbed Kern Knotts Crack in nailed boots and ascended Napes Needle the following year.

At the start of the war he moved to west Cumbria as a trainee engineer at Drigg and was a regular visitor to the farm owned by fell runner Joss Naylor's parents. His early climbing was encouraged by Jim Birkett and Charlie Wilson and he gained much experience on gritstone. Stan reckoned that if you could climb on that you could climb on anything. He often climbed solo in Birkett's company. In the summer of 1941, on the advice of George Basterfield a distinguished member of the FRCC which Stan had just joined, he helped in the removal of three dangerous blocks from the shoulder of Napes Needle, thereby altering the shape of the club's emblem. This caused some controversy, but it was recognised that the blocks were dangerous and their removal justified.

As an engineer Stan's occupation was reserved and he missed the first two years of the war, but after that he joined the Air Force and trained as a pilot, only to be

sent back to work at Lillyhall for High Duty Alloys a firm specialising in aircraft components.

While living in the Lakes, Stan became increasingly involved in mountain rescue, very often searching for airmen who had crashed in the Fells. He was also involved in the rescue of Wilfred Noyce, later of Everest fame, when he fell from Shark's Fin on Great Gable. The difficulty of this rescue underlined the need for a more co-ordinated approach to mountain rescue in the area and Stan was heavily involved in the creation of the team. He also encouraged George Fisher to open a climbing shop in Keswick as at that time the only supplier of quality mountain equipment was Robert Lawrie in London.

After the war Stan climbed in the Swiss Alps and among other peaks he ascended Mont Blanc and Monte Rosa. He recalled being very well treated by the locals as they regarded the British as the saviours of Europe.

In 1949 he took a job in Fort William and joined Lochaber MRT. He moved in the circles of Murray, MacInnes and Patey. In the fifties his career as an engineer took him all over the world: to Australia, India and Saudi Arabia. He climbed the mountains of Oman even though 'the locals thought we were off our heads'. He spent four years working as resident engineer on a big water and waste project at Al Ain in UAE and in his spare time worked out some rock routes on Jebel Hafeet.

As well as a mountaineer, Stan was also a skier and a member of the Lake District Ski Club. He also skied in Austria, France, Italy and Switzerland: St. Moritz being his favourite destination.

His final climb was Gillercombe Buttress in Borrowdale at the age of 86. Even then only illness involving a loss of balance prevented him carrying on, but he kept skiing until he was almost 90. Stan spent his final years in Keswick where, according to those who know, he was regarded as a local legend.

(Editor's note: I am most grateful to Jean Robson for supplying the photograph and the information from which this obituary is written and particularly for Issue 88 of The Update published by George Fisher of Keswick which contained an article on the life of Stan Thompson).

P.J.B.

WILLIAM DOUGLAS NICOLL j. 1972

WILLIAM NICOLL WAS BORN in 1922, and died aged 92 in January 2015. He was a 'son of the manse', and his father, Reverend William J. Nicoll, looked along Loch Rannoch to his opposite number, Reverend A.E. Robertson, at Bridge of Gaur. He was a friend of Ken Andrew – the author of the first Southern Uplands District Guidebook, and it may be through his association with him that he came to join the Club. Certainly he was a keen hill-walker, who recorded two completions of the Munros, the first in 1966 (no. 68) and the Donalds in 1989. He also attempted the Corbetts (or the 2,500ft Dochartys), but may have fallen just short. Unfortunately he gave up his membership of the Club around 2006, and so no obituary appeared for him.

This is not an obituary, but a mere note. We know that he lived in Ayr throughout his period of membership, that he worked there as a pathologist, that he was married to Margaret Hart Graham and had four children, but little else. When he died, his daughter Pamela got in touch with the Club, and most generously donated his books, papers and photographs, a vast collection. His books have been dispersed to our Library or to members. His papers – meticulous diaries and logbooks – are now deposited in the National Library as Acc.13874. His photographs – a topographical record of all the hills he visited – await cataloguing.

Robin N Campbell

Obituaries for Bill Jones, Bill Sproul and Peter Stewart will appear in the 2019 edition.

PROCEEDINGS OF THE CLUB

At the committee meeting in October 2017 the following were admitted to the Club. We warmly welcome:

CHRISTOPHER GRAFTON (60)
STUART J. MCLEOD (39)
JOHN G. PARK (54)
HUGH SIMONS (24)
OLLY STEPHENSON (49)

And at the April 2018 meeting:

SOPHIE GRACE CHAPPELL (54)
CALLUM JOHNSON (26)
ANDY MUNRO (48)
DAVID STRANG (52)
TIMOTHY L. TAYLOR (35)
FORREST J. TEMPLETON (57)
ANNA-MARIE D. WELLS (28)

The One-Hundred-and-Twenty-Ninth AGM and Dinner

2 December 2017

This year's event was back at The Carrbridge Hotel following the successful Dinner in 2015. The booking method for the Dinner has been updated and now members can avail themselves of the choice of using direct bank transfer or sending a cheque. The direct method seemed to appeal and well over half used this option. Also the bookings came in quicker, indicating that a few taps on the computer keypad or a phone is preferred to finding an envelope, finding the cheque book, collecting a stamp, checking the Dinner Sec's address and then finally finding a letter box. A small number of tickets were printed for those who wished one for posterity.

The weekend weather was reasonable, but this did not lure many members away from the excellent afternoon presentations. The first was from a team led by Rob Lovell, our Publications Manager. Rob explained the proposed strategy of maintaining the highest standard of paper guide books but in parallel using new technology to record and circulate route descriptions via a digital platform. This would support the Club's constitutional aim of maintaining a comprehensive record of all new routes and free up effort to be dedicated to new editions of traditional guidebooks. Rob, Martin McKenna and Neil Adams then showed a trial app for Polney Crag now available as an example of what could be available in the future.

The second part of the afternoon was a presentation by Ken Crocket based on his first book in the trilogy of Mountaineering in Scotland. This covered the period up to 1914 and Ken highlighted the standard of winter climbing then was only surpassed in the 1950s.

The AGM followed and conformed to a familiar pattern of regular reports being accepted with little comment. However some members did note that the Trust accounts are in an unusually healthy state following large bequests. There is a new post on the committee with the title of Information Convenor. The initial role of this position will be to ensure that the Club continues to utilise Information Technology in an optimal way.

The AOB section generated more discussion, including further information on attempts by the Journal Editor to get the Accident Reports back into the Journal. There seems to have been some progress and the Club should start to receive the information from the Mountain Rescue teams, although volunteers will be needed to turn the Scottish Mountain Rescue data into Journal format.

Finally a club member spoke to encourage those in the meeting to consider joining the Scottish Arctic Club. The Club exists to foster interest in Arctic Travel and exploration and in recent years has not been attracting sufficient new members.

After the AGM there was only a short wait for Dinner. Members must have been hungry as they positively raced through to the Dining room when summoned. Once well fed the President, Simon Richardson, gave a summary of a very successful climbing year which had club members leading some of the hardest new routes in Scotland (summer and winter) and in particular Uisdean Hawthorn establishing a new line on Arjuna in the Indian Kishtwar Himalaya. One literary highlight which Helen Forde presented, was that our President was the winner of the Guidebook Category at Banff Mountain Book Festival for his book *Chasing the Ephemeral: 50 Routes for a Successful Scottish Winter*. The successes of the club summarised, Simon handed over to our invited speaker Ian Parnell. Ian is no stranger to some of the hardest winter routes achieved in Scotland. However he explained that he started on many of the traditional routes, gaining experience and valuable skills as he served his apprenticeship. One early encounter was on a winter ascent of Tower Ridge. At some point he caught up with two older climbers and questioned which was the best way on. He was surprised that they were pretty non-committal about his options, leaving him to make his decision himself. He later found out this was Malcolm Slesser and Norman Tennent.

'Behold our jolly faces' Photo: Chris Huntley

I should finally thank Curly Ross for leading the Club Song and Helen Forde who designed the Menus. This year's theme for the menus was the 50th anniversary of the BBC televising multiple routes being climbed on the Old Man of Hoy.

The Dinner formalities closed with the invitation for as many as wished, to join the President on Sunday morning for a gully climb on the cliffs of Creagan Cha-No. In the end this was a well attended climb. 18 members and guests walked up to the top of the crag from Coire na Ciste car park and then descended down the usual descent gully with a static rope in place in case there were any difficulties. A traverse northwards then took us to the edge of the rockier buttresses and a fine but previously unclimbed gully. Simon went first and by judicial use of multiple ropes and some shuttling of ropes back down the crag all 18 climbed the route. A group photo on the top definitely had all the characteristics of two lines in the Club Song:

> And lots of other places shall behold our jolly faces
> When we go up to the mountains in the snow...

Hence the gully name Hobnailers' Gully.

Chris Huntley

Graeme Morrison emerging from the top of Hobnailers' Gully (I/II) on Creagan Cha-no. Graeme was perfectly kitted out for a traditional gully climb being dressed in tweed trousers, woollen hat and ventile jacket. He used a wooden ice axe and had the rope tied around his waist. Photo: Simon Richardson.

Lakes Meet, Robertson Lamb Hut, Langdale

1–3 September 2017

The Lakes Meet 2017 took place once again in the comfortable confines of the Wayfarer's Robertson Lamb Hut in Langdale. Good weather made for an impressive list of climbs ascended, upon most of Langdale's wonderful crags and buttresses.

My 1973 edition of the Fell & Rock Langdale Guide (the one with the red cover) was edited by Allan Austin. He records in the first ascent section a climb

Amy Goodill on the first pitch of Gimmer String. Photo: Simon Richardson.

that he, Metcalfe and Miller had first climbed 10 years earlier – with a footnote:

All the pitches had been previously climbed: - the Direct Start to Kipling Groove had been Led by J. Brown in 1952; [I like the way the great man is reduced to his initial 'J'] *the Rib had been climbed from the Crack with the aid of a piton; R. Smith and J. Moriarty had linked K.G. and the Rib with the aid of another piton. It only remained to remove the pitons and string it together.* [p242, J.A. Austin, 1973 Great Langdale Guide, FRCC.]

Gimmer String was among the many ascents done on the Meet and the Simon Richardson, Amy Goodill team enjoyed excellent autumnal sunshine and ideal climbing conditions on 'the String' – unintentionally invoking a little bit of SMC resonance in doing so.

Over 40 routes were ascended during the meet including:

Raven Crag: Revelation, Elevation, Ophidia, Mamba, Baskerville, Rowan Tree Groove, Jingo, By Jingo, Ramrod and Centipede.

White Ghyll: Slab Route 1 & 2, Haste Not (the latter by William Forbes and Jed…who were just visiting the meet), Ethics of Heather and Perhaps Not.

Gimmer: Ash Tree Slabs, D Route, Asterisk, Interlude, North West Arête, Poacher, Gimmer String, Bracket & Slab and A Route.

The rain which had been forecast led many to Sticklebarn Crag on the Sunday morning – mostly on the promise of easy access and a three star very severe route. Sure enough, on a near perfect 40ft buttress an obvious line – Main Wall Crack VS*** – offered scope for near continuous climbing by as many as we could manage before the rain spattered in. Several other routes were climbed before a five minutes retreat to the eponymous hostelry beneath the crag.

Hill walks included Blencathra, several Marilyns, and several Wainwrights too. It is fair to say everyone went home satisfied with the quantity of climbing achieved on the meet.

Attendees: Mike Watson, Fiona Reid, Brian Shackleton, Stuart Murdoch, Jane Murdoch, Chris Ravey, Nick Walmsley (guest,) Donny McLeod, Nikki Mcleod

Bob Reid on Slab Route, White Ghyll. Photo Bill Forbes.

(guest), Lisa Hutchison, Simon Richardson (President), Amy Goodill, Simon Fraser, Duncan Reid (guest, CAF), Guillaume Breuil (guest, CAF), Fraser Reid (guest), Dave Broadhead, Fay Brown (LSCC), Jeff Banks, Tom Wright (guest), Helen Brown (guest) and Bob Reid.

Bob Reid

Skye Winter Meet, Glen Brittle Memorial Hut

23–5 February 2018

Despite the cold, settled weather prevailing on Skye, and the excellent winter climbing conditions at the time, only Stan Pearson and Steve Kennedy ended up attending the meet. They were the lucky ones as sunny, frosty weather and seemingly endless névé coating the main ridge and buttresses were enjoyed throughout the weekend. The unusual conditions on the ridge were such that it was probably easier on this occasion to negotiate large sections when compared with the terrain usually encountered in summer. Rare winter conditions indeed for the Cuillin which lasted for around three weeks and resulted in numerous reported winter ridge traverses. Geoff Cohen and John Hutchinson had also planned to attend but their planned warm-up climb on the Friday in Kintail (Coire an t-Slugain) proved more challenging than expected for Geoff and resulted in a wee detour to Raigmore Hospital to deal with a dislocated elbow. Their company was missed but as the only remaining members in attendance, Stan and Steve enjoyed the exclusive use of the hut for the whole weekend.

Saturday dawned clear with a widespread frost which led to Stan and Steve climbing a new route on the left flank of the north face of Am Basteir. The route followed a system of ramps extending rightwards in two long pitches, at Grade III, to finish on the main ridge. Conditions were quite serious due to the extensive areas of ice and hard snow in Coire Basteir and crampons were donned from just above the Basteir Gorge. The pair continued the short distance to the summit and

Stan Pearson on Am Basteir after completing a new route with Steve Kennedy. Sgùrr nan Gillean's Pinnacle Ridge in the background. Photo: Steve Kennedy.

were rewarded with splendid views along the ridge. A celebratory dram was enjoyed later that evening, despite Stan's announcement that he had committed himself to a 'dry February'.

On Sunday, with the clear, sunny weather continuing, an easier day was enjoyed exploring the upper reaches of Coire Lagan, encountering a well-frozen lochan and some spectacular ice falls stretching down the approach slabs.

This was the third successive annual winter meet to Glen Brittle and, whilst winter conditions on Skye are undoubtedly fickle, excellent climbing conditions have been encountered on two of the meets, namely 2016 and 2018. With that in mind, and the increasing number of new winter routes recorded on Skye in recent years, there should hopefully be an upturn in interest from Club members in attending in future years. Thanks go to John Fowler for making the arrangements. Incidentally, Geoff has made a good recovery.

Steve Kennedy

SMC Ski-Mountaineering Meet, Nevache, Hautes Alpes, France
March 2018

Following last year's excellent meet, Anthony Walker, Chris Dickinson, Richard Bott and Gavin Swinton reunited at Nevache for another week's touring. We were joined at various times by Adam Kassyk, Bastien Demange (ex Glenmore Lodge) and Jacques Caraplis (neighbour). While there was snow up to our oxters or more, it was not always as skiable as hoped, and the chilly mistral put a stop to any thoughts of lingering.

The week kicked off with Chris, Gavin and Richard checking out the superbly wild, and tautological, Vallon du Vallon, above Nevache. Richard noted avalanche activity at the narrowest part of the valley and returned to Nevache by the demanding path, while Chris and Gavin continued up and over the Collette du Vallon for an alternative route down to the village on the crustiest snow of the week. Unable to comprehend how the locals in front managed to ski it in style, Chris and Gavin concluded that it must simply be down to their competitors' superior gear!

Day two saw probably the best snow of the week, on the hill opposite the chalet, the popular Croix de Carail, where we teamed up with the locals for a superb 800m blast down through the larches on fresh powder. At some point Chris, having been behind the rest of the group, disappeared altogether. The possibility of a rescue party was mooted, so Anthony begged a lift back to the chalet to raise the alarm only to find Chris already sunning himself on the terrace, beer in hand.

Discussing the next day's fun, someone mentioned Crevoux. An immediate chorus of assent came from those in the know, and soon persuaded the others that a day's lift-served off-piste was the perfect antidote to dodgy snow and hard graft. For some, a short skin up to the highest ridge led to a brilliant powder descent. Quel plaisir!

While Anthony was still recovering from flu we were joined by Adam Kassyk for a visit to the Cervières area near Briançon. Access to the Cime de la Charvie (2881m) is usually protected by a steep and often icy gully, fortunately now filled with soft snow. A delightful wild and open valley leads to the final steeper slopes and gullies below the summit. The latter proved too icy and challenging so a

Col du Chardonnet: Gavin Swinton, Richard Bott and Chris Dickinson.
Photo: Anthony Walker.

retreat on variable snow was effected down to the excellent pub in Cervières. Meanwhile the languishing Anthony received reports of a massive powder avalanche in the same area, and was somewhat concerned until he got news of the safe return of the party. Happily, there had been no casualties in the avalanche, though it was a salutary warning of the potentially unstable condition of the heavy snow pack.

Friday saw the four of us driving round to Pont de l'Alpe in the Guisane valley, to make the crossing back to Nevache via the Col du Chardonnet. Having narrowly avoided tripping over the almost buried chimneys of the lower chalets, a straightforward climb led up to the Col de l'Aiguillette. Despite the fine views of the Écrins, the cold wind moved us quickly on to the Crête du Chardonnet and the eponymous col from which the hoped-for powder descent revealed itself to be the usual mixture of slab, crust, sastrugi etc. A long traverse and a restful beer in the sun at the Refuge du Chardonnet were followed by the harum-scarum path (or the rocky bluffs favoured by some) down to Nevache.

On the final day, Chris left early for a tour of the Gran Paradiso area, while the remainder of the party were joined by neighbour Jacques to ski the Vallon du Creuzet from the door of the house. The crusty snow lower down did not augur well for the descent, but higher up an exposed traverse and powdery corner led on to a beautiful tree covered plateau followed by the final slope up to the Col de Lenlon (2500m). The high powered French contingent continued to the impressive Fort de Lenlon, while the slower (but wiser?) Scots picked their way down through the hard-pack, crust and occasional excellent powder. The final kilometre of shiny crust led down to the Forestière ski de fond track. Here a heated Franco-Scottish debate as to the best way back to the road stretched the Entente Cordiale a little, until lawyer Richard, regardless of legal consequences, broke the deadlock by heading up the track. Though a counter-intuitive move, this allowed for a pleasant descent to the river and bridge in good snow. Honour and Entente Cordiale were restored with the aid of useful quantities of beer. A memorable end to a varied and demanding week.

Anthony Walker

Easter Meet, Kinlochewe Hotel, Torridon

5–8 April 2018

The 2018 Meet was held in the Kinlochewe Hotel where the proprietors had changed, although there was no discernible difference in the public rooms and our archive of SMC photographs was still on the walls in pride of place.

The weather from Edinburgh north although fairly clear displayed a surprising amount of snow on the hills, improving in clarity and even sun towards Torridon.

On Friday evening John Hay had kindly invited the even larger than usual group to his evening reception in his delightfully characterful property on the shores of Loch Torridon. As we all crammed in shoulder to shoulder, the drinks and delicious plates of John's salmon and venison whisked by, and the members who had never experienced this splendid eccentricity before, stood by bemused, but happily joined in with a glass in their hands. It was a great pleasure to award him Honorary Membership of the Club after over 50 years of loyal service.

On Saturday before dinner, David Stone took the usual historically posed photograph, with the new proprietor's wife acting as the curious maid looking out of the window behind us. Back indoors we were treated to an excellent showing of Robin Campbell's collection of photographs displaying the many tangents that were Harold Raeburn's life. Robin enlivened the varied monotone and sepia images with his lively presentation. The Dinner was excellent but with unexplainably slow service. Gratis whisky from the proprietors provided adequate compensation. Slesser's ghost is still with us.

Hills ascended by many combinations of members included Slioch, Beinn an Eoin, Beinn na Eaglaise, Meall a' Ghlas-Leothaid, Meall na h'Araid, Creag Rainich, Beinn na Ramh, Beinn Alligin via Deep South Gully, Meall Aundrary, An Cuaidh, Bidein Clann Raonaild, Sidhhean Mor, An Ruadh Mheallan, Beinn Ghobhlach, Meall an Doirain, Fionn Bheinn and Meall a' Ghuibhais. The distinctly cool conditions meant that few ropes if any were uncoiled.

The meet had a splendid turnout and present were the President, S Richardson, R Aitken, R Archbold, G Ashton, S Atkinson, P Biggar, D Broadhead, P Brian, R Campbell, R Chalmers, G Cohen, A Coull, B Findlay, H Forde, C Forrest, J Fowler, J Hay, L Hutchison, G Irvine, H Irvine, A James, P Macdonald, W McKerrow, G McNair, T Prentice, K Robb, R Robb, R Ross, R Simpson, C Stead, D Stone, G Strange and N Williams. Our guests were C Anton, F Brown, G Fellows and J Preston.

Thanks to John Fowler for arranging the Easter Meet. We will visit Dundonnell in 2019.

Helen Forde

Easter Meet 2018 : Kinlochewe

Standing (L to R) : Peter Biggar, Calum Anton (guest), Jonathan Preston (guest), Gerrie Fellowes (guest), Robin Campbell, Raymond Simpson, Noel Williams, Bob Aitken, John Fowler, Bill McKerrow, Phil Gribbon, Kenny Robb, Brian Findlay, Fay Brown (guest), Paul Brian, Dave Broadhead, Gill Irvine, Alison Coull, Gordon McNair, Rob Archbold, Bob Ross, Hamish Irvine, Campbell Forrest, Roger Robb, Geoff Cohen, Simon Fraser, Lisa Hutchison, Colin Stead, Greg Strange, Geoff Ashton, Andy James, Peter Macdonald

North Wales Meet

4–11 May 2018

Chris Dickinson, Ian Crofton, David Myatt and Grahame Nicoll at Cwm Glas Mawr.
Photo Grahame Nicoll.

In the end just four members – David Myatt, Grahame Nicoll, Chris Dickinson and Ian Crofton – attended the meet, held in the smaller of the two Climbers' Club huts in the Llanberis Pass, Cwm Glas Mawr. This delightful cottage lies up and round the hillside from the CC's larger hut, Ynys Ettws, and, although capable of sleeping nine, was a perfect fit for a smaller, sprawling party. Surrounded by hawthorns, wood sorrel and a solitary oak, the cottage has a small terrace that catches the evening sun, and looks out across the valley at Clogwyn y Grochan and Carreg Wastad.

The start of the meet coincided with May Bank Holiday Weekend, and the three days of it were blessed with clear skies and glorious sunshine. To avoid the largest crowds, Chris and Ian opted for an interwar / Edwardian / Victorian theme on mountain crags, taking in The Parson's Nose, Kirkus's Route in Cwm Silyn, and Amphitheatre Buttress on Craig yr Ysfa. After his fall three years before, Ian was glad to return to mountain rock climbs in such safe hands, and even managed to lead the odd pitch. David and Grahame made use of the sunshine to opt for sterner stuff, taking in three good routes not far from the hut, followed by Crucible in Cwm Silyn and Llithrig on Cloggy.

The weather then broke, although the forecast snow showers failed to turn up. Choosing their venues wisely, David and Grahame managed to climb several routes between periods of rain, including a number on Clogwyn y Grochan, Lower Pen Trwyn and Holyhead Mountain. Chris and Ian eventually found Craig y Clipiau near Blaenau Ffestiniog through the mist and piles of slate waste, but by the time they reached the crag the heavens had opened. They did manage to grab some short, challenging routes on Craig Caseg Fraith Isaf in the Ogwen Valley until more rain appeared, and spent a final day at Tremadog, finishing in a chilly wind on the aptly named Grim Wall.

Thank you to David Myatt for organizing the meet, and to the CC for providing such a lovely venue.

Chris Dickinson on the Parson's Nose looking towards Lliwedd. Photo: Ian Crofton.

Ian Crofton

Skye Spring Meet, Allt Dearg Cottage
5–12 May 2018

We were too early for the superb weather which the whole country experienced a few weeks later. There was still a lot of snow in the Cuillin and the weather was wet and windy for much of the week. No climbing was done though Alan Smith and Peter Wilson did several short routes at Kingussie crag on their way to Skye.

Although Skye has become a famous location for dinosaur footprints, none were found at Staffin Slip and Port Earlish on Sunday. However, the large quernstone quarry on the tip of Rubha nam Brathairean was more conspicuous. Hundreds of quernstones were extracted from this site probably in Viking times.

The peaks visited on Monday were Sgùrr a' Mhadaidh (Tom Prentice, Alan Smith and Peter Wilson), Bruach na Frithe (Dave Broadhead, Raymond and Linda Simpson), plus Am Basteir (Geoff Cohen). Despite soaking wet rock Noel Williams found a good scramble on the flank of Druim nan Ràmh beyond the Bloody Stone.

Possibly the best spell of the week was on Tuesday afternoon when Geoff had already given up and left early. The sun came out and Tom, Alan, Noel and Peter did a south to north traverse of Beinn na Crò – a fine hill with great views.

Tuesday/Wednesday saw Dave, Tom and Peter bagging Beinn na Greine, a Marilyn above Portree.

On Thursday, though the weather was not great, Peter Macdonald, Tom and Peter Wilson crossed Bealach Coire an Lochain to bag Sgùrr Coire an Lochain. Paul Brian and Robin Campbell did a circuit of Preshal Beag and rescued a lamb, John Mackenzie did a round of Fionn Choire and Noel visited Greshornish where *A Drop in the Ocean* looked impressive.

Robin Campbell, John Mackenzie, Paul Brian, Tom Prentice, Eve Mackenzie and Peter Wilson soak up the sun on the morning we left. Photo: Noel Williams.

Descending the north ridge of Beinn na Crò. Photo: Noel Williams.

Friday saw most people head out on the track past Leallt to the old diatomite workings. Three then managed to traverse Creag a' Lain in windy conditions.

Those present: Paul Brian, Dave Broadhead, Robin Campbell, Geoff Cohen, Peter Macdonald, Eve Mackenzie (guest), John Mackenzie, Tom Prentice, Linda Simpson (guest), Raymond Simpson, Alan Smith, Noel Williams and Peter Wilson.

Noel Williams

JMCS REPORTS

Edinburgh Section: for the first time in living memory we passed 100 paid up members this year. A fair number of them came to the AGM and Dinner in Blair Atholl in November 2017, no doubt attracted by the prospect of Andy Nisbet as our guest speaker. Andy had kindly agreed to sacrifice what could have been a new routing weekend to show us slides of how winter was 30 to 40 years ago, i.e. longer, snowier and colder.

At times, the winter of 2017/18 felt like those times were returning, especially in March during our CIC weekend when a strong, freezing east wind howled round the hut all night, the normal water supply was buried (crampons were useful to reach its replacement) and climbing in one's belay jacket was the norm – assuming that one could summon the resolve to leave the comfort of the hut. Most people who did get out stayed as low as they could, enduring spindrift whipped in every direction by the wind blasting round the corries; ironically, the hardy few who made it to the plateau reported that it was the calmest place they'd been all day. After that weekend, hopes were high for a stellar April, but the mildness from the South West overcame the Beast from the East all too soon.

Our Annual Newsletters (available in the Library section of our website) reflect the spread of members' interests and activities. The 2017 Newsletter has a particularly wide range. There are articles about (and photos of) rock climbing in the Alps, the Lakes, the North West of Scotland and locally around Edinburgh, ski mountaineering in Norway and France and expeditioning to Antarctica. No-one wrote about hill walking or mountain biking, but you can take it for granted that they happen every weekend (although several members have been affected by the plague of bike thefts that afflicts Edinburgh at the moment).

If you are interested in joining the Edinburgh JMCS, we always welcome new faces. Please come along to our Monday or Wednesday night activities and meet and climb with some of the existing members. We climb indoors during the winter on Monday and Wednesday evenings, usually at Ratho on Wednesdays and at Ratho and/or Alien Rock on Mondays. During the summer we will be inside or out, depending on the weather; you can see where we are going by looking at our website which also lists our forthcoming weekend meets. Just Google Edinburgh JMCS. It is probably best to contact Nils Krichel, the Membership Secretary, beforehand to make sure there has been no last minute change of venue.

Our huts are available for booking by kindred Clubs; please contact the Custodians whose names are shown below. We have the Cabin in Balgowan, between Laggan and Newtonmore, and the Smiddy at Dundonnell in the North West.

The present committee includes: Honorary President, John Fowler; President, Thomas Beutenmuller; Vice President and Smiddy Custodian, Helen Forde (30 Reid Terrace, Edinburgh EH3 5JH, 0131 332 0071); Secretary, David Small (5 Afton Place, Edinburgh, EH5 3RB, <secretary@edinburghjmcs.org.uk>); Treasurer, Bryan Rynne.
The Cabin Custodian, Ali Borthwick (01383 732 232, before 9 p.m. please); Membership Secretary, Nils Krichel <nils.krichel@gmail.com>.

David Small

Glasgow Section: another busy and active year. The 2017 AGM was held in the Ben More Lodge Hotel, Crianlarich on Saturday 11 November. It was reported that there are 83 current members in total, 42 ordinary members and 41 life members. We had one new member recorded as joining in 2017.

The club organised a full schedule of more than 20 weekend meets in 2017 including successful weekends at each of the five SMC huts. There are meets every two weeks for most of the year, but only a single meet in August. The meets change from year to year, but as a rule cover the whole of Scotland and sometimes beyond. Venues included Karn House in Aviemore, Milehouse, Blackrock, Muir of Inverey, The Smiddy, the new Braedownie Hut and Tarf Bothy, as well as camping and bivi meets in Cairngorm and on The Cobbler. In the late spring and summer there are midweek evening meets to various central belt rock climbing venues. There are also midweek indoor climbing meets at The Glasgow Climbing Centre at Ibrox.

One of the more popular meets with JMCS members is the late May workmeet to the club hut at Coruisk on the Isle of Skye. The free boat trip from Elgol perhaps contributes to that popularity. The hut itself continues to be a busy at weekends, with overseas clubs now making regular bookings. New mattresses, blankets, pillows and comfy chairs were all added to the hut in 2017. Romantically, it has also become a recognised wedding venue, although there are a significant number of weddings that make do with just the landing stage. If any SMC members are planning to stay on Skye (or even get married there) please contact the hut custodian directly <iain-sneddon@hotmail.co.uk> or via the Glasgow JMCS website <www.glasgowjmcs.org>.

The club newsletter has a new lease of life under the editorship of Dr Ole Kemi. Four issues are published per year, circulated via the JMCS website in February, May, August and November. The newsletter welcomes contributions from all authors, not just members. Ideas and contributions for future issues, from folk either sitting on a story, or an idea of a story, then please contact the editor. Contributions may be long or short, or just photographs and may span the range of reminiscences of old times and stories, never-before told stories, pictures, poetry, quizzes, announcements and anything else resulting from the creative minds of mountaineers.

Notable Scottish routes climbed by members in 2017 included, in winter, the Cumming-Crofton Route on Beinn a' Bhuird, which included the traditional stay in the Slugain Howff; Tower Face of the Comb and Gargoyle Wall on Ben Nevis, The Cuillin Ridge on Skye, The Hoarmaster and a few more of the mixed lines in the Northern Corries. As readers will know, this winter's cold snaps were short-lived, but club members responded quickly when conditions arrived to snatch ascents, some indeed very notable given the difficult winter conditions.

In summer, the more significant climbs by members included Haystack on the Shelterstone, where an alpine start allowed a midday finish just in time for the arriving thundery weather (so all in all very alpine), swimming to routes on Muckle Stack of Duncansby, the excellent Land of the Dancing Dead on Creag Shomhairlie, and Unicorn in Stob Coire nan Lochain.

Another notable achievement was yet another member becoming a Corbett compleater, rounding off with a memorable club meet in Muir of Inverey in June, where Sgòr Mor was ascended to the tunes of a bagpipe and a large crowd providing a Guard of Honour.

Members' overseas trips included climbing in Lofoten and Stetind during a period in late summer that unfortunately turned out to be quite wet, so success was somewhat limited, alpine climbs or skiing in Chamonix, the Queyras, the Stubaital, and Gran Paradiso; rock climbing in Wilder Kaiser, Aosta, Frankenjura, and also in Chamonix; and finally trekking in New Zealand, including the Sabine-Travers trek that included the high level Robert Ridge and a scramble up Mt. Angelus.

In mid-April, during settled weather, as members of a group of five ski mountaineers, including two SMC members, two JMCS members successfully completed the excellent Urner Alps ski mountaineering tour from Andermatt to Engelberg, with a visit to the summit of the Sustenhorn(3503m) being the high point of the tour. In July two members scaled Mont Blanc de Cheilon (3870m) and The Tete Blanche (3710m) then finished the week with an ascent of the superb 15 pitch Voie Normale (or Voie de l'Y, French 5a) on the Miroir d' Argentine in Western Switzerland (see article). In November two JMCS ex-presidents climbed the remote Mount Usborne (705 metres) the highest point of the British Overseas Territory of The Falkland Islands. During their return to the UK, the same two trekked The Inca Trail to visit the impressive ruins of Machu Picchu.

Office Bearers: President, Iain Sneddon; Secretary, Phil Smith; Treasurer, Justine Carter. The Honorary President is Neil Wilkie after his own very successful presidential term of office. Our Honorary Member is Iain Cumming.

Colwyn Jones and Ole Kemi

Lochaber Section: as in previous years we started 2017 with a members' slide show, Davy Ford taking us on a trip to various locations around Europe and closer to home. This proved to be one of the most entertaining evenings ever held, with Davy teaming up with George Archibald to narrate the various stories held in the images displayed.

The club held weekend meets to Ling Hut in Torridon, Lochranza on Arran, Inverardran Cottage in Crianlarich and the Naismith Hut in Elphin. A considerable number of years had elapsed since we were last on Arran and this meet proved very popular with the members, with the Lochranza SYHA providing an excellent base for the weekend. Although the weather on the Saturday was not too great, with some strong winds and rain, some members ascended the higher mountains of the island. I am sure it will not be long before we return to this island and sample more of its natural and culinary delights.

For the first time the club held its annual dinner and AGM at the Nethy Bridge Hotel which proved to be a great hit with the members, not least for its central location and excellent hospitality. During the AGM it was proposed that we arrange a trip to Europe for the summer of 2019 and four options were suggested for the meets committee to consider. Following a member survey on the various options for location, method of travel and type of accommodation it was decided to go to Slovenia, with most selecting this on the basis that they had not been to this part of Europe before.

Steall Hut in Glen Nevis has continued to provide a good income stream for the club, which subsidises the weekend meets and it is also hoped will assist with the financing of the trip to Slovenia. This year we started a series of work weekends to the hut. We worked on the wiring, including changing the lighting to LEDs and installing electric heating in one of the rooms. See <www.steallhut.co.uk> and Mountaineering Scotland Huts Directory for further information and how to book.

To contact the club <iamacleod@btinternet.com>

Office Bearers: President, Malky Thomson; Secretary, Iain MacLeod; Treasurer, Ken Scoular; Hut Bookings, Ewan Kay; Hut Custodian, George Bruce.

Iain MacLeod

London Section: we continued to run a varied meets programme, comprising a mix of climbing, walking and mountain biking. The highlight was probably our visit to the Costa Blanca in March, when 10 of us enjoyed warm days and cloudless skies. A dose of winter sunshine lifts the spirits after a damp and dreary winter especially a wash-out of a meet in Glen Coe in February! April saw us in the Lake District using the excellent Agnes Spencer Memorial Hut in Patterdale for the first time, while in May it was back to our home turf in Snowdonia in the Ogwen Valley and on the cliffs of Gogarth. In June, we visited the Gower Coast and in early August celebrated David Hughes' 80th birthday at our cottage in Bethesda, with assorted curries washed down with the local Ogwen brew. It was time to visit the Peak District in September, which is probably the most convenient venue for our small membership, now residing mostly in the Midlands.

In the summer, members were active in North America and in the Alps. Maybe it's a symptom of our increasing average age but sailing is now a regular feature for several members. This included off the south coast of England and in the Hebrides. In the latter, a rough passage across to South Uist contrasted with warm, balmy weather and swimming in Loch Scavaig on our return to Skye.

The year ended with a well-attended AGM and dinner at the Swallow Falls Hotel near Betws-y-Coed, which proved to be an excellent venue.

The section hut would benefit from more use so if kindred clubs and spirits fancy a few days experiencing the delights of Snowdonia including its classic routes don't hesitate to contact us. New members are also very welcome regardless of age though some younger blood would not go amiss!

A special thank you is due to David Hughes, who in 2017 retired after serving as our Treasurer for 19 years. David has made a massive contribution to the section, not just keeping our finances in order but for most of this time organising our winter meet in Scotland every February. David has now moved to be nearer his daughter in Blandford in Dorset but we keep in touch.

Officer Bearers for 2018: President, Andy Hughes; Secretary, John Firmin <john.firmin3@btinternet.com>; Treasurer, Gordon Burgess Parker; Hut Custodian, David L Hughes <davidlewishughes@hotmail.com>.

John Firmin

Perth Section: the Perth Section is now known as The Perth Mountaineering Club but we remain proud of our roots in the JMCS. We are a small club with between 70 and 80 members about half of them regularly active on the hills. Despite the frequently dreadful weather, this was a better year for the club. Attendances at meets are up and there are new active members. On checking the numbers for the winner of the most frequent attender of meets I found we have 36 active members but there are others attending just the midweek climbing sessions.

There were some low points. In April Jeff convened a mountain biking meet for just himself in Galloway making it less well attended by members than my trip with Pamela up Mount Taranaki in New Zealand in March! Conveners were also inventive: Alison changed her meet from rain-drenched Arran to the Cobbler, encouraging three others to join her. On the other hand the Invergarry meet in January and Glen Brittle meet in August were very well attended and very successful.

Listing all the meets here would be tedious but it suffices to say we continue to enjoy the mountains in a variety of ways from climbing and walking both winter and summer to skiing and mountain biking. We learned the hard way that mountain biking in the winter is not such a good idea one icy day at Dunkeld.

Wednesday evening climbing continues to be popular both indoors and out and attracts new members. Many were even going to both the Dundee wall and the new Perth wall every week.

The joint lecture with the PSNS is part of what is now called the 'Perthshire Science Series' and an entertaining and informative presentation was given, at our invitation, by the Professor of Mountain Studies at the University of the Highlands and Islands, Martin Price. In March we entered and once again won the Mountain Mind Quiz. Congratulations to the A team of Grahame and Mel Nicoll and Paul Grace.

On a sad note we lost both Ken Laye and Des Bassett in the summer. Ken was active with the club in the '70s and did much of his walking and climbing with his wife Liz. Des on the other hand was our current Treasurer and Honorary President when he passed on. He was a club stalwart from his retirement in 2000 till just before his death. We will all miss him.

Someone who bridges these two eras is Ron Payne and although he is still very much alive, he has moved to the deepest South of England to be near his family. So, sadly, he will not feature on many meets now and we thank him for long service to the club.

The Dinner this year was once again well attended with 19 members and one guest, Rosie Bassett, Des's widow. It was a natural occasion to pay tribute to Des and his enjoyment of mountaineering in all senses of the word.

As part of our drive to keep the club relevant and to build our membership and meet attendance we carried out a survey of members. We will continue our programme of one weekend and one day meet each month but the plan is to add in more social events and you may even see us resplendent in the new PMC T-shirts complete with the JMCS logo on the climbing walls and crags.

Office Bearers: President, Dennis Underwood; Vice President, Wendy Georgeson; Secretary, Tim Storer; Membership Secretary, Wendy Georgeson.

For a full list of office bearers, more information and details of how to contact the club visit our website at <http://www.perthmountaineering-club.co.uk/>

Alasdair Dutton

SMC ABROAD

ALPS – MONT BLANC RANGE

Rick Allen and I teamed up for a couple of weeks alpine climbing in the Mont Blanc range in early summer 2017. It had been a very warm and dry spring and I was astonished how dry the mountains looked as I travelled from Geneva to Chamonix on 22 June. It was more like September than late spring.

Our first objective was a new route on the Grande Fourche (3610m), which is situated between the Aiguille du Tour and the Chardonnet, and is most often climbed from the Tour Glacier. The south-east face of the mountain above the Saleina Glacier was particularly intriguing as its 500m central spur was unclimbed. Of course, we were not the first SMC members to explore this beautiful cirque on the Swiss side of the range. In 1906 Ling and Raeburn made a first ascent on the North-East Face of the Aiguille d'Argentière – an attractive but rarely climbed mixed route.

After a night in the Albert Premier Hut we crossed the Fenêtre de Saleina and started up our spur in bright sunshine next morning. We expected to climb the route in a day and were traveling light, but we underestimated the difficulties, and by early afternoon we were only a quarter of the way up the route. But June days are long and the weather forecast was good so we pressed on up easier climbing on the upper part of the spur in the full knowledge that we would be spending a night out.

We settled down on a good ledge just below the summit as dusk fell and were a little surprised when it started to drizzle. We were even more surprised when the drizzle turned to rain and we spent the night curled up in our lightweight waterproofs willing morning to arrive. There was no point in complaining so we spent the night being as cheerful as possible. Cold muscles meant it was slow going next morning as we made our way over the summit in thick cloud and down to the Tour Glacier. Feeling rather traditional we named our 19-pitch creation the Scottish Route and graded it TD, 6a.

The weather had now entered an unsettled phase but we made the most of it with short rock routes in the Aiguilles Rouges and a wintry traverse of the Aiguilles d'Entrèves from the Torino Hut.

On 3 July we were back at the Albert Premier Hut all set for the big objective of the trip – a traverse of the East–West spine of the Aiguille du Chardonnet (3824m) starting from the Saleina glacier and finishing along the Forbes Arête. Rather surprisingly, this prominent structural feature had not been climbed in its entirety. The upper part of the ridge is taken by the popular Forbes Arête but the lower two-thirds that rise from the Saleina Glacier had not been followed.

The route took three days and required a full repertoire of alpine tricks and techniques. Rick climbed a difficult Scottish-style ice gully by finding a cunning through-route under a chockstone and I chimneyed my way up snowy offwidths in rock shoes. When the rock blanked out at the end of the first day and we were unable to continue any further, we bivouacked hoping for fresh inspiration in the morning. Warm sunshine next day provided the impetus to climb a blank corner then teeter along a sensational crenellated ridge of monolithic towers, followed by several pitches of tip-toe traversing across thinly ice-covered slabs.

After a second bivouac we joined the Forbes Arête, which was fun, but it took far longer than expected because conditions were lean after the warm spring. We front pointed black ice around the pinnacles on the ridge before reaching the

Rick Allen low down on the East Ridge Integrale on Aiguille du Chardonnet (TD).
The E–W traverse from the Saleina Glacier ending with the Forbes Arête took 3 days.
Photo: Simon Richardson.

summit mid-morning. The descent was pretty testing too – the initial snow couloir had been reduced to rubble and black ice – and worse, the glacier below Col Adams Reilly was cut by two enormous bergschrunds. It was lucky we had two 60m ropes.

We arrived back at the hut at 8 p.m. and somehow I managed to catch my flight from Geneva at 7 a.m. next morning. We called our route the East Ridge Integrale and gave it the ubiquitous TD grade.

Simon Richardson

CANADA – COAST MOUNTAINS

In August 2017, I visited the Canadian Coast Mountains with Micha Rinn from Germany. We climbed three new routes, but the stand out climb was the first ascent of the 1300m South–West Face of Monarch Mountain.

Monarch (3555m) is one of the highest mountains on the range, but it is very remote and rarely climbed. The story began in 1997 when I first climbed in the Canadian Coast Mountains with Dave Hesleden. We traversed the mountains north of Mount Waddington and on the horizon was a very prominent solitary peak. On our way home we met Don Serl, guidebook writer and pre-eminent Coast Mountains climber, who revealed that the peak was called Monarch Mountain. The mountain had poorer weather than Waddington, Don explained, and was very rarely climbed – maybe one ascent every three or four years. I was intrigued and resolved to try it some day.

Three years later Don crowned his Coast climbing career with a four-day ascent of the North Ridge of Monarch – the fourth route on the mountain and by far the most difficult. I took a deeper interest in the mountain and realised that the south-west face was huge, well over 1200m-high, and also unclimbed. Unfortunately I could not find any photos of the face. The standard route of ascent is from the east and only a handful of people had ever seen this side of the mountain, so the south-west face remained a big unknown.

Then in April 2007, light airplane pilot and mountain photographer John Scurlock flew around Monarch and took a remarkable series of photos. These showed that the south-west face was defined by a magnificent line of two stepped spurs that led directly to the summit. John published his images on the Internet and Don and I considered making an attempt but other commitments got in the way.

As one of the largest unclimbed walls in the Coast Mountains it was a prominent target but attempts by other teams were thwarted by bad weather or difficult planning and then Don retired from serious climbing. After our success on the Diamond Ridge on the Grandes Jorasses in 2016, Micha and I were looking for a similar objective for the following summer, and Monarch immediately came to mind.

We flew in to Monarch Icefield by helicopter on 28 July. Helicopter access is the standard way of approaching the Coast Mountains because approaches are so long. We camped on the col between Monarch and Page Mountain and acquainted ourselves with the area with a new route up the North Ridge of P2625m to the west. We then climbed Monarch by the West Face. This was the second route climbed on the mountain in 1953 and has seen very few ascents since. It provided an interesting and somewhat demanding mountaineering route of Difficile standard and would be our descent route.

The 1300m S.W. Face of Monarch Mountain (3555m) in the Canadian Coast Mountains. Game of Thrones (ED2) takes a line up the two stepped spurs in the centre of the wall. Photo: John Scurlock.

Finally on 4 August we started up the south-west face. Rather than follow the crest of the lower of the two spurs we climbed a more direct line to its left before bivouacking at the foot of the impressive second spur at half height on the face.

The climbing had become gradually more difficult during the first day and was particularly challenging on day two. Unlike the mostly excellent granite of the Waddington Range, Monarch is comprised of metamorphosed volcanic rock. This was very solid in the upper half of the route, but it was very compact with few protection possibilities, and rather alarmingly all the holds sloped downwards! We had numerous long runouts, and at times were worried whether the route would go, but fortunately we found a climbable line.

At the top of the second pillar the upper ridge provided easier climbing. We bivouacked for a second time 70m below the top and were on the summit early next morning. The descent of the West Face went smoothly, and we were greatly helped by our prior knowledge of the route.

We called our 1300m-high route Game of Thrones and graded it ED2 5.10a. It is similar in difficulty and scale to the Walker Spur on the Grandes Jorasses but more serious. We would not have been able to descend from above half height because the compact nature of the rock would have quickly exhausted our rack.

After a day's rest we made the first ascent of The Sugarloaf (2620m) which lay at the end of a long pinnacled ridge to the north of P2625 that we had climbed earlier in the trip. Although not technically difficult this proved to be almost a route too far as we soon realised that we were still very tired from the Monarch ascent. We flew out two days later as the weather began to turn.

Simon Richardson

USA – RED ROCK, NEVADA

In early October 2017, Tom Bohanon and I spent several days climbing moderate classics in Red Rock Canyon. The rock climbing on the superbly textured sandstone was exquisite, but the mountaineer in me yearned for something more adventurous. Bo was keen to travel new ground too, so from 7 to 8 October we climbed the prominent buttress to the left (south) of South Gully on the East Face of Mount Wilson – the dominant wall in the area. We started up a steep hanging chimney on the left side of the rib and climbed eight pitches up cracks, grooves and chimneys to an easing where the rock transitions from crimson to yellow in colour. We bivouacked on a good ledge and next day climbed eight more sustained and varied pitches up further cracks, corners and chimneys to gain the south ridge. From there we scrambled up to and over the twin summits of South Wilson, before continuing more easily to the main summit and descending First Creek Canyon and reaching our truck at midnight. We called our 16-pitch route Tickled Rib and graded it 5.8+.

Simon Richardson

Photos (360° panorama): Noel Williams.

NEW ZEALAND December 2017

A quarter of a century ago my friend Willie Jeffrey spent 18 months in New Zealand and when he eventually returned home he brought me a poster of Mount Aspiring – the Matterhorn of the Southern Alps. Willie had climbed the mountain in winter conditions and endured a cold bivouac not far below the summit. It looked a truly spectacular mountain but not having climbed it myself, I didn't feel I could hang the poster in our home.

My late friend Derek Fabian wrote a very amusing article for the 1997 *Journal* about how, via a wine and cheese party, a beat-up campervan and on his second attempt, he managed to climb the mountain in his sixties. I was hugely impressed. A couple of years later in the *Journal* Alan Hunt described soloing the mountain on his round the world sailing trip (1994–7). The idea of following in their footsteps remained a dream while I was teaching.

Once I retired I learnt that Paul Brian had had a couple of attempts but hadn't been lucky with the weather. I tried to interest him and his pals in having another go, but after chewing it over for a while they decided they weren't interested. They gave the impression that they'd maybe left it too late.

My daughter Lucy had been round the world in her gap year and now wanted to revisit New Zealand with her partner Mike. She tried to persuade mum and dad to go as well, but by now the thought of that long air journey was starting to put us off too.

If we were going that far we'd want to go for at least five weeks, but Lucy and Mike could only manage three. However, Lucy persuaded us that we could spend Christmas together down under before going our separate ways. Next thing you know we'd booked our flights.

Now Mike's young and very fit and works as a rope access technician. It turns out he'd done a little bit of sports climbing, but not trad. He'd never been to the Alps, though I'd enjoyed an afternoon with him on Castle Ridge. Might he be interested in climbing Mount Aspiring? If he and Lucy only had three weeks to 'do' New Zealand, they might be reluctant to set aside four or five days for an attempt on a mountain.

Then I discovered that Mike Dixon had done Mount Aspiring earlier in the year. I had a very hurried conversation with him at the first Northern District Meeting of the autumn. He mentioned that the weather was awful when he was there and that you have to be very lucky to find a weather window on a short visit.

But sometimes the stars align…

Lucy and Mike decided to hire a campervan, while Carolyn and I intended staying in motels and so plumbed for a car instead. We only booked two places before we left home – a couple of days in a hotel in Christchurch to get over jet lag when we arrived, and four days in a house in Wanaka over Christmas.

Mike Bauermeister on the summit of Mount Aspiring.

As soon as we got into our rooms in Christchurch I went online to check out the forecast for Mount Aspiring. There is a superb website called <mountain-forecast.com>, which gives weather forecasts for major mountain summits around the world. They were predicting days of storm for Mountain Aspiring, but then a window of perfect weather for the Friday before Christmas, after which it would start to break down again. Would it be possible to snatch an ascent?

We arranged to get early access to our accommodation in Wanaka and left Christchurch on Wednesday morning. After stopping off at various scenic spots on the way, eight hours later we were making ourselves at home in a commodious house on the outskirts of Wanaka.

Early next day I popped into the town to buy a camping stove and a couple of gas cylinders, as well as a mug and eating utensils. I enquired about staying in the Colin Todd Hut, but I wasn't sure if or when we'd get there. All I knew was that we wouldn't be popular if we missed Christmas with the rest of the team. I discovered there was running water at the hut so we didn't need to melt snow.

Mike and Lucy arrived on cue in their campervan. Next I contacted Aspiring Helicopters and they said the weather was currently too bad for us to be dropped off at Bevan Col, though there was an outside chance it might improve later in the day, in which case they'd give us a call. So we started packing for the hill just in case. I had to pop into town again as we didn't have a billy, though we later discovered we didn't need one as the hut was well equipped.

At 3 p.m. we got a call from the helicopter people to say that they had contact with a guide at Bevan Col. It was too cloudy to fly at the moment, but if we headed down to their base we might just be lucky later. And we were.

As soon as we jumped out of the helicopter at Bevan Col the guide and his client jumped in. After being stormbound for days we guessed that the client was probably having to abandon his attempt because he'd run out of money. I teased Mike that I might not charge him the standard NZ$5,000 guiding fee if we managed to climb the mountain.

Once we'd dropped down onto the Bonar Glacier we put the rope on. I pulled out a couple of prusik loops for Mike and gave him some rudimentary instruction on glacier travel. It was supposed to take only about 1½ hours to the Colin Todd Hut, but mist descended when we were halfway there and we went too far west. We ended up approaching from much lower down on the Shipowner Ridge than usual, but still made it to the hut by 6.30 p.m.

A guide and two clients were established in the hut. They planned on doing the North-West Ridge the next day – the same route as ourselves. Guides normally march their clients up a snow feature called The Ramp because it's the quickest route to the summit. However, the guide explained that a large section of it was missing snow already this season so that option was out of the question. We intended going up the Shipowner Ridge from the hut and then turning right along the North-West Ridge to the summit. We assumed the guided party would be doing the same.

I couldn't believe it when the other party started clattering around at 2.30 a.m. As the guide cooked breakfast for his clients he tried to impress on them the need to keep moving once they set off. He said they wouldn't be stopping to rest and any food would need to be eaten when the other client was climbing.

We had no intention of setting off this early, so tried to snatch some more sleep. Mike's phone alarm went off at 4 a.m. and we were soon scoffing some breakfast. As we headed up the ridge from the hut we noticed three headtorchs way over to our right. This was quite puzzling. They seemed to be slightly lower than we were. We wondered if the party was abandoning its attempt. At this point we stopped to put on our crampons but I only took a few steps and one came completely off my boot. I had bought a new pair of boots for the trip and stupidly hadn't checked how well my crampons fitted. The boots didn't have a welt so there was nowhere for the heel clamp to grip. When I'd discovered this the previous day I'd fitted the crampons as tightly as possible and they seemed to be OK. Maybe I'd not taken enough care in the dark.

By the time we set off again the other party was starting to head uphill again. We wondered if the guide knew something we didn't. At first we continued up the ridge, but after umming and ahing decided to follow the lights of the other party after all. This was the best decision we made all day.

We eventually realised we were cutting a major corner by slanting diagonally up a huge snowfield. We kept going at a steady plod. One of my crampons then came off again and this was clearly a concern. I decided to thread the crampon straps under the laces of my boots and fortunately this seemed to do the trick.

The guided party was roped together, but we were soloing so gradually started to catch them up. We arrived not far behind them at a big rockband just as it started to get light. The other party had traversed a long way leftwards at the base of the rockband, but we headed directly up onto the rock. We traversed left across a steep wall using an amazing jug. When we moved out onto easy slabs we caught sight of the other party again just above us on a snowfield. We later discovered that this snowfield is known as the 'Kangaroo Patch' because of its distinctive shape.

To our amazement it soon became clear that the other party was retreating. The guide was lowering his clients one by one back down the snow. He raised his eye brows in exasperation as we soloed by. He said not to take the steep rock buttress on the crest above but to slant across its left flank instead.

We now had the mountain to ourselves. When we reached a big snow patch on the exposed left flank we put crampons on again and kicked our way up by its top edge. I was impressed with how at home Mike seemed to be on snow.

Once we were back on the crest there was lots of great scrambling along the narrow ridge, though the rock was not always the best. There was then a long stretch of easy ground before we reached the snowy and much steeper upper section of the mountain. The snow was quite icy and I was glad I'd decided to take out two ice tools each. I wouldn't have been surprised if Mike had wanted to put the rope on at this point, although that would certainly have slowed us down. To my relief he shot off ahead of me. I was being careful because of my crampons (and old age!), but eventually joined him on the very sharp summit. Wow, what a breathtaking view! I have rarely been happier. It was 10.30 a.m.

Since we had plenty of time we decided to descend by the route we had meant to go up earlier. We really enjoyed returning this way. It was more interesting, but also quite complex and so proved much more time consuming. It involved four abseils and several climbing pitches, a couple of which felt about Severe, though we may not have gone the best way.

Mike traverses the steep wall below the Kangaroo Patch. Photo: Noel Williams.

Descending from the summit of Mount Aspiring. Photo: Mike Bauermeister.

A couple of keas were waiting for us when we arrived back at the hut.

The next day we stomped back across the Bonar Glacier to Bevan Col. From there – to hell with the expense – we managed to get a helicopter flight straight back to base in oodles of time for Christmas.

Noel Williams

NORWAY - EIDFJORD

In February 2018, Tom Bohanon and I visited Eidfjord in central Norway. The Internet hailed this deep valley east of Bergen as an 'ice climbing Mecca' with 'potential for hundreds of new routes' but typical of much of Norwegian climbing, information was scant. High profile American climbers had visited the area in 2010, but it was difficult to distinguish hype from reality. It turned out that several of the 2010 'new routes' had previously been climbed by Norwegians, and the genuine new additions, 300m WI6s, looked completely out of our league.

We climbed in Rjukan for five days before visiting Eidfjord. Although busy, Rjukan proved a good warm up. Bo already had some good water ice leads under his belt from Colorado, but it was especially useful for me to teach myself to climb steep ice again. Eidfjord was a different experience to Rjukan with longer approaches (but less snow), no guidebook and no other climbers. As a consequence the routes were not stepped out and were a grade harder than their Rjukan equivalents.

We started off by climbing on the south-west facing cliff above Tveito on the Eidfjord-Geilo road. The cliff lies to the left of a prominent left-slanting icefall, and is comprised of two tiers separated by a band of trees and seamed with

Simon Richardson climbing Gates of Mordor (WI4) on Tveito Crag in Eidfjord, Norway. Photo: Tom Bohanon.

Scottish-style gullies. We had no idea whether these had been climbed before but we named the eight-pitch left-hand gully cutting through both tiers Gates of Mordor (WI4), and the right-hand gully on the lower tier Good Country for Old Men (WI4). We descended by abseiling the upper gully of Gates of Mordor and then from trees. Two days later we climbed the long curving couloir directly above Hjolmo (12 pitches, mainly WI3 to WI4 with a pitch of WI5 at the top). We found footsteps up the route and it looked like it had been ascended a day or two before. We abseiled down the route using v-threads.

Simon Richardson

REVIEWS

The Archies: Paul Fettes & others (P. Fettes, 2017, hardback, 223pp, ISBN 978-1-527211-33-9, £19.99).

'If Munro were alive today he wouldn't come up with the Munros. He would come up with the Archies!' In this bold statement, the irrepressible enthusiasm of the author is revealed from the outset. The story dates back to 2014 when Paul Fettes and his merry band of 56 accomplices began planning an epic fund-raising endeavour in support of The Archie Foundation, a charity which supports children's healthcare on Tayside. Paul describes his re-classification of the Scottish mountains coming to him 'in a flash'. Suitable experts duly consulted, a plucky upstart of a list is born to challenge Munro's original, bringing together all Scottish summits over 1000m with a drop of 100m on all sides. The Archies total a neat 130 in number, stretching from An Teallach to Ben Ime, and from Ladhar Bheinn to Lochnagar.

At heart this book is a highly detailed account of the team's 16-day continuous relay across the Archies. We are introduced to an ever-changing cast of participants, including a good number of SMC members and other weel-kent faces together with many talented athletes who keep their cuddly baton, Rabbie, moving at a furious pace. With a fresh author for each chapter, we gain an insight into the often moving personal stories behind the team who battle against the inevitable poor weather to walk, run, paddle and bike across the Archies. There are some great stories in here, such as those madcap midnight rendezvous that start to seem quite natural when there is a great project under way. With the whole enterprise planned in minute detail on an Excel spreadsheet the unexpected is of course always threatening to derail everything. Thus the reader is given insider access to the comical late-night messages that keep things on track: 'Mate, Archie calls. Ben Cruachan needs done tomorrow. Easy 10km up and down big path. Could be as early as 9 a.m. but you know how these things slide.' (This to an already tired team member collapsed on a sofa on the opposite side of the country.)

The book will certainly appeal to those who enjoy 'new twists on old hills'. In order to make the relay work, the team tackle some really imaginative routes, and I found myself unfolding sheet after sheet of OS maps to make sense of the impressively complex logistics. The maps within the book itself are not quite detailed enough to do the story justice, though it does come with a generously sized Archies wall-chart.

In the end, what really shines through are the wonderful friendships between the participants. Anyone connected even indirectly with the original Archie Mountain Challenge will enjoy this as a memento of a 'bonkers and wonderful' adventure. Whether or not the metric Archies come to supersede their archaic Imperial ancestors is really beside the point. Long days in the hills with good friends and an ambitious objective will never get old.

Johannes Petersen

Beyond The Secret Howff: Ashie Brebner (Luath Press, 2017, paperback, ISBN 978-1-910745-87-8, £9.99).

Born in 1935 into a working class family in Aberdeen, Ashie Bebner tells the story of his experiences and adventures, initially working as a mechanic in an envelope factory, with climbing and skiing forays to the Cairngorms, and then, in his own words, to 'escape from a life of industrial servitude to soar in my element, the great outdoors.' Ashie covers a great deal of ground from bothy-based skiing and the challenges of getting around by public transport in the 1950s to taking naturalists to what were then fairly remote and inaccessible venues in the north-west of Scotland, Skye and the Outer Hebrides.

Much of the charm of the book lies in the abundance and breadth of the anecdotes that are peppered throughout its pages. For example, when working in a factory in the early days, Ashie recalls that married women were not allowed to work in the factory. Initially puzzled as to why this should be, he explains the reason: after two world wars there were so many single women whose potential husbands had been killed, it had been decided that single women would be given priority for employment. Another early factory memory was his job of putting the belt on and off the main pulley shaft while it was still running. If any clothing got caught throwing the belt back on, he could be seriously injured, and there had indeed been several fatalities sustained by mechanics throwing the belt from the wrong side. Health and Safety in the 1950s were more limited than today, and this exposure to risk at work presumably informed his attitude to adventures on the hills.

Simply getting to the hills in these early years of the 1950s involved a commitment to long bus journeys, with even longer walks to bothies while carrying what must have been huge rucksacks. For a while Ashie and his pals used a 20-year-old, eight-seater, Armstrong Siddeley that they had bought for £20. They could not afford the expensive antifreeze for the large radiator and so in winter they drained the radiator whenever the car was left overnight, and then refilled it again for the journey home.

The building of the Secret Howff in 1953 was a labour of love that provided much fun and also a great base for exploring the eastern Cairngorms. Carrying in all the materials was a major task, especially as they did not want the estate owners to know what they were up to. In the evenings they would brew up in the howff while listening to live opera via a radio broadcast from Italy — quite a feat of communications in the 1950s!

Ashie and his friends were Scottish ski mountaineering pioneers, and it is fascinating to follow some of their trips on the map. They used wooden ex-army skis with very simple bindings. Ashie briefly mentions that he skied down the Black Spout on Lochnagar in 1956. This is a Grade 1 gully and is a challenging descent on modern equipment. Skiing it on ex-army skis in the 1950s is an impressive achievement, especially considering all skills were self-taught with no uplift facilities. (There are photographs online that were taken on the day.) I had expected to be reaching for maps of the Cairngorms and other Scottish areas but I had not anticipated needing to look out a Norwegian map to follow the routes that were done from a base near Finse — a popular Nordic ski area.

In the 1960s Ashie took the bold step of giving up work in Aberdeen and setting up *Highland Safaris*. This was the beginning of a life in the outdoors, taking clients to all corners of the highlands and islands to enjoy a wide variety of flora and fauna, geology, history and culture. Income was supplemented in quiet times with a range of projects including a comprehensive survey of Ben Wyvis to ascertain its potential as a ski resort, and working with the RSPB to make a film about golden eagles. *Highland Safaris* took clients to Cape Wrath, Skye and the Western Isles in addition to many uninhabited islands including Mingulay, Handa, Eilean nan Ròn and the delightful Càrn nan Sgeir. On Mousa they waited in semi-darkness within the 2000-year-old broch for the arrival of storm petrels returning from the sea with fish for their chicks which were nesting in the walls.

The final chapter has a poignant feel, as Ashie looks back to the early days and revisits the howff to find it still in good condition. Although he and his pals never intended it to be 'secret', it has become a tradition to keep its location relatively unknown, and it is refreshing that this obscurity endures in these days of information overload.

Beyond The Secret Howff is not a mountaineering book, nor is it purely for naturalists. It is the story of one man's broad-ranging passion for the Scottish highlands in all their diversity. I thoroughly enjoyed reading it, and I recommend it.

Roger Wild

Bothy Tales: John D Burns (John D Burns.com, 2018, paperback, 205pp, ISBN978-0-9955958-2-8, £7.99).

This is a collection of stories, some of them true, that are set in various highland bothies and told for some reason in the present tense. As a form of accommodation, Burns likens the bothy to a medieval inn. Had he himself lived in those days he would surely have worn sackcloth and borne a penitential cross. In a typical episode as the November night descends we find him humping a coal-laden rucksack across some pathless bog or (having at last located the elusive howff) struggling ineffectually to kindle a fire. His fellow occupants are 'the good, the bad and frequently the ugly', and not uncommonly the mice too. The accommodation is dark, dank and draughty.

In fairness to the author I should confess that his reviewer is not – to mix Greek and Gaelic stems – a bothyphile. I would sooner have a tent over my head, and nothing in this book will serve to convert me. That euphoric hour of grace, when the crackling logs are piled high and the 12-year-old Glenlivet is amply dispensed (to paraphrase Horace trans. Smart), is preceded and succeeded by too much misery and attended by too much squalor, all of which Burns starkly describes. His own fondness for bothy life he ascribes to childhood experience of the fishing hut, and indeed the chapters touching on this and recalling his father are among the most satisfactory in the book.

Mountaineers should also relish the few passages in which he emerges from his smoky hovel and climbs into the clean air of the Cairngorms, or grapples with the NE Ridge of Aonach Beag. Any reader who enjoyed Burns's previous book, *The Last Hillwalker*, will affirm that he can write engagingly about climbing. In recalling an attempt to light a fire or describing the incendiary revenge of a scorned lover he may not match Jack London or Ronald Frame, but on the hills he comes into his own. He excels especially when drawing on his mountain-rescue experience: 'Only luck saved us from catastrophe; enthusiasm and inexperience are a dangerous mix in this game of ice and iron.'

Here and there the author revisits a scene of his youth, be it the Pennine Way or Lochnagar, and comments on the changes that 40 years have wrought in accommodation, equipment, or bodily vigour. Some bothies such as Gelder Shiel have been greatly improved, and in many instances this has been the work of the Mountain Bothies Association. Though Burns does mention the MBA in passing, he might perhaps have paid a fuller tribute to that organisation and its selfless volunteers. Its members and indeed all bothyphiles will doubtless find much to enjoy in this book.

Graeme Morrison

Mountaineering in Scotland – Years of Change: Ken Crocket (Scottish Mountaineering Trust, 2017, 371pp, hardback, ISBN 978-1-907233-24-1, £25). This is the second volume in Ken Crocket's trilogy on the history of mountaineering in Scotland and covers the period from 1914 to 1971. 'Years of Change' is an appropriate subtitle, for this is the era in which climbing in Scotland evolved from an exclusive activity practised by a small number of the professional and upper middle classes to a recognised sport accessible to the majority. It is also the period when the equipment and style of ascents emerged from the relatively rudimentary activity practised by the Victorian and Edwardian climbers to the beginning of the modern age.

For the generation who started climbing, as I did, in the 1970s, the period of 55 years covered in this book is the legacy we inherited and drew our inspiration from. The writings of W.H. Murray, Tom Patey and Robin Smith fired our imagination, and stories surrounding the exploits of John Cunningham, the Creagh Dhu and others on the wilder edge (who left little in the way of written records) fuelled our evening conversations in the pub. It was an era that seemed to us to be populated with characters whose personalities and antics were larger than life. It was also a time when there was a great leap forward in the technical difficulty of climbs being undertaken, and when many of the really great lines in Scotland were first ascended, some of which, particularly in winter, are now recognised as world class.

Mountaineering is part of the cultural heritage of Scotland, so this is a history worth documenting not just for climbers but for posterity. As a guidebook writer (*Glencoe and the Southern Highlands*), mountaineering historian (*Ben Nevis – Britain's Highest Mountain* and *Mountaineering in Scotland – The Early Years*) and one time editor of the *Scottish Mountaineering Club Journal*, Crocket is well qualified to write this book. He was also active in the final years of the step-cutting era and witnessed the introduction of front pointing and modern protection techniques, so in the latter part of the book is able to draw on his own recollections.

Crocket has clearly read widely around his subject and makes good use of the information available in mountaineering journals, biographies and other published material as well as private climbing diaries, personal interviews, correspondence and on-line searches. His approach is broadly chronological and the content is presented in an engaging narrative style. The text is divided into fifteen chapters, and there is a good balance in the coverage given to the individual decades and the stories behind the climbs. Crocket is objective in his assessment and gives fair credit to the contribution made by visiting English climbers where this is due. There is also a considerable amount of background information on social, economic, meteorological and other matters which, although only loosely related to the story of mountaineering in Scotland, gives a context to the events described. In addition there are numerous short biographical sketches, not just of well known individuals, as might be expected, but of the shadowy and little-known. These contextual and biographical inclusions add considerable value to the text.

Of particular interest is the documentation of the advances made in the development of climbing equipment. In the early part of the book ascents are being made with a hemp rope tied directly to the waist, minimal protection and the maxim that *the leader must not fall*. This gradually changed over the years with the introduction of shorter ice axes, the occasional use of a piton and, after the Second World War, the availability of nylon and kernmantel ropes, vibram boots, specialised rock-shoes, slings and nuts for protection, all of which have made climbing much safer and to some extent easier. The volume ends with the development of dropped picks on ice axes and the introduction of the front-pointing technique that has revolutionised winter climbing. Crocket describes these changes in revealing detail, and there was a fair amount of information here that I was not previously aware of.

Another facet that is well covered in this book is the growth in the number of climbing clubs. This accelerated in the mid-1920s with the formation of the Junior Mountaineering Club of Scotland (JMCS) and a number of locally based climbing clubs, particularly around Glasgow. The different clubs reflected the expanding social profile of those drawn to the outdoors, with the SMC and the JMCS still firmly middle-class and the Creagh Dhu, Ptarmigan and others having an almost exclusively blue-collar membership. This gradually changed as mountaineering experience, rather than social class, became the dominant criterion for membership, and new clubs emerged like the Edinburgh-based Squirrels and the Aberdeen-based Etchachan Club, both of which would make significant contributions to the evolution of Scottish climbing.

One of the more striking facts about this period is the astonishing rise in the technical difficulty of the climbs being undertaken. In the 1920s the hardest routes would have been Severe with the occasional Very Severe, and Grade III and occasionally IV in winter. By 1970 climbs were regularly being made which today are graded E2 or occasionally E3, in summer, and Grade V or VI in winter. Improved protection and equipment undoubtedly contributed to this but so did an expansion in the number of active climbers with a more determined and competitive attitude, improvements in transport which meant that people could climb regularly at weekends, and better access to information with the publication of detailed guidebooks. Alongside this was the exploration of the climbing potential in the more remote parts of Scotland, particularly in the Cairngorms and the Northern Highlands, and the discovery of superb new crags like Carnmore in the Fisherfield Forest.

The one thing I found a little disappointing about this book was the illustrations. Around a quarter of these I was already familiar with, while a number of others are printed about the size of a passport photo, which is too small, and would have benefited from being in a larger format. There are, however, a number of pictures of historic interest that, as far as I am aware, have not been previously published: for example, the first JMCS meet at the Cobbler in 1925; a Cambridge University group at the CIC hut in the early 1930s; and the first front-pointing ascent of Point Five Gully. Other interesting images that capture something of the era are a Creagh Dhu group outside the Dungeon Ghyll bar in Langdale in 1956, Bob Richardson with his Austin A40 in Glen Coe in the early 1960s, and a quizzical-looking Robin Campbell in poor winter conditions on Pinnacle Ridge of Sgùrr nan Gillean. In the acknowledgments, Crocket states the difficulty he had in obtaining suitable photographs from the period, so any lack in this area is probably not for want of trying.

The book is nicely produced and in the same format as several recent Scottish Mountaineering Trust (SMT) publications, with an illustrated hardback cover, white paper for the text, and a satisfyingly large font that makes for easy reading. The foreword is written by Andy Nisbet who, although not active in the period covered by this book, is probably Scotland's most prolific exploratory mountaineer of any era. Each chapter is well referenced, directing one to the main sources and a wealth of additional reading for those so inclined. The references are listed at the end of each chapter rather that at the end of the book, which is a more convenient way of cross-referencing. There are two useful indexes, a general one and a list of routes.

Inevitably there are occasional small mistakes and typographical errors: on p11, for example, C.F. Holland died in 1968 not 1986, and on p37 J.H.B. Bell died in 1975 and not 1976, but these errors are of little consequence. As the late Peter Hodgkiss once said to me when I commented on the number of typographical errors in a book of mine that he published: 'Peccadilloes, Mike; the Bible is in its two hundred and eighty-fifth edition and still has typographical errors, so we've got no chance'. I have no idea how many editions of the Bible there are, but I got the point.

This book is an excellent, well researched and very readable overview of Scottish climbing in its middle years, and a worthy addition to the first volume, *Mountaineering in Scotland – The Early Years*. It must be a daunting task to take on such a large body of work, and Crocket is to be congratulated on doing such a fine job in chronicling this.

Michael Cocker

The Ogre: Doug Scott (Vertebrate, November 2017, hardback, 192pp, ISBN 978-1-911342-79-3, £20).

We all know the old story about buses. You wait for what seems like ages then suddenly two come along, one after the other. The same thing now seems to apply to books by Doug Scott. First in 2015 the long-awaited first part of his autobiography *Up and About*, and now hard on its heels *The Ogre – biography of a mountain and the dramatic story of the first ascent*. If you have not yet had the chance to read the former, then Geoff Cohen's excellent review (*SMCJ* 2016, p310) gives a good overview, with some important caveats that the publisher seems to have taken on board. This latest offering is a much thinner volume, with a mere 178 pages compared with the over-detailed 404 pages of the autobiography. The cover features a striking black-and-white photograph of the mountain, and the text is generously illustrated with a variety of excellent images, mostly in colour. Full marks to Vertebrate Publishing for a very high-quality publication, which is printed and bound in Scotland. A short preface explains that this is 'a biography in two parts: the first concerned with geological evolution and exploration from ancient times; the second more personal, covering the first ascent and the drama of the descent with my two broken legs and Chris Bonington's smashed ribs'.

Geographically, historically and politically the Karakoram mountains which once formed the imperial frontier of British India have long held a fascination for intrepid travellers and armchair explorers. Now part of Pakistan, the area has been extensively documented by a number of writers, and although Part One comprises fewer than 60 pages, Doug makes an excellent job of covering a lot of material, split into seven easily read chapters. He readily acknowledges a variety of sources, and I can strongly recommend interested readers to follow some of these up, particularly the more modern and easy-to-access accounts. One small niggle here: I noticed that some of the authors mentioned in the text do not appear in the short 'Further Reading' list, while others do. In the Acknowledgements at the back the phrase 'at short notice' may explain this. Readers of this Journal may be particularly interested in Chapter 5, entitled 'Scottish Contribution to Empire'.

Taking up more than two-thirds of the book, Part Two is very much the main course, served up in the form of an old fashioned chronological expedition account: 'The Climbers'; 'March to Base Camp'; 'Climbing the Ogre', and so on. Accompanied by Mo Antoine, Chris Bonington, Paul 'Tut' Braithwaite, Nick Estcourt and Clive Rowland, his 'Ordeal on the Ogre' has already been covered in Chapter 6 of Doug's stunningly illustrated *Himalayan Climber* (1992), which mentioned some bad feeling following dissent among the party. The preamble to the new account makes much of 'newly discovered diaries, letters and audio tapes', but apart from a lot more detail it reads to me like the same old story. Even with the new material there is no attempt to recount events and situations through the words of the other participants, leaving me feeling that Doug has missed the opportunity to be a bit more creative and imaginative in re-telling the story. I also wonder why, 40 years after the event, the sudden rush to produce this book? Why not wait to cover it in the next volume of autobiography? Whatever the reasons, it remains a gripping story, brought to life again by the effective use of many superb photographs closely matched to the text. A number of these will be familiar from the earlier account, but the generous space given to some of the full-page portraits makes them particularly striking. Only ever having known Clive clean-shaven, I barely recognised the 'Man of the Mountains at the top of the Red Pillar' (p 119), while Dennis Hennek's portrait of a very battered Bonington in Askole (p 164) almost matches the suffering shown in the classic shot of Herman Buhl on his return from the summit of Nanga Parbat.

We learn from the dust jacket notes that since 1965 Doug has made forty-two expeditions to the high mountains of Asia, and while he may have been a bit reticent about setting his achievements down in print he has been tirelessly touring the UK and lecturing about them ever since. We are also reminded that in 1995 he founded Community Action Nepal (CAN), a UK-based registered charity whose aim is to help mountaineers to support the mountain people of Nepal. There can be few outdoor enthusiasts who have not had the chance to hear him speak at a nearby venue. While the Ogre epic still seems to be a popular show, 40 years after the first ascent in July 1977, I wonder how many people, after the talk, can name the other members of the expedition? With Tut and Nick down at base camp, debilitated by injury and illness, Clive and Mo (who is now, sad to say, deceased) supported the successful summit pair on the climb, then needed all their reserves of strength and skill to help their badly injured companions on the long and arduous descent. Last year Clive recounted his version of the story to the Club's Northern District, when a large crowd of us crammed into a small room, transfixed. My immediate reaction afterwards was that without Clive and Mo's support, the other two would simply not have survived. In the first paragraph of the 'Afterword' (p171) Doug has the grace to quote Al Alvarez's biography of Mo, *Feeding the Rat*: 'Between the rescue and the ensuing publicity, a curious conjuring trick took place. Mo and Rowland effectively vanished from the story'. Now, with the record finally set straight, Doug promises that 'over the next few years I intend to produce books about Kangchenjunga, Makalu, K2, Nanga Parbat, Everest and Baffin Island', and Clive has almost finished writing his memoirs. I can't wait!

Dave Broadhead

The Magician's Glass: Ed Douglas (Vertebrate, 2017, 192pp, paperback, ISBN 978-1-911342-48-9, £14.95).
The Magician's Glass is a collection of eight essays on climbing, written by author and journalist Ed Douglas over the six years 2009–15. The title draws a connecting

thread through the articles. In each, Ed depicts a particular way in which an individual personality has projected his ego on to the mountains. The mountains, though physically impassive, act as a mirror – a magician's glass, to use the author's metaphor. The reflections from this glass give us insight and understanding into the varied motivations of mountaineers.

The subtitle 'Character and Fate…' suggests a darker shade in the narratives. Following the journalistic imperative Douglas has chosen well-known climbers for most of his biographies, particularly those who aroused controversy in their careers and whose lives were attended by tragedy. Tomaz Humar, Patrick Edlinger, Cesare Maestri and Ueli Steck provide fascinating subjects for profile. The stories of their natural talent, rise to fame and eventual demise will attract the voyeuristic curiosity of the wider public. Self-obsession and hubris taint the brilliance and simplicity of youth. Their fates have a similar resonance – egos can outgrow the original passion. The essay 'Crazy Wisdom' has a more general theme, the corruption and exploitation of Sherpa culture by acquisitive Western mountaineers, and Ed's thesis is decidedly bleak, rather too much so in my opinion. The quality of the research and personal insight that support each piece is impressive.

Two chapters of more upbeat mood book-end the collection. In the title essay Ed examines the lives of two lesser known but highly able British climbers of the 1970s and 1980s, Nick Colton and Tim Leach. The pair retreat from high on the *South East Pillar* on Annapurna III, one of the world's most stunning mountaineering challenges. Having climbed two-thirds of the way up the route and without any critical crisis they recognise their limitations and turn back. Afterwards they pursue different courses in life. In Colton's case the death of his friend Alex McIntyre contributes to an epiphany. He becomes a family man and an advocate of competition and sport climbing, and so his passion becomes fun once more. Leach becomes an architect and divorces ego in favour of his talent for geometry and design in a way that can inspire not destroy.

The final essay, 'Lines of Beauty', profiles the climbing artist Andy Parkin. Here we sense a more creative, personalised approach to the mountains where all that is good must spring from love of the landscape. Sadly, it seems that the enigmatic Parkin is not overly loquacious so Ed has to pad the narrative with his own reflections, but his subject reveals something of a more authentic and enduring mountain philosophy. Sure enough, he climbs hard, but in all he does the essential purpose is to better know the beauty of the mountains.

I was left feeling a little fatalistic on finishing the book. A stressful day on bullet-hard snow and in strong winds guiding a party over An Teallach led me to macabre thoughts. At a few points a slip in any of the party would have likely spelled disaster to us all. I imagined that Ed Douglas might swoop down in the aftermath and pen an exposé on the fate of ambitious mountain guides, with a title something like 'Game's Up Martin Moran'!

It is testimony to the quality of Ed's writing that his work can provoke such imaginative reaction. *The Magician's Glass* is a riveting, if rather joyless, read.

Martin Moran

Wild Wanderings: Phil Gribbon (Luath, 2018, paperback, 224pp, ISBN 978-1-9107-4594-6, £9.99).
This is a collection of 34 short tales, many of which have been previously

published in the *SMC Journal* and elsewhere in the past. Several of the tales have sketches by the author at the start of the text, complementing the overall layout of the book. The collection has been brought together into a single volume including some colour photographs by David Meldrum, who has also edited the book and provided a useful synopsis and 'who's who' at the start of the book to assist the reader who may be less familiar with the author's style and use of pseudonyms.

There is a short forward by Chris Bonington and an introduction by Peter Biggar, the Hon. Editor of the *SMCJ*. Peter's introduction in particular provides a fascinating and vivid insight into the character of the author, whom he has known for 50 years and with whom he has shared many adventures, both in Scotland and further afield in Greenland. I hesitate to pick out any of Peter's observations but definitely recommend that one should read the introduction before embarking upon reading the tales themselves. Some of the adventures shared with Peter Biggar are of course included as separate tales in the book.

The author draws on a remarkable lifetime of experiences in the mountains, stretching from his younger years in his native Ireland to his many expeditions abroad, particularly to Greenland and the Arctic which drew him back time and time again during the 1960s and 1970s. During this time he became based in St Andrews where he became a physics professor and an increasingly well known and respected figure in the Scottish mountaineering scene. Phil joined the SMC in 1970, and since 2014 he has been an honorary member. His contribution to exploration in the Arctic was finally recognised in 2014 when he received the Polar Medal from HM Queen Elizabeth. It is to the landscape of Scotland, however, that Phil has always returned, whether to climb in summer and winter or simply to explore his adopted country on foot or by canoe, as others have done and doubtless will continue to do.

In his introduction, Chris Bonington states: 'Somewhat after the questioning and irreverent style of Tom Patey and Geoff Dutton, these stories paint a whimsical, yet at times profoundly analytical picture of our sport and its practitioners'. Additionally, however, I would suggest that the various tales give a useful picture of mountaineering in times which many of today's activists have not experienced, before the advent of mobile 'phones, climbing topos, a proliferation of climbing paraphernalia, reliable weather forecasts and paths that lead one effortlessly from carparks to the CIC Hut and such places. There seems less uncertainty today than there used to be, and perhaps we are the worse for it.

Whilst many of the tales are somewhat whimsical, some are written in a more serious manner and remind us of the perils to be faced in the high mountains in particular. Tale Nine is from the expedition that the author took part in to the Tien Shan mountains in China, and relates how the remains of a Japanese climber, who had disappeared 20 years before, are discovered on a glacier. Phil provides some thoughts as to what happened but ends the piece 'I hate to speculate any further, but what do you think?'

Undoubtedly those familiar with Phil's way of writing will greatly enjoy this book. Those less familiar will be helped along by the synopsis and who's who that is provided for each tale. I personally found it best to dip in and out of the book. Having just returned from a few day away during which I climbed the *Cioch Nose* in Applecross again after 25 years, I re-read Tales 17 and 18 and enjoyed them all the more!

Brian Shackleton

The 21 Escapes of Lt Alastair Cram: David M Guss (Macmillan, 2018, hardback, 432pp, ISBN 978-1-5098-2956-9, £18.99).

Alastair Lorimer Cram was a member of the Club from 1930 until his death in 1994. Until I read Guss's book, my knowledge of him had come almost entirely from the gracious obituary that Geoff Dutton and Bill Murray contributed to the *Journal* (35/186 (1995), 745–8), in which he was characterised as 'one of our most accomplished, courageous and civilised members'. Renowned chiefly for his many escapes from POW camps, Cram had always seemed worthy of a substantial memoir, if not the full-length biography that has at last been written.

Cram was born in 1909, the only child of a solicitor who later became a sheriff. Encouraged by parents who were fond of the outdoors, he made long forays into the Cairngorms even as a boy, and excelled as an athlete at school and at Edinburgh University, where he briefly held the Scottish half-mile record. He was then apprenticed to a legal practice in Edinburgh, before presently joining the family firm of solicitors in Perth. Having been a founder member of the Perth JMCS, he climbed widely in Scotland, the Alps and the Jotunheim in the pre-war years, becoming in 1938 the eighth person to have completed the Munros and just the third to have done all the Tops. Several notes in the SMCJ record his Alpine seasons and exploratory climbing. For example, he wrote as follows of what is now known as Cram's Route on No 1 Buttress of Sgòran Dubh: 'Wintry conditions had fourteen times forced the writer to abandon attempts on this piece of rock, but the ascent was completed with Miss E C Baily, Edinburgh, on 21st July, 1935.' He was a man who persevered.

David M Guss's book barely touches on Cram's early life, but opens in medias res with his capture in 1942 in the Western Desert, where he was serving as an officer in the Royal Artillery. The author admits to a lifelong fascination with escape stories, and gives us several detailed chapters on Cram's escapes from Italian and later German captivity. Some of these heroic episodes have previously been recounted, for example by Cram's cell-mate Jack Pringle (in his *Colditz Last Stop*) or by George Millar (*Horned Pigeon*), but Guss has additionally had access to the files of MI9 (the British government agency secretly established to assist POWs) and above all to Cram's own notes, which were helpfully scanned for him by our own archivist, Robin Campbell. These pencil-written journals of the escapes – which Cram misleadingly entitled 'Mountaineering Notes' – are so barely legible that Guss eventually enlisted the help of a cryptographer, but they have enabled him to compile a fascinating account of Cram's prison existence, his escapes from trains, camps and hospitals, and his solitary flights through the Italian countryside or Czech cities. To Guss the narrative is paramount, and the reader is given few insights into his subject's state of mind; but in one evocative passage we have Cram's own description of life on the run: 'I now know how a beast approaches a human habitation by night for I have been one. Mingled in with the wood perfumes comes something alien, the stale odour of decaying human food, the sour sweet smell of human bodies, the foul acrid stink of dogs and the ammoniac pungency of domestic beasts. Instantly is caution. The hearing is consciously focused upward through the woods, for it needs sweet water and food…'

Although Cram seems to have preferred solitary escapes, he was drawn later into collaborative enterprises with colourful characters such as the burly gold prospector, Buck Palm – 'a South African Hercules' – or the mining engineer and expert tunneller, Allen Pole. Guss describes how a well planned escape from Gavi was compromised by the last-minute inclusion of the SAS founder, David Stirling, who at 6'5" and lacking even a word of Italian was a highly conspicuous fugitive. We learn that Cram himself, who had fair hair and 'piercingly blue eyes', was known throughout these various camps as the Baron, after his aristocratic namesake Gottfried von Cramm, the pre-war German tennis ace. And we even encounter other imprisoned Scottish climbers of that period, in the persons of Tommy Wedderburn and Bill Murray.

Guss controversially dismisses as 'semi-fictional' Murray's passage about Cram in The Evidence of Things Not Seen. While Murray was seemingly wrong to locate Cram's protracted interrogation by the Gestapo in Dachau instead of Prague, his account remains broadly correct; and he can surely be forgiven for believing that the hitherto resilient Cram was afterwards 'in no condition for further prison life'. Pringle described him 'looking like a ghost of his former self…. I knew Alastair pretty well and I could see that he was shaken.' Whether Cram, who had previously been hospitalised after feigning appendicitis (and only narrowly avoided the ministrations of a German surgeon), was again play-acting, as stated by Guss, or had genuinely suffered a breakdown, as assumed by Murray, both authors agree he was moved to a psychiatric hospital. In April 1945 he made his final escape – the twenty-first by Guss's reckoning – and reached safety behind the advancing Allied lines.

In the closing months of the war Cram transferred briefly to the SAS, and was awarded the Military Cross in recognition of his many courageous escapes. He subsequently, while still in the Army, worked in a legal capacity for the War Crimes Group. Later still he became a judge in Kenya and then Nyasaland (now Malawi), before eventually retiring to Edinburgh. Throughout his time in Africa and in retirement, he and his wife Isobel travelled widely and climbed in all continents, besides finishing a further joint round of the Munros. As Guss remarks, '… it's difficult to determine whether he was a mountaineer who spent his spare time sitting on the bench or a judge with a singular passion for climbing.' Long after Cram's death his widow was befriended by Guss and was able to assist him in writing the book. On her own death in 2016 Isobel Cram left a generous bequest to the Club.

While there is little of immediate mountaineering interest in this book, we have every reason to suppose that Cram's adroitness at escape and survival owed much to his climbing prowess. Though not quoted by Guss, he wrote as follows: 'Twenty years of hillwalking and mountaineering provided a background of stamina, route-finding and ability to walk safely over rough country by night. All these things, small enough in themselves, proved useful in the escapes….' He also maintained fitness in prison by following JP Müller's now-forgotten regimen of physical jerks, to the bemusement of his fellow inmates; and when at large he had the great advantage of proficiency in the French, German, Italian and latterly Czech languages.

For all that Cram's audacious escapes are now so fully described, he remains a reserved and enigmatic individual whose motivation eludes scrutiny. Indeed, in this regard it is no criticism of Guss to say that Dutton and Murray's four-page tribute is as revealing as this lengthy narrative. Did his determination to escape spring from sense of duty or love of freedom? Whence came the fortitude to endure beatings, isolation, threats and interrogation? In an early monograph (again not quoted by Guss) we encounter conventional religious sentiments, while Cram's later writing hints at asceticism and mystical energy. A fuller account of his childhood and schooling, which are barely mentioned in the book, would perhaps have furnished clues while also serving to create a more rounded biography. Cram's delightfully laconic sense of humour, admired by Dutton and evident in his many SMC Abroad notes in the Journal, goes unremarked by Guss.

Relatively few prisoners of war sought to escape. Guss writes: 'In Murray's case, there was little need for the Germans to dissuade him from escaping. Like the great majority of prisoners he simply settled into the routine of camp life, preferring "the course of self-improvement" to the unknown dangers of the world beyond the wire.' The reader who detects in this a whiff of disparagement should bear in mind not only that fugitives were likely to be shot on recapture (especially later in the war), but also that the whole camp would incur retribution. Moreover, brutal reprisals were visited on any local peasant who was kind and brave enough to offer shelter. Would it seem facile to draw a parallel with the climber's frequent dilemma: by pursuing a personal adventure, am I entitled to risk not just my own life but the safety or peace of mind of others?

Guss writes crisply and has done his research thoroughly. The many sources of information for the book are listed in an appendix, though the lack of any reference numbers in the text makes it laborious for the reader to identify these, and it is sometimes unclear whether a passage is derived from Cram's notes or another document. There are several interesting photographs and helpful maps, and the book is handsomely produced and refreshingly free from misprints.

It is good to see a kindly searchlight shone upon this remarkable human being. To quote Bill Murray, 'The man was indomitable. I salute his memory.'

Graeme Morrison

Journals of Kindred Clubs: Alpine Journal, Vol 121 (2017); New Zealand Alpine Journal 2016; Wild Land News No 92, (Winter 2017-2018).
At almost 500 pages, the peerless *Alpine Journal* is now so extensive that division into sections has become a necessity. Thus its 40-odd articles are grouped under such headings as Modern Times, Far Flung Places, India, History, etc. The best writing often resists classification, however, and it is amusing to find an account of the Eiger Direct in Science & Nature while John Cleare's entertaining piece about the 1967 Old Man of Hoy broadcast is deemed Art & Photography and 'Filming the Summit of K2' is History. No matter; this dry taxonomy is sprinkled with watercolours and drawings from Paul Mellon's collection, ably 'curated' by Robin Campbell. An 1819 watercolour of Loch Scavaig whimsically precedes the MEF section, whereas Ruskin's Macugnaga landscape introduces Far Flung Places.

In a journal that offers such a wealth of readable articles, it is invidious to praise only a few, but I enjoyed Simon Richardson's account of the Diamond Ridge on the Grande Jorasses. Though placed in Modern Times, it is, he says, a route that could have been climbed 80 years ago. Scottish interest is served not only by the Old Man of Hoy piece but also by Richardson's summary of Scottish winter climbing (rather thin in 2016–17) and Geoff Cohen's dignified obituary of Des Rubens.

Only just our junior, the New Zealand Alpine Club celebrated its 125th anniversary in 2016, but its magazine-like journal has a youthful, forward-looking air. Nor is the coverage insular: fully a third of its 144 pages describe climbing abroad, with admittedly a tilt towards the southern hemisphere. In New Zealand itself, where south faces are shaded and June brings the snows, there are interesting accounts of a new winter line on Mount Aspiring and Grade 27 rock climbs in the Darrans.

Readers with an interest in footwear will be intrigued by Grant Hunter's 'Nailing Rubber', which is subtitled 'The awkward transition from hobnails to rubber soles in New Zealand's Mountains.' Although the first Vibram soled boots had been brought back from Italy at the end of the second world war, we learn that it was common practice well into the 1970s to add Tricouni edge-nails at the instep – ideal for the 'bush-bash', it seems.

Throughout the *NZAJ* the photographs are abundant and excellent, but I especially admired those of Taulliraju (5830m) in Peru. These accompany descriptions of the first ascents of the West Ridge and East Rib by predominantly New Zealand parties in 2016, which are also well summarised in the *AJ*.

In her presidential preface to the *NZAJ*, Penny Brothers draws attention to the Sustainable Summits conference held recently at Aoraki, which discussed 'practical solutions to minimising our footprint in alpine environments, response to climate change, the impact of increased visitor numbers, and the challenge of waste management'. Conservation is also Ed Douglas's editorial theme in the *AJ*, where he cannot imagine the current US president sharing a snowy camp in Yosemite with Theodore Roosevelt, as did John Muir a century ago. 'Quite what John Muir would have made of Donald Trump and his decision to withdraw the US from the Paris climate agreement can only be guessed at… How we as mountaineers respond is a personal choice but as humans who interact with nature in a unique and profound way, I feel we have something unique to offer.'

That we can and should safeguard our mountains is the mainspring of the Scottish Wild Land Group, whose modest 40-page newsletter is informative, thought-provoking and readable. There are articles about proposed gold mining at Cononish and the Eisgein wind farm in Lewis. Having read the latter piece I was surprised to see Beryl Leatherhead (in an otherwise admirable editorial) writing that 'we have renewable power generation established as a necessary contributor to endeavouring to combat global warming.' In reality such power generation has marred our landscape while barely affecting carbon dioxide emissions. I dare to suggest it is neither necessary nor desirable.

Wild Land News also contains an authoritative essay by James Fenton on the National Scenic Areas in relation to wild land, and this is complemented by Mel Nicholl's article on the John Muir Trust's 'Keep It Wild' campaign, in which she argues that wild land should enjoy the same safeguards as National Parks and NSAs: 'Getting a clear commitment from Government to protect WLAs would mean an end to protracted planning applications and Public Local Enquiries.' Indeed; and to remind us what is at stake, there are some delightful photographs of the Cairngorms, together with Andrew Painting's thoughtful reappraisal of Nan Shepherd's *The Living Mountain*. As he observes, 'There is always an element of anxiety when reading about wild land in Britain, or indeed visiting it; one feels the precariousness of its existence keenly.'

Graeme Morrison

Art of Freedom – The Life and Climbs of Voytek Kurtyka: Bernadette McDonald (Vertebrate Publishing, 2017, hardback, 256pp, ISBN 978-1-911342-51-9, £24).
This is an inspiring book about an extraordinary man. I approached it with caution, being suspicious of hagiography, but I became totally gripped by the chapters recounting Voytek's incredible climbs in the Karakoram and Nepal (even though

I had read previous accounts of many of these), and finally I felt uplifted by the philosophy that informs both his climbing and his life.

Kurtyka's father was a writer and Voytek sees himself as a creative artist. His approach to climbing seeks beauty of line and purity of style. He has no interest in slogging up trade routes; he never went near Everest. As perhaps the most outstanding high altitude mountaineer of his generation he is rare in combining these achievements with a very high level of rock climbing skill.

In the late 1970s Voytek teamed up with Alex Macintyre and John Porter to climb long, dangerous and ground-breaking routes on Koh-e-Bandaka in the Hindu Kush and Changabang in Indian Garhwal. The accounts of these climbs are full of colourful anecdote, but good as they are, they do not have quite the immediacy of Porter's own accounts in his recent book *One Day as a Tiger*.

Then in the early 1980s Voytek turned his attention to the Karakoram, and in company with Jerzy Kukuczka accomplished traverses of Broad Peak and Gasherbrum II, a rapid ascent of Gasherbrum I and, with Robert Schauer, the West Face of Gasherbrum IV (sometimes called the *Shining Wall*). This last is often considered his greatest achievement – a beautiful face demanding seven bivouacs above 7000 metres, and several days without food or water. There is not a great deal of technical description, rather McDonald has got Voytek to try and express the profound emotions that he experienced on these climbs, and to analyse the mental contortions and tricks that his brain played, while his body coped with an unimaginable ordeal.

The previous year they had perfect weather on their traverse of the three summits of Broad Peak. Camping at a col at about 7300 metres Voytek had an intensely spiritual experience, 'a sense of unity with space and light'.

I found these beautifully written chapters almost painfully moving. They brought back to me in shocking depth the intensity of feeling that these remote high-altitude bivouacs engender. Coincidentally, Des Rubens and I (with Clive Rowland and Paul Nunn) were attempting Gasherbrum III at the same time that Voytek was on Gasherbrum IV; so although his climb was in a completely different league from our (failed) attempt, I felt a personal connection to the events described.

McDonald presents a fascinating analysis of the parting of the ways between Kurtyka and Kukuczka, as the latter pursued an ambition to collect all the 8,000 metre peaks, an objective that Voytek considered 'a transformation of the climbing art into a vanity fair'. The analysis broadens into a discussion of specifically Polish factors, historical and cultural, that might account for the unrivalled successes of Polish mountaineers in Himalayan climbing in that period, especially in winter. The fact that, earlier in the book, there are several accounts of very hard winter climbs in the Tatra helps the reader who hasn't been to Poland to understand the kind of climbing to which these mountaineers were accustomed. Like the Scottish winter mountains, but even more so, experience of the Tatra in all weathers and conditions provided a superb training for 'the art of suffering' in the greater ranges.

After the split with Kukuczka, Voytek teamed up with the Swiss climbers Loretan and Troillet. With Loretan he climbed a very difficult new route on the Trango Tower. The change to steep rock climbing on a relatively low peak makes a welcome change from the chapters about persevering at the highest altitudes. But soon enough we are back at the latter, with the so-called 'night-naked' climbs of Cho Oyu and Shishapangma. The trio simply soloed at night, taking no sleeping bags or tents and absolutely minimal food and climbing gear (not even harnesses on Shishapangma). Troillet and Loretan had already proved this approach on the north side of Everest. The Swiss pair were significantly younger than Voytek and a little faster. On Shishapangma they did not wait for him even at the summit; he had to descend entirely alone and became so tired that he had two unplanned (and 'unclothed') bivouacs – one at 7800 metres!

A late chapter tells the tale of his obsession to succeed in soloing a 7c+ in Poland; at the age of 46 he was keeping up with climbers twenty years his junior. The detail of the mental and physical preparations for his climb is told with great insight. 'He needed to move dynamically with just the right amount of pressure to glide upward like liquid.' ... 'in the cosmos of crimpers and slopers, a ballast of flank robbed me of any grace and lightness.' On training: 'The chest becomes girdled in strength that binds soul to body. The waist is bound tight, promising lightness and beauty. And the shoulders, tensioned and poised, promise unbreakable strength.' We mortal readers can only mutter sarcastically, 'I wish!'. But perhaps these quotations illustrate the care with which language is used in the book. A Polish translator, Julia Pulwicki, is credited, but Bernadette McDonald also explains that Voytek himself is a most fastidious writer. I think all three deserve great credit for the quality of the writing.

A final chapter attempts to draw threads together to help us understand Voytek's complex character – his abhorrence of egocentricity, his penchant for illegal climbing, his opinion of climbing grades: 'the nefarious cult of the number took the noble art of ascent and made it one-dimensional, robbed of its soul and artistry.' His daughter is quoted: 'his perfectionism was hard to live up to'; and McDonald occasionally casts a gentle glance at the contradictions in his attitudes and behaviour which, in his maturity, he is well aware of.

Much is passed over briefly: his four attempts at K2, two attempts on Makalu and two attempts on the Mazeno Ridge of Nanga Parbat (where our members Sandy Allan and Rick Allen eventually triumphed). But in my view this results in a better balance for the book as a whole and keeps it of moderate length.

The publishers should be complimented on the quality of the hardback, both in design and production. It is a nice book to look at and handle – not an unimportant consideration for book lovers. The photos are generally well reproduced and offer a good balance between people and mountains (though there are no photos of him crag-climbing – perhaps as a result of his private soloing?). It is a pity there are no maps to show western readers the areas of Poland where he climbed; and the armchair reader might have welcomed a few maps to locate his high mountain climbs. The covers are replete with praise from respected climbing writers such as Jim Perrin and David Roberts, and top-level mountaineers such as Steve House and Silvo Karo. I cannot but agree with their encomia. It is an outstanding achievement.

Geoff Cohen

There's Always the Hills: Cameron McNeish (Sandstone Press, 2018, hardback, 332pp, ISBN 978-1-910985-95-3, £19.99; ISBNe: 978-1-910985-96-0).
I ground to a halt before actually reaching the body text; ISBN we should all understand, but what is an ISBNe? Of course the lower case 'e' is the clue, as this book is also being sold simultaneously in a Kindle edition. If one goes to Amazon, like a moth to a light, there it is, yours for £5.69. At a whopping 45Mb file size, this could be cumbersome in a reader, owing obviously to the number of photographs, most of which have the same smiling beardy.

To continue the ISBN theme, however, Amazon have the Kindle listed with the same ISBN as the hardback; but don't worry, either code will take you to the right page. The hardback seems to be discounted from £19.99 to £15.58. Whew! Can we now continue please? Well no, because in part of the electronic blizzard that predated the publication of this book, I became so fatigued on Twitter at seeing promotional references to this book by a character with the handle 'sandstonebob' (presumably the publisher at Sandstone Press), that I blocked his tweets. I very much doubt whether McNeish actually needs so much of this, as he has a large and loyal following in the walking world. Perhaps I should have written 'very large'.

The crucial word in the foregoing paragraph is 'walking', for this is a book, and a story within, that concerns walking and not climbing. The author did have an early life, beginning in Glasgow, which very nearly paralleled mine. My early life however was led in a tougher area of that great and grimy city, where I quickly learned the basics of wall climbing as a means of escape from tenement back yards, fleeing from the clutches of warring youths bigger than myself. I was self-taught, and needed no instructor. Like McNeish, my family moved to the south side, where I continued my growth spurts in a more suburban area, much of which included exploring miles away from home in some of the leafy parks. McNeish makes a comment here, with which I sympathise, regarding the sadly shrinking circumference within which modern kids are allowed to play. Like him I ran risks, some of which, looking back, I regard as hair-raising.

McNeish can give no obvious trigger as to why he became attracted to the outdoor life, but there is some regret that his father died before his time, with fags as the usual culprit. Perhaps some escape mechanism prompted him to head for the puffy clouds of cumulus in the great outdoors. This takes us forward and quite neatly to magazines, skipping, as did the author, any higher education. He would eventually edit *The Great Outdoors* magazine for two decades.

Everyone, without exception, that McNeish interacts with is his best buddy. Well, almost everyone. Weir would not talk to McNeish for a couple of years, following criticism from the bearded one about the misogyny of the SMC. But as McNeish readily admits in his book that he is not a team player, he could do little about that sorry state, not being a member and therefore unable to vote for women to be admitted, as many of us did. Tom of course was one of the opponents of that change, but a civilised one who kept his enthusiasm for a boys-only club muted in public. The SMC admitted women members in 1990, so this argument is now an old one.

McNeish would in the future have another, more serious contretemps with the SMC, but it is not described here, and it's perhaps best not to resurrect old, murky incidents. But his career seems to have been given many useful kicks by various contacts, as often happens to the lucky ones, or those who worked hard where they were and were spotted as such. I am sure he was a hard-working Youth Hostel *Obergruppenführer* for example, doing his duties conscientiously, if without full enthusiasm. He certainly ended up in some scenic areas, excepting a newly concreted Aviemore. And it was the Cairngorms which beguiled him early on, so much so that he and his good lady eventually found their niche at Newtonmore, where they no doubt became adept at shovelling snow off the drive every winter. He seems to have lost his Glasgow accent along the way, which is a shame, but probably a necessity if one is going to be warbling on film without the extra expense of subtitles.

Much of the book is naturally taken up with walking, and the walks became longer and longer, as do many of the descriptions in this book. If you are, as you probably will be, a keen walker, it is best to have a good collection of maps to hand as you read. I suggest that the book would have been better had some of the photographs of the bearded one been replaced by maps, indicating the routes that McNeish and his friend and now neighbour the director Richard Else concocted, as a series of walks for TV. The longest and easily most arduous walk must be the (unofficial) 'Scottish National Trail', which runs northward from Kirk Yetholm in the Borders to Cape Wrath, some 864km. If any reader might be interested in reading how and why he chose their lines, this is when a map would be most useful in following the details.

Inevitably there are a few bits I disagreed with. Although WH Murray was one of Scotland's greatest outdoor writers, inspiring many a youthful reader in the past, it is risky to say that he was the greatest, as styles change and new authors add their input to the genre. I am also not as easy-going as the author seems to be with the faults behind wind farms, including the wasteful production costs and their visual damage to some wild land views. They are neither clean nor green, and McNeish offers little justification for his enthusiasm here. (For a fresh and interesting critique of this topic see *Wind Farms and Tourism in Scotland*, prepared by Dr David S Gordon and published by Mountaineering Scotland in November 2017.)

This autobiography will doubtless be welcomed and enjoyed by those who follow McNeish. Unlike Murray's books, I don't think it will inspire youth; it's more of a read for the experienced walker who is looking for more from his or her walking, including long, scenic trails outwith Scotland.

Ken Crocket

Literature of the Gaelic Landscape: John Murray (Whittles Publishing, 2017, paperback, 256pp, ISBN 978-184995-363-4, £16.99).
Most people have close relationships with places from their formative years, but for Gaels the importance of place is particularly strong. Murray explains how place names in the Highlands are linked to experiences and legend, and how this is expressed in Gaelic poetry.

Donnchadh Bàn Mac an t-Saoir, Duncan Ban MacIntyre (1724–1812), one of the most famous of the Gaelic bards and born at Drumliart near Inveroran, worked as a gamekeeper in Glen Lochay. He composed (he could not read or write) *Òran Coire a' Cheathaich* – Song of the Misty Corrie, that celebrates the quality of the landscape there in terms of wildlife and plants; it had what we would now describe as rich biodiversity. He lost his job to another man for the likely reason that he was reluctant to implement the changes that were being proposed for land use. Was he an eighteenth century eco-warrior?

Later, when working as a gamekeeper for the Auch Estate near Bridge of Orchy, he composed his masterpiece *Moladh Beinn Dòbhrain* – In Praise of Ben Dorain. As well as eulogising the landscape, the flora and the fauna, he includes descriptions of hunting and mentions 23 places by name – all identified by Murray. The poem is structured like a pibroch (the classical style of bagpipe music). As far as I know there is no corresponding pibroch, but a short version of the poem is used as a Gaelic song.

Duncan Ban moved to Edinburgh in 1764 and spent the rest of his life there. He did revisit Coire a' Cheathaich and Ben Dorain, and wrote laments about what he found. The landscape had changed dramatically. Murray writes (p88):

'Whether such biodiversity really did exist in the Misty Corrie (as described in *Òran Coire a' Cheathaich*), without doubt the place which Donnachadh Ban describes in his lament *Cumha Coire a' Cheathaich* was much altered since his time as a gamekeeper'.

The reason was over-grazing by sheep. Duncan Ban must have left Glen Lochay around 1750, so that marks the time when the landscape there started to change. We still think of Glen Lochay and Ben Dorain being part of the magnificent scenery of Scotland, but it was clearly much better before sheep farming became prevalent. From what Murray tells us, Duncan Ban was a master wordsmith who left a very important legacy – a magnificent evocation of the style of the Scottish landscape pre-1750. I do not enjoy descriptive poetry but reading Murray's book has made me want to read *Moladh Beinn Dòbhrain* and has added to the wistfulness that I feel about the lost opportunity of learning Gaelic from my parents when I was young, so that I might have read it in Gaelic.

Of the 23 place-names mentioned in *Moladh Beinn Dòbhrain* only eight are not on the OS map. Murray notes that the Ordnance Survey started mapping towards the end of the nineteenth century, and that knowledge of some place names are likely to have been lost owing to clearances. Some years ago a letter published in the *Scots Magazine* suggested that the Ordnance Survey (OS) were misled by the people in the glens. Were all the minor features named on the OS maps really named? And some of the names are just silly! For example, the pass between Ben More and Stobinian is *Bealach-eadar-dha-Bheinn* – 'Pass between the Two Hills'. Every pass is between two hills so the name does not make sense. My reaction to the letter was as follows: firstly, I suspected that the writer had never heard the fine rhythm of the spoken Gaelic for the pass name; secondly, I knew of no other bealach with that name in Scotland so the name defines the place uniquely; and thirdly, I thought that the name, interpreted as 'the pass between the two hills', was very appropriate, because when viewed from Killin, Ben More, Stobinian and the bealach dominate the western horizon. Gaelic Landscape shows that the OS created a very important historical record about which the writer to the Scots magazine had no awareness.

One of the poems analysed is *Òran na Comhachaig*, the Song of the Owl, by *Domhnall mac Fionnlaigh nan Dan*, Donald Mackinlay of the Verses. This sixteenth-century song is 'used as a celebration of the hunt, the deer and a hymn of praise for Craig Ghuanach', the 631m hill at the southwest end of Loch Treig. Murray lists the thirty place names in the song, of which five are unidentified. Though Murray does not mention this, the tune for *Oran na Comhachaig* is played on the pipes with the title *Craig Ghuanach* (or *The Hawk that Swoops on High*). The tune is also used in the modern (1930s) *Mingulay Boat Song*.

Murray says of Sorley MacLean (1911–1986) that 'a great deal of his work would be abstract were it not for the use of landscape as a symbol'. His poem *An Cuilithionn*, The Cuillin, has 62 references to place-names. *Hallaig* is about the clearances in Raasay where MacLean was born. Based on Murray's descriptions, I think that I would prefer to read the poems of Duncan Ban to those of Sorley Maclean. Stories of the clearances are so poignant that I find it difficult to read about them. However I found John Murray's analysis of Maclean's poetry to be very readable.

The final chapter in the book is about the novels of Neil Gunn that are based in the north-east – Caithness and Sutherland. Gunn wrote in English but Murray finds that his style is very much in the Gaelic tradition, with frequent reference to place-names.

If, as you walk the bens and glens of the Scottish Highlands, you would like to improve your understanding of the cultural heritage of the places that you visit, *Gaelic Landscape* is the book to read.

Iain A MacLeod

Among the Summer Snows: Christopher Nicholson (September Publishing, 2017, 169pp, hardback, ISBN 978-1-910463-60-4, £14.99).

It seems only proper that in reviewing this book I declare an interest at the outset. In early summer 2016 I was contacted out of the blue by the author. In his e-mailed note he told me he intended to travel north to Scotland from his English base and embark on a month-long journey around the Highlands in late summer of that year, looking for vestiges of the previous winter's snow. The ostensible aim of this trip was to facilitate writing a book on snow patches. He asked if I, as someone who is reasonably well informed on this obscure subject, might be interested in meeting up and discussing it. A walk was also suggested. Intrigued, and always keen to meet up with like-minded chionophiles, I said that I should be very pleased to do so, if our schedules permitted. Unfortunately, though, our calendars didn't align whilst he was in Scotland, so for the most part he made the various journeys into the hills alone. The results of his expeditions and associated musings are captured in his latest book, *Among the Summer Snows*.

It is a brave author who attempts to build an entire book around the highly niche subject of snow patches on the Scottish hills. Indeed, when I first picked the hardback up I was slightly sceptical, imagining that Nicholson would toil to carry the reader through multiple chapters of basically doing the same thing (i.e. walking up into a corrie and looking at months-old or years-old snow). It is with considerable relief I can report that not only has Nicholson pulled it off; he has done so with great credit, and not a little empathy.

The book starts off by describing Nicholson's practical preparations, as well as concerns about his physical condition. He voices reservations about aching limbs, as well as his own fitness and age. Will his 60-year-old frame be able to carry him through the month-long walking holiday he had planned? From these worries he neatly side-steps into his own back-story, complete with a description of the tragic loss of his wife (and mother to his children) to cancer when she was comparatively young – an event you feel he has never fully recovered from. 'How could he?' one might reasonably ask. He also delves into episodes of his childhood history, with a description of how he was first inspired and stirred by snow. This is important because when one hears tales like these from folk who are interested in long-lying snow they tend to ape each other. Nicholson's description is no different, and it conveys a warmth and elucidation to the reader that would otherwise perhaps baffle them, especially one who doesn't share this interest.

The main body of the book, though, is taken up with the author stravaiging alone in the very highest of Scottish hill ranges looking for often tiny scraps of snow. The descriptions of what he finds when he does achieve his goals are delightful. Like a child he likens them to deeply-ingrained shapes that are present in his head. One particular patch reminds him of the famous Sutton Hoo Viking helmet, and another prompts him to be reminded of someone lying down as if at rest.

Nicholson is a gifted writer, with an enviable ability to describe the landscape and what dwells and is present in it. Throughout the story there are vivid descriptions of plants, landscape and wildlife: subjects which he clearly also has a passion for. I enjoyed these, and also his regular referencing of eighteenth and nineteenth century authors who had observed patches of snow hundreds of years before him. Unusually, the story sometimes read like a Wikipedia entry, branching off to recall some lost poem, unrelated to snow or even the outdoors. In this regard it reminded me of Sebald's *The Rings of Saturn*, as I was never quite sure where Nicholson was going to venture next. This is not a criticism: indeed, it added a series of welcome deviations.

I confess that I nodded in agreement at some of the descriptions Nicholson gave throughout the book. These were purely out of recognition of the inevitable highs and lows that a snow patch finder goes through over the course of an average season. One particular section, in which Nicholson describes the horror of realising the last snow in the Cairngorms might have melted, had me smiling wryly in sympathy and camaraderie: *A chink of light. The cloud had briefly lifted from the ridge to the south of the summit, near Sgòr an Lochain Uaine, the Angel's Peak. It sank back, but I was encouraged, surely the wind would blow it off soon .... So here I was, on my knees, late one day in the summer of 2016. My heart in my mouth. Absurd. Is this what it had come to? It: me, the world, human history. The winter would bring more snow, so why did it matter, it did not matter, not really, not at all, the old argument raged away in my head, but at that point it mattered at least enough to keep me there. I needed to know if the snow had survived.*

This passage is perhaps too idiosyncratic to be fully appreciated by every reader, but for those who indulge in snow-spotting in late summer and autumn the sentiment will be all too familiar. And this, I suppose, is part of the book's one inherent weakness. Because of its singular thesis it is not likely to have wide-ranging appeal. A good deal of it is given over to describing something that is just too esoteric for your average reader.

Why Nicholson ventures into the hills to look for old snow is never really clear to the reader. This is largely owing to the fact – as Nicholson himself concedes – that he doesn't truly know why himself. Again, this is something I can empathise with. It is the only question I struggle to answer when asked.

Despite its undoubted quirks, *Among the Summer Snows* is both deeply charming and highly appealing to anyone who has an open mind and doesn't care for genres or pigeon-holes. Nicholson's quest for his summer snow is something that anyone who has wonder in their hearts cannot fail to be impressed or moved by.

Iain Cameron

Into the Mountain – A Life of Nan Shepherd: Charlotte Peacock (Galileo, October 2017, 333pp, hardback, ISBN 978-1-903385-56-2, £20).
This is the first biography of Nan Shepherd, and the author's first book. In the 1930s Nan Shepherd was one of Scotland's best known writers. Three novels, *The Quarry Wood*, *The Weather House* and *A Pass in the Cairngorms*, as well as a volume of poetry, *In the Cairngorms*, were all published while she was in her thirties. These books established her reputation as one of the most highly respected members of the Scottish Modernist movement.

Then, much later, came *The Living Mountain*, a short but powerful reflection on her experiences walking in the Cairngorms. This book was rejected in 1945 by a publisher, and was consigned by Nan to a drawer in her bedroom. It was not until 1971 that the manuscript was unearthed, being finally published in 1977, but

Nan died in 1981 before the true and lasting success of this work was realised.

The biography's opening pages convey how enigmatic and elusive Nan Shepherd was, with a talent for silence. Born a late Victorian in 1893, she lived through a period of dramatic change during the twentieth century. Opportunities for women were expanding: the right to vote, access to higher education, and entry to the professions. She remained at home and studied English at Aberdeen University, becoming a lecturer at the Aberdeen Teacher Training College, which she enjoyed although she could never marry while remaining in this profession. Progress was slow in Aberdonian society; and although it was heavily patriarchal, limited expectations were not just down to Scottish male attitudes. Paradoxically it was often conservative women like the aunts in *The Quarry Wood*, satirised as the epitome of staid middle-class respectability, who upheld these patriarchal prejudices. Young women, who realised there must be more for them in life than the roles allocated to them by society, echoed Nan Shepherd's recurring theme to 'get leave to live' and try to find space for oneself.

The author was unable to find much in the way of personal notes or diaries, many of which had been destroyed, necessitating the use of two alternative sources for her research. Firstly there were quotations by friends and contemporaries which helped create a reliable and accurate frame for the biography of a woman who was the antithesis of garrulous and, according to her friends, would often reply to a question with an enigmatic gesture that revealed more than any outpouring of opinions. Secondly all of Nan's own books, if researched assiduously, are found to be autobiographical.

So was she considered to be a feminist? In all of Nan Shepherd's actions she rebelled against power structures, laws or social conventions that conspired to keep women servile, while at least on the surface she appeared to conform. Her walking in the hills was partly to prove that this was something a woman could do on her own. But in this activity, and in her deep love for the mountains, lochs and rivers, she found an escape from those disturbed and uncertain years between the two world wars. When her need for escape became more insistent, in the early 1940s, the hills were different from the present day, as there was almost nobody there. This suited Nan, who would rather walk alone than with the wrong companion.

Nan Shepherd's head adorns a £5 note. Photo: John Fowler.

Nan Shepherd.

Sketch:
Helen Forde

   In this keenly researched and well written biography you can read of her travels
abroad, and of the friends, poets and authors she met and was influenced by, and
whom she in turn influenced. Despite all the comprehensive research, I was left
with the rather bare threads of this woman's warp and weft: the fact that she lived
all her life in the same house, 'Dunvegan', in Cults, even in the same small
bedroom; and that her much loved brother Frank, who was tall and red-haired like
herself, died after serving in the Great War. A mother, who seemed to be an invalid
most of her life and was confined to house and garden, is shown in sharp contrast
to her restless, roaming daughter who loved and indeed craved the tirling of the
winds and rain on the Cairngorm summits.
   On the cover of this biography, *Into the Mountain*, is a photograph of Nan –
the same image that appears on our £5 bank notes. This was taken in a
photographer's studio at the age of sixteen, and she is quoted as 'just fooling
about' as she tied a piece of the photographer's film around her head with a bauble
on it, just for fun. This is the closest the reader ever really gets to the spirit of the
girl, as Neil Gunn summarised it in his final letter to Nan: 'You're like a lovely
day in the hills.'
   This is an intriguing introduction not only to Nan Shepherd herself but also to
the other literary work coming out of Scotland at this time, and it may serve to
draw a wider readership into the mountains.

                                                                    Helen Forde

The Top 500 Summits: Barry Smith (Where2walk Publishing, December 2016, hardback, 342pp, ISBN 978-0-9956735-0-2, £25).

This listing is a personal classification of the top 500 summits in Britain and Ireland, and the book itself is of a substantial coffee-table type. The author has put together a combined list of the hills of Britain and Ireland which are over 2,500 feet and have a 500-foot drop between them. This resulted in a list of 488 summits, so the next twelve highest summits were added to make the list up to 500.

For Scotland, this means a list that includes the Munros (less 82 that do not meet the 500-foot drop criteria) and all the Corbetts. There are notable omissions in the Munros that do not meet the 500-foot drop: for example, Cairngorm and Aonach Mor.

The list then has 17 summits in the Lake District, the Cheviot and two summits in the Pennines. There are 21 in Wales (including four in the Brecon Beacons) and 29 in Ireland (two of which are in Northern Ireland). The bulk of the book is therefore material on the Munros and the Corbetts, as these cover 430 of the 500 summits. Readers are invited to take up the challenge and log their compleation on the website of the author's brother.

The summits are divided geographically into day walks, with a photograph, diagram and comments about the route and the day from the author or his friends or family with whom he walked over the years. The route description is largely restricted to the author's route. In that respect, it is really a personal diary recollection of a lifetime of walking, and indeed the author emphasises at various points that the book is not a guidebook.

It isn't entirely clear who this work might be aimed at. It is a book that you might browse through if you plan to do any of the summits. However, anyone doing the hills that are listed in Scotland would probably be doing the full list of Munros and Corbetts and using the existing guidebooks. Similarly, the hills that are listed outside Scotland have their own guidebooks. I am not sure that the idea of having a book that combines some of the Munros, all the Corbetts and hills that are Corbett-size and above outside Scotland is sufficient to justify buying the book. Those who have already ticked Munros and Corbetts might find the book useful and interesting for extending the challenge to the rest of Britain and Ireland. Although it is not a guidebook, I noticed some slightly odd comments here and there. For example, against a photo of the West Ridge of Sgùrr nan Gillean: 'This route should be avoided. One slip could be disastrous.'

Overall an interesting idea, but the jury is out on whether the 500 summits will take off as a recognised addition to the many existing hill lists.

Alison Coull

The Outer Hebrides – Scottish Mountaineering Club Climbers' Guide: Rab Anderson, Kevin Howett and Colin Moody, Scottish Mountaineering Trust Publications Ltd. 2018. ISBN 978-1-907233-18-0. £29.95

This is a big guidebook in every sense of the word and it has clearly involved a vast amount of work by the authors and editor. Although produced to the highest quality, it is not a pocket guide, being A5 in size and weighing close on 1kg! The inclusion of history sections, The Bernera Islands, The Shiants, The Uists, Eriskay and Lingeigh (all available on-line) would have taken it well over a bag of sugar! No doubt the decision to combine Lewis and Harris with the Bishop's Isles was commercially driven but two near pocket-sized guidebooks would have been much more user-friendly.

There is undoubtedly something quite magical about climbing in the Outer Hebrides. Despite the many marine and climatic challenges, not to mention midge attacks, it is also hugely rewarding. The day I abseiled down Sròn an Dùin, on Mingulay, with Kevin Howett in 1993 – the first climbers to do so – remains a vivid and special memory. There was a sense of being on the edge of all things, at the wild interface of Scotland's oldest rocks and the vast Atlantic Ocean – adventure climbing in its purest form.

So what about the content of this guide? It is clearly well-researched and given the huge number of routes included, has few obvious errors. I could have a personal gripe about the misspelling of my name (page 452) and the lack of acknowledgement for my one and only first ascent on Harris (for the record, 'The Corner' on Creag Mò was climbed on 13 June 1971) but that would be churlish.

The illustrations range from the truly inspirational e.g. The Scoop (page 215) and Prophecy of Drowning (page 337) to the good and the mundane. However, the great majority of photos are in the first two categories. The photo-diagrams are sharp (a few obviously taken from the sea) with belays indicated on some of the longer multi-pitched routes. Access to the islands is well covered and access to the start of routes – critical information when abseiling down big sea cliffs – is clearly described.

There is no doubt that this guide is a labour of love and will undoubtedly inspire many more visits. It is to be hoped that future visitors will enjoy not just the excellent rock climbing but also the scenery and wildlife and take great care not to have an adverse impact upon either.

So well done to Rab, Kevin and Colin, you've produced a book to be proud of!

In conclusion, this guidebook is a treasure trove of trad climbing – it could even be claimed that there is no greater concentration of high quality routes in any other climbing area within the UK. If you disagree, buy it and go to the edge!

Graham Little

******

ERRATA
'...thou art full of error;'
(*Measure for Measure.* 1.2: 49–50)

In the 2017 edition of the *Journal*:
On the front inside cover Julian Lines is wrongly credited with making a Grade IX ascent: it should be E9 7a.
- p. 173 In the description of *Asphodel* the name *Heather Mourning* should read *Extra Thyme.*
- p. 233 End of fourth paragraph should read: 'This gave a total of 20 and 32 respectively...'
- p. 284 Pat Ingram (not Ingham) attended the Lakes Meet.
- p. 326 At the end of the second paragraph there is an unfulfilled footnote. It should read: For further discussion see *SMCJ* 2013 pp.651–2.

ORDERING THE SMC JOURNAL

Members should automatically receive a copy of the Journal when it is published. Members wishing to order extra copies or non-members wishing to place a regular order should contact the Distribution Manager, Roger Robb, by **e-mail** <journal.distribution@smc.org.uk>.

SMC JOURNAL BACK NUMBERS

Back numbers of the Journal may be obtained from Clifford Smith:
16 House o' Hill Gardens, Edinburgh, EH4 2AR.
e-mail: <journal.archive@smc.org.uk>
tel: 0131-332 3414   mob: 07748 703515

The following years are available: post and packaging are extra.

	Year
£5.00	1972
	1977
	1978
	1979
	1980
	1983
£5.50	1985
£5.70	1986
	1987
	1989
	1990
	1991
	1992
£6.95	1993
	1994
	1995
£8.95	1996
	1997
	1998
£11.95	1999

	Year
£12.95	2000
	2001
	2002
	2003
	2004
£13.95	2005
	2006
	2007
	2008
£14.95	2009
	2010
	2011
	2012
	2013
	2014
£16.95	2016
	2017

SCOTTISH MOUNTAINEERING CLUB HUTS

Bookings can be made to stay at any of the five Club Huts by contacting the relevant Custodian.

CHARLES INGLIS CLARK MEMORIAL HUT, BEN NEVIS
Location: (NN 167 722) On the north side of Ben Nevis by the Allt a' Mhuilinn. This hut was erected by Dr and Mrs Inglis Clark in memory of their son Charles who was killed in action in the 1914–18 War.
Custodian: Robin Clothier, 35 Broompark Drive, Newton Mearns, Glasgow, G77 5DZ.
e-mail <cic@smc.org.uk>

LAGANGARBH HUT, GLEN COE
Location: (NN 221 559) North of Buachaille Etive Mor near the River Coupall.
Custodian: Bernard Swan, 16 Knowes View, Faifley, Clydebank, G81 5AT.
e-mail <lagangarbh@smc.org.uk>.

LING HUT, GLEN TORRIDON
Location: (NG 958 562) On the south side of Glen Torridon.
Custodian: Patrick Ingram, 119 Overton Avenue, Inverness, IV3 8RR.
e-mail <ling@smc.org.uk>.

NAISMITH HUT, ELPHIN
Location: (NC 216 118) In the community of Elphin on the east side of the A835.
Custodian: John T Orr, 8 Fleurs Place, Elgin, Morayshire, IV30 1ST.
e-mail <naismith@smc.org.uk>.

RAEBURN HUT, LAGGAN
Location: (NN 636 909) On the north side of the A889 between Dalwhinnie and Laggan.
Custodian: Clive Rowland, Inverene, Links Place, Nairn, IV12 4NH.
e-mail <raeburn@smc.org.uk>.

SCOTTISH MOUNTAINEERING CLUB GUIDEBOOKS

Published by THE SCOTTISH MOUNTAINEERING TRUST

HILLWALKERS' GUIDES
The Munros
Munros GPS data sets – from
The Corbetts and other Scottish hills
The Grahams & The Donalds
The Cairngorms
Central Highlands
Islands of Scotland including Skye
North-West Highlands
Southern Highlands

SCRAMBLERS' GUIDES
Highland Scrambles North
Highland Scrambles South
Skye Scrambles

CLIMBERS' GUIDES
Scottish Rock Climbs
Scottish Winter Climbs
Scottish Sports Climbs
Inner Hebrides & Arran
Ben Nevis
The Cairngorms
Glen Coe
Highland Outcrops South
Lowland Outcrops
North-East Outcrops
Northern Highlands North
Northern Highlands Central
Northern Highlands South
Skye The Cuillin
Skye Sea-Cliffs & Outcrops
The Outer Hebrides

OTHER PUBLICATIONS
Ben Nevis – Britain's Highest Mountain
The Cairngorms – 100 Years of Mountaineering
A Chance in a Million? – Scottish Avalanches
Hostile Habitats
The Munroist's Companion
Scottish Hill Names – Their origin and meaning
Mountaineering in Scotland: the Early Years
Mountaineering in Scotland: Years of Change

e-BOOKS
Please see <https://www.smc.org.uk/publications/ebooks>

APPLYING FOR MEMBERSHIP OF
THE SCOTTISH MOUNTAINEERING CLUB

The following notes are provided outlining the principles by which climbers may be admitted to membership of the Club.

The Committee does not lay down any hard and fast rules when considering applications but considers each case on its own merits. Candidates must be over 18 and have experience of mountaineering in Scotland in both summer and winter. This experience should have extended over a period of at least four years immediately prior to application and should not be confined to just a single climbing district.

The normally expected climbing standards include:

- Experience of winter climbing including several routes of around Grade IV standard and the ability to lead climbs of this level of difficulty.

- Rock climbing experience including climbs of Very Severe (4c) standard and the ability to lead routes of this level of difficulty. In considering applications, emphasis will be placed on multi-pitch climbs in mountain locations.

- The ascent of at least 50 Munros of which at least one third should have been climbed in snow conditions.

In short, the candidate should be able to show – by producing a detailed list of climbs – that they are competent to lead a variety of outings in the mountains of Scotland in both summer and winter. The technical standards specified refer to applicants currently active and may be varied at the discretion of the Committee for older candidates provided that the applicant's routes reflect a reasonable standard for their time. Climbing in the Alps and elsewhere is taken into consideration. Candidates who do not fulfil the normal qualifications listed above but who have made special contributions to Scottish mountaineering in the fields of art, literature or science may receive special consideration.

It is essential that each candidate, before applying, should have climbed with the member proposing the application. It is also desirable that a candidate should be introduced to a member of the Committee before the application is considered. Application forms must be obtained on behalf of candidates by members of the Club who may not propose or support candidates for election during their own first two years of membership. The annual membership fee is £40.00 (£30.00 for those aged 65 and over) which includes the Club Journal.

A fuller version of these notes for members wishing to propose candidates is available from the Club Secretary who is happy to advise candidates and members on any aspect of the application process. Please contact John R R Fowler, Honorary Secretary at:

e-mail: <jrrfowler@tiscali.co.uk>
tel: 0131 226 4055.

OFFICE BEARERS 2017–18

Honorary President: Neil Quinn
Honorary Vice-Presidents: Robert T. Richardson and Robin N. Campbell
President: Simon M. Richardson
Vice-Presidents: Chris M. Huntley and Bob Reid

Hon. Secretary: John R.R. Fowler, 4 Doune Terrace, Edinburgh, EH3 6DY. **Hon. Treasurer**: J. Morton Shaw, 7 Kirkbrae Terrace, New Deer, Turriff, AB53 6TF. **Hon. Membership Secretary**: Geoff Cohen, 198/1 Grange Loan, Edinburgh, EH9 2DZ. **Hon. Meets Secretary**: John R.R. Fowler. **Hon. Editor of Journal**: Peter J. Biggar, Hillhead, Craigton, North Kessock, Inverness, IV1 3YG. **Hon. Librarian**: John C. Higham, 9 Balfleurs Street, Milngavie, Glasgow, G62 8HW. **Hon. Archivist**: Robin N. Campbell, Glynside, Kippen Road, Fintry, Glasgow, G63 0LW. **Hon. Custodian of Images**: David Stone, 30 Summerside Street, Edinburgh, EH6 4NU. **Hon. Reporter on Accounts**: David Small, 5 Afton Place, Edinburgh, EH5 3RB. **SMC Website Manager**: Michael P. Watson, 57 Mortonhall Park Crescent, Edinburgh EH17 8SX. **Convener of Publications Sub-Committee**: Rab Anderson, 24 Paties Road, Edinburgh, EH14 1EE. **Convener of Huts Sub-Committee**: Andrew M. James, 41 Urquhart Road, Dingwall, IV15 9PE. **Information Officer**: John A.P. Hutchinson, 11 Sandfield Avenue, Milngavie, Glasgow, G62 8NR. **Rep. to Mountaineering Scotland**: Brian R. Shackleton, 4A Campbell Road, Edinburgh, EH12 6DT. **Committee**: Neil G.F. Adams, David Myatt, Alison J. Coull, Colin A. Simpson, Fiona J.L. Reid and Simon Yearsley.

Journal Information

Editor:	Peter Biggar, Hillhead, Craigton, North Kessock, Inverness, IV1 3YG. **e-mail** <pjbiggar149@btinternet.com>
New Routes Editor:	Andy Nisbet, 20 Craigie Avenue, Boat of Garten, PH24 3BL. **e-mail** <newroutes@smc.org.uk>
Photos Editor:	Ian Taylor, 15, Pulteney Street, Ullapool, Ross-shire, IV26 2UP. **e-mail** <itandtf@hotmail.com>
Reviews Editor:	Graeme Morrison, 42 Orchard Drive, Edinburgh, EH4 2DZ. **e-mail** <g.d.morrison@btopenworld.com>
Distribution:	Roger Robb, Blaven, Upper Knockbain Road, Dingwall, IV15 9NR. **e-mail** <journal.distribution@smc.org.uk>
Back Numbers:	Cliff Smith. **e-mail** <journal.archive@smc.org.uk>

INSTRUCTIONS TO CONTRIBUTORS

The Editor welcomes contributions from members and non-members alike. Priority will be given to articles relating to Scottish mountaineering. Articles should be submitted **by the end of April** if they are to be considered for inclusion in the Journal of the same year. Material is preferred in electronic form and should be sent by e-mail direct to the Editor. Most common file formats are acceptable. Those without e-mail can send hard copy by post to the Editor's home address.

Illustrations not relating to an article should be sent to the Photos Editor. All images should be high resolution and have explanatory captions including the source. Books for review should be sent to the Reviews Editor by the end of May.

The Editorial team reserves the right to edit any material submitted.

INDEX OF AUTHORS

INDEX OF PEOPLE

Bold numerals denote an article by the person; *italic* numerals denote an image of the person.

INDEX OF PLACES & GENERAL TOPICS

Italic numerals refer to a picture; *fn* indicates a footnote.
FA = first ascent; FWA = first winter ascent.

INDEX OF PHOTOGRAPHERS & ARTISTS

INDEX OF REVIEWS

(Reviewers in brackets)